Women in the Criminal Justice System

Tracking the Journey of Females and Crime

Women in the Criminal Justice System

Tracking the Journey of Females and Crime

Edited by

Tina L. Freiburger
University of Wisconsin–Milwaukee
Milwaukee, Wisconsin, USA

Catherine D. Marcum
Appalachian State University
Boone, North Carolina, USA

CRC Press
Taylor & Francis Group
Boca Raton London New York

CRC Press is an imprint of the
Taylor & Francis Group, an **informa** business

CRC Press
Taylor & Francis Group
6000 Broken Sound Parkway NW, Suite 300
Boca Raton, FL 33487-2742

© 2016 by Taylor & Francis Group, LLC
CRC Press is an imprint of Taylor & Francis Group, an Informa business

No claim to original U.S. Government works

Printed on acid-free paper
Version Date: 20150610

International Standard Book Number-13: 978-1-4822-6049-6 (Hardback)

Visit the Taylor & Francis Web site at
http://www.taylorandfrancis.com

and the CRC Press Web site at
http://www.crcpress.com

To my mom, Mary Freiburger, and my sisters, Tammy, Debbie, and Julie.

Tina L. Freiburger

To my mother, my hero.

Catherine D. Marcum

Contents

Preface

The role of women in the criminal justice system has evolved since its inception. Once viewed as an emotional and illogical species incapable of most crimes, the evolution of criminological theory and policy has shaped a different perspective for women as offenders. The treatment of female offenders and victims, a role often fused, has changed to better address their needs and challenges. In addition, women are becoming a present and important stakeholder in law enforcement, court systems, and corrections.

The purpose of this edited book is to present the current state of the female presence in the criminal justice through the contributions of experts in criminology. Research from scholars in the academic field and government studies, statutes, and other material were gathered and summarized. Key concepts, statistics, and legislative histories are discussed in every chapter. It is the desire of the editors to educate and enlighten a wide audience, from those who are completely unfamiliar with the topic as an entirety to individuals who need more specific information on a particular issue facing women in the criminal justice system. This book should be a useful guide to students, academics, and practitioners alike.

Thank you to Carolyn Spence and the staff at CRC Press/Taylor & Francis Group for their assistance and patience with the preparation of this manuscript. It was wonderful to work with a group of individuals who shared the same vision for this book. We hope it is a great success.

Editors

Tina L. Freiburger is an associate professor and chair of the Department of Criminal Justice at the University of Wisconsin–Milwaukee, Wisconsin. Her main areas of research include gender and racial/ethnic disparities in the judicial system, issues in juvenile justice and the processing of juveniles in the criminal justice system, and women in the criminal justice system. She has published numerous articles in various criminal justice and other social science journals.

Catherine D. Marcum is an associate professor of criminal justice at Appalachian State University, Boone, North Carolina. Her areas of research include cybercrime, correctional issues, and sexual victimization. She has published numerous articles in various criminal justice and other social science journals, as well as authored and edited multiple scholastic books.

Contributors

Michele P. Bratina
Department of Criminal Justice
Shippensburg University
Shippensburg, Pennsylvania

LeAnn N. Cabage
Department of Sociology
Iowa State University
Ames, Iowa

Kelly M. Carrero
Department of Educational Leadership and Special
    Education
Shippensburg University
Shippensburg, Pennsylvania

Jeffrey W. Cohen
Criminal Justice
Social Work Program
University of Washington–Tacoma
Tacoma, Washington

Beverly R. Crank
Department of Government and Justice Studies
Appalachian State University
Boone, North Carolina

Kimberly D. Dodson
Law Enforcement and Justice Administration
Western Illinois University
Macomb, Illinois

Georgen Guerrero
Department of Sociology and Criminal Justice
University of the Incarnate Word
San Antonio, Texas

George E. Higgins
Department of Justice Administration
University of Louisville
Louisville, Kentucky

Carly M. Hilinski-Rosick
Department of Criminology and Criminal Justice
University of Tampa
Tampa, Florida

Stephane J. Kirven
Criminal Justice Department
Sacred Heart University
Fairfield, Connecticut

Susan Marcus-Mendoza
Department of Human Relations
University of Oklahoma
Norman, Oklahoma

Wendy Perkins
Department of Criminal Justice
College of Professional and Applied Studies
Urbana University
Urbana, Ohio

Doshie Piper
Department of Sociology and Criminal Justice
University of the Incarnate Word
San Antonio, Texas

Amy Poland
Department of Criminal Justice
St. Joseph's College
Patchogue, New York

Danielle Romain
Department of Criminal Justice
University of Wisconsin–Milwaukee
Milwaukee, Wisconsin

Corina Schulze
Department of Political Science and Criminal
    Justice
University of South Alabama
Mobile, Alabama

Alana Van Gundy
Department of Justice and Community Studies/
    Political Science
Miami University
Oxford, Ohio

Katherine Winham
Kent School of Social Work
University of Louisville
Louisville, Kentucky

Introduction

Males have historically received the greatest amount of attention in the criminal justice system. This has largely been due to the overrepresentation of males in the system, putting their needs and issues at the forefront of the criminal justice system and the study of crime. Male overrepresentation is found in all parts of the system, from offending, to rates of victimization, to being employed within the system. The underrepresentation of females in the system has led some to the question of whether we should be concerned with females at all. This line of thought argues that because women make up such insignificant numbers in the system, it is a waste of resources to focus on their needs and issues. Others, however, argue that it is important to be concerned with females. This book takes the stance of the latter argument, believing that a focus on females in the system is important. Despite their minority status, women still make up a significant number of offenders and victims in the system, and their numbers appear to be increasing. Women also bring special issues to the system that should not be ignored. In addition, the presence of women in criminal justice careers is increasing. This book examines issues of women in the criminal justice system, paying special attention to their experiences as victims, offenders, and practitioners in the system.

Female Treatment and Involvement in the Criminal Justice System

The first section of this book provides an introduction to issues of female treatment and involvement in the criminal justice system. It provides a foundation for understanding women's treatment and involvement in the criminal justice system by placing women in the criminal justice system within a historical context, providing an overview of the theoretical explanations for female criminality, and explaining how male dominance in the criminal justice system has shaped that system.

A history of gender and social control in the criminal justice system is provided in Chapter 1. It begins by explaining the concept of gender and what *doing gender* means for males and females as masculine and feminine traits are reflected in men and women's actions. The chapter further provides an overview of how laws and social contracts have reinforced gender differences throughout history.

Chapter 2 discusses female crime and theory; this discussion includes an overview of the relationship between traditional criminological theory and feminist criminology. After describing the typical characteristics of female criminals, the chapter analyzes the ability of traditional criminological theory to explain female crime. The major traditional criminological theories of rational choice, traits, social structure, social processes, critical and developmental are discussed. Next, an overview of the theoretical history is provided. Liberal, Marxist, socialist, postmodernist, and critical race feminist theories are also explained. The chapter further explains the advancement of the field of feminist criminology and its recent advancements.

Many discussions of gender and the criminal justice system focus solely on females, ignoring males. Gender, however, is something that shapes the lives and experiences of both males and females. Chapter 3 discusses crime as a male-dominated activity. The implications of this male dominance for girls and women are also discussed, followed by a discussion of the implications of male dominance for boys and men.

Women and Victims

Females' relationship with the criminal justice system as victims of crime has arguably received more attention than their involvement in other areas of the criminal justice system. This is true despite the fact that females' actual representation in this area is lower than males. The National Crime Victimization Survey collects data on victims of crime in the United States. Using a probability sample that represents all individuals over 12 in the United States, it provides valuable information as to who is most likely to be a victim of a crime. According to the 2013 National Crime Victimization Survey, men were more likely to be victims than females. In fact, when examining who is more often victimized by a stranger, males are almost twice as likely as females (1,192,190 males were victimized by a stranger compared to 620,110 females). When examining victimizations that occur in which the offender and the victim know each other, however, females are more likely to be victimized by an intimate partner, a relative, or a friend/acquaintance than males (Lauritsen & Rezey, 2013).

The second section of this book discusses women as victims. It pays special attention to offenses for which women are overrepresented as victims and explores the historical and current challenges faced by female victims. How the criminal justice system has adjusted to these specific victims' needs is also explored.

Chapter 4 presents a discussion on females' experiences with intimate partner violence. It begins with an overview of the history of intimate partner violence and proceeds into a discussion on the current state of intimate partner violence. The chapter further provides information on the prevalence of intimate partner violence. The characteristics of the victims and offenders of intimate partner violence are also discussed, along with the criminal justice system and community response to intimate partner violence. This chapter further examines the cycle of violence and the issue of stalking.

Sexual assault and the evolution of rape are discussed in Chapter 5. This chapter describes the prevalence of sexual assault and the characteristics of victims, offenders, and the incidences of sexual assault. It further discusses the history of rape, the handling of sexual assault and rape cases in the legal system, and the evaluation of sexual assault and rape laws. The system's current handling on sexual assault and rape cases is also discussed.

Chapter 6 provides a definition of human trafficking and an overview of the history of sex trafficking in the United States. The different types of sex trafficking networks are also described. It further explains the extent of human trafficking in the United States and in several other countries. The chapter also explains the police response to human trafficking, including the contemporary legislation and laws to combat human trafficking.

Chapter 7 discusses women's roles as victims and offenders in cybercrime. It discusses issues such as child pornography, cyberbullying, cyberstalking, digital piracy, and hacking. Females' engagement and dominance in prostitution is also discussed.

Women as Offenders

Males have always engaged in crime at higher rates than females, and this continues to be true today. According to the Uniform Crime Reports, in 2012 males accounted for over 80% of violent offenses and almost 63% of property crime. In fact, the only category in which women made up a larger percentage than men was for prostitution and commercial vice crimes. These percentages are similar to those reported 10 years earlier in 2002, when males made up almost 83% of arrests for violent offenses and over 69% of arrests for property offenses. When changes within gender groups are examined, however, a different picture emerges. From 2002 to 2012, the rates of male arrests for violent offenses decreased almost 15%, and for females the rate of violent offenses decreased less than 3%. For property crime, rates of male arrests have decreased by almost 7%, while rates for female arrests have increased almost 25% (Federal Bureau of Investigation [FBI], 2012).

These changes have led some to argue that the gap between male and female offenders is decreasing. Others, however, argue that these numbers are more of a reflection of changes in arrest patterns and the handling of female-perpetrated crimes. Regardless of which explanation is correct, more females are entering into the criminal justice system than before, or at the very least, the number of males entering the criminal justice system is decreasing at a higher rate than the number of females entering the criminal justice system. As females make up a larger percentage of offenders in the system, it is increasingly important that their needs be addressed and more resources be devoted to understanding their experiences, offending patterns, and treatment in the system.

The third section of this book discusses women as offenders. It covers specific types of female offenders, addressing their prevalence and the current issues surrounding these women and their needs. Treatment of female offenders is also explored.

In Chapter 8, violent women are discussed. This chapter provides an overview on the prevalence of violent offending among women and girls in relation to the prevalence among men. It also discusses the possibility of the closing of the gender gap and women and girls' violent offending. The chapter further discusses female violence in intimate partner relationships, in gangs, and in serial murder. It also covers theoretical explanations for female-perpetrated violence and the treatment of violent women in the criminal justice system.

In Chapter 9, the role of females in the War on Drugs is discussed. This chapter provides an overview of the history of women's drug use and women's contemporary drug use. It then discusses drug policies and legislation. Issues surrounding pregnancy and substance abuse and the intended and unintended consequences of laws to deal with these issues are also discussed. This is followed by a discussion of punishment, treatment, and harm reduction programming for women's substance abuse issues.

Chapter 10 discusses the provenance of female theft. It provides an overview of important legislation and laws. It details women's involvement in the common property crimes of robbery, burglary, motor vehicle theft, shoplifting, larceny, and fraud.

Women's involvement in white collar thefts of embezzlement and check fraud is also discussed. Theoretical considerations for female theft are further examined.

In Chapter 11, prostitution is defined and sex work is discussed. This chapter provides an overview of the history of prostitution and the contemporary legislation addressing prostitution. Next, it discusses the punishments for engaging in prostitution and the solicitation of a prostitute. Other crimes that often surround prostitution and males' involvement in prostitution are also addressed. Last, the chapter discusses violence against prostitutes and the changes within prostitution that have occurred due to globalization and technology.

Mothers who kill their children are discussed in Chapter 12. This chapter provides an overview of the history of filicide and notable cases of filicide in the United States. Legal issues regarding the prosecution and defense of filicide cases are also discussed. The characteristics of both the victims and offenders of filicide are presented and victim–offender relationships are examined. Finally, this chapter discusses the reasons why mothers kill their children.

Chapter 13 addresses the issues surrounding incarcerated females. It provides an overview of the history of women in prison. It also discusses the current rate of female imprisonment and issues facing current female prison populations. The chapter also describes programming for women in prison and the challenges that women face when they exit prison.

Women and Employees

Criminal justice professions such as police officer, probation officer, correctional officer, and lawyer have long been considered male-dominated careers. Women's representation in these occupations, however, has increased greatly during the last several years. Although females' first participation in these occupations was limited to specific roles, their involvement has expanded so they now perform all the same duties as their male counterparts. The fourth section of this book examines the experiences of women practitioners in the fields of policing, corrections, and the courts.

Chapter 14 provides an overview of the history of women in the policing profession. It explains women's early roles as matrons and traces their progression to policewomen. This chapter also discusses the current representation of females in the policing profession, their experiences as police officers, and women's performance in policing.

In Chapter 15, women in the judicial system are discussed. This chapter provides a historic overview of women's role in the court system and explains women's journey and the struggles they faced as they entered into law schools and the legal field. Women's experiences with discrimination and sex-based harassment in the legal profession are also discussed. The chapter further provides a discussion of women as judges in the court system.

Chapter 16 provides a discussion of women employees in the field of corrections. This chapter overviews the challenges of women working in the correctional system, including women working as correctional officers, parole agents, and probation officers. It further discusses what is required to work in corrections, the history of women working in corrections, the obstacles that women face in corrections, and the future of women's work within the field of corrections.

References

Federal Bureau of Investigation (FBI). (2012). *Ten-year arrest trends by sex. Table 33.* Retrieved from   http://www.fbi.gov/about-us/cjis/ucr/crime-in-the-u.s/2012/crime-in-the-u.s.-2012/tables/33tabledatadecoverviewpdf

Lauritsen, J. L., & Rezey, M. L. (2013). *Measuring the prevalence of crime with the National Crime Victimization Survey.* Technical Report. Washington, DC: U.S. Department of Justice.

History of Gender and Social Control in the CJ System

1

CORINA SCHULZE

Contents

For much of American history, men have made laws, arrested, judged, incarcerated, guarded, and policed our society. Only recently has women's influence on the criminal justice system become a rigorous subject of debate in academia (Belknap, 2015). Still, many scholars are prone to discuss this "influence" through scholarly resurrections of exceptional women, like Margaret Brent (1601–1671), or exceptional groups of women (prison matrons). Beyond these history lessons lie philosophical discussions that are variations of the difference/equality debate: whether the influx of women practitioners has made a "difference" or if women have assimilated into a male-dominated culture (e.g., Garcia, 2003; Martin, 1999). Yet even while acknowledging that women's role within the system is substantially rich in history and impact, it remains an inescapable truth that women are treated as intruders in an essentially masculine space. Many larger questions about gender, the criminal justice system, and society remain unanswered. The history of the criminal justice system and the history of social control are inseparable and codependent but rarely examined as such.

Aside from victimization, the numerical underrepresentation of women in every aspect of the criminal justice system had been seen as grounds to dismiss the role of women from criminology and related disciplines. Indeed, masculine hegemony had been so deeply woven into all that is criminal justice that it appears to have collapsed into itself, creating an oxymoronic masculine vacuum from which no real discussion of gender could escape. Academics who are interested in utilizing gender as a conceptual framework still face difficulty in challenging long-standing and persistent approaches to knowledge production. Male interests and epistemologies have prevailed in explaining women's behavior whether it is in relation to victims, offenders, professionals, or policies. The paradox of a male-dominated academic discourse is that underlying assumptions and explanations about men's criminality also explain men's superiority (and ability to govern other men's criminality). Take, for instance, the quality of aggression. Men's victimization and women's criminality have presented many opportunities to see the bigger picture, but instead have been explained away through sexist and often contradictory theories that utilize "common sense" (Belknap, 2015).

The criminal justice system operates within a larger set of systems that is governed and shaped by the social and political context of the current day. Public interest in women's and girls' criminality vacillates between projections of feminism gone wild (women behaving badly), women gone wild (and thus in need of help), or worrying about wild women (crazy women). There is no shortage of well-researched and documented evidence of gender's salience as a basis to judge offenders, victims, and major policies (e.g., Chesney-Lind, 1989; Chesney-Lind & Eliason, 2006). In short, gender is as relevant today as it was in the 1600s (the first precursor/stirrings of the U.S. government), but it is certainly more visible, particularly in criminology. Still, though gender discrimination is generally frowned upon, centuries of institutionalized discrimination are difficult to erase from the hearts and minds of citizens. What Collins (2000) dubs the "structural domain of power," all those institutions and their interrelationships that characterize U.S. society, is generally resistant to change (p. 277).

Women, lacking the rights afforded to full citizens for most of American history, have been subjected to social controls emanating from a number of political and social institutions, notwithstanding the criminal justice system. The following discussion is centered on the criminal justice system, loosely defined as the institution comprised of a web of courts, police agencies, correctional facilities, and the laws that sustain it, as well as other social institutions ranging from as small as the family to as large and amorphous as the media that have served to reenforce and perpetuate notions of women's inferiority. Uncovering the mechanisms by which the criminal justice system has been gendered entails an understanding of women and other social groups' subjugation more generally.

The subsequent section will offer a brief description of how gender and social control are conceptualized in relation to the criminal justice system along with definitions of terms used throughout this chapter. As gender is not the only way in which human beings organize themselves, other socially determined categories like race are included in the discussion. The U.S. criminal justice system has its roots in the colonial period and thus the historical component of this chapter begins in the 1600s. Specifically, women's subjugation under the law is traced to the set of laws known as coverture that in effect gave husbands legal ownership of their wives. Women's legal rights were incorporated with those of the husband upon marriage. The earliest women's rights advocates like Elizabeth Cady Stanton saw the end of coverture as the catalyst in gaining equal rights for women (Holton, 1994). The system of coverture set a precedent that women's bodies do not belong to them since their labor and their offspring were considered a husband's property. The final section of the chapter examines some of the laws and social practices that designated women's bodies as public property. Special attention is paid to current day practices that perpetuate traditional beliefs about the relationship between women and men, women and government, thereby women and the criminal justice system.

Doing Gender in a Gendered Social Hierarchy

> An understanding of how gender is produced in social situations will afford clarification of the interactional scaffolding of social structure and the social control processes that sustain it.
>
> **West and Zimmerman (1987, p. 147)**

Before understanding the meaning of this quote, the use of gender, as a noun, an adjective, and as a verb, requires a brief explanation. *Gender*, as understood here, refers to the social construction of the concept whereas *sex* refers to the anatomical sex designated at birth (West and Zimmerman, 1987). Our focus here is on gender although it should be noted that biological sex is also a debatable concept (try searching the Internet for a clear definition of biological sex). Nevertheless, due to a history of treating sex assignments as rigidly binary, male and female, discussions of gender have also generally followed this pattern. Though limited by this binary, social understandings of gender, masculinity and femininity, are everchanging and vast in their breadth and diversity.

The distinction between sex and gender might seem simple but the everyday conflation of biological sex with gender suggests that society has been unable to separate the two concepts. Speaking of women as naturally or innately passive, for example, demonstrates this confusion. To speak of the passivity of women is to talk about gender, not sex, because it is socially constructed and has been assigned to the category of femininity. Failing to recognize this distinction is what eventually gives way to logically sound arguments that women belong in the kitchen and men on the battlefield. More concerning has been the tendency of the criminal justice system to conflate the two concepts (Belknap, 2015). Some women who are aggressive, for example, are viewed as biological aberrations as they possess a quality that has been designated as strictly male. Therefore, they may be treated more harshly than their equally culpable cohorts or even their aggressive male counterparts, who are behaving according to their nature.

This suggests that gender is not static and instead is something that is made, collectively and individually produced, and is *dynamic* (West and Zimmerman, 1987). Gender expressed as the object of a verb means that gender can be part of an intransitive verb (doing gender), or something that is being done to something, a transitive verb (gendering criminal justice). *Doing gender* refers to the active process that reinforces and perpetuates sex stereotyping and gender binaries (West and Zimmerman, 1987). Miller (1998), for example, studied how robbery is a way of *doing masculinity* in that the very commission of the crime reinforced masculinity. For criminologists, a better understanding of the array of masculinities has paved the way for better theories of criminal behavior and victimization in men and women (e.g., Messerschmidt, 1993). Work now addresses heteronormativity in the criminal justice system in addition to exalting a particular type of masculinity. Miller, Forest, and Jurik (2003), for example, found that police work tends to privilege a heterosexual viewpoint that, combined with masculine values, embraces violence as much as it seeks to contain it.

Violence and crime are as closely interconnected as are violence and masculinity (Harris, 2000; Messerschmidt, 1993). Women's criminality, then, is truly deviant. Criminal men break legal codes not societal conventions and are, more-or-less, "normal" in the sense that they are conforming to the "boys-will-be-boys" mentality. Criminal justice work is similarly masculine, created by a majority male workforce that generally ascribes to the largely masculine value system (Messerschmidt, 1993; Prokos and Padavic, 2002).

The insights and work of feminist researchers as well as others who challenge the essential tenets of criminological theories have forever changed the discipline. Just as there are many criminological approaches, there are many feminism(s) (Gelsthorpe, 1992), but for the sake of simplicity, herein feminism will refer quite loosely to the body of work and the social movements that address patriarchal social structures and gender projects.

For a long time, criminology has been dominated by two methodological approaches. The first approach, a commitment to the "Lombrosian project" (Garland, 1992), refers to the study of crime in a strictly scientific way, which can limit and constrain knowledge. The second approach is the "governmental project," which refers to the science of creating efficient criminal justice institutions (Garland, 1992). Consequently many feminist and critical theories specifically address theories of knowing, particularly the scientific enterprise (Daly & Chesney-Lind, 1988). Feminist criminology today is composed of research, theories, and methods that examine how the criminal justice system and criminology is affected by social constructions of gender (Miller & Mullins, 2006). Unfortunately, some evidence suggests that the research of feminists in criminology continues to be also devalued (Chesney-Lind, 2012) likely because feminism, as understood by the public, is devalued, ridiculed, and generally dismissed as passé.

The criminal justice systems is gendered just as any other system, but is distinct in that it has been so patently defined and saturated by masculinity (Harris, 2000; Messerschmidt, 1993). So seemingly obvious is this observation that scholars have by and large neglected to consider how the criminal justice system and all its attendant effects might be gendered. Feminist criminologists have critiqued theories and practices that do not take gender into consideration, noting that this failure, as Smart (1990) speculated, makes it difficult to "see what criminology has to offer feminism" (p. 84). Daly (1998) later suggested that we should try to see how crime is a correlate of gender, "rather than analyze gender as a correlate of crime" (p. 99). Notwithstanding such critiques, feminist researchers have not abandoned ship and continue to shape the contours and understanding of the discipline.

The study of gender and institutions is inevitably also a study of social control, which in turn should highlight other important social demarcations. These would include, but not be limited to, oppressions due to race, sexuality, and class. An understanding of "intersectionality" (Crenshaw, 1989), recognizing oppressions as overlapping and mutually constitutive, is useful in examining how gender has operated as a mode of social control. Gender may be dynamic but it is also a social structure that manifests itself in a number of ways and on a number of social dimensions (Risman, 2004). People can also "do race" and behave in ways that have been racialized or, in a similar process, deracialized (see Omi & Winant's seminal 1994 *Racial Formation*). It is helpful to examine gender in isolation given its theoretical utility to understanding other types of social control and its historical neglect by scholars, but to limit the discussion to gender only would be insufficient.

W.E.B. Du Bois was the first American sociologist to thoroughly document how crime, concomitant to law, is reflective of the current hierarchy of social groups (Du Bois, 1899). Though largely focused on explaining the cause and effects of African American disenfranchisement, his work extended the discussion from taking groups and slavery as givens to one that recognizes the complex sociocultural history of domination and subordination, of racialization and deracialization. This cultural perspective of crime is echoed in Donald Black's (1983) treatise on crime and social control, which examines how crime can be considered "self-help" and how laws tend to penalize those with the least amount of power. In short, identifying how social control is organized and maintained and by whom is integral to understanding the criminal justice system.

Public policies are in a state of constant evolution in response to changes in societal norms. See, for example, how the meaning of juvenile status offenses has changed over time and how differently girls and boys have been sanctioned for those same offenses (Chesney-Lind & Shelden, 2004; Feld, 2009). It is a cyclical process, in that policies and practices affect outcomes, which in turn affect conceptualizations about crime and gender. Ideas about gender inform ideas about criminality, victimization, and the contours of the criminal justice system. Understood this way, the criminal justice system has always been about women as much as it has been about men. As Simone de Beauvoir famously postulated, women's social position as "other" can afford them with a unique perspective that may allow for more critical, objective reflection of social arrangements. Black feminism(s) has built on this idea pointing out that intersectional approaches can help explain, for example, the experiences of white men precisely because of this "outsider" perspective (Collins, 2000).

Laws and Social Contracts

Law is but one way to exert social control, but it is arguably one of the most influential. Du Bois and then later critical race theorists point out that law is not value-neutral but is instead laden with deeper social meanings that affect social group standing. They have been used to reinforce gender roles, sometimes in obviously sexist ways and at other times with more subtlety (Belknap, 2015). Only recently has law turned to combat gender discrimination, destroying centuries of legal precedent.

An example of subtle sexism is the U.S. Supreme Court decision in *Stanton v. Stanton* (1975) struck down a Utah law which relinquished parents of legal obligations for girls at 18, but boys at 21. While by today's standards this law could be viewed as a benefit to girls more than boys, the law reflected a long-standing belief that boys require more time to become breadwinners, and girls would remain in the custody of their parents until married. This is traceable to the 1600s when American settlers delayed marriage until the male was deemed financially responsible (Mays, 2004). The period of minority (Title 15, Chapter 2, Section 1) has been amended such that it is gender-neutral but it is arguably still *heteronormative*, the privileging of a heterosexual viewpoint, in that the marriage provision remains. This provision states that parents are not legally responsible for children who marry. Utah's stance on same-sex marriage has been historically oppressive and was only recently (October 2014) overturned via judicial intervention.

While laws derive power from the weight and support of the government, the long-standing beliefs that define proper gender roles rely on the stubbornness of the individual and society's contentment with the status quo for survival. A poll conducted by the Pew Research Center (2013) found that Americans still by and large believe that children are better off with a mother who stays at home rather than a father. Much of this could be said to derive from the conflation of gender with biological sex.

Theorists have argued that the survival of modern society depends on the *social contract* in which individuals relinquish rights to the government in exchange for protection. Thomas Hobbes, John Locke, and Jean-Jacques Rousseau are possibly the most cited for social contract theory, though the philosophy stems from early Greek philosophers. All three of the aforementioned philosophers thought that gender and biological sex were inseparable. Moreover, most understandings of the social contract implicitly assume a contract between men and the government, leaving women out altogether. Explaining women's historically inferior place in society, Carole Pateman (1988) identifies the *sexual contract*, in which women relinquish rights to men in exchange for protection. Specifically, women relinquished most of their social, economic, and political rights in hopes that they would be protected by (and from) men. Without regressing into what preceded what, Pateman understands the sexual contract as a precursor and explanation of women's place in the social hierarchy. The marriage contract refers, collectively, to the body of laws that has legitimized men's domination over women (and to a lesser extent, men) and has therefore been intimately tied to the criminal justice system as a whole.

The Marriage Contract

The argument that gender inequality can be traced to the institution of marriage is not a new one. Contrary to popular belief, however, it was not the "radical women" of the 1960s that first suggested this rather incendiary proposition. John Stuart Mill (1869) argued in *The Subjugation of Women* that marriage, which he compared to slavery, was at the heart of women's inequality. Activists in the first women's movement noted that marriage reform was an important and necessary step to freeing women from male tyranny. This is not to say that all activists opposed marriage; rather that all activists recognized the dangers inherent to a system in which women were entirely dependent on men.

For much of U.S. history, women were controlled by either their household or the criminal justice system. As women were considered property of their fathers, marriage meant that the transference of ownership would pass to the husbands. Since women lacked legal rights to their own bodies, options outside of marriage were limited. Losing a husband was for some women tantamount to becoming orphaned and some were forced to fend for themselves sometimes through prostitution and theft. The criminal justice system became a surrogate, albeit an abusive parent to many women who "failed" to find a husband who could be responsible for her or lost a husband due to illness, war, or desertion. While women lost rights in marriage (stated differently, "when fathers lost rights"), men, as husbands, actually gained additional rights including, but not limited to, the right to rape.

In examining early colonial America prior to the formalization of social control (e.g., codified laws and prisons), we can see that religion and sin were prevailing concerns (Mays, 2004). In these times, social control was largely exerted through the community, which was the primary institution of justice, and legal recourse was sought after only in the most extreme of circumstances. Even when legal remedies were utilized, the formal modes of conflict resolution were controlled by men. These proceedings were primitive in nature, relying heavily on puritan values and less on the logic and professional expertise we would expect today. Accordingly, the most common type of crime women were accused of was related to their sexual (mis)behavior and the most effective form of punishment was to publicize and humiliate offenders (Mays, 2004). This preoccupation with sexuality continues today, particularly in young girls, and is inherited from efforts to control women's sexuality (Chesney-Lind & Shelden, 2004).

Implicit to this bygone system were beliefs and values regarding women's inability to protect themselves due to their frailty and inferior mental, physical, and moral qualities. This did not usually result in more benevolent treatment by officials likely because most cases of female deviance were handled by families (Mays, 2004). So, women who came to the attention of the criminal justice system may have been considered particularly ungovernable or were accused of especially heinous crimes. While few records from this time exist, women seemed limited in the types of crime committed because they had limited mobility in that they were confined to their respective households. Unmarried women were therefore most likely to be accused of criminal behavior and their crimes were usually related to their sexual (mis)behavior (Mays, 2004).

America has had a long history of marriage as a "cure" for social ills (Onwuachi-Willig, 2005). In the 1600s, it could be said that marriage really was a primary goal for women, but certainly not solely for romantic reasons. Marriage offered some protection from external factors as well as economic security. Women were generally forbidden to own land, obtain professional educations, and support themselves. The handful of women that have gained the attention of scholars by virtue of their extraordinary accomplishments were from extraordinary social circumstances in which brothers, fathers, husbands, and other men with the means to do so supported their education, though usually in secret.

Due to the English-inspired common law of coverture, wives had no real legal rights. Understandably in such a system, domestic violence was a nonissue with only the most serious cases of physical abuse and murder ever coming to the attention of courts. Physical violence was arguably the lesser concern because marriage was an economic necessity. As Mays (2004) found, a reputation of chastity and fidelity, both venerated qualities in a woman, may have been most vulnerable to abuse. The benefits of marriage, such as they were, were not available to all women, particularly African Americans.

As colonial America grew, so too did the institution of indentured servants and, later, slavery. Slave owners recognized the potential significance of marriage to African Americans and other enslaved people. Marriage among slaves was illegal because married men would have ownership over wives, children, and property (Harris, 1996). Laws governing women's reproduction ensured that children of enslaved mothers belonged to slave owners (Onwuachi-Willig, 2005). This proved to be enormously profitable for slave owners for hundreds of years until the Thirteenth Amendment abolished slavery. Children of slaves were deemed illegitimate and consequently eligible for government assistance. To remedy this potential drain on government, marriage was encouraged among African Americans to ensure that men would be financially responsible for the family. Modern-day equivalents can be found in initiatives like Bush's 2002 Healthy Marriages Act, which singled out black mothers as contributing to overall poverty and crime levels (Onwuachi-Willig, 2005). Many policies supporting the institution of marriage conveniently forget that women are disproportionately victimized by domestic violence and may thus have good reason to be "single."

Race and class have always moderated the relationship between gender and the potential benefits of marriage. The progressive movement of the early nineteenth century relied heavily on social stereotypes of women's inherent femininity and morality thus allowing mostly upper-class, educated white women to lobby against alcohol and other moral vices and usher in a new world of social work. Some of these activists (who generally had good intentions) stressed marriage as a solution for poorer, immigrant, and women of color because they conceptualized the family as consisting of a male breadwinner and a female who is the primary caregiver. Many activists in the progressive movement came to realize that criminality and poverty were linked and women's position in society explained their consequent involvement in the criminal justice system. Still, their efforts were largely targeted at poorer white women and in many cases resulted in a "net-widening" effect in that more women were sanctioned for behavior that men were not. Moreover, African American women were not privy to the "benevolence" of well-meaning reformers.

Women's inferior political and social position explained why, for much of American history, they were either under the control of their husbands/fathers, the criminal justice system, or, for many African American women, under the control of slave owners. Laws and norms of behavior relating to sex explain much of women's underrepresentation and therefore men's *over*representation. It is therefore curious that their involvement, whether it as victims, offenders, or professionals, was not more prominent in academia. As researchers have noted, women have been "invisible" and thus less important to scholarship and public policies (Belknap, 2015; Chesney-Lind & Eliason, 2006). Evidence of this invisibility can be found in the lack of theorizing about the import and necessity of reproduction and families to the development modern civilization.

Women's Bodies as Public Property

Quite obviously, reproduction is the key to human survival and yet has gained little to no attention in academic theories about human behavior and social relations (Hartsock, 1983). The medical establishment and criminal justice system had complementary, albeit confusing, views about women and criminality. Many theories that addressed women's criminality presented women as either mentally ill and/or driven by overactive sex drives which was eagerly promoted and supported by the medical wisdom of the day (Belknap, 2015). The same sex drive seen as driving criminality in women was identified as the transgressor in most crimes that disproportionately affected women, like stalking and sexual assault. Ironically, sexual assaults were not criminalized because men were seen as victims of their own sex drives and thus could not be held responsible for their behavior. Part of this acceptance of male aggression toward women was due to the fact that women did not have the same legal rights and privileges as their male counterparts and in the greater sociopolitical context.

Centuries of such thinking and institutionalization resulted in a national epidemic of violence against women and necessitated the 1994 Violence Against Women's Act (VAWA) which recognized violence as a pervasive and systemic problem. Among the usual feminist suspects, the American Medical Association was also a major proponent of the act. The intended and primary target of VAWA was the criminal justice system, which was seen as most in need of reform. This belies a complex sociopolitical relationship between the medical establishment and the criminal justice system. Scholars now suggest that the history of gender and the medical profession is inseparable to the study of American government (Borst & Jones, 2005). Regardless of which institution, medical or criminal justice, is more enlightened at the moment, it should be clear that without major social change, VAWA's effects are limited (though by no means negligible).

Early Americans generally favored bigger families but nevertheless viewed birth control and reproductive health as important. Quite possibly, this was due to the high rate of mortality for pregnant women and the threat of venereal diseases like syphilis (Mays, 2004). Indeed the evidence suggests that, despite what the moniker "puritan" might suggest, cures for venereal diseases and modes of contraception were discussed somewhat freely (Mays, 2004). Even abortion was not criminalized until much later. The contours of women's rights may have changed, but one cannot necessarily say for the better.

Treating women's bodies as vessels of state property has its origins not only in the marital contract, but in laws that claimed that children born to enslaved mothers were also slaves. This was known as "hereditary slavery" and in 1662 Virginia was the first state to pass a law that legitimized this practice. When viewed through the cultural lens of that time period, laws like this served as tacit encouragement of rape. The male sex drive narrative, in combination with the monetization of African women and children's bodies, help explain why rape was more likely to be treated as a method to increase one's property value than as a felony. The rape of women with the purpose of impregnation, incidentally, has been a tactic used in many wars, many occurring in this century, and is due to a shared understanding of a woman's body as the property of the invader (Enloe, 2000). One can easily see how the transition from coverture to complete ownership of what happened inside women's bodies was an easy one, especially if the medical community offered "scientific" corroboration.

Slave owners encountered little difficulty in arguing, and legally codifying, ownership over women's internal organs. Not soon thereafter laws were written that encapsulated all women, "free" or not. Thus, the necessity of regaining control over women's bodies has remained a central tenet of different women's rights movements. Paternalism, the idea that women must be protected from themselves by a benevolent state, can be found in the history of the medical profession and is most visible today in discussions about contraception and reproductive rights (Wynn and Trussell, 2006). Now, however, the linkage of abortion to any related issue about women's reproductive rights can render it untenable in the political realm.

For a better part of the eighteenth and nineteenth centuries, doctors provided "gender-neutral" health care and relied heavily on the efforts of midwives when it came to women (Borst & Jones, 2005). Issues, like reproductive rights, would have remained private without the efforts to extricate by various women's social movements and groups (Bone, 2010; Parry, 2011). The criminal justice system and other systems of social control often worked in tandem to silence leaving activists little choice but to turn to public speaking and other ways of disseminating information (Bone, 2010). When it looked as if women were successful in raising public awareness, laws were passed to make such activities illegal. Take, for instance, the 1873 Comstock Act that prohibited the "obscene," material that could potentially educate people on subjects like contraception and reproductive health. This rather vague and therefore broad decree led many states to pass laws that criminalized even *speaking* about contraception (McFarlane & Meier, 2001). So effective were these resulting laws and actions taken by the criminal justice establishment that related topics became socially taboo even when decriminalized (Bone, 2010) and affected most of the medical community to the point of gross negligence (Reed, 1978).

Even today, simply speaking about reproductive rights can result in public censure and humiliation. Take, for instance, the case of Rush Limbaugh (1951–) calling Sandra Fluke (1981–) a "slut" for testifying in Congress about women's right to birth control. In 2012, the then-law student Fluke was asked to testify about the importance of providing health care at religious institutions like Georgetown, the school she was attending. Limbaugh responded by pronouncing Fluke a prostitute on his radio show. That Limbaugh is a proud, serial sexist is less important than his being quite possibly the most popular (and well-paid) radio talk show host in recent history (and the dubious distinction of coining the moniker "femi-nazi"). In other words, misogynic viewpoints are not a thing of the past.

Tempting as it might be to pass judgment on America's past from today's privileged standpoint, the power of public opinion should not be underestimated and any naysayers are therefore particularly remarkable. Victoria Woodhull, known for having both beauty and brains, flaunting her sexuality (in public! and for wearing pants!), also being the first woman to run for president, and run a newspaper, (abbreviated list), was such a person. Sadly it is the rather uncharismatic Anthony Comstock, the one who arrested her, who is most often cited in American government texts. Woodhull's influence affected thousands of Americans who, by all accounts, saw her as one of the most famous people of that time.

Her personal infamy aside, the social revolution she was a part of and inspired has been woefully underappreciated (though a cursory Internet search will yield many a website dedicated to her extraordinary life).

A more recognizable figure in U.S. history books is Margaret Sanger (1879–1966), perhaps the most influential leader of the contraception and reproductive rights movement. Sanger saw the importance of forcing previously "private" issues into the public discourse, and purposefully broke the law to do so (Parry, 2011). Not until the 1960s, did birth control become widely available but social norms regarding women's sexual behavior affected how doctors treated women who sought to obtain it. Many informal and institutionalized barriers, like the requirement in some states to be married, further prevented women from obtaining birth control. Indeed, the topic has retained its controversial nature well into the twenty-first century.

Feminists have documented a myriad of ways in which the United States continues to regulate and criminalize women's bodies. The National Advocates for Pregnant Women (NAPW) was established in 2001 because women's bodies, particularly women of color, continue to be a source of political contestation. In 2001, Regina McNight, an African American woman, was convicted of homicide because of her use of cocaine during pregnancy; even though evidence of cocaine's negligible effects was presented at trial. The American Civil Liberties Union (ACLU) was able to overturn her case, but not until after she served more than 8 years. Hundreds of similar cases demonstrate a continuing preoccupation with women's bodies and how race mitigates perceptions and treatment in the media as well as the criminal justice system.

Case Study 1

In 2013, a Tennessee woman was arrested for assault for taking illegal drugs while pregnant. While morally objectionable, this case represents a continuing trend in governmental attempts to control women's bodies through criminalization even though the medical community overwhelmingly has rejected such attempts. The American Medical Association, the American Academy of Pediatrics, the American College of Obstetricians and Gynecologists, the American Public Health Association, and many more related professional organizations are against such legislative efforts, so the criminal justice system's treatment of pregnant women should be considered a women's rights violation (NAPW). Moreover, the government's regulation of contraception and reproductive rights has criminalized the behavior of licensed medical professionals while concomitantly legalizing discrimination against women. The Supreme Court's 2014 ruling in *Burwell v. Hobby Lobby* is an example of the latter in that employers are allowed to deny contraceptive coverage. The decision largely framed the issue as one involving religious rights not women's rights. Notably the only women justices on the Supreme Court dissented with the majority opinion.

As tends to be the case, governmental views of pregnancy and the sanctity of human life are contradictory and dependent on race and class. A recent California State Auditor's (2013) report found that female prisoners, disproportionately women of color, had been sterilized without first obtaining consent. Controlling reproduction due to perceptions about who is most worthy of parenthood has a long history, most notably in the nineteenth and twentieth eugenics movements, and has been supported by the government, the public, and even some feminists but, perhaps most significantly, afforded scientific *legitimacy* by the medical community.

Critical conflict theorists inspired by the writings of Karl Marx (a questionable proponent of women's liberation having stated that "social progress can be measured exactly by the social position of the fair sex, the ugly ones included") have focused on women's enslavement under capitalism. Later Huey P. Newton, founder of the Black Panther Party (a revolutionary group not known for its welcoming stance on women), attempted to galvanize support for women's emancipation from their inferior social status (Jeffries, 2002). The interrelationships between movements for women's rights and African American men and women's rights are often hidden from the popular discourse and usually discussed in isolation from one another. However, there is a close association traceable to early American and later to what many identify as the official beginning of the women's rights movement at Seneca Falls. Frederick Douglass, quite possibly one of the most famous African American men in U.S. history, was the only man to support Elizabeth Cady Stanton when she became the first woman in the United States to publically demand the right to vote (though it should be noted Margaret Brent, mentioned at the beginning of the chapter, did precede her by a couple hundred years). Whatever the reasons for these blind spots in history, women's rights to reproductive health and contraception have always been of crucial importance to revolutionaries and social movements diverse in purpose and ideology.

Men's bodies, especially in reference to their contributions to reproduction, are rarely the subject of heated political debate, unless in reference to the victimization of women (Wynn & Trussell, 2006). "Proper" women do not typically enjoy sex with more than one partner (and the degree to which women enjoy sex with just one partner is a debatable subject) and must constantly fend off the advances of men. Wynn and Trussell (2006) illustrate this double standard by contrasting the rhetoric surrounding the emergency contraceptive pill (plan B) to the uproar caused by the discovery that hundreds of convicted sex offenders had been taking Medicaid-covered Viagra in 14 states. In essence, women were seen as incapable of making moral decisions as a result of a drug, and thus in need of protection, whereas the men were depicted as victims of a gender that victimizes women. Sexism, like other "isms," often sends out messages that are contradictory and confusing.

Concluding Thoughts

The marital contract may have provided the initial scaffolding necessary to extend the criminal justice system's control over women's bodies, but social understandings about gender and gender roles provided an enduring foundation. Laws were important in preventing women the right to an education, to work, and to participate in politics; but it was the social condemnation and censure that perhaps was most influential. Both men and women were actively hostile to changes proposed by women's rights advocates and encouraged the criminal justice system to arrest and degrade women who dared challenge the status quo. Typical portrayals of "radical" feminists tend to recognize men and women in contemporary social movements. However, these so-called radicals, who took on an entrenched and oppressive system of laws and societal conventions, even encouraging active rebellion, can be found among the earliest advocates for women's rights (Holton, 1994). The complex history of women's rights advocates within the antislavery and later civil rights movements is often homogenized and whitewashed promoting the falsity that contemporary feminism(s) is dangerous and, perhaps most damning, no longer relevant.

The Declaration of Rights and Sentiments drafted at the Seneca Falls Convention in 1848, declaring women's equality, was a radical call for change, yet is still a relatively unknown event in American history. It set the tone for women's rights movements that followed and led even more men to join the fight for equality. Men's impact in these movements has also been silenced as a consequence of refusal to see history, and consequently society, as gendered. This silence is a primary component in the definition of *patriarchy* as Johnson (1997) identifies such a society as "male-identified": things considered good and "normal" are, in effect and practice, masculine (note he also adds "male-dominated" and "male-centered" to the definition). This explains women's invisibility from history books and criminology because, in actuality, patriarchy itself is invisible to the vast majority of participants. An understanding of patriarchy in its most literal sense, rule by men, can stymie progress because it presents numerical increases in women as the solution to dismantling such a system. By pointing to successes of women in business, in politics, and in other institutions like the criminal justice system is perpetuating the notion that all it's going to take is more women behaving like men…or a hope that having women will transform the culture.

Public property as women's bodies might have been, women's experiences and viewpoints are conspicuously absent from the tomes of scholarly work having been relegated to the private and thus invisible sphere. Much of American history has been (re)written such that groups and individuals who were in some way or another enslaved, exploited, unpopular, radical, or viewed less deserving of full citizenship are cast in supporting roles. Unfortunately, many still consider the mention of individual African American men and women (or the designation of a month) as homage enough to the African American experience. Think of the difference between a friend, who knows how you think and what you value, and an acquaintance who, though perhaps well-meaning, does not understand where you came from or why that might be important and valuable. Who might better tell your story? More importantly, *why* might someone like that provide a more complete picture?

Discussion Questions

1. How have understandings of sex and gender affected women and men as criminals, as criminal justice professionals, and as victims?
2. When is gender more important than sex in explaining differences between men and women? When is sex more important than gender?
3. How has the institution of marriage affected women's treatment in the criminal justice system? Do you think our current understandings of marriage help explain criminality and victimization?
4. What justifications are given for the omission of women from the study of criminal justice and in criminology? Why are these reasons insufficient?
5. How does an understanding of intersectionality help understand women's treatment in the criminal justice system? What modern-day examples of intersectionality can you find in the media?

References

Belknap, J. (2015). *The invisible woman: Gender, crime, and justice* (4th ed.). Stamford, CT: Cengage Learning.

Black, D. (1983). Crime as social control. *American Sociological Review, 48*(1), 34–45.

Bone, J. E. (2010). When publics collide: Margaret Sanger's argument for birth control and the rhetorical breakdown of barriers. *Women's Studies in Communication, 33*(1), 16–33.

Borst, C. G., & Jones, K. W. (2005). As patients and healers: The history of women and medicine. *OAH Magazine of History, 19*(5), 23–26.

California State Auditor's Report. (2013). Sterilization of female inmates. Retrieved August 2, 2014 from the California's State Auditor website, http://www.auditor.ca.gov/pdfs/reports/2013-120.pdf

Chesney-Lind, M. (1989). Girls' crime and woman's place: Toward a feminist model of female delinquency. *Crime & Delinquency, 35*, 5–29.

Chesney-Lind, M. (2012). Campus crime beat: The challenges of doing feminist criminology in the academy. *Women & Criminal Justice, 22*(1), 54–67.

Chesney-Lind, M., & Eliason, M. (2006). From invisible to incorrigible: The demonization of marginalized women and girls. *Crime, Media, and Culture, 2*, 29–48.

Chesney-Lind, M., & Shelden, R. G. (2004). *Girls, delinquency, and juvenile justice* (3rd ed.). Belmont, CA: Wadsworth publishing.

Collins, P. H. (2000). *Black feminist thought: Knowledge, consciousness, and the politics of empowerment* (2nd ed.). New York: Routledge.

Crenshaw, K. W. (1989). Demarginalizing the intersection of race and sex: A Black feminist critique of antidiscrimination doctrine, feminist theory, and antiracist politics. *University of Chicago Legal Forum, 139*, 139–167.

Daly, K. (1998). Gender, crime, and criminology. In M. Tonry (Ed.), *The handbook of crime and justice*. Oxford, UK: Oxford University Press.

Daly, K., & Chesney-Lind, M. (1988). Feminism and criminology. *Justice Quarterly, 5*, 497–538.

Du Bois, W. E. B. (1899). *The Philadelphia Negro: A social study*. Philadelphia, PA: University of Pennsylvania Press.

Enloe, C. (2000). *Maneuvers: The international politics of militarizing women's lives*. Berkeley, CA: University of California Press.

Feld, B. C. (2009). Violent girls or relabeled status offenders? An alternative interpretation of the data. *Crime & Delinquency, 55*(2), 241–265.

Garcia, V. (2003). "Difference" in the police department: Women, policing, and "Doing Gender." *Journal of Contemporary Criminal Justice, 19*(3), 330–344.

Garland, D. (1992). Of crimes and criminals: The development of criminology in Britain. In M. Maguire, R. Morgan, & R. Reiner (Eds.), *Oxford handbook of criminology*. Oxford, U.K.: Oxford University Press.

Gelsthorpe, L. (1992). Feminism and criminology. In M. Maguire, R. Morgan, & R. Reiner (Eds.), *Oxford handbook of criminology*. Oxford, UK: Oxford University Press.

Harris, A. (2000). Gender, violence, race, and criminal justice. *Stanford Law Review, 52*(4), 777–807.

Harris, C. I. (1996). Finding Sojourner's truth: Race, gender, and the institution of property. *Cardozo Law Review, 18*, 209–332.

Hartsock, N. (1983). The feminist standpoint: Developing the ground for a specifically feminist historical materialism. In S. Harding & M. B. Hintikka (Eds.), *Discovering reality*. Boston, MA: Ridel.

Holton, S. S. (1994). "To educate women into rebellion": Elizabeth Cady Stanton and the creation of a transatlantic network of radical suffragists. *The American Historical Review, 99*(4), 1112–1136.

Jeffries, J. L. (2002). *Huey P. Newton: The radical theorist*. Jackson, MS: University Press of Mississippi.

Johnson, A. G. (1997). *The gender knot: Unraveling our patriarchal legacy*. Philadelphia, PA: Temple University Press.

Martin, S. E. (1999). Police force or police service? Gender and emotional labor. *The Annals of the American Academy of Political and Social Science, 56*(1), 111–126.

Mays, D. A. (2004). *Women in early America: Struggle, survival, and freedom in a new world.* Santa Barbara, CA: ABC-CLIO.

McFarlane, D. R., & Meier, K. J. (2001). *The politics of fertility control.* New York: Seven Bridges.

Messerschmidt, J. W. (1993). *Masculinities and crime: Critique and reconceptualization of theory.* Lanham, MD: Rowman and Littlefield.

Miller, J. (1998). Up it up: Gender and the accomplishment of street robbery. *Criminology, 36*(1), 37–66.

Miller, J., & Mullins, C. W. (2006). The Status of feminist theories in criminology. In F. T. Cullen, J. Wright, & C. Belvins (Eds.), *Taking stock: The status of criminological theory* (Vol. 15). New Brunswick, NJ: Transaction Publishers.

Miller, S. L., Forest, K. B., & Jurik, N. C. (2003). Diversity in blue: Lesbian and gay police officers in a masculine occupation. *Men and Masculinities, 5*(4), 355–385.

Omi, M., & Winant, H. (1994). *Racial formations in the United States* (2nd ed.). London, U.K.: Routledge.

Onwuachi-Willig, A. (2005). The return of the ring: Welfare reform's marriage cure as the revival of post-bellum control. *California Law Review, 96*(6), 1647–1696.

Parry, M. (2011). Pictures with a purpose. *Journal of Women's History, 23*(4), 108–130.

Pateman, C. (1988). *The sexual contract.* Redwood City, CA: Stanford University Press.

Pew Research Center. (2013). Pew Research Center Survey conducted April 25–28. Retrieved August 2, 2014 from http://www.pewsocialtrends.org/2013/05/29/breadwinner-moms/1/

Prokos, A., & Padavic, I. (2002) "There oughtta be a law against bitches": Masculinity in police academy training. *Gender, Work, & Organization, 9*(4), 439–459.

Reed, J. (1978). *From private vice to public virtue: Birth control since 1830.* New York: Basic Books.

Risman, B. J. (2004). Gender as a social structure: Theory wrestling with activism. *Gender and Society, 18*(4), 429–450.

Smart, C. (1990). Feminist approaches to criminology, or postmodern woman meets atavistic man. In L. Gelsthorpe & A. Morris (Eds.), *Feminist perspectives in criminology.* Philadelphia, PA: Open University Press.

West, C., & Zimmerman, D. H. (1987). Doing gender. *Gender and Society, 1*(2), 125–151.

Wynn, L. L., & Trussell, J. (2006). The social life of emergency contraception in the United States: Disciplining pharmaceutical use, disciplining sexuality, and constructing zygotic bodies. *Medical Anthropology Quarterly, 20*(3), 297–320.

Female Crime and Theory

2

ALANA VAN GUNDY

Contents

The goal of this chapter is to discuss the theoretical history of female crime and the relationship between traditional criminological theory and feminist criminology. First, a description of the characteristics and gender-specific variables of female offenders will be presented. Second, the history of traditional criminological theory and its ability to explain female criminality will be discussed. The chapter will then describe the current state of feminist criminological theory and its different forms. It will then conclude with a discussion of the advancements that have occurred within the field of feminist criminology.

Background

Male offenders comprise the majority of offenders being arrested, charged, convicted, and imprisoned within the criminal justice system. As a result, the field of criminology has paid little attention to understanding female criminality and has neglected to create policies designed to address or treat female offenders until recently. Traditional criminological theory was simply applied to female offenders in the same manner as at the time females that committed crimes were viewed as more "male-like," and therefore, criminologists operated under the assumption that male-centric theory would apply to a female offender.

Traditionally, female criminality has been strongly impacted by the social context and the concept of societal gender role expectations. In other words, female crime has historically been treated as a norm violation in which women are viewed as being double-deviant—violations of role expectations or "womanhood" in addition to violations of criminal law (Belknap, 2001). Punishments for these double violations have often been gender specific and have included burning at the stake, branding, or women being forced to wear a letter, having their breasts ripped off their chests, the brank or Scold's Bridle for idle gossiping, and masks to prevent women from opening their mouths—each a punishment that was specific to females that engaged in socially constructed norm or criminal violations.

While gender specificity was apparent with regard to role expectations and punishments for speaking/gossiping/adultery, it remained nonexistent in the field of criminology. Theorists continued to argue that traditional criminological theory applied to women that engaged in crime as equally as it did to males. Society continued to informally sanction females for violations of role expectations and punish in the same manner as males for violations of criminal law. This has resulted in a steady increase in female offending, an acceleration of the female prison population, and a sustained lack of understanding on the impact of criminal law and policy on female behavior.

Despite the increase in the rates of female offending over the last three decades, males continue to make up the large majority of those processed in the criminal justice system. This continued to leave females of microscopic interest to researchers, public policy makers, and theorists alike until the 1970s and 1980s. The Women's Movement of the 1970s and Bell Hooks 1984 book titled *Feminist Theory: From Margin to Center* began to stimulate attention to the peripheral status of women in society and contributed to the emergence of the field of critical feminist theory. In conjunction with the steady increase in the female prison population that began in 1985, those familiar with crime statistics, criminological theory, and criminal policy began to take a second look at how well traditional criminological theory was able to explain female criminality, including the gender-specific characteristics and reasons for engaging in criminality that were specific to females.

Female Offenders

Throughout the history of crime and punishment, there has been a gender gap in crime. Males and females are both more likely to be involved in lower-level and nonviolent criminal activity than they are to be involved in serious, violent crime, but women are less likely to engage in criminal activity in totality (Schwartz & Steffensmeier, 2008). While there is participation by both genders in each type of criminal activity, females have historically offended at higher rates than males at only one criminal activity: prostitution. Criminology has conceded that female offenders commit less crime in general than males, are less dangerous and violent, and are less likely to recidivate, be a professional criminal, or be involved in multiple crime typologies than males (Carlen & Worrall, 1987; Immarigeon & Chesney-Lind, 1993; Silvestri & Crowther-Dowey, 2008).

The demographic characteristics of male and female offenders also show important points of convergence and divergence. The profiles of male and female offenders are similar in that they are both primarily from a lower socioeconomic status background, are under-educated, show histories of drug and alcohol abuse and addiction, are disproportionately of minority status, are from broken homes, and evidence mental and physical health issues.

While these characteristics hold for both genders, there are some significant differences. While both males and females come from a low socioeconomic status, females are more likely to be responsible for dependents, either children or their parents (Bloom, Owen, & Covington, 2003). Females are also more likely to have multiple mental and physical health problems (e.g., co-occurring disorders such as bipolar and depression) in comparison to one primary problem for males. One of the most significant points of divergence is the previous physical and sexual abuse history. While male offenders show a higher prevalence to be victims of sexual or physical abuse in comparison to the general public, studies have shown that up to half of female offenders have been sexually and/or physically abused prior to incarceration (Beck, 2000).

Females differ biologically, sociologically, and psychologically from males. Thus, a fair assumption is that the reasons for engaging in criminal behavior will have a different origin than the origin for male criminality. Studies consistently find that women are less aggressive than men (Moffitt, Caspi, Rutter, & Silva, 2001; Wright, Tibbetts, & Daigle, 2008), prone to different medical conditions (McQueen, 2006), experience higher levels of social control by family members and social/structural institutions, have different relational experiences (Eagly, 1987), are more likely to be at risk from those closest to them, and are impacted by personality and psychological traits in different ways than males (Thomas & Pollard, 2001). Despite these differences, traditional criminological theory has historically been utilized to explain, predict, and treat female criminality.

Traditional Criminological Theory

Traditional criminology originated from research, publications, and models that focused primarily, if not solely, on explaining male criminality. Each criminological theory creates a model that focuses on specific variables that are proposed to be related to the origin, existence, and desistance of crime. They attempt to answer commonly asked questions about crime and make statements about the relationship between crime and related variables (Akers, 2000; Vold, Bernard, & Snipes, 1998). There are six broad categorizations of traditional criminological theories:

1. *Rational choice*: This classical form of criminological theory was conceived in the eighteenth century. Rational choice theory views crime as offense and offender specific and argues that crime is a choice and that individuals make a distinct and rational choice to engage in criminal behavior. The premise of rational choice theory is that individuals consider personal and situational factors, determine whether the risks outweigh the benefits, and make an individual decision to engage or not engage in crime. Policy initiatives of rational choice theory include swift, harsh, and certain punishment in order to make the costs and risks outweigh the benefits of the criminal behavior. Influencers of rational choice theory include Cesare Beccaria and the concept of the social contract, Jeremy Bentham and his theory of utilitarianism, and James Q. Wilson's, the creator of the concept of broken windows theory.

2. *Trait theory*: The premise of trait theory is that biological makeup and genetics control human behavior. These theories argue that human behaviors such as attachment, aggression, violence, and impulsivity interact with the environment to cause

antisocial or deviant behavior. Trait theory is divided into two categories: biosocial theories (biochemical conditions, neurophysiological conditions, arousal, genetics, and evolutionary theory) and psychological trait theories (psychodynamic and attachment). Policy initiatives include dealing with antisocial behavior prior to the behavior occurring (primary prevention), provided to those that are at risk for criminal behavior (secondary prevention), and after the punitive process to impact recidivism (tertiary prevention). Influencers of trait theory include Charles Darwin's evolutionary theory, Cesare Lombroso and positivist criminology, John Bowlby and attachment theory, and Sheldon and Eleanor Glueck's research on psychopathy.

3. *Social structure*: Social structure theory focuses on the impact that the social structure (such as economics and poverty) has on criminal behavior. The three categories of social structure theories include social disorganization theory (deteriorated neighborhoods, inadequate social control, and conflicting norms and values), strain theory (unequal distribution of wealth causes frustration and may result in antisocial methods of achievement), and cultural deviance theory (subcultures are developed and offer opposing or antisocial ideologies). Policy initiatives of social structure theory include cleaning up neighborhoods and improving the community structure, offering social welfare programming, attempting to bridge the gap between cultural norms, and supporting for community-based programming (e.g., community-based policing). Influencers of social structure theory include Emile Durkheim and his views on the division of labor, Robert Merton and anomie theory, and Robert Agnew's general strain theory.

4. *Social process*: Social process theory focuses on the process of human interaction. This human interaction can be positive and prosocial or negative and antisocial. The process can be impacted by family, peers, education, and those in authority. The three categories of social process theory include social learning theory (all behavior is learned, including criminal), social control theory (associations with others can impact behavior), and social reaction theory (those labeled as negative will act as such). Policy initiatives of social control theory include providing strong prosocial role models to those at risk in order to impact their learning, increase bonds and associations with others that lead to prosocial behavior, and diversion programs that bypass the system to avoid designating or labeling an individual in a negative manner. Influencers of social process theory include Edwin H. Sutherland's differential association theory, Walter Reckless's containment theory, Travis Hirschi's social bond theory, George Herbert Mead's concept of the generalized other and symbolic interactionism, and Edwin Lemert's labeling theory.

5. *Critical criminology*: The premise of critical criminology is that social conflict impacts criminal behavior. This conflict is a result of societal unrest and is experienced differently by those that lack power (based upon gender, race, and class) and that the working or lower class of society is exploited by those that have control. Critical criminology is a Marxist-based viewpoint of society that argues that crime is a socially construed variable created by those in power to control the lower classes through legislation. There are four theories of critical criminology: left realism (crime is a function of relative deprivation under a capitalistic system), feminist theory (gender inequality), power-control theory (economic inequality), and peacemaking criminology (punitive strategies are counterproductive).

Policy initiatives of critical theories focus on decreasing conflict, inequality, and competition, and support the utilization of restorative justice and reintegrative shaming. Influencers of critical criminology include Karl Marx and his theories of economic struggle and social conflict, James Messerschmidt's masculinity theory, Freda Adler's liberation theory, and Meda Chesney-Lind's concept of the invisibility of women.

6. *Developmental theories*: Developmental theories focus on the onset, continuation, and desistance from criminal behavior or what is called the criminal trajectory. These theories integrate components of all previously discussed theories such as sociological, psychological, economic, and biological components. The two categories of developmental theory include life course theory (criminality is a dynamic process that is influenced by multiple variables) and latent trait theory (human and criminal development is controlled by a stable master trait that develops from the beginning of an individual's life). Policy initiatives of developmental theories focus on multisystemic treatment models that provide personal, social, educational, economic, and family services to young children and adults and continued treatment as an adult, throughout an individual's life course. Influencers of developmental theory include Robert Sampson and John Laub's life course theory, Rolf Loeber's persisters and desisters' theory, Michael Gottfredson and Travis Hirschi's theory of self-control, and Terrie Moffitt's developmental theory of crime.

Each of these categories includes two or more subtheories that propose additional variables deemed to be related to criminality. The theories are widely tested, and the theories that have the most measurable outcomes have strong and consistent findings either positively or negatively related to the proposed variables (e.g., Travis Hirschi's social bond theory is one of the most often-tested theories, and its findings remain largely consistent). The variables as proposed here offer strong, distinct viewpoints of what causes crime and how to address, treat, and to some extent deter criminality. However, the one thing that they each hold in common with the exception of conflict theory is the lack of attention paid to the impact, interaction, and importance of gender to criminality.

Theoretical History of Female Crime

The evolution and history of female criminality evolved from a mere mention in the early 1800s to sparse books dedicated solely to female offenders and their behavior. These founding books led to a revolutionary addition to criminology in the form of feminist criminology. The field of feminist criminology became a focus of research as a resultant convergence of factors: books calling attention to the types of crimes committed by women and the different reasons they were committed, the Women's Liberation Movement, increasing engagement by women in criminal activity, and the continued economic marginalization of women, in particular women of minority status.

In 1895, Cesare Lombroso was one of the first criminologists to call attention to the female offender (Lombroso & Ferraro, 1895). He had previously focused exclusively on male offending, viewed crime from a positivist viewpoint, and argued that genetics would determine criminality. Lombroso and Ferraro's work was one of the first published efforts at attempting to understand female crime. *The Female Offender* focused on the anthropological differences between men and women's skulls, brains, facial and cephalic anomalies, and body typology, and studied the "born" criminals, occasional criminals, hysterical offenders, crimes of passion, suicides, and female lunatics (Lombroso & Ferraro, 1895). He was followed by the works of Sigmund Freud as described next.

Sigmund Freud and Dora

In the late 1800s and early 1900s, Sigmund Freud analyzed the case of a "hysterical" girl named Dora (Freud was hired by Dora's father to help and analyze her "condition"). Consistent with the social times, the lack of focus on female criminals, and the state of criminological theory, Freud held off from publishing his case study as he felt it would "put people off"; however, his full case study was later published. It provides valuable insight into both the social context of the times and early criminology while foreshadowing things to come in later developments of criminological theory.

Freud introduces Dora's case with the following disclaimer "Now in this case study— sexual questions will be discussed with all possible frankness, the organs and functions of sexual life will be called by their proper names, and the pure-minded reader can convince himself from my description that I have not hesitated to converse upon such subjects in such language even with a young woman" (p. 3). He also focuses on interpreting her dreams, examining her lesbian tendencies, and exposes what he considers to be her repressed desires. Freud notes that Dora is 18 years old, the product of a dominant father that was well off yet stricken with illness and an absent mother, and that the father and daughter were drawn together by the usual sexual attraction (p. 14). He also describes her as suffering from nervous coughing, severe migraines, spurts of unconsciousness, sexual delusions, a victim of sexual trauma (he later convinced Dora she was actually in love with the perpetrator), and a "girl of intelligence and engaging looks" (p. 16). Freud's analysis of Dora's behavior consistently focused on her identification with others, including her father, her brother, her aunt, and her cousin, all of which he felt she was envious of.

His dream analysis of Dora focused on her recurrent dreams as she reported to him. According to Freud, dreams are unfulfilled wishes that are held in the unconscious. When Dora reported dreaming about her house burning down and her father standing by her bed to save her and her mother attempting to retrieve a jewelry box, Freud explained to her that she had heard her father say that he was afraid of fire, that Dora herself viewed her father standing by her bed in lieu of the individual that caused her sexual trauma, and the jewelry represented her sexual organs (she wanted to protect her sexual organs from being taken). Dora later had a dream in which she went to her home and found a letter from her mother stating that her father had died, and then after following her mother's instruction to go to the station, she found herself back at home where the maid notified her that both her mother and father had passed away. Freud explained the meaning of this dream to be latent for Dora's dreams of revenge toward others.

Additional Works

In 1931, Cecil Bishop wrote *Women and Crime*, and he titled his first chapter "The New Outlook." This new outlook posited that by the time of publication, women had "won most of their objectives and they have good reason to be jubilant at their success" (p. 3). Bishop's book foreshadowed later arguments of equal opportunity by arguing that as women gain emancipation, they become unhappy as a result, they become more "criminally minded" (p. 4). Similar to Lombroso and Ferarro, Bishop focused on the crime of prostitution, but unlike previous criminologists, he did focus on additional relationships between gender and housing (deeming substandard housing as hell on earth), employment (male domination in the workforce), drugs (specifically cocaine), homosexuality (which he referred to as perversion), media and literature subjugating women, and venereal disease. Bishop and his multifaceted approach to viewing female criminality laid a foundation for the later evolution of the importance of power, dominance, social structure, and socioeconomic status and their impact specifically *on women*.

Additional support for the unique impact of social, economic, and psychological factors were presented in writings by Otto Pollak, Freda Adler, and Carol Smart. Otto Pollak (1950) argued that women were in fact not less criminal than men, but simply were able to mask their criminality better than males because they are more adept at deceit. Additionally, he argues that this gender-specific adeptness at deceit results in biased crime statistics, lower prosecution rates, and a misunderstanding or unwillingness to examine the female victim's preference (family and children). Similar to Bishop, he also argues that women's emancipation has led to an increase in female criminality, and he discusses specific biological (physical weakness, physiological overdevelopment of girls, generative phases of female development) and social factors (differential association, creation of criminal desire, accessibility of victim) specific to female criminality.

Freda Adler's book *Sisters in Crime* also contributed to the history of feminist theory by examining the crime patterns of women, identifying additional crime typologies, and focusing on interacting variables such as race and class. Her work discussed the acceleration of female criminality in areas outside of the stereotypical prostitution by focusing on their involvement in violent crimes such as robbery and drug-related criminal activity. She stated that her book "offers a psychosocial perspective through which female criminal behavior can be understood as a natural extension of normal female behavior, which is itself both a product and producer of the larger forces which mediate all human interaction" (Adler, 1975, p. 3).

One of the most influential and important books in the history of feminist criminology is *Women, Crime and Criminology: A Feminist Critique* by Carol Smart (1976). The social context (Women's Liberation Movement, etc.) at the time of her writing was ripe for a critical analysis of criminology's lack of focus on female offenders and criminology. Smart's analysis was one of the first publications to commit to analyzing female offenders and the state of female crime solely from a feminist perspective. Although she continued the discussion of stereotypical female crimes such as prostitution and shoplifting, her main focus was on the treatment of females by law enforcement, the courts, and corrections and the interaction between female behavior and histories of sexual abuse, mental illness, and sexual politics. She also reviewed studies that were available up to the time of her publication, and in the last chapter of her book, she calls for a shift of criminology to include "a non-separatist social science….because women and men do not act separately in the social world, they are not independent of each other and their inter-relationship is a vital fact of life" (p. 179). This statement foreshadowed the blurred gender lines that are now an important component of gender and crime studies, and the themes presented in her book strongly impacted the evolution of feminist criminology.

Last, in 1988, Kathleen Daly and Meda Chesney-Lind published a journal article showcasing five strong consistent elements that must be considered when examining crime from a feminist perspective. They include (verbatim from Daly & Chesney-Lind, 1988, p. 504) the following:

1. Gender is not a natural fact but a complex social, historical, and cultural product; it is related to, but not simply derived from, biological sex difference and reproductive capacities.
2. Gender and gender relations order social life and social institutions in fundamental ways.
3. Gender relations and constructs of masculinity and femininity are not symmetrical but are based on an organizing principle of men's superiority and social and political–economic dominance over women.
4. Systems of knowledge reflect men's views of the natural and social world; the production of knowledge is gendered.
5. Women should be at the center of intellectual inquiry, not peripheral, invisible, or appendages to men.

These elements provided a stimulus for those interested in female crime with a strong framework from which to draw from for theoretical models and concepts. Daly and Chesney-Lind's work was followed with a flurry of publications focused on creating new ways to examine female crime, the importance of additional variables in theoretical models, and a renewed focus on critical feminist theory.

Critical Feminist Theory

Critical feminist theory places females at the center or core of the model and focuses on gender-specific relationships and variables that are unique to the female gender. Feminist theory views crime as a result of a social structure that is patriarchal, commodity or capitalism based, and formulated on gender inequality. Therefore, the theory links criminality to gender conflict created by political, economic, and social inequality; physical and sexual victimization that is a result of male domination; and forces that control power relationships both in the workforce and at home. Components presented by Bishop, Pollak, Adler, and Smart are included in the current forms of feminist criminology.

The premise of feminist theory follows Daly and Chesney-Lind's five elements as listed earlier. Additionally, it heavily focuses on the idea that gender is socially constructed. Thus, gender roles, ideologies, and behavior are learned as a product of interaction throughout an individual's life course. This learning process interacts with additional demographic variables such as class and race/ethnicity, structural variables such as economics and politics, and biological/psychological variables that are related to both gender and sex. As a result, there is not one distinct way of viewing female criminality from a theoretical perspective, but instead there are multiple forms of feminist crime models that offer important additions to the understanding of female criminality. They are liberal feminist theory, Marxist feminist theory, radical feminist theory, socialist feminist theory, postmodernist feminist theory, and critical race feminist theory (Renzetti, 2013; Van Gundy, 2014).

Liberal Feminist Theory

Liberal feminist theory focuses on the gender roles proscribed by society, the patriarchal division of labor, and the impact of gender roles on equality. It originated from the political and social movements that focused on gaining equal rights for women such as the National Organization for Women and the Congressional Caucus for Women's Issues (Renzetti, 2013). The key premise of liberal feminist theory is that males and females are both equal in all aspects, that they should have the same equal human rights, and that opportunities should be equal for both males and females. Theoretical models that are based on liberal feminist theory must measure for blocked opportunities, the gender-specific impact, or consequences of opportunity or lack thereof, and suggest the reconstruction of social and gender roles to reflect equality for both males and females.

Marxist Feminist Theory

At the core of Marxist feminist theory is the concept of social class and its impact on women. According to Marxist theory, capitalistic societies are structured such that they result in the oppression of women. This oppression is apparent in the political, social, and economic spheres of life, and in order to appropriately understand the female experiences of oppression, power must be considered. The power structure that occurs in capitalistic society results in females being victimized at higher rates than males (especially physical and sexual abuse), females increasingly being engaged in criminal activity (opportunities are not available to those that are oppressed), and females less likely to earn or maintain job opportunities (particularly in male-dominated fields). Theoretical models that are based on Marxist Feminist Theory must include variables measuring feelings of and actuality of oppression, and the impact that subordination or oppression has on victimization, and would suggest that as long as societies remain capitalistic, females will remain a minority (Van Gundy, 2014).

Radical Feminist Theory

Radical feminist theory focuses on male dominance or patriarchy as the main component of gender inequality. Radical feminists argue that females are and will remain the most oppressed social group in general society, regardless of whether or not the society is capitalistic (Renzetti, 2013). This viewpoint of feminism argues that multiple variables such as biology, sexuality, and social construction interact to result in structural oppression and violence against women, and that an explicit relationship between society and patriarchy result in gender and structural oppression. This interactional theory suggests that until society as a whole rejects patriarchy, women will remain oppressed. As such, they must stand together as women and know, profess, and exude their value. Theoretical models based on radical feminist theory focus on the impact of victimization on women, consider the lack of structural and educational support for women, and suggest that as long as social institutions are male dominated, female criminality will be impacted in a multitude of ways (Renzetti, 2013; Van Gundy, 2014).

Socialist Feminist Theory

Socialist feminist theory combines the emphasis of Marxist theory with the premise of radical feminist theory to focus on both gender and class as equally important variables. Socialist feminists reject radical feminist idea that patriarchy is the root of all evil and Marxist theory that only economics or capitalism is the sole driving force in the oppression of women. It extends Marxist theory in four important ways: extends the definition and meaning of material conditions, emphasizes human subjectivity, analyzes the relationship between multiple variables, and suggests a conscious group effort to improve conditions for females (Van Gundy, 2014). Theoretical models that are based on socialist feminist theory include components of gender and/or class (and the interaction between the two) and suggest that in order to understand female criminality variables such as gender socialization, the division of labor at home and work, the economic marginalization of women and the concept of home and family as a safe spot for women (where their subordinate status places them at risk for victimization).

Postmodernist Feminist Theory

Postmodernist feminist theory argues that ideals, norms, and categorizations surrounding sex and gender are a social construction of language. This social construction is created by individuals with power, and it is learned by society and individuals to be the "truth" (Renzetti, 2013). Importantly, the created categories are heavily impacted by social context, meaning that throughout different cultures, geographical locations, and so forth, gender is constructed in a different manner according to society and those that control it. Theoretical models that stem from the postmodernist viewpoint of female crime would need to measure the belief, norm, and value system of the culture in which the variable was being measured, understand how the concepts were translated or taught, the consequences for their violations, and would suggest that gender not be viewed in black-and-white terms (e.g., blue for boys and pink for girls) but as a fluid construct that would change with time and social context.

Critical Race Feminist Theory

Last, critical race feminist theory includes the interaction between gender and race. This theoretical viewpoint argues that women of color hold a "doubly subordinate" position in society as they are a minority both in gender and in race/ethnicity. Both categories of minorities are oppressed and subordinate to the dominant ruling class, and therefore the consequences that result are much more difficult for those who hold this status than for those that hold one minority status (or none). It has been argued that critical race theory is distinct from other feminist theories primarily by its emphasis on various demographic variables such as "gender, race, ethnicity, social class, sexuality, age, national origin and physical ability" (Renzetti, 2013, p. 66). Critical race feminist theorists argue that an understanding of criminality would be incomplete without the inclusion of race and an examination of the intersectionality of gender and race. They argue that women's lives are multifaceted, in particular, minority women's lives, and that the unique experiences of women of color must be studied (Collins, 2000).

Theoretical History

Utilizing early case studies of female offenders (such as Freud), women were placed into categories of social deviance. Those categories were primarily focused on sexuality/sexual desires, looks (pretty or ugly), and those that violated the "womanhood" norms such as feeling shame, being materialistic, and being immodest. While most of the early cases discussed female offenders from an antiquated nature, what is interesting is that they each utilize or call attention to repression, medical issues, sexual trauma (in many cases, training the victim that she is not actually a victim but a willing participant), and suicidal tendencies, all of which contribute to the foundation of feminist criminology. One such example of this is W.I. Thomas's case studies presented in his book titled *The Unadjusted Girl*.

W.I. Thomas and *The Unadjusted Girl*

In 1923, W.I. Thomas published a book of case studies, which he deemed "a study of individuals who, having failed in one way or another to adapt to socially dominant standards of behavior, turn to delinquency, crime, prostitution, or some other form of social maladjustment" (p. 8). He states in his book that among women offenders "we have the thief, the prostitute, the blackmailer, the vamp, and the charity girl" (p. 11) and focuses primarily on crimes of adultery, illegitimate birthing, and sexual passion. His concept of female crime and deviance was situated in the framework of male deviance; in other words, he would discuss the importance of love, relationships, and the desire to respond to children (or wishing for responses from others) and how that impacts females in different manners than it does males.

In his book, Thomas primarily refers to the women as a number (i.e., Number 17, Number 18, etc.) but sometimes uses their real names, provides demographics (e.g., nationality, age, marital status, husband's occupation, references beauty/looks, hair color, social nature and personality, amount of children), and includes verbatim from the women their thoughts, desires, and psychology. Here are a few examples of cases that Thomas includes (verbatim):

- *No. 33*—I myself drove out my good and true husband in a shameful manner and placed the guilt at his door, and although he is angry he is decent enough not to say anything to anybody. He takes the blame on himself. All my friends and acquaintances think that he is really the guilty one. I have been married for the last 11 years and up to two years ago, I thought that somehow I should end my life peacefully, although I have caused many a quarrel….my tongue is sharp and burning….quite often I would start to fire away at the table and he would get up, leave the house, and go to a restaurant. When he returned he had some more. And according to my behavior my husband began to treat me roughly….I am a snake by nature and this is not my fault; that's how I am. My friends meet him and they tell me that he does not say a word about our tragedy. He says "I am doing the best that I can and when I am able to give a home to my children, then I will worry about them." And I am afraid that someday he will take away the children from me and then I shall be left alone like a stone (pp. 55–56).

- *No 38*—I had been looking for Margaret, for I knew she was a striking instance of the unadjusted who had within a year come with a kind of aesthetic logic to Greenwich Village. She needed something very badly. What I heard about her which excited me was that she was 20 years old, unmarried, had never lived with a man or had any of that experience, had worked for over a year on a socialist newspaper, and a socialist magazine, was a heavy drinker and frequenter of Hell Hole, that she came from a middle-class family but preferred the society of the outcasts to any other. Greenwich Village is not composed of outcasts, but it does not reject them, and it enables a man or woman who desires to know the outcast to satisfy the desire without feeling cut off from humanity. Hell Hole is a saloon in the back room of which pick pockets, grafters, philosophers, poets, revolutionists, stool pigeons, and the riff-raff of humanity meet. Margaret loves this place and the people in it—so they told me—and there she did and said extreme things in which there was a bitter fling at decent society (p. 73).

- *No. 45*—My sweetheart remarked that she would like to have a great deal of money. When I asked her what she would do with it, she replied that she would buy herself a lot of beautiful dresses. When I said that it was alright to have them but it ought to be all right without them too, she protested that she loved fine clothes and this to such extent that—here she made a remark which I am ashamed to let pass my lips. I would sooner have welcomed an open grave than to have heard those words. She said that she would sell her body for a time in order to procure nice clothes for herself. And since that day I go around like a mad person. I neither eat nor sleep. In short, I am no more a man. She afterward excused herself, claiming that it was said in a joke, and that as long as one talks without actually doing it there is no harm in it. But this is not reassuring to me. I have a premonition that she would go further than mere talk after marriage, for if she carries such notions in her head now, what might happen after we are married (p. 83).

- *No 46*—A young girl may be taught at home and church that chastity is a virtue, but the newspapers and the movies feature women in trouble along this line, now painting them as heroines, now sobbing over their mystery and pathos. Apparently they get all the attention and attention is the life blood of youth. The funny papers ridicule marriage, old maids, and bashful men. The movies, magazines, street conversation, and contemporary life are filled with the description of lapses that somehow turn out safely and even luxuriously. If the modern young girl practices virtue she may not believe in it. The preliminaries to wrong doing are apparently the accepted manners of the time. When the girl herself lapses it is frequently because of lack of a uniform, authoritative definition of the social code (p. 84).

- *No 57*—The experiences of Commenge in Paris are instructive on this point. "For many young girls" he writes "modestly has no existence; they experience no emotion in showing themselves completely undressed, they abandon themselves to any chance individuals whom they will never see again. They attach no importance to their virginity; they are deflowered under the strangest conditions, without the least thought or care about the act they are accomplishing. No sentiment, no calculation, pushes them into a man's arms. They let themselves go without reflection and without motive, in an almost animal manner, from indifference and without pleasure." He was acquainted with 45 girls between the ages of 12 and 17 who were deflowered by chance strangers whom they never met again; they lost their virginity in Dumas's phrase, as they lost their milk-teeth, and could give no plausible account of the loss....In the United States, Dr. W.T. Travis Gibb, examining physician to the New York Society for the Prevention of Cruelty to Children, bears similar testimony to the fact that in a fairly large proportion of "rape" cases, the child is the willing victim (p. 100).

Theoretical Advancement

Applications of traditional criminological theories such as rational choice (which women have to be considered rational, not hysterical as early case studies deemed them to be), trait (biological gender differences), social structure, social process, and developmental theory continue to focus on the characteristics of women, the violations of norms, values, and womanhood. Works by Bell Hooks and Daly and Chesney-Lind stimulated a change in this way of thinking and proffered the ability for criminology to place women at the center of the theory as a way of explaining the different characteristics, origins, types of crimes, and conditions that apply specifically to women.

Utilizing the six different forms of feminist criminology as outlined in the following, a modern-day case study would advance cases such as Dora and Thomas's examples in the following ways:

- Examine the impact that proscribed gender roles, the understanding of gender roles, and the household and workplace division of labor have on women (liberal feminism).
- Study the impact of social class on women (Marxist feminism). For example, the aforementioned case of Dora, was she upper/middle/lower class? Did that contribute to her hysteria (the pressure and social status of her father who paid for her to be "studied")? And with Thomas's examples—were the majority of the women nonworking, did they have access to resources, where was their position in the system of stratification?
- Observe the impact of male dominance on the women being studied (radical feminism). Dora identified multiple cases of male dominance, both her father, the male who sexually abused her, and later in the book, additional men. Cases available as presented by Thomas—almost all of them were housewives and mothers (fitting with the social context). How does status and lack of freedom/dominance impact the females? Why do they feel guilty for feelings that are natural/how do they deal with that guilt?
- Understand the impact of gender and class on the ability to work, the freedom of choice, and its impact on social, medical, physical, and psychological issues (socialist feminism).
- Integrate variables such as the social construction of gender and intersectionality of gender and race as a means of understanding the relationship between gender and crime (postmodernist and critical race). The presented cases were published close to 100 years ago. The social context during that time did not consider, nor value, the impact that race has on life choices. These forms of feminist criminology are a very valuable advancement for the understanding of how society constructs gender roles and of how minority women are "double-punished" by violating additional expectations and norms placed on them due to their race and gender status.

While qualitative case studies are difficult to find in the level of detail in Freud's and Thomas's books, they do exist. What is different about the more recent cases is the inclusion of feminist explanations of crime, the utilization of the feminist theoretical framework, and a deeper understanding of the role that gender plays in the personal and professional choices that women make, regardless of whether those choices are law abiding or deviant. Feminist criminology has advanced traditional criminology in multiple ways, although continued work is necessary.

Discussion Questions

1. How has feminist criminology advanced the state of traditional criminological theory?
2. How has the evolution of feminist criminology impacted the ability to understand female crime and criminality?
3. Choose one of the traditional theories presented in the chapter. Compare and contrast how it would explain the offending behavior of males in comparison to females.

References

Adler, F. (1975). *Sisters in crime*. New York: McGraw-Hill.

Akers, R. L. (2000). *Criminological theories: Introduction, evaluation, and application* (3rd ed., p. 310). Los Angeles, CA: Roxbury Publishing Company.

Beck, A. J. (2000) Prisoners in 1999. *Bureau of Justice Statistics Bulletin*, NCJ 183476. http://www.bjs.gov/index.cfm?ty=pbdetail&iid=928.

Belknap, J. (2001/2007). *The invisible woman: Gender, crime, and justice* (3rd ed., p. 513). Belmont, CA: Thomson/Wadsworth.

Bishop, C (1931) *Women and crime*. London, U.K.: Chatto and Windus.

Bloom, B., Owen, B., & Covington, S. (2003). *Gender-responsive strategies: Research, practice, and guiding principles for women offenders*. Washington, DC: U.S. Department of Justice, National Institute of Justice.

Carlen, P., & Worrall, A. (1987). *Gender, crime, and justice*. London, U.K.: Open University Press.

Collins, P. H. (2000). *Black Feminist thought: Knowledge, consciousness, and the politics of empowerment*. New York: Routledge.

Daly, K., & Chesney-Lind, M. (1988). Feminism and criminology. *Justice Quarterly, 5*(4), 497–538.

Eagly, A. H. (1987). *Sex differences in social behavior: A social-role interpretation*. Hillsdale, NJ: L. Erlbaum Associates.

Hooks, B. (1984). *Feminist theory: From margin to center* (2nd ed.). Boston, MA: South End Press.

Immarigeon, R., & Chesney-Lind, M. (1993). Women's prisons: Overcrowded and overused. In R. Muraskin & T. Alleman (Eds.), *It's a crime: Women and justice* (pp. 242–259). New York: Prentice Hall.

Lombroso, C., & Ferraro, W. (1895) *The female offender*. New York: The Appleton Company.

McQueen, S. (2006). Cardiovascular disease. In R. L. Braithwaite, K. J. Arriola, & C. Newkirk (Eds.), *Health issues among incarcerated women*. New Brunswick, NJ; Rutgers University Press.

Moffitt, T. E., Caspi, A., Rutter, M., & Silva, P. A. (2001). *Sex differences in antisocial behaviour: Conduct disorder, delinquency, and violence in the Dunedin Longitudinal Study*. Cambridge, U.K.: Cambridge University Press.

Pollak, O. (1950) *The criminality of women* (p.180). Philadelphia, PA: University of Pennsylvania Press.

Renzetti, C. (2013) *Feminist criminology*. London, U.K.: Routledge, Taylor & Francis Group.

Schwartz, J., & Steffensmeier, D. (2008). The nature of female offending: Patterns and explanations. In R. T. Zaplin (Eds.), *Female offenders: Critical perspectives and effective interventions* (2nd ed., pp. 43–75). Burlington, MA: Jones & Bartlett.

Silvestri, M., & Crowther-Dowey, C. (2008). *Gender & crime: Key approaches to criminology*. Los Angeles, CA: Sage Publications.

Smart, C. (1976). *Women, crime and criminology: A feminist critique*. London, U.K.: Routledge and Kegan Paul.

Thomas, A., & Pollard, J. (2001). *Substance abuse, trauma, and coping: A report on women prisoners at the Dame Phyllis Frost Centre for women*. Cariniche Pvt. Limited.

Thomas, W. I. (1923). *The unadjusted girl*. New York: Little, Brown and Company.

Van Gundy, A. (2014). *Feminist theory, crime, and social justice*. London, U.K.: Anderson Publishing.

Vold, G. B., Bernard, T. J., & Snipes J. B. (1998). *Theoretical criminology*. New York: Oxford University Press.

Wright, J. P., Tibbetts, S. G., & Daigle, L. E. (2008). *Criminals in the making: Criminality across the life course*. Los Angeles, CA: Sage Publications.

Criminal Justice as a Male Enterprise

3

JEFFREY W. COHEN

Contents

Crime is a predominantly male enterprise. By this, I mean that men and boys are significantly more likely to be involved with the criminal and juvenile justice systems. As I will explore in this chapter, males are more likely to commit crimes, more likely to be victimized by crime, and more likely to be arrested, convicted, and sentenced to criminal sanctions (e.g., prison and probation). These trends have led to a system that has been primarily designed to address male offending and offenders. Criminological theorizing and criminal justice policy and practice have historically ignored the experiences of females as victims and offenders. Moreover, situating male offending as normative has led to a relative lack of attention paid to the experiences of male victims and offenders as gendered beings. Drawing on (pro)feminist calls to bring gender to the fore of criminological thinking, this chapter outlines how male dominance in offending and victimization has had serious implications for both females and males. We begin with a brief overview of evidence supporting the claim that crime is a predominantly male enterprise.

Male Dominance in Criminal Justice

The most widely used database for estimating rates of crime commission in the United States is the Federal Bureau of Investigation's Uniform Crime Reports (UCR). The UCR offers a yearly count of arrests (or crimes known to the police) across local, state, and federal jurisdictions in the United States. While the UCR suffers from important methodological limitations, it nonetheless serves as the most consistent source of offense data in the country. According to the UCR, males represent the majority of those arrested for both violent and property crimes. For instance, in 2012 (the most recent year for which complete arrest statistics were available at the writing of this chapter), males represented 73.8% of all arrests, 80.1% of arrests for violent crimes, and 62.6% of arrests for property crimes.

Table 3.1   Proportion of Arrests, by Sex

	2003	2008	2011	2012
All arrests				
Male	76.8	75.8	73.9	73.8
Female	23.2	24.2	26.1	26.2
Violent crime[a]				
Male	82.1	81.7	80.5	80.1
Female	17.9	18.3	19.5	19.9
Property crime[b]				
Male	69.0	65.3	62.6	62.6
Female	31.0	34.7	37.4	37.4

Source: FBI's Uniform Crime Reports. http://www.fbi.gov/about-us/cjis/ucr/ucr.

[a] Includes murder and nonnegligent manslaughter, forcible rape, robbery, and aggravated assault.

[b] Includes burglary, larceny theft, motor vehicle theft, and arson.

These sex-based differences in arrests are consistent with previous years, as indicated in Table 3.1, and mirror historical trends going back decades.

It should be noted, however, that the so-called gender gap in offending (i.e., the higher rates of crime commission among males as compared to females) has been steadily, albeit slowly, decreasing over time (Pollock, 2014). This is particularly the case for property and other nonviolent crimes (e.g., drug crimes). As Pollock (2014) points out in her review of sex differences in arrest statistics over time, "any differences of women's contribution to crime must clearly differentiate violent crime from property crime to give the most accurate picture" (p. 55). In an analysis of gender gap trends for violent crimes over a 23-year period, Steffensmeier, Zhong, Ackerman, Schwartz, and Agha (2006) noted that the gap in arrests remained stable for more serious forms of violence (i.e., homicide and rape/sexual assault), but decreased for more minor forms (i.e., criminal assault). They concluded that "there has been no meaningful or systematic change in women's involvement in crimes of interpersonal violence and in the gender gap during the past couple of decades" (p. 93). In other words, while the gap between male and female offending in terms of nonviolent property crimes continues to shrink over time, primarily through dramatic decreases in arrests for males as opposed to dramatic increases for females, the violent crime gap has remained relatively stable. Moreover, males continue to commit (or at least be arrested for) property crimes at higher rates than females.

Not only are males consistently more likely to be arrested, they are also much more likely to find themselves under the supervision of correctional authorities at both the state and federal levels. In every year from 2003 to 2012, over 90% of state and federal prison populations have been male (see Table 3.2). When considering noncustodial correctional authorities, the story is slightly less dramatic but fundamentally the same. For instance, in 2012, males made up 76% of the probation population (Bureau of Justice Statistics, Annual Probation Survey, 2000, 2011, 2012) and 89% of the parole population (Bureau of Justice Statistics, Annual Parole Survey, 2000, 2011, 2012).

The fact that males are significantly more likely to be arrested and placed under correctional supervision probably comes as little surprise to anyone with even a cursory familiarity with crime and criminal justice. News and popular media outlets consistently portray

Table 3.2   State and Federal Prison Populations by Sex, 2003–2012

	2003	2004	2005	2006	2007	2008	2009	2010	2011	2012
% Male	93.1	93.0	93.0	92.8	92.8	92.9	93.0	93.0	93.0	93.1
% Female	6.9	7.0	7.0	7.2	7.2	7.1	7.0	7.0	7.0	6.9

Source: Carson, E.A. and Mulako-Wangota, J., Bureau of Justice Statistics, *Count of total jurisdiction population,* July 14, 2014, Generated using the Corrections Statistical Analysis Tool (CSAT)—Prisoners at www.bjs.gov.

Table 3.3   Victimization in the United States, Percent by Victim's Sex, 2003–2012

	2003	2004	2005	2006	2007	2008	2009	2010	2011	2012
Violent victimization										
Male	52.3	52.8	58.2	53.2	55.0	51.9	48.7	50.8	55.2	54.2
Female	47.7	47.2	41.8	46.8	45.0	48.1	51.3	49.2	44.8	45.8
Rape/sexual assault										
Male	6.0	2.4	7.3	22.4	4.6	11.3	6.5	5.6	4.3	37.8
Female	94.0	97.6	92.7	77.6	95.4	88.7	93.5	94.4	85.7	62.2
Robbery										
Male	51.6	57.0	72.9	58.6	57.4	51.6	64.5	53.2	60.9	67.1
Female	48.4	43.0	27.1	41.4	42.6	48.4	35.5	46.8	39.1	32.9
Aggravated assault										
Male	58.4	62.9	60.7	57.5	61.0	52.8	55.0	56.8	57.0	57.5
Female	41.6	37.1	39.3	42.5	39.0	47.2	45.0	43.2	43.0	42.5
Simple assault										
Male	53.6	51.9	57.4	53.5	55.8	54.9	47.7	52.6	56.5	52.7
Female	46.4	48.1	42.6	46.5	44.2	45.1	52.3	47.4	43.5	47.3
Personal theft/larceny										
Male	33.1	51.6	44.5	49.9	61.7	59.5	39.1	58.1	32.3	43.2
Female	66.9	48.4	55.5	50.1	38.3	40.5	60.9	48.2	67.7	56.8

Source: Bureau of Justice Statistics, *Number of violent victimizations, personal thefts/larcenies, serious violent victimizations, rape/sexual assaults, robberies, aggravated assaults, and simple assaults by sex 2003–2012,* July 14, 2014, Generated using the NCVS Victimization Analysis Tool at www.bjs.gov, 2014a.

males as more violent and criminal than their female counterparts. Despite more recent (and relatively unfounded) suggestions of a *wave* of female violence and crime, females are still more likely to be portrayed as victims than offenders. However, these portrayals belie the reality of crime statistics in the United States, where males find themselves not only at greater likelihood for criminal justice intervention (i.e., arrest and incarceration), but also at greater risk for victimization, and violent victimization in particular.

The National Crime Victimization Survey (NCVS) is the most widely used database for estimating victimization rates within the United States. Based on a nationally representative household survey, the NCVS collects data related to both violent and nonviolent person crimes as well as property offenses. According to data from the NCVS, males consistently make up the majority of those who experience violent victimizations in the United States.* As indicated in Table 3.3, from 2003 to 2012, males made up the majority

---

* Included in the NCVS's measure of violent victimization are rape/sexual assault, robbery, aggravated assault, and simple assault.

of violent victimizations in every year except one, 2009. When broken down by type of violent victimization, males represented the majority in all years in all categories except rape/sexual assault. The greater likelihood of sexual victimization among females is an issue that is taken up later in this book. For now, it is important to recognize that males are significantly more likely to experience all other forms of violent victimization as measured by the NCVS.

When considering personal theft/larceny (the only nonviolent person crime reported by the NCVS), the picture is a bit murkier, with 5 of the last 10 years showing a male majority and 5 showing a female majority. The fact that personal theft/larceny is not a violent crime may help explain these more balanced trends. In other words, sex-based differences in victimization are greater for violent crimes compared to nonviolent person and property crimes. These trends in victimization mirror the arrest trends discussed previously. Whether considering those who commit crimes or those who are direct victims of crime, it is clear that the criminal justice system is primarily focused on male bodies. Over time, male dominance in criminal justice systems has had negative implications for females and males.

Implications of Male Dominance in Criminal Justice for Women and Girls

Given the fact that males are significantly more likely to be involved with the criminal justice system, it is little surprise that females have been historically ignored within the criminological discourse. As Chesney-Lind and Pasko (2013) point out, "the extensive focus on disadvantaged males in public settings has meant that girls' victimization and the relationship between that experience and girls' official delinquency has been systematically ignored" (p. 16). The same can be said for women's experiences of victimization and official criminality.

There is little doubt that early theories of criminality and delinquency ignored the experiences of women and girls. In her critique of mainstream criminological theory and research, Belknap (2007) points to the near-total exclusion of females. This near-total exclusion of women and girls in early theorizing has two important implications. First, women and girls who do violate the law are seen as also violating gender norms, and, therefore, as abnormal and abhorrent. Second, those women and girls who violate the law are subject to a criminal justice system almost exclusively designed to deal with males, leaving many of their needs unattended.

Female Crime and Delinquency as Gender Violation

As Belknap suggests, "female lawbreakers historically (and to some degree today) have been viewed as 'abnormal' and as 'worse' than male lawbreakers—not only for breaking the law but also for stepping outside of prescribed gender roles of femininity and passivity" (p. 32). The idea that female criminality and delinquency are abnormal is reinforced by the trends discussed earlier. It follows, as Belknap suggests, that those women and girls who engage in criminal or delinquent behavior are seen as violating gender roles and norms, and, therefore, more problematic and deserving of harsher treatment than males, for whom crime and delinquency are seen as at least partially normative. This kind of thinking is particularly true when women and girls engage in violent behavior.

The process through which female violence and aggression is constructed as abnormal and abhorrent often begins with the establishment of perceived sex differences. It then moves to a reinforcement of those perceived sex differences in both academic and popular discourses. Specific instances of female aggression and violence are then highlighted as examples of gender-norm violation. Finally, these comparatively rare examples are strung together as evidence of an epidemic or wave of female violence. This drama is played out across a variety of contexts, from minor forms of aggression (see Case Study 1) to serious violence, including homicide (see Hannah Rosin's *The End of Men and the Rise of Women* [Rosin, 2012] for a troubling example of how this narrative takes hold in popular discourse).

Case Study 1: The Criminalization of Girls' Bullying Behaviors

In their recent analysis of the construction of school bullying as a social problem, Cohen and Brooks (2014) put forth the argument that the trend toward the criminalization of school bullying is partly grounded in gender-based assumptions about girls' and boys' behavior. Early academic and popular constructions of school bullying established distinct sex differences in terms of the ways in which boys and girls bullied. For instance, in a 1993 *New York Times* article, professor of educational psychology Jan N. Hughes was quoted as saying, "Aggression in boys is different from aggression in girls ... Girls are aggressive by excluding others and saying mean things. Boys are aggressive by hitting and getting into fights" (October 28, 1993). The establishment of these sex differences in bullying, which were grounded in the existing academic literature, worked to construct particular expectations about the behavior of boys and girls. Violation of these expectations was sometimes constructed as particularly troubling, as illustrated by assistant professor of psychiatry Eugene V. Beresin: "I'm more concerned about grade-school girls than boys who fight with peers ... If I see a 10-year-old girl who's getting into fights, I start thinking about underlying biological problems" (quoted in the *New York Times*, March 24, 1994). As this excerpt suggests, physical aggression on the part of boys is not only expected, but also seen as normative. Among girls, however, physical aggression is viewed as a symptom of biological or psychological abnormalities in need of serious intervention.

Similar to early theories of female criminality, girls' aggression and bullying was also constructed as hidden. For instance, in a *New York Times* feature article (February 24, 2002), the following was quoted from Rachel Simmons's book about girls' bullying entitled *Odd Girl Out: The Hidden Culture of Aggression in Girls* (Simmons, 2002): "girls frequently attack within tightly knit friendship networks, making aggression harder to identify and intensifying the damage to the victims." This construction of girls' aggression as hidden and dangerous is similar to Otto Pollack's theoretical argument that lower rates of female criminality could be explained by their greater ability to hide their crimes through the use of deceit (see Belknap, 2007).

The news media also continually described girls involved in bullying as catty, nasty, and manipulative members of cliques, supporting the framing of girls' bullying within existing essentialist notions of gender. These popular news media constructions echoed the academic literature and reinforced perceived inherent differences between girls' and boys' performances of bullying. While some claimsmakers recognized the cultural and social roots of this essentialism, many simply accepted it as fact. Once established, those young women who violated the gender norms of bullying were cast as even more sinister than those who bullied from within its confines.

For example, the 2010 bullying-related suicide of 15-year-old Phoebe Prince in South Hadley, Massachusetts, marked a dramatic shift in responses to school bullying. Those who bullied Prince were seen to have violated the gendered norms related to bullying by engaging in what had been previously established as a boy's domain— physical and direct verbal bullying. In response, the local community lashed out through increased outrage and troubling expressions of actual and threatened vigilantism. Moreover, in what seems to be the first time in U.S. history, those who engaged in the school bullying of Phoebe Prince were criminally charged in relation to her suicide. Cohen and Brooks (2014) suggest that the vitriolic community responses and filing of criminal charges were partially fueled by the violation of gender norms in relation to bullying.

As this case study illustrates, sex differences in school bullying behaviors were first established and then reinforced through popular and academic discourse. A form of gender essentialism took hold, in which girls' bullying was framed as almost exclusively relational (nonviolent) and boys' bullying was framed as almost exclusively physical (violent). Incidents of physical bullying on the part of particular girls (e.g., those who bullied Phoebe Prince) were then situated as violations of established gender norms. Those who violated the established norms were cast as especially sinister and in need of severe punishment (e.g., the filing of criminal charges).

The notion that female crime, delinquency, and violence are abnormal makes some sense on its face considering the degree to which females, in general, are more law abiding compared to males. The problem, however, is that some women and girls do violate the law and find themselves the target of criminal justice authorities. This brings us to the second important implication that male dominance in criminal justice has for women and girls—that those who do engage in crime and delinquency are subject to a system that has been almost exclusively designed to deal with males. This is perhaps no more evident than in the case of prison policy.

Female Imprisonment and Male Dominance in Criminal Justice Systems

It is little secret that the United States has the highest rates of imprisonment in the world. And, as was discussed earlier in this chapter, males make up the overwhelming majority of prisoners in both state and federal institutions. What is perhaps less well known is that the United States' love affair with incarceration has had dramatic impacts on females. As shown in Table 3.4, incarceration rates have increased much more rapidly for females as compared to males. From 1982 to 2012, females experienced a 350% increase in their rates of incarceration compared to a 172% increase for males. Interestingly, since 2007, females have experienced a decrease in incarceration rates, as have males since around 2008. Similar to trends during the incarceration boom, the decrease in female incarceration rates since 2007 has outpaced the decrease for males. This at least suggests that correctional policy has a somewhat more immediate effect on females than males, although we should not lose sight of the fact that males consistently make up over 90% of state and federal prison populations.

Table 3.4   Trends in Incarceration Rates[a] by Sex

	30-Year Trend (1982–2012)	20-Year Trend (1992–2012)	10-Year Trend (2002–2012)	5-Year Trend (2007–2012)
Female	+350.0%	+80.0%	+3.2%	−9.5%
Male	+172.0%	+42.4%	+0.1%	−4.7%

Sources: Female: Bureau of Justice Statistics, *Imprisonment rate of sentenced female prisoners under the jurisdiction of state or federal correctional authorities per 100,000 female U.S. residents*, December 31, 1978–2012, Generated using the Corrections Statistical Analysis Tool at www.bjs. gov, 2014b; Male: Bureau of Justice Statistics, Imprisonment rate of sentenced male prisoners under the jurisdiction of state or federal correctional authorities per 100,000 male U.S. residents, December 31, 1978–2012, Generated using the Corrections Statistical Analysis Tool at www.bjs.gov, 2014c.

[a] Number incarcerated per 100,000 in the U.S. population.

Unfortunately, the dramatic increases in female incarceration rates over the past 30 years have taken place within a system originally designed to deal with male offenders. As such, gender-sensitive treatment for female offenders has been historically lacking. In a somewhat unexpected turn, the important liberal feminist emphasis on equality among the sexes has played a role in the relative lack of gender-sensitive treatment for female prisoners. As Katherine van Wormer (2010) notes about adult corrections, "a focus on equality that is equated with sameness lingers—this misunderstanding of the true spirit of equality often results in identical treatment models for men and women" (pp. 3–4). van Wormer suggests that the implementation of gender-neutral policies grounded in the liberal feminist call for equal treatment has led to what is often referred to as *equality with a vengeance*. Bloom and Chesney-Lind (2007) describe how a focus on equality has unintentionally led to problems for female inmates: "This equity orientation translated into treatment of women prisoners as if they were men. Since this orientation did not change the role of gender in prison life or corrections, women prisoners receive the worst of both worlds" (p. 556).

The impact of male dominance in criminal justice was somewhat successfully challenged by the liberal feminist argument for increased equality among the sexes. However, because criminal justice systems remained male oriented, the notion of equality was framed within a male standard. Equality for female prisoners meant being treated like male prisoners. Instead of taking into consideration important differences in the experiences of male and female offenders, gender-neutral policies were the dominant mode of operation. However, since males (in general) occupy a structurally advantaged group within the U.S. society, they are not viewed as having a gender. As such, what many frame as gender-neutral policies within criminal justice systems are more appropriately described as gender-blind. For females, these gender-blind policies and practices have led to a prison system that has been slow to address their needs.

Take, for instance, the trends in sexual victimization presented earlier in this chapter. As was noted, the NCVS clearly shows that sexual victimization is the one type of violent crime females are consistently and overwhelmingly more likely to experience. Feminist pathways literature has pointed to the significant effect that prior victimization has on the likelihood of women to engage in offending behavior. For example, drawing on interviews with female inmates in a maximum security prison, DeHart (2008) found that the combination of multiple victimization experiences (including sexual victimization) worked to limit women's access to "legitimate pathways to life" (p. 1378). She suggests, "Given the restricted options and negative influences illustrated in these women's stories, failure to choose a pathway involving crime seems more remarkable than having chosen such a pathway" (pp. 1377–1378).

Combined with a gender-blind approach to prison policy, female inmates are often left to deal with the lasting impact of prior victimization experiences on their own. Moreover, the prison experience often exacerbates the problem. Similar to the higher rates of sexual victimization among women in the general population, female inmates also experience higher rates of sexual victimization than their male counterparts while serving time. For instance, among their sample of prisoners in one-state prison system, Wolff, Blitz, Shi, Bachman, and Siegel (2006) found that rates of inmate-on-inmate sexual victimization were over four times higher for females compared to males.

The relationship between sexual victimization, offending, and the prison experience is just one example of the myriad ways that a male-dominated criminal justice system has worked to the detriment of female victims, offenders, and prisoners. Other scholars have pointed to additional aspects of women's and girls' lives that have been ignored within a male-dominated criminal justice system, including mental illness, drug use, and mothering. The negative consequences of male dominance in criminal justice for females are certainly important to consider. In fact, this book is in part focused on the need to further incorporate females' experiences of victimization and offending into criminological theory and criminal justice policy and practice. However, it would be an oversimplification to assume that male dominance in criminal justice has worked to the general advantage of men and boys. In addition to ignoring the experiences of female offenders and victims, criminological theory and criminal justice policy and practice have also generally ignored the gendered aspects of men's and boys' lives. We end this chapter by considering the negative implications of male dominance in criminal justice for men and boys.

Implications of Male Dominance in Criminal Justice for Men and Boys

It may seem counterintuitive to think that male dominance in criminal justice has functioned to ignore the lived experiences of men and boys. However, upon closer examination, it becomes clear that the taken-for-granted nature of male offending has had this effect. The feminist call to "account for the myriad ways that *gender matters*" (Chesney-Lind & Pasko, 2013, p. 22; emphasis in original) points not only to the dearth of theorizing around female experiences, but also to the lack of attention paid to the gendered experiences of men and boys. This seeming contradiction is actually a common attribute of all forms of privilege, wherein the privileged group is not seen as possessing the characteristic under consideration (e.g., white is not considered a race; heterosexual is not considered a sexuality). And like other forms of privilege, a criminal justice system steeped in male privilege ultimately works to the disadvantage of all, including many of those who occupy the privileged status.

The lack of focus on men and boys as gendered beings is also tied to what Messerschmidt (2006) refers to as the reification of gender. The reification of gender entails an exclusive focus on sex-based differences between males and females. These sex-based differences are then grounded in purported (and often exaggerated) biological differences between the sexes, making them appear concrete and innate. In their analysis of research published in criminological journals, Cohen and Harvey (2006) note that researchers almost exclusively rely on rudimentary measures of sex (e.g., checking male or female on a survey) in order to draw wide-ranging conclusions regarding the relationship between gender and crime (see also Cohen & Martin, 2012; Martin, Cohen, & Champion, 2013). This combined with the trends described at the beginning of this chapter helps reinforce the notion of an inherent difference between males and females in relation to criminal offending, further entrenching the reification of gender within criminology and criminal justice. As an example of this process in action, let us return to the discussion of sexual victimization.

Sexual Victimization as a Gendered Experience for Men

It was noted earlier that the NCVS has consistently shown significantly higher rates of sexual victimization (i.e., rape) among females compared to males. Combined with the important contributions of feminist scholars, the NCVS data have led to necessary improvements in the ways we think about and respond to the sexual victimization of women and girls (although continued efforts in this arena are warranted). However, as Stemple and Meyer (2014) point out, our reliance on the NCVS and UCR data hides the very real and damaging experiences of male victims of sexual violence. Part of the problem, as they point out, is the kinds of sexual victimization that have been emphasized by researchers, policy makers, and the broader public, as well as how those forms of victimization have been defined.

For instance, from its origins in 1927 until 2013, the FBI's UCR defined rape as "The carnal knowledge of a female forcibly and against her will." This definition worked to exclude any forms of sexual violence that did not include a male perpetrator and female victim, force, and/or penetration. In essence, the UCR explicitly ignored all sexual victimization of males and any other forms of sexual victimization experienced by females. This definition also ignored rapes and other sexual victimizations that occurred in nonheterosexual contexts. According to the new definition, adopted in 2013, rape now includes "penetration, no matter how slight, of the vagina or anus with any body part or object, or oral penetration by a sex organ of another person, without the consent of the victim" (Federal Bureau of Investigation, 2014). While this new definition addresses the exclusion of male victims and recognizes a wider range of sexual victimization experiences, it still suffers from a significant problem that serves to mask men's and boys' experiences.

In their review of several nationally representative government surveys, Stemple and Meyer (2014) provide a more nuanced and complex picture of sexual victimization. Drawing on data from the National Intimate Partner and Sexual Violence Survey 2010 (NISVS), the NCVS, the UCR, the National Inmate Survey, and the National Survey of Youth in Custody, they found "widespread sexual victimization among men in the United States, with some forms of victimization roughly equal to those experienced by women" (p. 19). In particular, they note that the NCVS and the UCR ignore the majority of male victimizations due to their emphasis on perpetrator penetration of victim. In contrast, the NISVS measures instances of both rape (penetration by perpetrator) and *made to penetrate*, where the victim is forced or coerced into penetrating the perpetrator. The latter form of victimization is much more prevalent among males. According to Stemple and Meyer's review, the NISVS data show that "the number of women who have been raped (1,270,000) is nearly equivalent to the number of men who were 'made to penetrate' (1,267,000)" (p. 21).

When we consider inmate populations, the picture is equally complex. Both the National Inmate Survey and the National Survey of Youth in Custody show that females experience significantly higher rates of inmate-on-inmate or juvenile-on-juvenile sexual victimizations. This finding is consistent with the NCVS data. However, both of these surveys also show higher rates of staff-on-inmate or staff-on-juvenile sexual victimizations among males than females (Stemple & Meyer, 2014). These findings are consistent with Wolff et al.'s (2006) analysis of sexual victimization in a state prison system showing higher rates of inmate-on-inmate sexual victimization among females and higher rates of staff-on-inmate sexual victimization among males.

Based on the results of their review, Stemple and Meyer (2014) call for "the use of gender-conscious analyses that avoid regressive stereotyping, to which both women and men are detrimentally subject" (p. 25). We can connect this call for gender-conscious analyses to two important issues already introduced in this chapter. First, researchers, policy makers, and the general public tend to emphasize sex differences in offending and arrest and ignore the higher rates of violent victimization among males compared to females. This framing of females as victims and males as perpetrators is perhaps no more apparent than in the ways we define, measure, and respond to sexual victimization. Second, this dichotomized view of male perpetrator and female victim is grounded in essentialist notions that reinforce the reification of gender that Messerschmidt and others argue against. The framing of sexual victimization in heteronormative and gender-essentialist ways also works to the detriment of men and boys who find themselves victims of sexual violence.

For instance, drawing on data from the Prison Climate Survey in Texas, Kristine Levan Miller (2009) found that "embarrassment is one of the primary reasons for inmates not to report a sexual assault" (p. 702). Miller linked this notion of embarrassment to the highly masculine prison environment, where sexual violence is used as a mechanism for emasculating victims. By acknowledging victimization, men and boys would be exposed to further challenges to their masculinity. Given the cultural messages regarding male victims as *weak* and in some way not masculine, it is not too far a leap to suggest that men and boys in the general population are equally reluctant to admit sexual victimization. This is just one example of how a male-dominated criminal justice system ignores the gendered aspects of men's and boys' lives in relation to victimization. But problems also arise when we fail to view men and boys as gendered beings in the context of their offending behaviors as well.

Rampage Shootings as a Gendered Performance for Men

By taking criminal or delinquent behavior (and violence in particular) for granted as an innate or biologically driven aspect of the male experience, we fail to recognize or address the ways in which gender socialization influences men's and boys' behavior. With some important exceptions (see, for instance, the work of Messerschmidt, 2000, 2006, 2014), the gendered aspects of male offending have been made invisible in mainstream criminology and criminal justice. Take, for instance, the phenomenon of rampage shootings that have garnered incredible media attention in recent years. The very fact that these shootings are almost exclusively committed by boys should raise serious questions about the manner in which we are raising young men. As Douglas Kellner notes, "While the motivations for the shootings may vary, they have in common crises in masculinities" (2014, p. 189). However, scholars have pointed to the utter lack of attention paid to the gendered aspects of these killings in popular media discourse. Kellner continues: "Media coverage of the phenomenon rarely, if ever, roots rampage killing in male rage and crises of masculinity, and fails to see how the violence is a pathological form of resolving crises in masculinity" (p. 189).

However, the general lack of attention paid to gender in this context came to a head in response to the 2014 rampage shooting near the University of California Santa Barbara. The reason for the increased attention to gender in the coverage of this shooting was driven by the shooter's manifesto, which included numerous misogynistic messages (see Case Study 2). It was clear from Elliot Rodger's manifesto that threats to his masculinity sat at the center of his actions. Not even popular media outlets could ignore the gendered aspects of his rampage shooting. Of course, feminist and pro-feminist scholars had been pointing to the gendered nature of school shootings since the late 1990s, when two young men committed a rampage shooting at Columbine High School in Colorado. More recently, Madfis (2014) provided a comprehensive investigation of the role of masculine identity in the lives of rampage killers. Through his analysis, Madfis suggests that "white heterosexual male entitlement fuses with downward mobility, subordinated masculinity, and other disappointing life course events in a way that drives some anguished individuals to retaliate in true hegemonic masculine form through large-scale acts of retaliatory violence and murder" (p. 68). As Case Study 2 illustrates, Elliot Rodger's rampage shooting was clearly prompted by a crisis of (hetero)masculinity. As this and the previous example regarding sexual victimization show, male dominance in criminal justice has not led to a nuanced understanding of men and boys as gendered beings. Quite to the contrary, the continuation of a male dominance in criminal justice that ignores the gendered aspects of men's and boys' lives negatively impacts not only women and girls, but all of us as well.

Case Study 2: A Gendered Analysis of Rampage Shootings—The Case of Elliot Rodger

On May 23, 2014, 22-year-old Elliot Rodger killed six people and injured another 13 near the campus of the University of California (UC), Santa Barbara, before committing suicide. Not surprisingly, this tragic event garnered widespread coverage in the popular news media. What was different, however, was the degree to which the popular discourse focused on gender dynamics. Prior to this rampage shooting, feminist and pro-feminist scholars had attempted to link extreme forms of school violence (such as school rampage shootings) to threats to masculinity. To their dismay, this narrative could not seem to gain traction in popular discourse. What made this shooting different was the blatantly misogynistic manifesto produced by the shooter and disseminated online. From the very first passage, it is hard to ignore the degree to which internalized threats to his masculinity fueled Rodger's violence:

Humanity…All of my suffering on this world has been at the hands of humanity, particularly women. It has made me realize just how brutal and twisted humanity is as a species. All I ever wanted was to fit in and live a happy life amongst humanity, but I was cast out and rejected, forced to endure an existence of loneliness and insignificance, all because the females of the human species were incapable of seeing the value in me.

Rodger would go on to write that "Cruel treatment from women is ten times worse than from men." After describing an incident in which a boy "who was tall and had blonde hair called me a 'loser', right in front of his girlfriends," Rodger noted "This is how girls are," continuing:

The most meanest and depraved of men come out on top, and women flock to these men. Their evil acts are rewarded by women; while the good, decent men are laughed at. It is sick, twisted, and wrong in every way. I hated the girls even more than the bullies because of this.

In describing his move to Santa Barbara at age 19, Rodger noted that he viewed it as

...giving the world one last chance to give me the life that I know I'm entitled to, the life that other boys are able to live with ease. If I still have to suffer the same rejection and injustice even after I move to Santa Barbara, then that will be the last straw. I will have my vengeance.

And just what was this life he was entitled to? Well, it primarily involved the accomplishment of hegemonic masculinity through sex with women:

All while I was suffering this lonely existence, other boys my age lived their happy lives of pleasure and sex. I can never forgive such an injustice, and it was my bid to overcompensate for it in the future. I had to make up for all the years I lost in loneliness and isolation, through no fault of my own! It was society's fault for rejecting me. It was women's fault for refusing to have sex with me.

Upon consideration of Elliot Rodger's manifesto, it would be quite difficult for popular news media or anyone else to ignore the gendered aspects of his rampage shooting. Arguments suggesting that his targeting and killing of both males and females is evidence that this was not an act of gendered violence ignore the complex dynamics of threats to masculinity. Applying a more nuanced gendered analysis sheds light on how Rodger was experiencing a crisis of masculinity. First, Rodger experienced an inability to perform his masculinity through the sexual conquest of women. He was, in this sense, denied access to hegemonic masculinity. Hegemonic masculinity is defined by Kellner (2014) as "the dominant form of masculinity in a culture at a specific period" (p. 190). One aspect of hegemonic masculinity in the United States is heterosexual prowess. In response, Rodger raged against both those who rejected him (women) and those who did not suffer the same rejection (men who had access to hegemonic masculinity through heterosexual sex). His rampage shooting can be seen as a response to this crisis of masculinity, where violence and weaponry (firearms in particular) serve as props in Rodger's performance of masculinity. While a more complete explication of this argument is beyond the scope of this chapter, this brief example helps illustrate how and why it is vital to apply a gendered lens to men's and boys' experiences.

Conclusion

The underlying theme of this chapter has been that crime is a predominantly male enterprise. Males are much more likely than females to be arrested, convicted, and sentenced to some form of criminal justice sanction. Males are also much more likely to be victims of crime. These trends are particularly apparent when considering violent crime and victimization. Early attempts to explain criminal and delinquent behavior explicitly ignored the experiences of women and girls. In what are now clearly seen as problematic androcentric approaches to criminology and criminal justice, females' experiences with offending were viewed as abnormal and abhorrent. Women and girls who violate gender norms by engaging in criminal or delinquent behavior have and continue to be positioned as particularly dangerous and in need of intervention. This male dominance in theory and policymaking has led to significant problems for women and girls who find themselves under the auspices of criminal justice systems. As feminist criminologists rightly point out, failure to attend to women's and girls' experiences at the individual, institutional, and structural level works to further victimize them within systems that are at least nominally intended to serve their needs.

However, male dominance in criminal justice has also worked to the detriment of men and boys. Partly based in the reification of gender and male privilege, criminology and criminal justice have also ignored the gendered aspects of men's and boys' lives. The notion of male dominance is grounded in a narrow and problematic understanding of gender that often unconsciously emphasizes perceived biological essentialism, denying that men and boys also experience gender in nuanced and complex ways that contribute to their offending and victimization, and shape the ways criminal justice actors respond to or ignore those experiences. As you make your way through the remainder of this book, I invite you to consider how the important work being done to better understand and address the experiences of women and girls as gendered beings within criminal justice systems can also shed light on the equally important work of understanding the experiences of men and boys as gendered beings.

Discussion Questions

1. In what ways does male dominance in criminal justice influence the experiences of women and girls as offenders and victims?
2. In what ways does male dominance in criminal justice systems influence the experience of men and boys as offenders and victims?
3. How might criminal justice systems incorporate more nuanced understandings of gender?
4. This chapter distinguishes between gender-neutral, gender-blind, and gender-conscious approaches to criminal justice policy and practice; what are these, and how are they different?

References

Adler, F. (1975). *Sisters in crime: The rise of the new female criminal.* New York, NY: McGraw-Hill.
Belknap, J. (2007). *The invisible woman: Gender, crime, and justice* (3rd ed.). Belmont, CA: Thomson Higher Education.

Bloom, B., & Chesney-Lind, M. (2007). Women in prison: Vengeful equity. In R. Muraskin (Ed.), *It's a crime: Women and justice* (4th ed., pp. 542–563). Upper Saddle River, NJ: Pearson.

Bureau of Justice Statistics. (2014a). *Number of violent victimizations, personal thefts/larcenies, serious violent victimizations, rape/sexual assaults, robberies, aggravated assaults, and simple assaults by sex 2003–2012*, July 14, 2014. Generated using the NCVS Victimization Analysis Tool at www.bjs.gov

Bureau of Justice Statistics. (2014b). *Imprisonment rate of sentenced female prisoners under the jurisdiction of state or federal correctional authorities per 100,000 female U.S. residents*, December 31, 1978–2012. Generated using the Corrections Statistical Analysis Tool at www.bjs.gov

Bureau of Justice Statistics. (2014c). *Imprisonment rate of sentenced male prisoners under the jurisdiction of state or federal correctional authorities per 100,000 male U.S. residents*, December 31, 1978–2012. Generated using the Corrections Statistical Analysis Tool at www.bjs.gov

Carson, E. A., & Mulako-Wangota, J., Bureau of Justice Statistics. *Count of total jurisdiction population*, July 14, 2014, Generated using the Corrections Statistical Analysis Tool (CSAT)—Prisoners at www.bjs.gov.

Chesney-Lind, M., & Pasko, L. (2013). *The female offender: Girls, women, and crime* (3rd ed.). Thousand Oaks, CA: Sage.

Cohen, J. W., & Brooks, R. A. (2014). *Confronting school bullying: Kids, culture, and the making of a social problem*. Boulder, CO: Lynne Rienner.

Cohen, J. W., & Harvey, P. (2006). Misconceptions of gender: Sex, masculinity, and the measurement of crime. *The Journal of Men's Studies, 14*(2), 223–233.

Cohen, J. W., & Martin, R. (2012). The four dimensions of gender. In D. McDonald & A. Miller (Eds.), *Race gender, and criminal justice: Equality and justice for all?* (pp. 17–34). San Diego, CA: Cognella.

DeHart, D. (2008). Pathways to prison: Impact of victimization in the lives of incarcerated women. *Violence Against Women, 14*, 1362–1381.

Federal Bureau of Investigation. (2014). *UCR program changes definition of rape: Includes all victims and omits requirement of physical force*. Retrieved from http://www.fbi.gov/about-us/cjis/cjis-link/march-2012/ucr-program-changes-definition-of-rape

Kellner, D. (2014). Diagnosing and preventing school shootings. In G. W. Muschert, S. Henry, N. L. Bracy, & A. A. Peguero (Eds.), *Responding to school violence: Confronting the columbine effect* (pp. 189–213). Boulder, CO: Lynne Rienner.

Madfis, E. (2014). Triple entitlement and homicidal anger: An exploration of the intersectional identities of American mass murderers. *Men and Masculinities, 17*(1), 67–86.

Martin, R., Cohen, J. W., & Champion, D. (2013). Conceptualization, operationalization, construct validity, and truth in advertising in criminological research. *Journal of Theoretical and Philosophical Criminology, 5*(1), 1–38.

Messerschmidt, J. W. (2000). *Nine lives: Adolescent masculinities, the body, and violence*. Boulder, CO: Westview Press.

Messerschmidt, J. W. (2006). Masculinities and crime: Beyond a dualist criminology. In C. M. Renzetti, L. Goodstein, & S. L. Miller (Eds.), *Rethinking gender, crime, and justice: Feminist readings* (pp. 29–43). Los Angeles, CA: Roxbury.

Messerschmidt, J. W. (2014). *Crime as structured action: Doing masculinities, race, class, sexuality, and crime* (2nd ed.). Lanham, MD: Rowman & Littlefield.

Miller, K. L. (2009). The darkest figure of crime: Perceptions of reasons for male inmates to not report sexual assault. *Justice Quarterly, 27*(5), 692–712

Pollock, J. M. (2014). *Women's crimes, criminology, and corrections*. Long Grove, IL: Waveland Press.

Rosin, H. (2012). *The end of men and the rise of women*. New York, NY: Riverhead.

Simmons, R. (2002). *Odd girl out: The hidden culture of aggression in girls*. New York, NY: Harcourt.

Steffensmeier, D., Zhong, H., Ackerman, J., Schwartz, J., & Agha, S. (2006). Gender gap trends for violent crimes, 1980 to 2003: A UCR-NCVS comparison. *Feminist Criminology, 1*, 72–98.

Stemple, L., & Meyer, I. H. (2014). The sexual victimization of men in America: New data challenge old assumptions. *American Journal of Public Health, 104*(6), 19–26.

van Wormer, K. (2010). *Working with female offenders: A gender-sensitive approach.* Hoboken, NJ: Wiley.

Wolff, N., Blitz, C., Shi, J., Bachman, R., & Siegel, J. (2006). Sexual violence inside prisons: Rates of victimization. *Journal of Urban Health, 83*(5), 835–848.

The Cycle of Intimate Partner Violence

4

CARLY M. HILINSKI-ROSICK

Contents

When you think about domestic violence, what do you think of? Chances are, you imagine a man hitting a woman (usually his wife), leaving a bruise or mark, in retaliation for some alleged transgression by the woman. However, domestic violence is not this simple. Rather, domestic violence includes a broad range of behaviors, couples, and relationship types.

Consider the following situations:

Joan and David have been married for 15 years; however, their marriage has been over for a long time. When Joan starts to bring up the subject of leaving, David threatens to hurt himself and says that he is not willing to live without Joan. He then throws her things and clothes into the yard, saying that if he cannot be with her, then no one can.

Jennifer is a young mother with two young children. She has been married to Mike for 5 years and has been staying at home taking care of her children for the past 4 years. Each day, Jennifer is frantic, trying to get dinner on the table by 5:30 p.m.

when Mike comes home from work. When he comes home and dinner is not on the table, he calls her a fat slob and tells her that she cannot do anything right. When Jennifer does not respond to Dan's comments and instead continues what she is doing, he often will take the food and dishes and throw them against the wall. He then storms out of the house, taking Jennifer's keys and wallet with him, and comes home drunk later that night. The next day, he comes home with flowers and apologizes to Jennifer, begging for her forgiveness, and promising that it will never happen again.

Nancy and Andrea are partners who have lived together for the past 10 years. Nancy does not allow Andrea to work outside the home and controls their finances. Andrea gets a small weekly allowance for personal items as well as money for grocery shopping. She must provide Nancy with the receipts from the grocery shopping and is not permitted to spend more than what Nancy allocates. Andrea has recently expressed an interest in going back to school to finish her college degree. Nancy refuses to allow Andrea to do this and tells her that if she is not happy with what she has, then she cannot have any of it. Nancy then takes away Andrea's weekly allowance and takes away her car keys, leaving her unable to leave the house.

Would you consider the earlier situations to be domestic violence, or intimate partner violence (IPV), as it is more recently called? The traditional view of domestic violence is violence that takes place between a husband and a wife (with the husband being the aggressor and the wife being the victim) and entailing some sort of physical abuse. As you read in these scenarios, no physical abuse actually occurred. Under the traditional definitions of domestic violence, these situations would simply be considered private relationship issues. However, these situations do constitute abuse. Just because the abuse is not physical does not mean that it is not IPV. As you will read in the following sections, more contemporary definitions of domestic violence now encompass a wide range of behaviors and relationships. Further, you will also learn more about the history of IPV, the nature and prevalence of IPV, the risk factors for and negative consequences of IPV, and how the criminal justice system treats victims and offenders of IPV.

History and Definition of Intimate Partner Violence

Historically, IPV was limited to physical violence that was perpetrated by husbands against their wives. There is some controversy, however, when it comes to how society treated this behavior in the past. Common belief is that violence against wives was a tolerated, and even condoned, behavior, as the man was considered the patriarch of his family and should be permitted to do what was necessary to control his wife and children (Dobash & Dobash, 1979). When examining laws from history, we can look as far back as the 1600s, when laws were on the books prohibiting violence against wives in America. By the 1870s, most states had similar laws on their books; however, the punishment of men who abused their wives was usually very informal. Thus, although there were laws prohibiting this type of behavior, there was little punishment involved for men who committed these crimes.

There are instances, however, of courts tolerating minor forms of violence committed by husbands against their wives, despite laws that prohibited these behaviors. When courts did not convict or uphold convictions of men who had physically abused their wives, it was generally minor violence and because of the view that the courts should not intervene based on the principle of privacy, and allowing husbands and wives to handle personal matters within the privacy of their home, without court intervention (Felson, 2002).

It was not until the 1970s that IPV emerged as a pressing issue and garnered any policy or research attention. The women's rights movement of the 1970s was integral in shedding light on issues such as IPV and rape and sexual assault. Those who advocated for women's rights argued that IPV was a result of a patriarchal social structure and that the male-dominated criminal justice system did little, if anything, to protect women. One of the most significant developments of this movement was the creation of domestic violence shelters, which provided women with places to go in order to get out of abusive relationships. These shelters also provided abused women with services and other assistance necessary to leave their abusive partner (Daigle, 2012). Further, the criminal justice system began to view IPV as a legal issue, not a private marital issue. Continued efforts to bring violence against women to the attention of lawmakers and the public were successful in the 1990s, with the passage of the Violence against Women Act (VAWA), which provided more than $1 billion to programs designed to address violence against women. Difficulties emerged, however, when it came to defining IPV.

The traditional term of *domestic violence* is limited in its spectrum. Domestic violence statutes typically were limited to violence between individuals who lived together, thus ignoring the potential violence between those who were once living together but were not any longer, individuals in romantic relationships who were not living together, and those who were in a casual relationship. Further, early domestic violence definitions included only violence perpetrated by husbands against their wives. We now recognize that relationship violence is neither unique or exclusive to married couples, nor something that is committed only by husbands and against their wives; IPV can be committed by males or females, in heterosexual and homosexual relationships, and in dating relationships. An intimate partner can be any number of people; it could be a current spouse, ex-spouse, a current or former boyfriend or girlfriend, or a dating partner. The term *intimate partner* is used in an effort to encompass a wide range of relationships that may involve violence.

Complicating matters even more is that IPV is not limited to physical violence. Emotional and psychological abuse can also be considered to be IPV. Controlling behavior, such as limiting an individual's access to bank accounts, a car, or the ability to come and go as they please also can be categorized as IPV. Isolating a partner from his or her friends and family is yet another example of IPV that does not involve any sort of physical contact. The current definitions of IPV are much more inclusive and extensive than the historical definitions and include a broad range of behaviors committed by many different individuals. Many states have been revising statutes to reflect this shift in definition as well. For example, in its domestic assault definition, the State of Michigan considers domestic assault in any situation where an individual assaults or assaults and batters his or her spouse or former spouse, an individual with whom he or she has or has had a dating relationship, an individual with whom he or she has had a child in common, or a resident or former resident of his or her household. This definition includes a wide range of different romantic partners (and nonromantic partners) and also acknowledges that both men and women can commit this type of assault (The Michigan Penal Code, Section 750.81).

Current State of Intimate Partner Violence

IPV, like rape and sexual assault, is an often underreported crime. For many reasons, victims of IPV are reluctant to report the crime to law enforcement officers. Many victims do not report IPV out of embarrassment, fear of retaliation from the abuser, financial dependence on the abuser, or lack of desire that charges be filed against the abuser; thus, it is difficult to know the full extent of IPV. Official statistics, like the Uniform Crime Report, often underreport IPV, since they include only crimes reported to the police. The most accurate statistics indicating the extent of IPV come from victimization studies, such as the National Crime Victimization Survey (NCVS) and other surveys focusing specifically on IPV, including the National Family Violence Survey, the National Violence against Women Survey (NVAWS), and the National Intimate Partner and Sexual Violence Survey (NISVS), which ask victims to self-report any victimizations they have experienced. Although victimization surveys also suffer from underreporting, the underreporting may be much less than official statistics, rendering these surveys the best estimates we have of IPV.

National Crime Victimization Survey

The NCVS includes information gathered from interviews of persons aged 12 and over from a nationally representative sample of the U.S. households. Household members are asked to report the number of victimizations they experienced in the 6 months preceding the interview, and if they report that they had been the victim of a crime, they are asked a series of questions about the specific characteristics of the incident, such as their relationship with the victim and the impacts of the victimization. The NCVS includes rape, sexual assault, robbery, simple assault, and aggravated assault committed by a current or former spouse, boyfriend, or girlfriend in its definition of IPV.

NCVS data indicate that between 1994 and 2011, the rate of serious IPV (rape or sexual assault, robbery, and aggravated assault) committed against women declined by 72%, with the greatest declines occurring between 1994 and 2001 (Catalano, 2013). Despite these declines, 4.7% of women and 1.5% of men were the victim of IPV in 2011. The most common type of IPV reported to NCVS interviewers was simple assault, comprising over half of all IPV victimizations (Catalano, 2013). Further, 50% of women who had been the victim of IPV suffered an injury, while 44% of men who had been the victim of IPV suffered an injury (Catalano, 2013). The NCVS is not without its limitations, however. Underreporting still may occur, as victims may be embarrassed to report their victimization to an interviewer. Further, the offender may also live in the same household, making it difficult for the victim to be forthcoming about the abuse.

Conflict Tactics Scale and the National Family Violence Surveys

In the 1978 and 1975 National Family Violence Surveys, the Conflict Tactics Scale (CTS) was used to measure levels and use of conflict tactics; the CTS was created by Straus and Gelles to examine conflict in intimate relationships. The National Family Violence Surveys found that in about 12.5% of the couples, the husband had perpetrated at least one violent act in the previous year. Interestingly, women also were found to have committed physical violence against their husbands about equally as often—about 12% of women had used some sort of physical violence on their husbands in the previous year. These findings were controversial at the time, as they went against conventional beliefs that it was always husbands abusing their wives and that women were not capable of this type of violence. Critics of the CTS noted that it does not take into account the motives of violence and argued that women may be using violence in relationships as a way to fight back against their husbands who initiated the violence. Further, critics argued that when women do commit violence in relationships, they were less likely to cause injury, compared to when a man commits relationship violence (Dobash, Dobash, Wilson, & Daly, 1992).

The original CTS has been revised and is now known as the revised Conflict Tactics Scale (CTS-2) (Straus, Hamby, Boney-McCoy, & Sugarman, 1996). The CTS-2 includes 78 questions that measure the use of conflict tactics in the domains of physical assault, psychological aggression, and negotiation. It also measures injuries and sexual coercion of and by an intimate partner. The CTS-2 asks respondents to indicate one of eight response options, which range from never to more than 20 times in the past year. For example, respondents are asked to note how many times in the past year, if any, they or their partner threw something at their partner that could hurt, pushed or shoved their partner, or slammed their partner up against a wall. Respondents also can indicate whether the action did not happen in the past year, but has happened sometime in the past.

National Violence against Women Survey

The goal of the NVAWS was to gather information about rape, physical assault, and stalking victimizations from a national sample of 8000 men and 8000 women over the age of 18. The NVAWS also asked the respondents about any psychological and emotional abuse perpetrated by current or former spouses and cohabitating partners (Tjaden & Thoennes, 2000). Of the survey participants, 22% of the women and 7% of the men reported that they had experienced physical assault by their current or former intimate partner at some point in their life. About 1.3% of women and less than 1% of men had experienced IPV during the previous 12 months. Women were more likely to report injuries, were more likely to report the assault to the police, and were also more likely to be the victim of recurring victimization (victimization by the same partner) (Tjaden & Thoennes, 2000). Although useful, the information gathered from the National Family Violence Surveys and the NVAWS is dated; a more recent effort to examine the prevalence of IPV is detailed in the following text.

National Intimate Partner and Sexual Violence Survey

In 2006, the Centers for Disease Control and Prevention (CDC) implemented the development of a new tool to gather information about the prevalence of intimate partner and sexual violence. The NISVS was created in response to the lack of sufficient data on the nature and extent of IPV and sexual violence and uses nationally representative data to shed light on the issue of IPV and sexual violence. The survey was first administered in 2010 and measured five types of IPV, including sexual violence, stalking, physical violence, psychological aggression, and control of reproductive/sexual health.

The NISVS found that over one-third of women in the United States had experienced rape, physical violence, and/or stalking committed by an intimate partner at some point in their life (Black et al., 2011). Nearly 6% of the women in the survey indicated that they had experienced violence committed by an intimate partner in the past 12 months. Further, over 25% of men reported that they had been the victim of rape, physical violence, and/or stalking at some point in their life, and about 5% reported that they had been the victim of this violence in the past 12 months (Black et al., 2011). These surveys also revealed information about the victims and offenders of IPV, which is discussed in greater detail in the following section.

Victim and Offender Characteristics

The IPV is not limited to one particular group in society. It crosses racial, gender, and socioeconomic groups. There are characteristics, however, that put some individuals at a greater risk for the IPV than others. Younger individuals and women, particularly black women, are more likely to be the victim of IPV than their older, male, and white counterparts (Rand & Rennison, 2004). The NCVS data indicate that black females are 2.5 times more likely to be the victim of IPV than white females, and this difference is most pronounced in women aged 20–24 (Rand & Rennison, 2004).

Overall, offenders are most likely to be male, and this finding applies in both heterosexual and same-sex relationships. Despite findings that the gender gap in IPV may not be as a large as once thought, men are much more likely to commit IPV than women (Archer, 2000). When males commit IPV, they are more likely to cause injuries, which may be because they are, in general, stronger than females and have the physical capabilities to cause injuries, they are more likely to use tactics that result in violence than women, such as using weapons, and they are also more likely to engage in intimate terrorism, which is rooted in a desire for power and control of the victim, and often leads to serious injuries (Johnson, 2006).

Additional risk factors for both IPV perpetration and victimization can be classified as individual, relationship, societal, or community. Individual risk factors include low self-esteem, low socioeconomic status, low academic achievement, aggressive or delinquent behavior as a youth, drug and alcohol abuse, depression, anger and hostility, antisocial personality traits, borderline personality traits, prior history of being physically abusive, having few friends and being isolated from people, emotional dependence and insecurity, belief in strict gender roles, desire for power and control in relationships, being a victim of physical or psychological abuse, and experiencing physical discipline as a child (CDC, 2014).

Relationship factors that are associated with a higher risk of IPV include marital conflict and instability, including divorce and separation, cohabitation without marriage (research has found that the rate of IPV is the highest among couples who are unmarried but are living together [Wallace, 2007], unhealthy family relationships and interactions, and dominance and control of the relationship by one partner). Community and societal factors can also impact IPV, including poverty, low social capital, weak community sanctions against IPV, and a strong emphasis on traditional gender norms (CDC, 2014).

Same-Sex Intimate Partner Violence

While IPV historically was believed to occur only between a married couple, expanded definitions of IPV encompass a variety of different relationships, including same-sex relationships. Current definitions of IPV typically do not specify the gender of the victim and the offender, which allows for same-sex IPV to be considered as the same as IPV in heterosexual relationships. Through the NVAWS, Tjaden and Thoennes (2000) found that women who lived with female intimate partners were less likely to experience IPV than women who lived with male intimate partners; however, more than 11% of women who lived with a female intimate partner reported that she had been raped, physically assaulted, and/or stalked by a current or former female intimate partner. Not surprisingly, men who lived with male intimate partners reported a higher number of incidents of IPV than men who lived with female intimate partners. The NVAWS found that 15% of men who lived with a male intimate partner reported that he had been raped, physically assaulted, and/or stalked by a male intimate partner, while only 7.7% of men living with a female intimate partner reported this type of violence (Tjaden & Thoennes, 2000). Individuals in same-sex relationships also may be the victim of a unique form of IPV: *outing* an individual. If a person has not disclosed to family, friends, or others that he or she is gay or lesbian, an abuser may reveal, or threaten to reveal, this information to others (Daigle, 2012).

Despite the recognition of IPV in same-sex relationships, it is even more difficult to measure the extent of IPV among same-sex couples than IPV among heterosexual couples. IPV is underreported to begin with and may be underreported even more among same-sex couples. One reason for this is fear of how criminal justice system officials will treat victims of IPV who are in a same-sex relationship. Victims often fear that they will be demeaned or will not be believed and are reluctant to report (Jaquier, 2010); further, many of the resources available to female victims of IPV are not available to same-sex IPV victims. Men who are the victim of same-sex IPV may have even more difficulties, as the vast majority of domestic violence shelters are for females only (Daigle, 2012). The next section discusses the criminal justice system response to IPV in both heterosexual and same-sex relationships.

Case Study 1: Intimate Partner Violence in Same-Sex Relationships

IPV in same-sex relationships has historically received little attention. In fact, it was not until recently that states even recognized that IPV could occur in same-sex relationships and created statutes that did not specify that the couple need to be married or that the victim and offender had to be one man and one women. More contemporary statutes recognize that IPV is not limited to married men and women and can, and does, occur in same-sex relationships as well.

Steven is a gay man who entered into his first relationship with another man, Dennis, when he was 22. Dennis came from a family where drugs, guns, violence, and crime were prevalent. His family did not accept his lifestyle, and Dennis believed that it was impossible to be happy in a same-sex relationship, but began a relationship with Steven anyway. In the beginning, their relationship was happy. Steven described Dennis as generous, sweet, and charming. However, 1 year into their relationship, Dennis began using drugs and alcohol again, after being sober for nearly 16 months. As the relationship turned tumultuous, Steven attempted to break up with Dennis. Dennis became hysterical and threatened suicide if Steven left him. Eventually, Steven gave in, even though he knew he needed to get out of the relationship.

Dennis's drug use escalated, and he was using needles to inject drugs, putting himself at risk for HIV/AIDS and other diseases. As a result, Steven refused to engage in a sexual relationship with Dennis, which resulted in the first physical assault by Dennis. Dennis pushed Steven so hard into a wall that he put a hole in the drywall. Dennis apologized profusely and promised that it would never happen again. Like his drug use, Dennis's violence also escalated. He threatened a coworker and ultimately showed up at his house to confront him, where he then beat him with a club. Around the same time, Dennis told Steven that if he attended a party that he wished to go to, he would wait for him outside the party and shoot him when he left. Or, he said he would just crash the party and start shooting anyone there. Given his past behavior, Steven believed he was capable of this behavior and did not attend the party. As the months went on, Steven and Dennis found themselves in a cycle where violence would occur, Dennis would apologize and beg for forgiveness, promising that it would never happen again, and Steven would relent. Eventually, things escalated to a point where he locked Steven in his apartment and once again threatened to shoot him. As the night went on, Dennis repeatedly asked Steven how it felt to know he was going to die. He would then elaborate on how he was going to kill him, either with his knife or his gun. First, though, he told Steven that he was going to rape him.

After over 3 hours, Steven was finally able to escape from Dennis, who was much stronger and larger than him. The next day, he packed what he could fit into his car and left his house for good, staying with a coworker. He met with a victim advocate to explore his options, but the victim advocate was unable to provide much assistance to him, other than advising him to press charges or to take out a restraining order. There also were no shelters available to him, leaving him to find his own housing in a location safe from Dennis. Steven's situation is not uncommon. IPV occurs in same-sex relationships, just as it does in heterosexual relationships, yet the services available to male victims of IPV are severely limited.

Criminal Justice System Response to IPV

As discussed in the beginning of the chapter, IPV is something that has historically been viewed as a private matter between a husband and a wife, and was to be settled in the home without outside (especially criminal justice system) intervention. As the definition of IPV evolved, and as IPV started to receive more attention within the criminal justice system, the response of the police, courts, and community also evolved.

Police

There are a number of different reasons why police have historically been reluctant to make arrests in IPV cases. Some argue that police do not want to make arrests in IPV cases because they want to give the couple privacy and do not want to intervene in what they believe is a private matter. Others argue that police are reluctant to respond to IPV calls because IPV situations are thought to be dangerous to officers (Kanno & Newhill, 2009). Even further, some officers are hesitant to become involved because victims often refuse to press charges and officers may feel that an arrest is a waste of time (Wallace, 2007).

Even when police may want to make an arrest in an IPV situation, their ability to do so may be limited. In general, police are unable to make a warrantless arrest for misdemeanors. Police can typically make misdemeanor arrests only if they have an arrest warrant or if they witness the crime occur. Since many IPV incidents are considered misdemeanors, and since police officers most often arrive on the scene after the violence has taken place, they are often unable to make an arrest. These policies limited the options of law enforcement officers for many years, until the mid-1980s, when research examined the impact of arrest on IPV situations. In the early 1980s, Sherman and Berk (1984) examined the deterrent effect of arrest on perpetrators of domestic violence in the Minneapolis Domestic Violence Experiment, often referred to as the Minneapolis Experiment. Sherman and Berk were interested in examining how much of a deterrent it was to arrest a domestic violence perpetrator when police were called to the home, so they created an experiment to examine if arrest deterred IPV offenders in Minneapolis, Minnesota, in the early 1980s.

To make it a true experiment, Sherman and Berk created a set of color-coded cards that instructed officers to do one of three things: make an arrest that would result in one night in jail; advise the couple using the officer's judgment; or separate the two parties for a period of time. When an eligible call came in, officers would randomly be assigned a response based on the color-coded response cards. Officers were able, however, to deviate from the color-coded card if they felt that a different response was the best option (this impacted the validity of the results, however). Situations where they could deviate from the experiment included when the offense was a clear felony, when the officer felt threatened, and when the IPV victim requested action (Doerner & Lab, 2012). To measure the effectiveness of each of the strategies, researchers followed up with each IPV victim biweekly for 6 months after the IPV incident. The goal was to gather information about any subsequent violence committed by the suspect.

Characteristics of the victims and the offenders revealed a high rate of unemployment (60% were unemployed), a high likelihood of having a criminal record (60% had some sort of criminal history), with one-third of the offenders having a violent arrest history, 80% had assaulted their partner at least once in the previous 6 months, and half of all of the couples were not married at the time of the incident. There were two outcomes measured by the experiment. First, researchers examined whether police had to return to the residence for another domestic call during the 6-month follow-up period. Second, interviewers contacted the victims in each case to determine if there had been any incidents of IPV that occurred but were not reported to the police.

The official statistics (i.e., police records) showed that in the cases where officers issued a warning and separated the parties for a *cooling-off* period, there was a 26% recidivism rate, meaning officers had to return to 26% of the households for another domestic violence call within the follow-up period. For the cases where police counseled the victim and the offender, recidivism was 18%, and for cases where the offender was arrested, there was a 13% recidivism rate. The interviews also indicated that the counseling option had the highest recidivism rate, with 37% of the offenders reoffending when the officers' response was to counsel the victim and the offender. When the victim and the offender were separated, victims reported that 33% of the offenders recidivated, and once again, arrest had the lowest recidivism rate, with 19% of those who were arrested reoffending.

These findings clearly indicated that arrest has the most significant impact on recidivism in IPV case; however, Sherman and Berk (1984) offered words of caution when disseminating their findings. They called for replication studies before any policies were enacted, as the experiment took place in only one city in the United States, and they also argued for a presumption of arrest, which would call for arrest unless there are clear reasons why an arrest would be counterproductive, rather than mandatory arrest. They did not favor mandatory arrest in all misdemeanor domestic violence cases, even if their findings were replicated in a number of other jurisdictions and believed that arrest worked better for some kinds of offenders than others, and in some kinds of situations better than others. In short, they did not favor a one-size-fits-all approach for IPV cases.

Replication studies conducted in five different jurisdictions (Charlotte, NC, Dade County, FL, Colorado Springs, CO, Milwaukee, WI, and Omaha, NE) found results that contradicted Sherman and Berk's initial findings. The replication studies found that arrest had only a deterrent effect in one jurisdiction (Dade County), and in Omaha, Charlotte, and Milwaukee, arrest deterred offender initially but caused an escalation of IPV over time, meaning that over time, the domestic violence got worse and more frequent. One of the most significant findings, and one in line with Sherman and Berk's initial words of caution, was that arrest differentially impacted offenders, with employed offenders having lower recidivism rates with arrests. Unemployed offenders were more likely to engage in repeat IPV (Maxwell, Garner, & Fagan, 2001).

Despite Sherman and Berk's words of caution and the findings of the replication studies, many departments were quick to implement mandatory arrest policies for IPV cases, which require arrest by police officers when there is probable cause that a crime was committed and enough evidence exists for an arrest. By 2007, more than 20 states had mandatory arrest policies (Iyengar, 2007). Some states, however, now have a pro-arrest or presumptive arrest policy, similar to what Sherman and Berk proposed. These policies assume that an arrest will be made in each case, but allow an offender to make a decision not to arrest. The officer is then usually required to make a written justification why he or she did not make an arrest. One additional response is a permissive arrest policy, which does not mandate or presume arrest in IPV situations, but allows officers to determine who they should respond to IPV calls.

One last development in law enforcement's response to IPV is a dual arrest policy. In a dual arrest, the officer arrests both the victim and the offender. This policy is based on the assumption that many victims of IPV are also offenders and that IPV is a part of common-couple violence and is a mutual behavior. Research has found that dual arrest is more common among same-sex couples and when the offender is female (Hirschel, 2008). One of the downsides to dual arrest policies is that it may make victims fearful of calling the police in an IPV situation because they are afraid they are going to be arrested (Bui, 2001). Victims also may be reluctant to participate in the prosecution of their abusers if they were also arrested (Bui, 2001).

Courts

While law enforcement officers make the initial decisions on how to handle IPV cases, prosecutors play a significant role in the outcome of IPV cases. Once police make an arrest, prosecutors must make the decision on whether to formally charge the offender. Criticisms of prosecutors have centered on the idea that they were reluctant to file formal charges even when an arrest was made (Chalk & King, 1998; Hartman & Belknap, 2003). There is little research examining prosecution and conviction rates of IPV, making it difficult to make generalized statements about the court response to IPV cases.

Factors that have been shown to play a role in the prosecution of an offender include physical injury of the victim (Jordan, 2004), whether the victim or the defendant had been under the influence of alcohol or drugs at the time of the incident (Jordan, 2004; Rauma, 1984; Schmidt & Steury, 1989), the history between the victim and the offender (e.g., is there a history of abuse) (Schmidt & Steury, 1989), and whether the victim was willing to participate in the court process (Dawson & Dinovitzer, 2001). Some researchers also have found that the court's culture can impact the processing of IPV cases even more than existing laws (Currul-Dykeman, 2014).

Victim participation in the prosecution process is often integral to the prosecutor's case. However, in IPV cases, victims may be extremely reluctant to testify against the offender for a number of different reasons. They may still live with the offender, have children with him or her, be financially dependent on the offender, or fear retaliation if he or she testifies. In response to the reluctance of victims to participate in the prosecution of IPV cases, some jurisdictions have adopted no-drop prosecution policies. These policies require prosecutors to file charges in IPV cases and allow the cases to move forward even without the participation of the victim. Research has indicated that the dismissal rate of IPV cases has declined (Davis, Smith, & Davies, 2001); however, the policies have been criticized because they may be harmful to victims if the offender retaliates against the victim. Victims also may be reluctant to call police if they are aware of the no-drop policies. They may simply want the police to intervene in the situation and are not interested in seeing the offender prosecuted.

Recent court responses to IPV have included specialty courts of IPV cases. These courts exclusively handle IPV cases and focus on the treatment of the offender to identify the causes of the abusive behavior so that future violent behavior can be prevented. Evidence has suggested that participating in domestic violence courts reduced rearrests for IPV (Gover, MacDonald, & Alpert, 2003) and future offending against the same victims (Goldkamp, Weiland, Collins, & White, 1996).

One additional court response is a protective order (sometimes called a restraining order or personal protective order). These orders may be no-contact orders, where the offender is not permitted to contact the victim after a court hearing (this is generally ordered after an offender's arraignment or first court appearance). Orders also may prohibit an offender from coming within a certain distance of the victim. All states allow for protective orders for the protection of IPV victims, but the enforcement of them varies from state to state. Further, most eligible victims do not seek protection orders from the court. The NVAWS found that only 17.1% of female victims of IPV received protective orders, and only 36.6% of females who were the victims of intimate-partner-perpetrated stalking received protective orders (Tjaden & Thoennes, 2000).

Some jurisdictions are creating coordinated response teams to IPV, which consist of police, court officials, victim advocates, and social service providers. Communities that have these teams generally rely on victim advocates or social service providers to guide victims through the court process and provide other necessary services. Some law enforcement agencies will also bring a victim advocate or social service provider along on an IPV call, so that they can provide information to the victim on the services available to them immediately.

Community Response

Beyond the criminal justice system, the community also provides services to victims of IPV. The most significant perhaps being shelters available to IPV victims. The first domestic violence shelter opened in Minnesota in 1974. These shelters, which are typically in a secret location, allow victims to have a place of refuge. The location of the shelters is not advertised so that the victims can feel safe from their abusers. Research has shown that the time when victims are leaving their abusers is the most dangerous time for them; Wilson and Daly (1993) found that women who stayed with their abusive husbands were less likely to be killed than women who left them.

Domestic violence shelters are able to provide victims with a place to stay (usually short term, typically between 30 and 60 days), clothing and transportation, counseling, child care, and help with finding employment. These resources are necessary, as many victims of IPV are financially dependent on their partners and have been isolated from friends and family, who could provide a support system for them if they attempt to leave. Some communities have even created programs to care for the pets of victims of IPV who leave their abusers. Research has shown that not wanting to leave a pet behind is a significant reason why some women do not leave an abusive relationship, and many domestic violence shelters will not allow women to bring their pets with them, resulting in them returning to their abusive relationships, or not leaving them in the first place.

Cycle of Violence

Revictimization is common among IPV victims. In general, research finds that many victims are abused again and many offenders offend again. The NVAWS found that female IPV victims in their study reported nearly seven physical assaults by the same person. Male IPV victims reported that they experienced, on average, 4.4 physical assaults by the same person (Tjaden & Thoennes, 2000). This revictimization and reoffending is not limited to the same partners, either. Many women find themselves in multiple different abusive relationships in their lifetime, and men often physically abuse their partners in multiple relationships as well.

This cycle of violence, as it is often called, was first discussed by Walker (1979). She argued that IPV takes on a pattern that involves different stages or phases. The first is the tension-building phase, where the abuser and the victim interact in a relationship that often includes positive behavior by the offender. As the relationship goes on, day-to-day pressures and other serious events built tension. These tension-causing events may be the precursor to minor violence. The tension then continues, though, into a more serious incident of violence, called the acute battering phase. During this phase, the abuser engages in serious physical abuse of the victim. The acute battering phase is followed by the honeymoon phase, where the abuser once again becomes calm and acts in a loving way. He or she often may beg for forgiveness and ensure his or her partner that the abuse will never happen again. Walker argues that if the two stay in a relationship, the cycle will start once again.

Given the statistics that show that IPV is likely to repeat itself, many people wonder why IPV victims do not leave their abusive relationships. Recall that the cycle of violence includes a phase where the offender is often charming and engages in positive behavior;

there is also a honeymoon phase, where the offender promises the victim that the abuse will never happen again and often begs for forgiveness. These periods of loving, appropriate relationship behavior can be very emotionally confusing to an IPV victim. Victims often see positive traits in the abuser and once loved him or her (or even still loves them), making it difficult for them to leave the relationship. Even when victims do leave the relationship, they often go back. Okun (1986) found that women leave an abusive relationship an average of six times before leaving for good and ending the relationship permanently.

Leaving permanently is difficult for many reasons. Many women are financially dependent upon their partners. They also may have children, and leaving would mean taking the children away from the other parent. Abusers also often isolate their victims from family and friends, making it difficult for victims to have a network of supportive people to help him or her leave. If they do have friends and family who could help, these individuals often may blame the woman or encourage her to try to work things out with her partner rather than leaving the relationship. Even still, some women may not leave due to religious reasons. Women who have strong religious beliefs and feel that divorce or separation is not an option may not leave. They also may fear disapproval from fellow members of their religion or their clergyperson. Finally, many women do not leave because they are scared. Recall that women who are leaving relationships are in the most danger, with women more likely to be killed after leaving their husbands than living with them (Wilson & Daly, 1993). To some women, staying in the abusive relationship is better than the alternatives available to them.

Case Study 2: Rihanna and Chris Brown: Intimate Partner Violence and the Cycle of Violence

Many people know singers Rihanna and Chris Brown for their top albums and songs played on the radio. However, in 2009, Rihanna and Brown were in the news for something much different. In early 2009, Brown severely physically assaulted Rihanna and threatened to kill her, over a series of allegedly sexual text messages Rihanna found on Brown's phone. Brown attacked her in his car, giving her injuries that resulted in hospital care. Shortly after the attack, Brown was charged with felony assault and felony criminal threats. During summer 2009, he issues a public apology to Rihanna via YouTube, saying "I wish I had the chance to live those few moments again... what I did was inexcusable... I'm truly, truly sorry that I wasn't able to handle the situation both differently and better... I will do everything in my power to make sure that it never happens again." Eventually, Brown pleads guilty to the assault, in exchange for no jail time. He was, however, ordered to serve 5 years of probation, complete 6 months of community service, and ordered to stay away from Rihanna. In 2011, a judge reduced the restraining order and allows Brown to speak to Rihanna, as long as he does not annoy or harass her.

During this time, both Brown and Rihanna had moved on from each other, dating others. In 2012, Rihanna and Brown once again team up, for two songs, one on each of their albums. Also in 2012, Brown got into a physical altercation with Rihanna's former boyfriend, Drake, at a New York City bar. Shortly after, Rihanna opened up about her feelings for Brown, saying on national television that he was the *first love* of her life. Brown and Rihanna then go on to share a kiss on the MTV Video Music Awards and are spotted around New York City in intimate moments. During this time, Rihanna also publicly proclaimed her support for Brown when he had to attend a probation hearing.

Both Brown and Rihanna received much public criticism for their actions: Brown for his abusive behavior and Rihanna for seemingly sticking by him and proclaiming her love for him after the assault. Brown and Rihanna's relationship is a real-life example of the cycle of violence. After a tension-building phase, Brown exploded in the acute battering phase, causing visible physical injuries to Rihanna, causing her to seek medical attention. He then issued a public apology, promising that the abuse will never happen again. In the honeymoon phase, Brown and Rihanna find themselves together once again, collaborating professionally as well as reestablishing their intimate relationship. Brown also reported that he grew up in a household where he witnessed his stepfather repeatedly physically assault his mother, showing support for the social learning explanation of IPV.

Today, Brown and Rihanna are no longer a couple, and Brown has been plagued by a myriad of legal troubles since the assault on Rihanna, including several physical altercations resulting in arrest, probation violations and revocation, positive drug tests, and jail time.

Stalking

Many states have also enacted laws that address threatening behavior and situations, including stalking. Stalking is a unique behavior, as there is no one universally accepted definition. Stalking has been recognized as a crime in the United States only since the 1980s. Currently, stalking is a crime in all 50 states and on the federal level. Although stalking statues differ from state to state, researchers have attempted to define stalking. According to Wright et al. (1997), stalking is "the act of following, viewing, communicating with, or moving threateningly or menacingly toward another person" (p. 487). Many states also require that these behaviors are repeated or coupled with other behaviors. For example, in the State of Pennsylvania, a person commits the crime of stalking when "(1) the person either engages in a course of conduct or repeatedly commits acts toward another person, including following the person without proper authority, under circumstances which demonstrate either an intent to place such other person in reasonable fear of bodily injury or to cause substantial emotional distress to such other person or (2) engages in a course of conduct or repeatedly communicates to another person under circumstances which demonstrate or communicate either an intent to place such other person in reasonable fear of bodily injury or to cause substantial emotional distress to such other person" (18 Pa. C.S. § 2709.1., 2003). A "course of conduct" is defined as "a pattern of actions composed of more than one act over a period of time, however short, evidencing a continuity of conduct." This is an important distinction, as stalking encompasses behavior that is repeated, rather than consisting of one single incident. Most states also require that the behavior cause some level of emotional distress. Stalking takes on many different forms, including following the victim; showing up at his or her work, home, or school; unwanted communication such as repeated phone calls, text messages, e-mails, or written communication; damaging the victim's home or property; monitoring Internet or phone use; threatening loved ones and pets; and posting information online or spreading rumors about the victim (National Center for Victims of Crime, n.d.).

Stalking estimates suggest that 1 in 12 women and 1 in 45 men will be stalked at some point during their lifetime (Baum, Catalano, Rand, & Rose, 2009). Further, nearly 3.5 million adults are stalked each year, and more than three-fourths are stalked by someone they know. Those who are divorced or separated are at the highest risk for stalking, and almost 30% of stalkers are current or former intimate partners (Baum et al., 2009). This has been termed *partner stalking* by Logan and Walker (2009). Stalking most often occurs when the victim of IPV tries to leave the relationship (Doerner & Lab, 2012). Beck (1992) also found that 90% of all women killed by a former intimate partner had been stalked by the offender prior to the homicide. In terms of the cycle of violence, the victim may leave after the acute battering phase. When the offender is unable to regain her trust during the honeymoon phase as has been possible in the past, he may resort to stalking or threats as a way to stop her from leaving or to regain control over her.

A new type of stalking, cyberstalking, has grown more prevalent due to increased use of the Internet and the ease of using technology to monitor the whereabouts and online activities of victims. According to the National Conference of State Legislatures (n.d.), "cyberstalking is the use of the Internet, e-mail or other electronic communications to stalk, and generally refers to a pattern of threatening or malicious behaviors." Social media sites like Facebook, Twitter, and Instagram often make it very easy for potential stalkers to locate their victims. By *checking in* to locations, victims are allowing others to see where they are, often at all times of the day. Cyberstalking also can involve posting information about victims, pictures, and videos on social media sites. Further, cyberstalking can include unwanted e-mails, messages through social media sites, and other unwanted behavior, such as frequenting the same message boards as a victim. Many states have created cyberstalking and cyberharassment statutes, or expanded existing stalking statutes to encompass electronic communications, such as e-mails and instant messages, as well.

Case Study 3: Intimate Partner Violence, Stalking, and Homicide

Stalking in intimate relationships is most common when a victim tries to leave the relationship, and estimates suggest that 90% of women who have been killed by an intimate partner were also stalked by that same partner prior to the homicide. The murder of Officer Kim Carmack of the Indianapolis (Indiana) Metropolitan Police Department (IMPD) is a sobering example of the links between IPV, stalking, and homicide. Carmack was married to a fellow IMPD officer, Sergeant Ryan Anders, for 6 years. Court documents showed that Carmack feared for her life, sought a restraining order against Anders, and described their marriage as one fraught with physical, sexual, and emotional abuse.

After their divorce was finalized, Carmack reported that Anders showed up places unexpectedly, accused her of having affairs with other IMPD officers, followed her to work, where he forced his way into her car and refused to get out for over 90 minutes, and showed up at her house where he once again forced his way in, took her cell phone, and began going through her text messages. Anders also allegedly may have tracked Carmack's whereabouts using a function that allows an individual to track an iPhone.

After receiving an internal tip, IMPD began to investigate the alleged domestic abuse between Carmack and Anders, and both were reassigned to administrative duties and had their department-issued weapons taken away. Carmack was assigned a domestic violence advocate and was given a safe place to live. Anders received counseling and mental health treatment.

Upon completion of the IMPD investigation, prosecutors prepared to file felony stalking charges against Anders, as a result of his consistent harassing and unwanted behavior. However, before they could file the charges, Anders found Carmack, who had left her safe home and returned to her previous home, and fatally shot her and then himself. Although an extreme example, this case illustrates the strong link between IPV, stalking, and homicide. Unfortunately, even though Officer Carmack was able to remove herself from the relationship, she was still in danger.

Consequences of Intimate Partner Violence

There are many negative consequences of IPV. Injury and death may result; women may be isolated from family and friends; professional lives may be affected; there are often severe negative psychological and emotional effects; and children are also at risk when a relationship is abusive, as there is a link between IPV and child abuse.

Injuries, or death, are two of the most obvious negative consequences of IPV. Rand (1997) found that over one-third of women who sought care in the emergency room for violence-related issues were victimized by a current or former spouse, boyfriend, or girlfriend. Further, Berios and Grady (1991) found that almost 30% of women who sought emergency room care for IPV required hospital admission, and more than 10% required some sort of major medical treatment. In terms of intimate partner homicide, women face a greater chance of being murdered by an intimate partner than men; 70% victims killed by an intimate partner are women (Catalano, Smith, Snyder, & Rand, 2009). When examining the overall number of female homicides (femicide), 33% of women murdered were killed by an intimate partner (National Coalition Against Domestic Violence, 2007). Further, IPV is the number one cause of homicide and injury-related deaths among pregnant women (Frye, 2001).

Psychological Outcomes

Physical injuries are not the only injuries that IPV victims suffer. They also experienced psychological and emotional trauma. Psychological abuse is one form of IPV itself, but physical abuse also can result in psychological trauma. According to the CDC (2010), IPV victims are more likely to suffer from depression, anxiety, posttraumatic stress disorder, and sleep disorders. Research also has found that women who were IPV victims have higher suicide rates and also are more likely to attempt suicide and have suicidal thoughts (Coker et al., 2002; Stark, 1984).

Impacts on Children

In addition to the negative impacts of IPV on the victim, there are often other victims as well. IPV is often linked with child verbal abuse, physical punishment, and physical abuse (Kerker, Horwitz, Leventhal, Plichta, & Leaf, 2000; Ross, 1996; Tajima, 2000). Most studies indicate that the rate of co-occurrence of IPV and child abuse ranges from 30% to 60% (Appel & Holden, 1998; Edleson, 1999b). Further, studies of children involved in the child welfare system find that IPV occurs in 30%–40% of the families in the child welfare system (Edleson, 1999a). In addition, research has suggested that children who are exposed to violence in the home suffer long-term consequences, such as behavioral and psychological problems, learning difficulties, limited social skills, exhibit violent, risky, or delinquent behavior, and suffer from depression or anxiety.

Summary and Conclusion

IPV is an issue that impacts people from every walk of life. It crosses racial, gender, and socioeconomic lines. IPV can impact men and women, those in heterosexual and same-sex relationships, those currently in relationships, and those no longer in relationships. IPV includes a broad range of activities and impacts a broad range of victims and affects many people. Statistics suggest that one in four women will be the victim of IPV at some point in their life. Given the prevalence of IPV, as well as the extreme negative consequences of IPV, the criminal justice system is constantly searching for the best way to address IPV, at the police, court, and community level. It is likely that some level of IPV will always occur in our society, but this level can hopefully be reduced through criminal justice system and community intervention.

Discussion Questions

1. If it were easier for women to leave abusive relationships (i.e., if the financial resources were readily available, if they were given a safe place to stay away from the abuser, etc.), do you think more women would leave? Is there anything that can be done to make it easier for women to leave abusive relationships?
2. What do you think the best law enforcement response to IPV is? Should there be a one-size-fits-all approach, like mandatory arrest, or should officers be able to use their discretion on how to deal with victims and offenders in IPV situations?
3. What changes could the criminal justice system make to best deal with victims of IPV who are not women? How can the criminal justice system serve men who have been the victims of IPV, whether in a heterosexual relationship or a same-sex relationship?
4. What is the best strategy to reduce IPV? Can the criminal justice system, social service agencies, and the medical community do anything to decrease the amount of IPV that occurs?

References

Appel, A. E., & Holden, G. W. (1998). The co-occurrence of spouse and physical child abuse: A review and appraisal. *Journal of Family Psychology, 12*, 578–599.

Archer, J. (2000). Sex differences in aggression between heterosexual partners: A meta-analytic review. *Psychological Bulletin, 126,* 651–680.

Baum, K., Catalano, S., Rand, M., & Rose, K. (2009). *Stalking victimization in the United States.* Washington, DC: U.S. Department of Justice, Bureau of Justice Statistics.

Beck, J. (1992, July 13). Murderous obsession. *Newsweek,* p. 60.

Berios, D. C., & Grady, D. (1991). Domestic violence: Risk factors and outcomes. *Western Journal of Medicine, 155*, 133–135.

Black, M. C., Basile, K. C., Breiding, M. J., Smith, S. G., Walters, M. L., Merrick, M. T., ... Stevens, M. R. (2011). *The national intimate partner and sexual violence survey (NISVS): 2010 summary report.* Atlanta, GA: National Center for Injury Prevention and Control, Centers for Disease Control and Prevention.

Bui, H. I. (2001). *In the adopted land: Abused immigrant women and the criminal justice system.* Westport, CT: Praeger.

Catalano, S. (2013). *Intimate partner violence: Attributes of victimization, 1993–2011.* Washington, DC: U.S. Department of Justice, Bureau of Justice Statistics.

Catalano, S., Smith, E., Snyder, H., & Rand, M. (2009). *Female victims of violence.* Washington, DC: U.S. Department of Justice, Bureau of Justice Statistics.

Centers for Disease Control and Prevention (CDC). (2010). *Intimate partner violence prevention: Consequences.* Atlanta, GA: Centers for Disease Control and Prevention. Retrieved from http://www/cdc/gov/ViolencePrevention/intimatepartnerviolence/consequences.html

Centers for Disease Control and Prevention (CDC). (2014). *Intimate partner violence: Risk and protective factors.* Atlanta, GA: Centers for Disease Control and Prevention. Retrieved from http://www.cdc.gov/violenceprevention/intimatepartnerviolence/riskprotectivefactors.html

Chalk, R., & King, P. (1998). *Violence in families: Assessing prevention and treatment programs.* Washington, DC: National Academy Press.

Coker, A. L., Smith, P. H., Thompson, M. P., McKeown, R. E., Bethea, L., & Davis, K. E. (2002). Physical health consequences of physical and psychological intimate partner violence. *Archives of Family Medicine, 9*, 1–7.

Currul-Dykeman, K. (2014). Domestic violence case processing: A matter of local legal culture. *Contemporary Justice Review, 17*, 250–272.

Daigle, L. (2012). *Victimology: A Reader.* Los Angeles, CA: Sage.

Davis, R. C., Smith, B. E., & Davies, H. J. (2001). Effects of no-drop prosecution of domestic violence upon conviction rate. *Justice Research and Policy, 3*, 1–13.

Dawson, M., & Dinovitzer, R. (2001). Victim cooperation and the prosecution of domestic violence in a specialized court. *Justice Quarterly, 18*, 593–622.

Dobash, R. E., & Dobash, R. P. (1979). *Violence against wives: A case against the patriarchy.* New York, NY: Free Press.

Dobash, R. E., Dobash, R. P., Wilson, M., & Daly, M. (1992). The myth of sexual symmetry in marital violence. *Social Problems, 39*, 71–91.

Doerner, W. G., & Lab, S. P. (2012). *Victimology* (6th ed.). Burlington, MA: Anderson Publishing.

Edleson, J. L. (1999a). *Problems associated with children's witnessing domestic violence.* Retrieved from http://www.vaw.umn.edu

Edleson, J. L. (1999b). The overlap between child maltreatment and woman battering. *Violence Against Women, 5*, 134–154.

Felson, R. B. (2002). Reasons for reporting and not reporting domestic violence to the police. *Criminology, 40*, 617–648.

Frye, V. (2001). Examining homicide's contribution to pregnancy-associated deaths. *Journal of the American Medical Association, 285*, 1510–1511.

Goldkamp, J. S., Weiland, D., Collins, M., & White, M. (1996). *Role of drug and alcohol abuse in domestic violence and its treatment: Dade County's domestic violence experiment, appendices to the final report.* Washington, DC: U.S. Department of Justice.

Gover, A., MacDonald, J., & Alpert, G. (2003). Combating domestic violence: Findings from an evaluation of a local domestic violence court. *Criminology & Public Policy, 3*, 109–132.

Hartman, J. L., & Belknap, J. (2003). Beyond the gatekeepers: Court professionals' self-reported attitudes about experiences with misdemeanor domestic violence cases. *Criminal Justice and Behavior, 30*, 349–373.

Hirschel, D. (2008). *Domestic violence cases: What research shows about arrest and dual arrest rates.* Washington, DC: National Institute of Justice.

Iyengar, R. (2007). The protection battered spouses don't need (Editorial). *New York Times.* Retrieved from http://www.nytimes.com/2007/08/07/opinion/07iyengar.html

Jaquier, V. (2010). The role of the gay male and lesbian community. In B. S. Fisher & S. P. Lab (Eds.), *Encyclopedia of victimology and crime prevention* (Vol. 1, pp. 313–314). Los Angeles, CA: Sage.

Johnson, M. P. (2006). Conflict and control: Gender symmetry and asymmetry in domestic violence. *Violence Against Women, 12,* 1003–1018.

Jordan, C. (2004). Intimate partner violence and the justice system: An examination of the interface. *Journal of Interpersonal Violence, 19,* 1412–1434.

Kanno, H., & Newhill, C. (2009). Social workers and battered women: The need to study client violence in the domestic field. *Journal of Aggression, Maltreatment, and Trauma, 18,* 46–63.

Kerker, B. D., Horwitz, S. M., Leventhal, J. M., Plichta, S., & Leaf, P. J. (2000). Identification of violence in the home: Pediatric and parental reports. *Archives of Pediatric Adolescent Medicine, 154,* 457–462.

Logan, T. K., & Walker, R. (2009). Partner stalking: Psychological dominance or "business as usual?" *Trauma, Violence, and Abuse, 10,* 247–270.

Maxwell, C., Garner, J., & Fagan, J. (2001). *The effects of arrest on intimate partner violence: New evidence from the spouse assault replication program.* Washington, DC: National Institute of Justice.

National Center for Victims of Crime. (n.d.). *Stalking resource center.* Retrieved from http://www.victimsofcrime.org/our-programs/stalking-resource-center/stalking-information

National Coalition against Domestic Violence. (2007). *Domestic violence facts.* Retrieved from http://www.ncadv.org/giles/DomesticViolenceFactSheet(National).pdf

Okun, L. E. (1986). *Women abuse: Facts replacing myths.* Albany, NY: SUNY Press.

Rand, M. R. (1997). *Violence-related injuries treated in hospital emergency departments* [Special Report]. Washington, DC: Bureau of Justice Statistics.

Rand, M., & Rennison, C. (2004). *How much violence against women is there?* Washington, DC: National Criminal Justice Reference Service.

Rauma, D. (1984). Going for the gold: Prosecutorial decision making in cases of wife assault. *Social Science Research, 13,* 321–351.

Ross, S. E. (1996). Risk of physical abuse to children of spouse abusing parents. *Child Abuse and Neglect, 20,* 589–598.

Schmidt, J., & Steury, E. (1989). Prosecutorial discretion in filing charges in domestic violence cases. *Criminology, 27,* 487–510.

Sherman, L. W., & Berk, R. A. (1984). The specific deterrent effects of arrest for domestic assault. *American Sociological Review, 49,* 261–272.

Stalking. 18 Pa. C.S. § 2709.1. (2003).

Stark, E. (1984, May). The unspeakable family secret. *Psychology Today,* pp. 42–46.

Straus, M. A., Hamby, S. L., Boney-McCoy, S., & Sugarman, D. B. (1996). The revised Conflict Tactics Scale (CTS2): Development and preliminary psychometric data. *Journal of Family Issues, 17,* 283–316.

Tajima, E. A. (2000). The relative importance of wife abuse as a risk factor for violence against children. *Child Abuse & Neglect, 24*(11), 1383–1398.

The Michigan Penal Code, Michigan Legislature Section 750.81. Retrieved from http://www.legislature.mi.gov/%28S%282iksoaassevdox55oqm2ws3a%29%29/mileg.aspx?page=GetObject&objectname=mcl-750-81

Tjaden, P., & Thoennes, N. (2000). *Full report of the prevalence, incidence, and consequences of violence against women.* Washington, DC: National Institute of Justice, Centers for Disease Control and Prevention.

Walker, L. E. (1979). *The battered woman.* New York, NY: Harper & Row.

Wallace, H. (2007). *Victimology: Legal, psychological, and social perspectives* (2nd ed.). Boston, MA: Pearson.

Wilson, M., & Daly, M. (1993). Spousal homicide risk and estrangement. *Violence and Victims, 8,* 3–16.

Wright, J. A., Burgess, A. G., Burgess, A. W., Laszlo, A. T., McCrary, G. O., & Douglas, J. E. (1997). A typology of interpersonal stalking. *Journal of Interpersonal Violence, 11,* 487–502.

Sexual Assault and the Evolution of Rape

5

DANIELLE ROMAIN

Contents

What images come to mind when you hear the term "rape?" Oftentimes, we think of high-profile cases that involve physical violence, victim injuries, and offenses perpetrated by strangers who stealthily attack an unaware victim. Case Study 1 provides an example of a case that received much media attention. Are these types of cases, the "stranger jumping from the bushes," typical of all rapes? Statistics from victimization surveys reveal that these are rare occurrences, yet this image often influences how we think about rape victims. This image has also impacted how cases of rape were treated by police, prosecutors, and legislatures. Historically, cases of rape were dealt with very differently than other forms of violent crime, often with law enforcement and the courts treating victims with disbelief. Major reform efforts to redefine the state response to rape were implemented in the 1970s and 1980s. The lasting impact of these reforms on the treatment of rape victims and rape cases continues to be discussed. This chapter will examine the history of the state response to rape, the role of rape myths and stereotypes on criminal justice responses to rape, and current responses by the criminal justice and medicolegal systems.

Case Study 1: Amanda Berry

On May 6, 2013, a young woman ran from a home, clutching a small child, and asked a nearby stranger for help. Amanda Berry, who had gone missing in 2003 from her part-time job in Cleveland, had been able to break free from the home where she was held captive for a decade. An additional two victims were found in the home when police arrived—Michelle Knight and Gina DeJesus—also kidnapped as teenagers from the Cleveland area by Ariel Castro. The victims were raped repeatedly, beaten, threatened, bound, and locked in a basement in inhumane living conditions. Due in part to the extreme nature of the false imprisonment and prolonged abuse, this highly publicized victimization might lead you to wonder how common aggravated rapes are. This chapter will present an overview of the prevalence of sexual assault, as well as risk factors that increase the likelihood of victimization (Caniglia & Blackwell, 2013).

How was the case handled by the courts? Prosecutors were quick to act in issuing charges, issuing a multitude of counts associated with the ongoing physical and sexual assault of these three women over the course of a decade. Ariel Castro was indicted by a grand jury with 977 counts on June 7 and 12, 2013, including 446 counts of rape (Caniglia & Blackwell, 2013). Further, although Castro avoided the possibility of a trial by pleading guilty to the majority of charges on July 26, 2012, Judge Michael Russo took a hardened stance in sentencing him. Castro received a life sentence and an additional 1000 years, in effect making a strong statement that sexual assault, torture, and kidnapping of these women were inhumane and not to be tolerated (Stanglin, 2013). Does this case represent the typical handling of sexual assault cases by the criminal justice system?

Sexual Assault Victimization

The terms "sexual assault" and "rape" have become common parlance, sometimes used interchangeably, to describe sexual victimization. Rape, commonly seen as the most serious form of sexual victimization, involves nonconsensual penetration of one's genital, anal, or oral area—whether by oral, digital, genital, or object (Federal Bureau of Investigation [FBI], 2013). Nonconsent may be due to an active decision by the victim, an inability to give consent due to incapacitation, or one's legal status. Traditionally, rape was defined as penile-vaginal penetration by the use of physical force, precluding coercive sexual experiences that were nonetheless nonconsensual from being labeled as rape (Estrich, 1987).

Sexual assault, a broader term for sexual victimization, defines any sexual act that involves nonconsent by the victim as a criminal act. This may include forcible rape (with the use physical force or threats of force), alcohol-facilitated rape (with an offender's use of drugs or alcohol to incapacitate), and coercive sexual assault (with the use of psychological threats, promises, and pressure). For example, if a teacher used physical force to engage in nonconsensual sexual intercourse with a student, it would be labeled forcible rape. If, however, the teacher threatened to fail the student or promised to give the student an "A" for engaging in nonconsensual intercourse, it would be sexual coercion. Additionally, sexual assault includes nonpenetrative sexual acts. Unwanted sexual contact involves touching, groping, or licking of genital, anal, or breast areas without consent. This may include forced contact or contact under coercion (Kilpatrick, Resnick, Ruggiero, Conscenti, & McCauley, 2007; Rape, Abuse and Incest National Network [RAINN], n.d. a).

Finally, statutory rape is a unique type of sexual assault offense, in that the victim's status as a minor precludes him or her from giving consent. States differ as to what the age of consent is, yet most states have set the age of consent at 16 (Department of Health & Human Services, n.d.). Furthermore, several states have adopted special laws, often called Romeo and Juliet laws, designed to protect adolescents who engage in noncoercive sexual relationships from criminal sanctions and the label of a sexual offender (Cohen, 2007; Koppelman, 2003). Sixteen states have a minimum age requirement for prosecuting the offender, which prescribes the minimum age of an offender charged with statutory rape. In over half of states, age differential laws have been created to determine the appropriate gap in age between parties engaging in noncoersive sexual relations. In Oregon, for example, if the parties' ages are within 3 years of one another, penalties are reduced or the parties are not held criminally liable (Department of Health & Human Services, n.d.).

Prevalence Estimates

Developing reliable estimates on the prevalence of sexual assault presents researchers with several problems. Official estimates, such as the FBI's Uniform Crime Report (UCR), have included only forcible rape and attempted forcible rape in their recording of sexual assault until very recently. As such, coerced and alcohol-facilitated sexual assaults were not recorded until January 2013 (FBI, 2013). In addition, official estimates include only crimes reported to the police, which for crimes such as sexual assault may be grossly underestimated (Tjaden & Thoennes, 2006). In 2012, the number of reported forcible rapes was 52.9 per 100,000 of the female population (FBI, 2013).

Given that official records have had relatively narrow definitions of sexual assault and that sexual assault is often underreported to law enforcement (Rennison, 1999), other sources of victimization data are often preferred by researchers and community stakeholders. The National Crime Victimization Survey (NCVS) provides estimates of the prevalence of sexual assault victimization, measured as whether an individual has experienced a sexual assault during the previous 6 months. In addition, it provides an estimate of the percentage of sexual assaults reported to law enforcement, as well as common reasons for deciding whether to report. In 2010, the rate of sexual assault was 0.7 per 1000 (Truman & Rand, 2011). The NCVS data have demonstrated a substantial decrease (~41%) in the number of sexual assault victimizations over a 10-year period (Truman & Rand, 2011).

Finally, additional victimization surveys have been developed to better capture the prevalence of sexual assault. These measures utilize less formal, legal language in defining sexual assault, unlike the NCVS survey. Two widely cited surveys include the National Violence Against Women Survey (NVAWS) and National Intimate Partner and Sexual Violence Survey (NISVS). Conducted in 1995–1996, the NVAWS is a national survey of men and women that provides lifetime and annual estimates of forcible rape and attempted forcible rape (Tjaden & Thoennes, 2006). From this survey, it has been estimated that approximately 18% of women and 3% of men have been victims of rape within their lifetime (Tjaden & Thoennes, 2006). An additional survey that has gained recent attention for its expansive definitions of sexual assault is the NISVS. In 2010, annual and lifetime estimates of forcible rape, alcohol-facilitated rape, sexual coercion, and unwanted sexual touching were measured (Black et al., 2011). Framed from a public health perspective, this survey has found even higher estimates of sexual assault. Over 18% of women report being raped in their lifetime, 8% report alcohol-facilitated rape, and almost half experienced other forms of unwanted sexual victimization (Black et al., 2011). The NCVS estimates that 188,380 rapes and sexual assaults were committed within a 6-month period of 2010 (Truman & Rand, 2011). The NISVS, by contrast, estimates that 1.3 million women were raped in 2010, with another 6.7 million experiencing other forms of sexual violence (Black et al., 2011).

Characteristics of Victims, Offenders, and Incidences

Common mental images of rape and sexual assault often invoke the stereotype of the stranger blitzing an unsuspecting victim from behind bushes, utilizing extreme physical force. The reality, however, of common risk factors and characteristics of sexual assault belies this image. Estimates from NISVS suggest that females are at an increased risk of sexual assault victimization, particularly during the late teenage years through the early 20s. In fact, two-thirds of all female victims of rape experienced their first victimization between the ages of 11 and 24 (Black et al., 2011). Similarly, although offenders of forcible rape can be found across all age groups, the typical offender is aged 16–30, and overwhelmingly male (FBI, 2013). Further, the NISVS estimates demonstrate a greater risk of rape within one's lifetime among Native American (~27%) and multiracial females (~34%) and a smaller risk among Hispanic females (~15%) compared to white (~19%) and black females (~22%) (Black et al., 2011). Similar trends are found for other forms of sexual violence, with almost 60% of multiracial females reporting lifetime experiences of unwanted sexual activity.

Among victims of sexual assault, it is not uncommon for more than one assault to occur within one's lifetime. Experiencing sexual abuse as a child increases one's risk of sexual assault as an adult (Black et al., 2011; Breitenbecher, 2001; Follette, Polusny Bechtle, & Naugle, 1996). Repeat victimization is also common, with one study finding that over three-quarters of all sexual assaults were experienced by less than 10% of respondents. Many of these victims experienced three or more assaults in a given year, and risk of a second victimization was highest within the first 30 days (Daigle, Fisher, & Cullen, 2008). Additionally, alcohol and drug use by the victim and offender has been associated with an increased risk of sexual assault. Data from the NVAWS find approximately 20% of victims were drinking or taking drugs prior to the rape incident, which was even more common among offenders (~67%) (Tjaden & Thoennes, 2006).

Characteristics of sexual assault incidences demonstrate that aggravated rapes (involving more than one offender, a stranger, victim injury, and/or weapon use) are much less common than simple rapes (nonstranger rapes where none of these aggravating factors are present). Susan Estrich (1987) is one of the pioneering feminist legal scholars to challenge traditional notions of rape, arguing that common stereotypes of what constitutes a "real rape" are based on aggravated rape situations and perpetuate rape myths. Rape myths are stereotypes of rape that are generally false or uncommon, yet influence people's perception of what rape is (e.g., consuming alcohol means it's not rape, women cannot be raped by intimate partners). These in turn place blame on the victim, rather than examining the offender's conduct (Lonsway & Fitzgerald, 1994). In NVAWS estimates, injuries were reported among only one-third of victims, and the most common form of injury was scratches and bruises (Tjaden & Thoennes, 2006). Further, although NVAWS measures only forcible rape and attempted rape, less than 40% of rapes involved physical assault of the victim—most often hitting or slapping (Tjaden & Thoennes, 2006). Given that other forms of rape (e.g., alcohol-facilitated) and sexual coercion do not, by definition, involve physical force, extensive physical harm is quite uncommon in sexual assaults. Weapon use is also rare—the NVAWS estimates only 11% of offenders had weapons on them at the time of the incident (Tjaden & Thoennes, 2006). Furthermore, most sexual assaults involve only one offender (Black et al., 2011).

Although it is commonly assumed that strangers are more likely to be perpetrators of sexual assault, the estimates from a variety of surveys suggest otherwise. NCVS data from 2010 find that approximately one-quarter of sexual assaults were perpetrated by strangers and less than 20% by intimate partners (Truman & Rand 2011). NISVS data, by contrast, suggest that intimates are much more likely to be perpetrators than acquaintances and strangers. Indeed, over half of rapes and three-quarters of sexual coercive assaults were committed by current or former intimates (Black et al., 2011). Thinking about the relationship between the victim and the offender is critical—as the victim/offender relationship influenced the state response to rape until the 1970s. Given commonsense notions of aggravated rape perpetrated by strangers—how might this widely held belief influence police and prosecutors? Juries? Women when conducting their daily routine activities?

Historical Treatment of Rape

The earliest known laws relating to rape can be found in the Hammurabi Code and early Mosaic Law (Brownmiller, 1975). In these laws, rape was defined as a grievance against men, the victim's father or husband, of the devaluation of the status of their daughter or wife. Women were essentially left out of legal proceedings and restitution. Indeed, if a woman was raped, her rapist faced a fine for spoiling her value in a bride price and at times women were forced to marry their rapists. The treatment of rape by the criminal justice system has undergone extensive changes, most prominently during the 1970s and 1980s. Prior to this time period, the state response to rape victims was based on common law approaches that often did not take sexual violence against women seriously, particularly if the victim knew the offender. This section will outline early responses to rape victims, followed by changes that occurred in the mid-twentieth century. Finally, a discussion of rape law reform will provide background on the reforms that took place, challenges faced, and evaluations of the effectiveness of these reforms.

Seventeenth-Century Logic through the Early Twentieth Century

The legal definition of rape prior to the 1970s in all states was rooted in the common law tradition of England. The traditional rape definition was "carnal knowledge of a woman (by a man who was not her husband) forcibly and against her will" (Decker & Baroni, 2011, p. 1083). Within this definition, it was not possible for wives to be raped by husbands (or common law relationships in some states), nor if the victim did not experience physical force. Further, the traditional definition equated nonconsent as utmost physical resistance by the victim. Only aggravated rapes, with physical force and extreme victim resistance, were likely to receive police attention, be charged by prosecutors, and face the possibility of conviction (Buchhandler-Raphael, 2011; Decker & Baroni, 2011).

Based on this legal definition, victims seeking to report a rape incident were scrutinized and investigated more so than suspects for their behaviors prior, during, and after the assault. Unlike other crimes—violent or property—the burden of proof regarding consent and resistance lay with the victim. Consent was assumed even when verbal indicators of nonconsent (e.g., saying no, crying, yelling) were given by victims. In fact, nonconsent and physical resistance were required throughout the duration of the offense. It was not enough to physically resist at the beginning, physical resistance was required during the entire incident, or consent would be assumed (Buchhandler-Raphael, 2011; *Reynolds v. State*, 1889). Further, in cases involving prior relationships, consent was determined to be assumed by the offender based on previous consensual sexual actions (Estrich, 1987).

Why might the traditional definition of rape have focused so closely on the behavior of the victim? The most often cited source influencing the development of rape laws prior to the 1970s was Chief Justice Sir Matthew Hale, who famously opined that rape accusations are "easily to be made and hard to be proved, and harder to be defended by the party accused, tho' never so innocent" (as cited in Estrich, 1987, p. 5). His words formed the basis for jury instructions that were specific to rape cases in many states, cautioning jurors that rape cases involve a he-said/she-said and a victim with a heightened emotional state. Jury instructions were rooted in the rape myth that women commonly file false reports. This mistrust of women's reporting was pervasive in influencing procedural laws for rape cases as well as police and prosecutors in investigating and charging rape cases (Estrich, 1987).

Additional requirements were placed on victims to support rape allegations that were not required of victims of other forms of crime. Evidentiary laws from the Model Penal Code required corroborative evidence—whether through the presence of witnesses or documented injury as indicative of force and resistance—for charging and conviction of rape. In addition, prompt reporting was a crucial factor in assessing the validity of a rape victim's claims (Decker & Baroni, 2011; Spohn & Horney, 1992). Delays in reporting, particularly in nonstranger rape cases, were viewed with suspicion that the victim had a motive to lie and file a false report—whether for revenge (e.g., the women scorned) or to escape trouble (e.g., out past curfew, cheating). Echoing Sir Hale's concerns about false reporting, these requirements perpetuated mistrust of women as rape victims and reinforced the view of women as liars and manipulative (Estrich, 1987; see also Miller, Markman, Amacker, & Menaker, 2012). Further, legal scholars and appellate judges worried that women alleging rape were easily confused, and often regretted their decision to engage in sexual activities. Combined with 1950s psychoanalytical views of women as fantasizing about rape, the concerns about ambivalent women falsely calling rape influenced appellate rulings and case law to disfavor women (Estrich, 1987).

Feminist scholars have argued that appellate courts, by requiring consent via utmost physical resistance, reinscribe gender inequality in access to law. The physical resistance requirement discredits female victims by creating a standard of conduct that ignores power imbalances between men and women requiring them to be like men (Buchhandler-Raphael, 2011; Estrich, 1987). Further, others have argued that by defining rape to exclude spouses and placing emphasis on victims' precipitating behaviors, the law "preserve[s] male rights to possess and subjugate women as sexual objects" (Spohn & Horney, 1992, p. 20). By defining "real rape" as aggravated rape, the state response involved a bifurcated system for dealing with aggravated and simple rapes.

Other criticisms have alleged that race has played a significant role in the processing of cases, as well as instilling public fear of minority men. Historically rape allegations involving black males and white females were racially and politically charged (Estrich, 1987; see also Crenshaw, 1991). Inequality in the handling of rape cases was a concern for feminists and civil rights activists. In fact, rape was punishable by death in some states until as late as 1977, and black men convicted of raping white women faced greater odds of receiving a death sentence than white men (Estrich, 1987). The sexual stratification hypothesis states that prosecutors, juries, and judges will systematically penalize black males more than white males for the crime of rape. The value of white women as victims—particularly when they are raped by black men—leads to disparate treatment based on the race of victim and offender. Some evidence has been found in support of disparate treatment from cases in the 1970s (LaFree, 1989), yet more recent research has not found differences in case processing between intraracial and interracial cases (Tellis & Spohn, 2009).

Rape Law Reform

Early calls for rape law reform came from grassroots feminists, concerned with the lack of attention by the criminal justice system to the crime of rape. Indeed, as part of the second wave of feminism, rape law reform sought to challenge traditional systems of patriarchy in the legal arena as well as in public discourse. Yet feminists of the 1970s were not the only proponents of changing the legal response to rape—conservatives, as part of the "get tough on crime" approach, were dissatisfied with what was perceived to be a growing crime rate, coupled with rehabilitation-focused corrections that appeared to be "soft" on offenders (Bachman & Paternoster, 1993; Parenti, 1999; Spohn & Horney, 1992). They sought tougher laws that would hold offenders (including rapists) accountable, while lobbying for more punitive and longer sentences. Although these two groups—feminists and conservatives—appear to be strange bedfellows, their coalition was successful in lobbying for changes to federal and state statute definitions of rape, as well as procedural requirements.

Grassroots reformers outlined several goals for changing the state response to rape victims. First, notably, reformers were concerned that rape went heavily unreported. Newly created national victimization surveys (e.g., NCVS) demonstrated the vast under reporting of rape (Bevacqua, 2000). They hoped that by increasing the proportion of sexual violence that did come to the attention of law enforcement, a sense of security and healing could begin for victims. Second, reformers were concerned with the high attrition rates of rape cases processed through the system. As high as 54% of cases were unfounded in Chicago, while the average percent nationally was 19%. These statistics, coupled with estimates that only one-third of charged cases resulted in convictions, led to the conclusion that rape was not being taken as seriously as other forms of violent crime (Estrich, 1987; Spohn & Horney, 1992). Finally, reformers were concerned that nonlegally relevant factors were influencing decision making by police, prosecutors, and juries. Factors such as the victim's sexual history, as well as what he/she did surrounding the offense, were thought to systematically exclude sexual violence committed by non-strangers as well as place undue burden on the victim in proving that she had been raped and was a "genuine victim."

Before rape law reforms were enacted, local women's rights groups began providing services for rape victims. Initially, the feminist response to rape was led by those who had been victims previously. The first rape crisis center (RCC) opened in Washington, DC, in 1972, providing advocacy, counseling, and referrals for victims of rape and other forms of sexual violence (Bevacqua, 2000). Additionally, RCCs provided education for the general public on rape myths and redefined traditional conceptions of rape as part of the larger system of patriarchy. Additional RCCs cropped up throughout the nation, providing increased attention to rape as a social problem, as well as grant- and legislation-writing assistance (Koss & Harvey, 1991). Local RCCs combined with national feminist organizations, such as the National Organization for Women, in placing rape law reform on the national agenda (Bevacqua, 2000).

From Rape to Sexual Assault

Rape law reform has taken on a variety of forms—including changes to state statue definitions, eliminating the marital rape exemption, changing evidentiary laws, and providing rape shield laws. States began changing their statute definitions of rape in the early 1970s. Many states moved from the term using "rape" to "sexual assault"—a term that for some feminists defined sexual violence as any other assault. The new label of sexual assault was thought to give equal treatment of rape by the criminal justice system. Yet other feminists were upset with the redefinition of rape as sexual assault, arguing that by emphasizing rape as violence, this definition perpetuated the ignoring of simple rape. Further, those that opposed the label of sexual assault felt that this new term paid little attention to the underlying power, dominance, and gender inequality present in rape and violence against women (Decker & Baroni, 2011; Estrich, 1987).

In addition to changes in statute language, the legal definition of rape was modified. One major change was the definition of rape to include any form of penetration. Remember, the traditional rape definition included only vaginal-penile penetration. Under rape law reform, any nonconsensual penetration—including oral and anal—by the mouth, digit, genitals, or object held by another person constituted sexual assault. Thus, unwanted sexual activities traditionally charged under sodomy laws became redefined as sexual assault in many states. A second key development in rape law reform was the removal of the physical force requirement; post-reform, only nonconsent was required for a victimization to be defined as sexual assault. Given the concern that physical (such as choking or punching) force is often not present in cases of nonstranger rape, focusing on the element of nonconsent allowed for sexual coercion to be labeled a criminal offense. In addition, concern over date rape (unwanted sexual activity with an acquaintance that may involve drugs such as rohypnol and alcohol) during the 1980s, led to acknowledgment of alcohol-facilitated rape as a criminal offense (Bevacqua, 2000; Estrich, 1987).

The expanded list of criminal offenses provided by these definitional changes led to the adoption of new offense statutes to differentiate between the severities of various sexual assaults. States developed degrees of rape and sexual assault to correspond to the level of force, injury, and type of contact that was sustained. For example, in the state of Wisconsin, Statute 940.225 includes four degrees of sexual assault. First-degree sexual assault (a Class B felony) requires severe injury to the victim, the use or threat of a weapon, or the presence of multiple offenders. This definition most closely fits aggravated rape. Second-degree sexual assault (a Class C felony) requires threat or use of physical force, injury, or psychological harm to the victim, and also includes special classes of victims: those with mental deficiency, or who are intoxicated and unable to give consent, and unconscious victims. Third- and fourth-degree sexual assault (a Class G felony and Class A misdemeanor, respectively) involve unwanted sexual contact with varying degrees of force or coercion.

Evidentiary Changes

Additional rape law reform changes included evidentiary laws, which removed the requirement of physical resistance and corroboration. Historically, appellate judges equated
nonconsent with utmost physical resistance; this shift toward eliminating the resistance
requirement acknowledged that women who are raped may verbally resist by screaming,
or if fearful, may only say no. Further, given that other violent crimes did not require victims to physically resist their attackers (e.g., robbery), the removal of this requirement was
aimed at increasing victim reporting and reducing case attrition. Remember, the second
evidentiary law, corroboration, was developed with the view that women may manipulate,
lie, or feel ambivalent about sex. Historically, some states required women to undergo polygraphs to prove they were not making a false report. The validity of polygraphs aside, treatment of victims in this manner perpetuated disbelief of victims by law enforcement and
prosecutors—leading to underreporting by victims. Further, witnesses and other forms of
evidence that add weight to the victim's allegations are often not present in simple rapes
(Decker & Baroni, 2011; Estrich, 1987).

Fight for Spousal Rape

Perhaps one of the greatest struggles of rape law reform was the removal of the prohibition
of naming one's spouse as a sexual offender. Indeed, California State Senator Bob Wilson
was quoted in 1979 upon hearing testimony regarding marital rape exemptions as saying,
"if you can't rape your wife, who can you rape?" (as quoted in Estrich, 1987). Part of the
reluctance to admit spousal rape to criminal sanctions lies in the belief that marriage, as
a contract, implies continual consent by a spouse to engage in sexual activity. Further,
patriarchal views of marriage purported that wives did not have determination over their
own bodies and had a duty to be available to their husbands (Brownmiller, 1975; Estrich,
1987). Feminists argued that this exemption violated women's equal protection under the
Constitution. The first state to repeal spousal exemption was Nebraska in 1978. Several
states followed in eliminating spousal exemption through the early 1980s, and by 1985,
10 states had removed the marital exemption. Yet there were also nine states that allowed
even the most aggravating of rapes committed by spouses to be excluded from prosecution
(Estrich, 1987). North Carolina was the last state to repeal spousal exemptions in 1993.
As of today, all 50 states allow for charges of sexual assault against spouses, yet there are
differences that persist in how marital sexual assaults are treated in some states. South
Carolina, for example, defines sexual assault by a spouse as occurring only with the use or
threat of force, and carries a less severe punishment than nonspousal rape (Hasday, 2000;
RAINN, n.d. b).

Ending the Victim on Trial: Rape Shield Laws

Finally, one of the most touted achievements of rape law reform was the development of
rape shield laws, designed to protect victims from having their sexual histories discussed at
trial during cross-examination by defense attorneys. Historically, rape victims were often
subject to greater levels of scrutiny than offenders—asked in detail about their virginity,
previous sexual encounters, and whether their behavior prior to the incident precipitated
the assault in any way. This might include questions on what the victim was wearing,

whether she had been drinking, or had danced provocatively with the offender. This invasion into one's privacy may have led some victims to think twice before reporting to police. Rape shield laws prohibit asking the victim about her sexual past while testifying. Defense attorneys and those in support of greater defendant rights challenged the constitutionality of these laws, citing the necessity of asking questions to in raising a consent defense as well as establishing the credibility of the victim as a witness (Wallach, 1996; see also Gershman, 1993). Feminists have argued, however, that this perpetuates a double standard of female sexual chastity by inquiring into the victim's sexual history while not allowing similar inquiries into the defendant's background (Estrich, 1987).

Michigan was the first state to adopt a rape shield law in 1974, demonstrating a more strict prohibition against inquiring into the victim's sexual history. Only in cases involving current or former intimates can defense attorneys ask questions about the victim's past relationship with his/her client, or to introduce evidence that fluids or diseases contracted by the victim were the result of another source (Spohn & Horney, 1992). Other states have adopted softer prohibitions in their rape shield laws, essentially allowing any reasonable inquiry into the victim's sexual history if a judge determines it is relevant. Further, in at least some states, questions supporting a motive to lie are allowed to impeach credibility. As of 2014, all states and the federal government have enacted some form of rape shield law (RAINN, n.d. c).

Evaluations of Rape Reform

Rape law reforms were enacted throughout the 1970s and 1980s across the United States, with varying implementation across states. Some states (e.g., Michigan) enacted rape shield laws, evidentiary laws, and statute redefinitions all at once, while others gradually introduced changes into their existing laws. Further, variation exists across states in statute definitions and strictness of rape shield laws. Several studies conducted in the 1980s and 1990s evaluated single and multiple jurisdictions to determine whether rape law reform had achieved its goals of increased victim reporting and decreased case attrition. Loh (1981), examined rape reform in Washington, and found no difference in the charging and conviction rates post-reform (see also Bachman & Paternoster, 1993). Several other studies, however, found increases in arrest (Marsh, Geist, & Caplan, 1982), charging (Polk, 1985), and conviction rates after reforms were implemented (Marsh et al., 1982; Polk, 1985).

Spohn and Horney (1992) conducted an evaluation of rape law reform from 1970 to 1984 in six cities. They found no change in victim reporting rates post-reform in three cities, with a delayed increase in reporting in Houston and a decrease in reporting in Washington, DC. In only one city, Detroit, was there an increase in reporting that was consistent with the time period of the reform. Further, criminal indictments by prosecutors and conviction rates did not change following rape law reform in four of the six cities. Although Detroit showed promise meeting the goals of reform through increasing the number and rate of criminal indictments, Houston actually decreased its indictments. Conviction rates remained unchanged, and relatively low, leading the authors to conclude that rape law reform had limited success. They attributed this to the factors prosecutors considered in screening cases continued reliance on victim resistance, corroboration, and prompt reporting. Further, as some feminists have pointed out, without changing public perceptions of sexual assault, changes to statute language and evidentiary requirements will have little influence on the handling of rape cases (Lonsway & Archambault, 2012).

Additional Reforms

In addition to rape law reform, the growing focus on victims' rights during the 1970s and 1980s led to federal legislation aimed at improving the experiences of victims in the police and court process. One of the first developments that provided funding, for programs and victim services, was the Victims of Crimes Act of 1984 (VOCA). This act created the Office for Victims of Crime, which provided a clearinghouse of information for criminal justice organizations regarding victimization. Second, VOCA provided funds for training of law enforcement, prosecutors, and judges on the causes and consequences of crime, as well as funding for victim/witness assistance programs (Office for Victims of Crime, n.d.).

Two additional legislative acts expanded funding and training for crimes that largely affect women as victims. The Violence Against Women Act of 1994 (VAWA) was enacted to increase responsiveness of law enforcement and prosecutors to intimate partner violence and sexual assault. This act provided over $1 billion in funding to agencies and criminal justice organizations that work with female victims, including rape crisis centers. The early focus of VAWA was to increase sensitivity training of staff working with victims of domestic violence and sexual assault, as well as to develop programming to meet the needs of these victims. In addition, VAWA provided rape shield laws for federal victims of sexual assault. Further, VAWA prohibited journalists and the media from releasing victim information (including name, address, and image), to increase the privacy and protection of sexual assault victims (The White House, n.d.). VAWA has been reauthorized by Congress several times, with an expanded scope of training and funding for programs affecting disabled women, victims of stalking, and the elderly (Office on Violence Against Women, n.d.). Finally, the DNA Sexual Assault Justice Act of 2004 provided federal funding to state agencies in order to process backlogged rape kits. As part of the Justice for All Act, this funding was meant to decrease the delay of court cases and provide a sense of closure for victims (Office of Justice Programs, 2006).

Advocacy and Specialized Services

Victims of sexual assault that have reported their victimization to law enforcement may have many questions, concerns, and needs. Fortunately, victim/witness assistance programs have been implemented by district attorneys' offices and some law enforcement offices to help victims navigate the criminal justice system. These programs employ specialists who explain the rights victims have, as well as information on the case, and provide resources, such as victim impact statements (Sims, Yost, & Abbott, 2005). Importantly, evaluative research suggests that victim/witness assistance programs may not be effective at alleviating the psychological consequences of victimization. Additional programs for victims of sexual assault have been offered through RCCs and other women-focused organizations, including case management, advocacy, and referrals for housing, counseling, and legal assistance (Bevacqua, 2000).

Another concern is the medicolegal response toward victims of sexual assault during emergency room visits. Historically, nurses treating sexual assault victims did not have training on the unique needs of sexual assault victims or on proper techniques for collection of forensic evidence (Corrigan, 2013). Victims reported being dissatisfied with treatment by medical professionals, particularly with their lack of empathy. In response to these challenges, the Sexual Assault Nurse Examiner (SANE) program was developed to provide training for nurses on the needs of victims of sexual assault (including empathy, referrals for services), as well as proper documentation and collection of evidence. SANE nurses are often first responders to victims of sexual assault who seek treatment for injuries and testing for diseases. Evidence collected by SANE nurses in rape kits includes documentation and photographs of injuries, swabs of skin and bodily fluids, containers for hairs and other pieces of physical evidence on the victim, and documentation of information obtained from the victim on the nature of the assault (Taylor, 2002). Research has shown that cases with rape kits collected by SANE nurses are more likely to be charged and result in higher conviction rates than cases without SANE examinations (Campbell, Patterson, & Bybee, 2012; Crandall & Helitzer, 2003). Further, victims who have worked with SANE nurses report feeling treated with respect and compassion (Fehler-Cabral, Campbell, & Patterson, 2011).

In addition to SANE programs, the state response to sexual assault has begun including a more collaborative approach toward working with sexual assault victims. Known as Sexual Assault Response Teams (SARTs), these teams include prosecutors, SANE nurses and medical responders, as well as victim advocates who work collaboratively to ensure that victims have the legal, medical, and psychological resources necessary to begin the process of healing (Smith, Holmseth, Macgregor, & Letorneau, 1998). Further, many prosecutors' offices have begun implementing specialized units that solely process sexual assault cases. Sexual assault units (also called sensitive crimes units or special victims units) are aimed at providing prosecutors with intensive knowledge and expertise for the handling of sexual assault cases. Understanding victims' needs, as well as in the unique challenges of prosecuting sexual assaults are common goals of these units. Often, prosecutors in these units work with victim/witness specialists, providing extra support for victims throughout the court process (Beichner & Spohn, 2005; Long & Wilkinson, 2011). Although the stated goal of specialized units is to increase prosecution and conviction rates through developed knowledge bases and sensitivity, evaluations of these programs suggest additional reforms are needed (Beichner & Spohn, 2005).

Current Responses to Sexual Assault

The controversy over the handling of sexual assault cases did not end with the rape law reforms of the 1970s and 1980s. In fact, the Philadelphia Police Department came under fire in 1999 for a history of miss-classification of rape cases dating from the 1980s. Faced with heavy workloads and backlogged rape kits, officers often classified initial reports as either unfounded or "investigation of person" (Fazlollah, Matzah, & McCoy, 1999). Actions of police officers and prosecutors during investigations may send a strong message to victims, potentially impacting whether a victim chooses to notify the police in the future. This section will examine the response of victims, police, and prosecutors to sexual assault incidences.

Reporting of Sexual Assault

Before any investigation or criminal sanctioning of an offender, victims must first decide to notify law enforcement that a sexual assault has occurred. As previously stated, one of the goals of rape law reform was to increase the victim reporting rate. Yet as we saw from several studies (e.g., Spohn & Horney, 1992), reporting rates of sexual assault did not substantially increase after rape law reform. What does the reporting rate look like today, and why might victims choose not to report? Research from victimization surveys between 1992 and 2000 suggests that one-quarter to one-third of all rapes and sexual assaults were reported to police (Rennison, 2002). By 2010, approximately 40% of all sexual assault victimizations were reported to police, suggesting that women are reporting more often today than prior to rape law reform (Truman & Rand, 2011).

Victimization surveys also routinely ask victims about the most important reasons behind their decision of whether or not to report to law enforcement. The most common reasons given for reporting to police include a desire to prevent future victimization, to seek justice, and because the victim defined the incident as a crime (Bureau of Justice Statistics [BJS], 2008). Additionally, victims are more likely to report the crime if the offender used a weapon or physical force on the victim, and if the victim was injured during the attack (DuMont, Miller, & Myhr, 2003; Felson & Parre, 2005).

Some of the main concerns of victims who chose not to report to the police include shame, fear of retaliation, and privacy violation (Felson & Parre, 2005; Sable, Danis, Mauzy, & Gallagher, 2006). Some victims anticipate that police and prosecutors will be skeptical of their allegations (Felson & Parre, 2005; Jones, Alexander, Wynn, Rossman, & Dunnuck, 2009). Additionally, research has shown that if the victim consumed alcohol before the assault, he or she is less likely to notify police (Felson & Parre, 2005; Jones et al., 2009), and that acquaintance rapes are much less likely to be reported, compared to stranger and intimate partner rapes (Felson & Parre, 2005; Gartner & Macmillan, 1995). One possible reason for this is that victims might not label the act as rape, perhaps because of the rape myths and victim blame regarding alcohol use and nonstrangers. Given the importance that victims place on skepticism by criminal justice personnel, we now turn to an investigation of state responses to sexual assault.

Police and Prosecutor Responses to Sexual Assault

Police are responsible for taking an initial report from victims, conducting a thorough investigation, conducting suspect identifications, questioning of suspects, and arresting when probable cause has been met (Lonsway & Archambault, 2012). As police serve as a vital first point of contact for victims, their actions with victims may subtly communicate any reservations about the strength of a case. Surveys of officers have demonstrated that rape myths continue to influence officers' assessments of victim credibility and likelihood of a conviction (Jordan, 2004; Page, 2010). This may lead to victims not following through with cases after the initial report is taken (Lonsway & Archambault, 2012; Murphy, Edwards, Bennet, Bibeau, & Sichelstiel, 2014).

How have arrest, charging, and conviction rates changed since rape law reform? Although there has been an increase in victim reporting to police since the late 1980s, arrest rates for identified suspects of forcible rape have tended to decrease. In fact, by the mid-2000s, approximately 25% of rapes reported to police resulted in an arrest. Of the cases that are reported to police, few result in a criminal charge. Between 8% and 25% of all sexual assault cases that are reported to police are charged by prosecutors, a statistic that is much lower than other violent crimes. Further, conviction rates are also much lower than comparable violent crimes, as less than one-quarter of charged cases results in a conviction (Lonsway & Archambault, 2012). Given these numbers, what might influence the attrition of cases that we have seen?

The decision by police to make an arrest, as well as the prosecutor to initiate criminal charges, is influenced by a myriad of factors. Some of the most important factors that police and prosecutors consider include the amount of physical and corroborative evidence, including rape kit results (Beichner & Spohn, 2005; Bouffard, 2000; Campbell et al., 2012; Tasca, Rodrigues, Spohn & Koss, 2013), and prompt reporting by the victim (Alderdren & Ullman, 2012; Beichner & Spohn, 2005). Yet factors that are consistent with the stereotype of *real rape* (e.g., stranger, weapon, injury, victim resistance) are also influential. Cases in which the victim was injured or a weapon was used are often more likely to result in a suspect's arrest and criminal charges issued (Alderdren & Ullman, 2012; Bouffard, 2000; Horney & Spohn, 1996). Perhaps most concerning is that several studies continue to find that intimate partner and acquaintance cases are treated differently than stranger cases (Alderdren & Ullman, 2012; Tellis & Spohn, 2008; Tasca et al., 2013).

Prosecutors have to assess the credibility of victims and witnesses when determining whether to charge a case. Factors such as prior criminal record and giving inconsistent testimony are often red flags for prosecutors, as their testimony can be impeached or discredited during a trial. Unlike for other types of violent crime, certain background factors and behaviors are often scrutinized more closely. Tellis and Spohn (2008), in their investigation of sexual assault cases in San Diego, found that if a victim is engaged in risky behavior before the assault (e.g., walked home alone at night, drank with the suspect in a bar), charges were less likely to be issued. They also found that this concern about victim behavior was more common in simple rape cases rather than aggravated rape cases. Think back to our earlier discussion on rape shield laws and the scrutiny of victims' behaviors before rape law reform. At least in cases involving nonstrangers, some of these concerns may still influence the handling of cases (Beichner & Spohn, 2012).

Another growing concern is the potential misuse of UCR classification codes by police, including unfounded and exceptionally cleared statuses. Unfoundings are classified by the FBI to include false reports (e.g., victim's recanted statement) and baseless reports (e.g., no conclusive evidence that a crime occurred). Given the attention to the Philadelphia Police Department over their misuse of this code, researchers have investigated whether this practice is widespread in other jurisdictions. Spohn and Tellis conducted an extensive investigation of police and prosecutor responses to sexual assault in Los Angeles County in 2008. They found that most unfounded cases were correctly classified and false reports were relatively uncommon (Spohn, White, & Tellis, 2014); however, cases that were determined to be unlikely to result in conviction were often *exceptionally cleared*, a UCR category that is reserved for cases without suspects located or uncooperative victims (Spohn & Tellis, 2010). Cases among acquaintances and intimate partners are more likely to be exceptionally cleared (Bouffard, 2000), while the presence of victim credibility factors (e.g., unemployed, alcoholism) is associated with unfounding decisions (Spohn et al., 2014).

Why might factors associated with the myth of *real rape* continue to influence decision making by police and prosecutors after rape law reform? Frohmann (1991, 1998) undertook extensive observations of court proceedings and conducted interviews with prosecutors in one California court in the late 1980s. She found that prosecutors examine cases for issues with victim credibility (e.g., possible motives to lie, inconsistent statements), as well as whether the case fits their understanding of what a *typical* rape is. These factors were based on concerns that juries would not convict a rapist if the crime did not fit rape myths or if the victim was not perceived as a *genuine victim*. Think back to the earlier discussion on reasons victims choose to not report. How might victims' concerns, combined with communication between victims, police, and prosecutors during the investigation and early charging decisions, influence a victim's decision to cooperate?

Special Topic: Sexual Assault at Colleges

As previously reported, sexual assault victimization risk tends to be highest for women aged 18–24. Further, research demonstrates that college women in this age group have a greater risk than women who are not attending college (Karjane, Fisher, & Cullen, 2005). An extensive amount of research has been conducted on the risk factors and consequences for victims of sexual assault at colleges and universities. One well-known victimization survey, the National College Women Sexual Victimization Study, has provided a stark picture of the pervasiveness of sexual assault and unwanted sexual experiences faced by college women. Conducted in 1997, this survey found that almost approximately 10% of college women experienced unwanted sexual contact in a given school year (Daigle et al., 2008; Fisher, Cullen, & Turner, 2000). While less than 5% of women are raped in a school year, one-quarter of women will have been raped over a 4-year period (Karjane et al., 2005). Further, college women face an increased risk of repeat victimization (experiencing a subsequent sexual assault)—with over 7% of college women indicating that they were sexually assaulted more than once. Almost half of repeat victimizations occurred within the first 30 days of the initial assault (Daigle et al., 2008). What are common risk factors for college women? Similar to what we see with the general population, college women are much more likely to be assaulted by acquaintances than strangers (Fisher, Cullen, & Daigle, 2005), and assaults are likely to involve the use of alcohol by both the victim and the offender (Abbey, 2002; Fisher et al., 2005). Further, research suggests that peer pressure as well as social situations common in college life (e.g., parties at fraternity houses and pub crawls) provide opportunities for sexual assault to occur (Abbey, 2002).

Case Study 2: College Sexual Assault

Anna, a student at William Smith Colleges in New York, had just begun her freshman year of college. She decided to attend a fall welcoming party with friends at a fraternity house, where she met a senior football player. After dancing for some time with him, and consuming several beers and mixed drinks, she followed him upstairs to find a quieter room. In the process, Anna lost track of her friends, who became concerned and began looking for her. At one point in the night, she texted a friend that she was afraid of the man she had met and that he had a group of men ready to hook up with her.

She was found several hours later by a friend in a community room, called the *barn*, crying while being visibly sexually assaulted by the football player she had met earlier. At least a handful of other students were in the room, watching, laughing, and taking pictures of the assault. Although she had no recollection of the night's events, the rape kit performed by a SANE nurse provided evidence of injuries consistent with multiple assaults or excessive physical force. Further, evidence was collected from DNA samples found on her clothing and body. Although a witness, Anna's friend, found the football player with his pants down in a posture that was suggestive of sexual activity, the football player denied that any assault took place. How might Anna's victimization have been similar to the risk factors mentioned in this section? Why would bystanders not help Anna?

The investigation conducted by the school took only 12 days and was closed without an arrest, charge, or penalty for the football players named as suspects in the case. Because Anna reported her assault to campus officials, their investigation and hearing were very different than if she had alerted police. A university panel conducted a hearing, in lieu of a criminal court case, and did not examine the results of the rape kit. When questioning Anna, the panel focused on what she drank, whether she had initiated any sexual act with anyone at the party, and the style of dance she used with the football player. She did not have access to a victim advocate, and the school published her name in a letter sent out to students to alert them of the assault. Further, Anna faced harassment and ridicule from fellow students, who claimed that she made up the rape for attention. Anna is not alone in her experience with reporting her victimization to campus officials. As many as 55 colleges were recently examined by the federal government for violating federal laws on reporting and handling of sexual assault and harassment cases. Accounts from victims similar to Anna have led to Congress drafting a bill that would increase transparency of school investigations. How might the panel's questions and handling of her case have impacted her healing? (Bogdanich, 2014).

During the 1980s, increased attention to sexual assault on college campuses led to the creation of several state and federal policies. The goals of these policies were to develop reliable estimates of the number of sexual assault victimizations on campuses as well as to create programs to prevent victimization and respond to victims' needs. The first federal response was the Student Right-to-Know and Campus Security Act of 1990, which later became known as the Clery Act, after Jeanne Clery, a freshman student who was raped and killed in her college dorm room in 1986. This act required that all universities (public and private) receiving federal funding publish annual reports on the prevalence of crime on college campuses and to provide information to students and faculty about campus safety policies (Karjane et al., 2005). Critics of the Clery Act argue that because sexual assault continues to be underreported, prospective and current students may have misinformation about the actual safety of college campuses. In addition, crimes committed off campus (e.g., private residences near campus) are not counted in official reports, providing a limited picture of crime near college campuses (Sloah, Fisher & Cullen, 1997). College victims are especially less likely to report their victimization to police. Less than 5% of sexual assault victims tell law enforcement or other campus officials about their assault; however, victims often seek support from friends (Fisher et al., 2005). One reason for such low reporting rates is that victims may not view their assault as a criminal act. Victims who have been assaulted by an acquaintance, particularly if alcohol or coercion was involved, may feel as if what happened was "wrong" but not against the law. Because of this misconception, advocates have called for increased educational programming on campuses to provide students with information that counters the *real rape* myth in order to increase the likelihood that victims will report their assault to law enforcement or campus safety officials (Karjane et al., 2005).

A second piece of legislation is the Campus Sexual Assault Victims' Bill of Rights Act of 1992, which requires more attention to victims' needs post-assault and further programming to prevent sexual assault on campus. Colleges have responded by developing official policies that prohibit sexually hostile school environments as well as initiating sensitivity training for campus law enforcement and safety officers. Finally, prevention programs are routinely offered on college campuses, including self-defense training and sexual assault awareness events, such as pamphlets distributed during freshmen orientation. Although these acts have increased attention to the problem of sexual assault on college campuses, there is additional work to be done. Recently, a sponsored bill entitled the Campus Accountability and Safety Act has been presented to Congress to increase funding for training of campus security and staff, as well as heightened university oversight to ensure compliance with the Clery Act (RAINN, 2014d).

Summary

The state response to rape has undergone vast changes over the past 40 years. Early reform efforts broadened the definition of sexual assault, changed evidentiary and force requirements, and limited inquiries into a victim's sexual history. Yet one of the main concerns of feminists before rape law reform—the perpetuation of myths about *real rape*—appears to continue today and influences victim reporting and legal outcomes. Victims, particularly college students, are less likely to report sexual assaults committed by nonstrangers, or if alcohol or drugs were involved. Further, police and prosecutors continue to screen cases differently based on the presence of weapons, use of force, and the relationship between victim and offender. To this end, rape law reform has had limited effectiveness in changing societal and criminal justice responses to sexual assault. To be sure, however, the state response to sexual assault victims has not been entirely negative. SANE and SART programs have changed the way that medical and legal practitioners interact with victims, and evaluations of these programs has generally been positive. Additional reforms, whether directed at colleges or law enforcement, continue to be drafted to provide training and oversight in the handling of sexual assault cases.

Discussion Questions

1. In what ways has rape law reform changed the current state response to victims of sexual assault? In what ways has the reform failed to leave lasting changes?
2. How do aggravated and simple rapes differ? How might these two types of rape present unique challenges for police and prosecutors?
3. Some feminists have criticized the redefinition of rape as sexual assault. What are the benefits of defining rape as rape? As sexual assault? Which, in your opinion, will lead to better responses by the state?
4. Take a look at the campus safety information for your college or university. What information does it provide for protecting college students from sexual assault? What services are available to victims? What, if anything, should be added to university programming to increase the awareness of sexual assault?

References

Abbey, A. (2002). Alcohol-related sexual assault: A common problem among college students. *Journal of Studies on Alcohol and Drugs,* (14), 118.

Alderden, M. A., & Ullman, S. E. (2012). Creating a more complete and current picture: Examining police and prosecutor decision-making when processing sexual assault cases. *Violence Against Women, 18*(5), 525–551.

Bachman, R., & Paternoster, R. (1993). A contemporary look at the effects of rape law reform: How far have we really come?. *Journal of Criminal Law and Criminology, 84*(3), 554–574.

Beichner, D., & Spohn, C. (2005). Prosecutorial charging decisions in sexual assault cases: Examining the impact of a specialized prosecution unit. *Criminal Justice Policy Review, 16*(4), 461–498.

Beichner, D., & Spohn, C. (2012). Modeling the effects of victim behavior and moral character on prosecutors' charging decisions in sexual assault cases. *Violence and Victims, 27*(1), 3–24.

Bevacqua, M. (2000). *Rape on the public agenda: Feminism and the politics of sexual assault*. Boston, MA: Northeastern University Press.

Black, M. C., Basile, K. C., Breiding, M. J., Smith, S. G., Walters, M. L., Merrick, M. T., Chen, J., & Stevens, M. R. (2011). *The national intimate partner and sexual violence survey (NISVS): 2010 summary report*. Atlanta, GA: National Center for Injury Prevention and Control, Centers for Disease Control and Prevention.

Bogdanich, W. (2014, July 12). Reporting rape, and wishing she hadn't. *New York Times*. Retrieved from http://www.nytimes.com/2014/0713/us/how-one-college-handled-a-sexual-assault-complaint.html?r=3

Bouffard, J. A. (2000). Predicting type of sexual assault case closure from victim, suspect, and case characteristics. *Journal of Criminal Justice, 28*(6), 527–542.

Breitenbecher, K. H. (2001). Sexual revictimization among women: A review of the literature focusing on empirical investigations. *Aggression and Violent Behavior, 6*(4), 415–432.

Brownmiller, S. (1975). *Against our will: Men, women and rape*. New York, NY: Simon & Schuster.

Buchhandler-Raphael, M. (2011). The failure of consent: Re-conceptualizing rape as sexual abuse of power. *Michigan Journal of Gender & Law, 18*(1), 147–228.

Bureau of Justice Statistics. (2008). *Criminal victimization in the United States, 2006 statistical tables*. Washington, DC: U.S. Department of Justice (NCJ 223436).

Campbell, R., Patterson, D., & Bybee, D. (2012). Prosecution of adult sexual assault cases: A longitudinal analysis of the impact of a sexual assault nurse examiner program. *Violence Against Women, 18*(2), 223–244.

Caniglia, J., & Blackwell, B. (2013, May 9). Cleveland city prosecutors charge Ariel Castro with kidnapping, rape in case of missing women. *The Plain Dealer*. Retrieved from http://www.cleveland.com/metro/index.ssf/2013/05/ cleveland_city_prosecutors_cha.html

Cohen, M. (2007). No child left behind bars: The need to combat cruel and unusual punishment of state statutory rape laws. *Journal of Law & Policy, 16*, 717–756.

Corrigan, R. (2013). The new trial by Ordeal: Rape kits, police practices, and the unintended effects of policy innovation. *Law & Social Inquiry, 38*(4), 920–949.

Crandall, C. S., & Helitzer, D. (2003). *An impact evaluation of a sexual assault nurse examiner (SANE) program*. Washington, DC: National Institute of Justice (NCJ 203276).

Crenshaw, K. (1991). Mapping the margins: Intersectionality, identity politics, and violence against women of color. *Stanford Law Review, 43*(6), 1241–1299.

Daigle, L. E., Fisher, B. S., & Cullen, F. T. (2008). The violent and sexual victimization of college women: Is repeat victimization a problem?. *Journal of Interpersonal Violence, 23*(9), 1296–1313.

Decker, J. F., & Baroni, P. G. (2011). No still means yes: The failure of the non-consent reform movement in American rape and sexual assault law. *Journal of Criminal Law & Criminology, 101*(4), 1081–1170.

Department of Health and Human Services. (n.d.). Statutory rape: A guide to state laws and reporting requirements. Retrieved from http://aspe.hhs.gov/hsp/08/sr/statelaws/summary.shtml

DuMont, J., Miller., K., & Myhr, T. L. (2003). The role of "real rape" and "real victim" stereotypes in the police reporting practices of sexually assaulted women. *Violence Against Women, 9*(4), 466–486.

Estrich, S. (1987). *Real rape: How the legal system victimizes women who say no*. Boston, MA: Harvard University Press.

Fazlollah, M., Matzah, M., & McCoy, C. R. (1999, October 29). Police checking into old sex cases: The department is reviewing hundreds of assault complaints in Philadelphia dating from early '98. *Philadelphia Inquirer*. Retrieved from http://articles.philly.com/1999-10-29/news/25508727_1_crime-statistics-review-thousands-of-sexual-assault-cases

Federal Bureau of Investigation. (2013, May 20). Frequently asked questions about the change in the UCR definition of rape. Retrieved from http://www.fbi.gov/about-us/cjis/ucr/recent-program-updates/new-rape-definition-frequently-asked-questions

Fehler-Cabral, G., Campbell, R., & Patterson, D. (2011). Adult sexual assault survivors' experiences with sexual assault nurse examiners (SANEs). *Journal of Interpersonal Violence, 26*(18), 3618–3639.

Felson, R. B., & Paré, P. P. (2005). The reporting of domestic violence and sexual assault by non-strangers to the police. *Journal of Marriage and Family, 67*(3), 597–610.

Fisher, B. S., Cullen, F. T., & Daigle, L. E. (2005). The discovery of acquaintance rape: The salience of methodological innovation and rigor. *Journal of Interpersonal Violence, 20*(4), 493–500.

Fisher, B. S., Cullen, F. T., & Turner, M. G. (2000). *The sexual victimization of college women.* Washington, DC: U.S. Department of Justice (NCJ 182369).

Follette, V. M., Polusny, M. A., Bechtle, A. E., & Naugle, A. E. (1996). Cumulative trauma: The impact of child sexual abuse, adult sexual assault, and spouse abuse. *Journal of Traumatic Stress, 9*(1), 25–35.

Frohmann, L. (1991). Discrediting victims' allegations of sexual assault: Prosecutorial accounts of case rejections. *Social Problems, 38*(2), 213–226.

Frohmann, L. (1998). Constituting power in sexual assault cases: Prosecutorial strategies for victim management. *Social Problems, 45*(3), 393–407.

Gartner, R., & Macmillan, R. (1995). Effect of victim-offender relationship on reporting crimes of violence against women. *Canadian Journal of Criminology, 37*, 393–429.

Gershman, B. L. (1992). A moral standard for the prosecutor's exercise of the charging discretion. *Fordham Urban Law Journal, 20*(3), 513–530.

Hasday, J. E. (2000). Contest and consent: A legal history of marital rape. *California Law Review, 88*(5), 1373–1505.

Horney, J., & Spohn, C. (1996). The influence of blame and believability factors on the processing of simple versus aggravated rape cases. *Criminology, 34*(2), 135–162.

Jones, J. S., Alexander, C., Wynn, B. N., Rossman, L., & Dunnuck, C. (2009). Why women don't report sexual assault to the police: The influence of psychosocial variables and traumatic injury. *The Journal of emergency medicine, 36*(4), 417–424.

Jordan, J. (2004). Beyond belief? Police, rape and women's credibility. *Criminal Justice, 4*(1), 29–59.

Karjane, H. M., Fisher, B., & Cullen, F. T. (2005). *Sexual assault on campus: What colleges and universities are doing about it.* Washington, DC: U.S. Department of Justice (NCJ 205521).

Kilpatrick, D. G., Resnick, H. S., Ruggiero, K. J., Conoscenti, L. M., & McCauley, J. (2007). *Drug-facilitated, incapacitated, and forcible rape*: A national study. Charleston, SC: Medical University of South Carolina, National Crime Victims Research & Treatment Center (NCJ 219181).

Koppelman, A. (2003). Lawrence's penumbra. *Minnesota Law Review, 88*, 1171–1183.

Koss, M. P., & Harvey, M. R. (1991). *The rape victim: Clinical and community interventions.* Thousand Oaks, CA: Sage Publications.

LaFree, G. (1989). *Rape and criminal justice: The social construction of sexual assault.* Belmont, CA: Wadsworth Publishing Company.

Loh, W. D. (1981). Q: What has reform of rape legislation wrought? A: Truth in criminal labelling. *Journal of Social Issues, 37*(4), 28–52.

Long, J. G., & Wilkinson, J. (2011). *Benefits of specialized prosecution units in domestic and sexual violence cases.* Washington, DC: U.S. Department of Justice (NCJ 244042).

Lonsway, K. A., & Archambault, J. (2012). The "justice gap" for sexual assault cases: Future directions for research and reform. *Violence Against Women, 18*(2), 145–168.

Lonsway, K. A., & Fitzgerald, L. F. (1994). Rape myths in review. *Psychology of Women Quarterly, 18*(2), 133–164.

Marsh, J. C., Geist, A., & Caplan, N. (1982). *Rape and the limits of law reform.* Boston, MA: Auburn House.

Miller, A. K., Markman, K. D., Amacker, A. M., & Menaker, T. A. (2012). Expressed sexual assault legal context and victim culpability attributions. *Journal of Interpersonal Violence, 27*(6), 1023–1039.

Murphy, S. B., Edwards, K. M., Bennett, S., Bibeau, S. J., & Sichelstiel, J. (2014). Police reporting practices for sexual assault cases in which "the victim does not wish to pursue charges". *Journal of Interpersonal Violence, 29*(1), 144–156.

Office for Victims of Crime. (n.d.). What is the office for victims of crime?. Retrieved from http://www.ovc.gov/publications/factshts/what_is_OVC2010/intro.html

Office of Justice Programs. (2006, April). Justice for all act. Retrieved from http://ojp.gov/ovc/publications/factshts/justforall/content.html

Office on Violence Against Women (n.d.). Legislation. Retrieved from http://www.justice.gov/ovw/legislation-0

Page, A. D. (2010). True colors: Police officers and rape myth acceptance. *Feminist Criminology, 5*(4), 315–334.

Parenti, C. (1999). *Lockdown America: Police and prisons in the age of crisis.* New York, NY: Verso Publishing.

Polk, K. (1985). Rape reform and criminal justice processing. *Crime & Delinquency, 31*(2), 191–205.

Rape, Abuse and Incest National Network. (n.d. a). Sexual assault. Retrieved from https://www.rainn.org/get-information/types-of-sexual-assault/sexual-assault

Rape, Abuse and Incest National Network. (n.d. b). Laws in your state: South Carolina. Retrieved from http://apps.rainn.org/crimedef/index.cfm?state=south%20carolina

Rape, Abuse and Incest National Network. (n.d. c). Aftermath: Working with the criminal justice system. Retrieved from https://rainn.org/get-info/legal-information/working-with-the-criminal-justice-system

Rape, Abuse and Incest National Network. (n.d. d). Eight senators announce bipartisan campus accountability and safety act. Retrieved from https://rainn.org/news-room/campus-accountability-and-safety-act

Rennison, C. M. (1999). *Criminal victimization 1998: Changes 1997–98 with trends 1993–98.* Washington, DC: U.S. Department of Justice (NCJ 176363).

Rennison, C. M. (2002). *Rape and sexual assault: Reporting to police and medical attention,* 1992–2000. Washington, DC: U.S. Department of Justice (NCJ 194530).

Reynolds v. State, 27, Neb. 90 (42 N. W., 1889).

Sable, M. R., Danis, F., Mauzy, D. L., & Gallagher, S. K. (2006). Barriers to reporting sexual assault for women and men: Perspectives of college students. *Journal of American College Health, 55*(3), 157–162.

Sexual Assault, Wisc. Penal Code, § 940.225 (2014).

Sims, B., Yost, B., & Abbott, C. (2006). The efficacy of victim services programs: Alleviating the psychological suffering of crime victims?. *Criminal Justice Policy Review, 17*(4), 387–406.

Sloan, J. J., Fisher, B. S., & Cullen, F. T. (1997). Assessing the student right-to-know and campus security act of 1990: An analysis of the victim reporting practices of college and university students. *Crime & Delinquency, 43*(2), 148–168.

Smith, K., Holmseth, J., Macgregor, M., & Letourneau, M. (1998). Sexual assault response team: Overcoming obstacles to program development. *Journal of Emergency Nursing, 24*(4), 365–367.

Spohn, C., & Horney, J. (1992). *Rape law reform: A grassroots revolution and its impact.* New York: Plenum Press.

Spohn, C., & Tellis, K. (2010). Justice denied: The exceptional clearance of rape cases in Los Angeles. *Albany Law Review, 74*(3), 1379–1421.

Spohn, C., White, C., & Tellis, K. (2014). Unfounding sexual assault: Examining the decision to unfound and identifying false reports. *Law & Society Review, 48*(1), 161–192.

Stanglin, D. (2013, July 26). Ariel Castro pleads guilty in Ohio abductions. *USA Today.* Retrieved from http://ww.usatoday.com/story/news/nation/2013/07/26/ariel-castro-cleveland-abduction-plea-deal-death-penalty-25890390/

Tasca, M., Rodriguez, N., Spohn, C., & Koss, M. P. (2013). Police decision making in sexual assault cases: predictors of suspect identification and arrest. *Journal of Interpersonal Violence, 28*(6), 1157–1177.

Taylor, W. K. (2002). Collecting evidence for sexual assault: The role of the sexual assault nurse examiner (SANE). *International Journal of Gynecology & Obstetrics, 78*(S1), 91–94.

Tellis, K. M., & Spohn, C. C. (2008). The sexual stratification hypothesis revisited: Testing assumptions about simple versus aggravated rape. *Journal of Criminal Justice, 36*(3), 252–261.

Tjaden, P. G., & Thoennes, N. (2006). *Extent, nature, and consequences of rape victimization: Findings from the National Violence Against Women Survey.* Washington, DC: National Institute of Justice (NCJ 181867).

Truman, J. L., & Rand, M. R. (2011). *Criminal victimization, 2009.* Washington, DC: U.S. Department of Justice (NCJ 231327).

Wallach, S. J. (1996). Rape shield laws: Protecting the victim at the expense of the defendant's constitutional rights. *New York Law School Journal of Human Rights, 13,* 485–521.

The White House (n.d.) The Violence Against Women Act, Fact sheet. Retrieved from http://www.whitehouse.gov/sites/default/files/docs/vawa_factsheet.pdf

Domestic and International Sex Trafficking

MICHELE P. BRATINA AND KELLY M. CARRERO

Contents

Case Study 1

Ashley K. is 11 years old and loves to draw pictures of animals. She lives with her mother, who is addicted to methamphetamines. Ashley's mother frequently brings unknown men into their home, and Ashley has been "woken up" by many of these men in the middle of the night. One autumn evening, Ashley is sitting outside of a pizza place in her neighborhood while her mom "entertains a friend." Ashley is gripping her empty stomach and shivering from the cool of the evening, when Ronnie J. approaches her and asks her if she would like a slice of pizza. Ronnie is a charming 31-year-old man, who seems to show genuine care for Ashley's well-being. Ashley cautiously accepts Ronnie's offer of pizza, and they chat about animals while she eats her pizza. Once Ashley is finished eating, Ronnie smiles at her, tells her he will see her around the neighborhood, and then he leaves. About a week later, Ashley sees Ronnie again. They share another slice of pizza and some laughs. For the next several months, Ronnie makes frequent visits to Ashley's neighborhood in an effort to gain her trust. By the end of the summer, Ashley has had enough of living with her mother and confides in Ronnie that she wishes she could just get away from it all. When Ronnie offers to let Ashley stay with him and his "cousin," Lorena S., Ashley quickly goes home and packs a bag. She lives with Ronnie and Lorena for a few weeks when Ronnie starts to become physically affectionate with Ashley. She has never known a father figure and welcomes the attention, although it made her uncomfortable at first. The physical affection soon becomes sexual, and Ashley is sure she and Ronnie are in love. Ronnie tells Ashley she could really help him out with the finances if she would go on a couple of "dates" with some of his "friends." Ashley doesn't like the thought of it, but obliges, feeling it is the least she can do for the man who saved her from her mother's house. After a few months of dating Ronnie's friends, Lorena tells Ashley that she has a really great opportunity for Ashley to bring big cash into the family. Lorena introduces Ashley to a very classy woman named, Giselle M. Giselle gives Lorena a nod of approval, and Lorena excitedly tells Ashley she has "landed the big job." After a big hug, Lorena tells Ashley that Ronnie will be so proud of her and they will see her later. Giselle takes Ashley to an apartment where there are about 20 other girls. It's not long before Giselle orders Ashley to get "prepped." Ashley gets her hair cut, nails done, and a new outfit. After getting fully prepped, Ashley is put on a private jet and flown to a secluded island in the Caribbean. Ashley and a couple of the other girls cannot believe they get to go on a trip to the Caribbean! The jet lands on the island, and they are taken by bus to an unbelievable mansion. The girls are giddy with excitement, but among their giddiness is an undercurrent of nervousness and anxiety. Ashley is scared, but calms herself when she thinks about how proud Ronnie must be of her now. When the girls arrive at the mansion, they are greeted by one of Giselle's friends, Cari J. Cari tells the girls the "rules" of the job—and the bottom line is—smile, do not get too drunk, and do as the client requests. Ashley and another young girl, Ratana P. (but she is known as "Crystal"), are told they will be giving a massage to the man who owns the island—someone by the name of Jeffery Epstein.*

America's Emancipation Proclamation of 1862 is a historical example of the tragic truth that people seek profit from the control and exploitation of others. President Lincoln's declarations were not the first—nor would they be the last—to vehemently denounce the use of human beings as slaves for any purpose at all. Notwithstanding any public denouncements, the truth is that, from time to time and place to place, people from various parts of the globe have been viewed as insignificant "others" who are, for a variety of cultural, social, or political reasons, more likely to be abused, exploited, and isolated from larger society. Fortunately, time has brought about significant progression of thought, and such views have been exposed as morally reprehensible and punishable under the laws of many nation-states across the globe for years. Particularly, in terms of sexual exploitation, the message has been clear: No human being, adult or child, man or woman, should be subjected to abuse of any form and the vices of others. Despite the bravado generated by key domestic and international policy makers on the prevention and punishment of sexual victimization, and particularly, violence against women, sex trafficking has become a significant and growing problem in the United States and internationally in recent years (Deshpande & Nauer, 2013).

This chapter seeks to (1) define human sex trafficking and discuss its major types; (2) discuss the scope of the problem in several countries, using the United States as a prime example; and (3) identify some of the factors that may foster sex trafficking worldwide. We conclude that trafficking in persons, particularly the sexual exploitation of children, constitutes a gross violation of human rights and a global threat to democracy and peace.

---

* The names and characters in this case example are fictional, except for Jeffery Epstein, also known as the Beach Billionaire. To learn more about the Jeffrey Epstein case, *see* Walter, V. & Sauer, M. (2008, June 30). Jail time for millionaire in teen sex scandal. *ABC News*. Retrieved from http://abcnews.go.com/Blotter/story?id=5278867.

What Is Human Trafficking?

Trafficking in persons, or human trafficking, is a violation of human rights standards and decency and has been described as a form of slavery in the twenty-first century (Ngwe & Elechi, 2012). Out of fear and coercion, victims designated by traffickers as "others" develop a sense of worthlessness, a sense of shame, and a compelled service to their controller(s). In recent years, trafficking, and its ability to result in severe trauma and addiction, has emerged as a critical issue in criminal justice on a global front. In addition to the traumatic stress related to exploitation, trafficking in persons is a highly profitable commodity. As an economic generator of billions of dollars every year, trafficking in persons victimizes millions of people around the world and, in the United States, despite its rich history, is one of the fastest growing criminal industries in the world today.

There are two common purposes for human trafficking: sexual exploitation and forced labor (Deshpande & Nour, 2013). Although much of what the American public hears about regarding human trafficking involves individuals who are smuggled into the United States and subjected to forced labor, it is important to understand that trafficking in persons—particularly sex trafficking—is a global issue, albeit one that is not uniformly addressed. Though the sexual exploitation, or sex trafficking of adults and children, has been viewed as morally reprehensible and legally prohibited in the United States and abroad under mixed laws for decades, for most of history, there was no clarification within international law as to what constituted sex trafficking. Consequently, lawmakers were lacking informed context as to the specific behaviors that needed to be abolished. A manageable and agreeable definition of human trafficking was first set forth in 2000 with the adoption of the *United Nations Protocol to Prevent, Suppress, and Punish Trafficking in Persons, Especially Women and Children* (also referred to as the "Palermo Protocol"):

> [T]he recruitment, transportation, transfer, harboring or receipt of persons, by means of threat or use of force or other forms of coercion, of abduction, or fraud, of deception, of the abuse of power or of a position of vulnerability or of the giving and receiving of payments or benefits to achieve the consent of a person having control over another person, for the purpose of exploitation. Exploitation shall include, at a minimum, the exploitation of the prostitution of others or other forms of sexual exploitation, forced labor or services, slavery or practices similar to slavery, servitude or the removal of organs.
>
> **UN General Assembly (2000, p. 2)**

Sex trafficking refers to the use of force or coercion to involve individuals in the commercial sex trade against their will. Child sex trafficking involves victims who are under the age of 18 who are engaged in commercial sex. Like trafficking related to forced labor, sex trafficking revolves around forced servitude to a trafficker or several traffickers, though the victim and circumstantial dynamics may differ to some extent.

History of Sex Trafficking in the United States

The commercial sex trade and prostitution have a rich history on an international level, but also in the United States. During the seventeenth and eighteenth centuries, it was common for people to be brought from Africa to the United States for the purposes of being sold to Americans and live in servitude. African slaves were forbidden to marry—particularly because they were considered property of American landowners. Consequently, if unwed, they had no rights, and rape was not prohibited under the law. Female slaves belonged to their master so had no legal right to refuse their sexual advances. Any man could have sex with female African slaves, but white females could not have sex with African American males, freed or enslaved. Many states had laws against interracial relationships. Female slaves were also raped by other African American males; like forced sex with their masters, the victimization was not punishable as the union might produce a child that would add to the property (Reddington & Kreisel, 2009). The United States abolished slavery in 1865 with the passing of the Thirteenth Amendment, forcing human traffickers to utilize underground networks.

Smuggling versus Human Trafficking

Sex trafficking is a profit-driven crime. Therefore, victims of sex trafficking can be found just about anywhere sex or sexual fantasy is exchanged for money. Almost every aspect of the sex industry serves as a forum for sex trafficking. Online images, pornography, street prostitution, residential brothels, escort services, and strip clubs are some examples of potential arenas human sex traffickers target to profit from their human sex slaves.

The key to understanding the prevalence of victimization is in understanding the relationship between supply and demand. Buyers of commercial sex are U.S. citizens and foreign nationals of any race or ethnicity. These are individuals who fall under a range of ages who are from diverse socioeconomic backgrounds. While the demand for commercial sex is gender-neutral, buyers tend to be primarily male.

People often confuse the concepts of smuggling and trafficking and hence use the terms interchangeably, as if talking about the same phenomenon. However, several factors distinguish the two concepts. *Smuggling* refers to a crime against a country's borders, whereas *trafficking* is a crime against a person. Smuggling involves illegal border crossing; sex trafficking involves forced commercial sex acts. The primary act implicated in smuggling is illegal transportation; in sex trafficking, transportation can be an element, but is not required. Although transport is implied because of the concept "trafficking," under federal statutes, trafficking does not require state or international border-crossing. Trafficking in persons involves the use of force, fraud, or coercion to attain sexual services, and it is not dependent on whether transport occurs. It is important to recognize that smuggling can serve as a gateway to trafficking—particularly if force, fraud, or coercion is used to compel an individual into commercial sex. A common example would be if debt incurred from smuggling was used as a means of control to force persons smuggled to perform sex acts.

Types of Sex Trafficking Networks

Countries with markets for sex trade are involved in some type of human sex trafficking network. While the demand and host country's government play a role in specifying the type of network most frequently found in the country, all sex trafficking networks share some common elements. Specifically, most sex trafficking networks consist of an enforced hierarchy of control, several means of advertisement of services, and service or working expectations for the victims.

In the United States, three primary sex trafficking networks have been identified: domestic networks (e.g., strip clubs, Internet, truck stops), Asian networks (e.g., Asian massage parlors), and Latino networks (e.g., Latino residential brothels) (National Human Trafficking Resource Center, 2011; "Types of Trafficking Cases in the U.S.," 2010). Victims of domestic networks can be minors and adults and may be U.S. citizens or foreign-born nationals. *Controllers* are people who are use force and/or coercion to keep the victims in sexual servitude. Typically, controllers are pimps, intimate partners, or family members. Victims are often recruited by a boyfriend or caretaker who offers promises of false employment. Common clientele are part of an open network, and victims work in locations that include streets, clubs, truck stops, or hotels. Advertisement for services can be found online, through word of mouth, or business cards. Moreover, service providers are often advertised under legitimate business models (e.g., escort service, private dancing). Victims involved in pimp-controlled trafficking networks are typically expected to service an average quota of about five customers per night 5–7 days a week. This averages out to approximately 1820 forced sexual encounters per year, resulting in an average annual income of about $588,000 for the pimp (National Human Trafficking Resource Center, 2011).

Victims working at Asian massage parlors are primarily Asian women. Typically, three to five women live on-site and rotate about every other week. Asian male and female controllers (female controllers are referred to as "Mamasans") recruit their victims through false job promises and often smuggle the women across international lines. Similar to pimp-controlled clientele, customers are a part of an open network and are charged anywhere between $60 and $90 per encounter (National Human Trafficking Resource Center, 2013). Asian massage parlor trafficking networks can be found in storefronts, office space, commercial areas, health spas, and nail salons. Services are advertised in the newspaper, phone books, and online. Victims servicing customers at Asian massage parlors are expected to work about 6–7 days per week, resulting in an average of about 2184 forced sexual encounters per year. Women who are working in the parlors are often required to pay "house fees." A parlor with three women working will earn over $500,000 per year.

Victims in Latino residential brothels are typically Latina women and minors. Their controllers are male and female Latinos. Clientele consist of primarily Latino males who typically pay $30 for about 15 minutes of service. Latino brothels can be found in residential areas, rural trailers, and apartments. Other fronts masked as legitimate businesses have included cantinas and escort delivery services. Controllers effectively advertise through word of mouth and business cards. In an average week, victims at Latino residential brothels service about 25 customers per day and work 7 days per week, resulting in each victim experiencing approximately 9100 forced sexual encounters per year. Traffickers targeting Latino brothels earn about $273,000 a year (National Human Trafficking Resource Center, n.d.).

Who Are the Victims-Turned-Offenders?

There is a common misperception that trafficking victims are almost always foreign nationals. Under the federal definition, victims can be foreign nationals and U.S. citizens. Both are protected since the implementation of Trafficking Victims Protection Act (TVPA) in 2000. Research indicates that there are specific characteristics belonging to both traffickers and their victims.

Victims of sex trafficking can be anyone, including U.S. citizens and foreign nationals; males and females; adults and minors; or strangers, friends, family members, or neighbors (Walker-Rodriguez and Hill, 2011). Trafficking in persons has no geographic or industry boundaries. According to the scant literature on physical locations where trafficking is likely to take place, sex trafficking mostly occurs in adult clubs, massage parlors, truck stops, and other areas with significant populations or tourism including a significant presence of military personnel. Note that while trafficking has been found in these places, this does not mean all people working in these industries are victims of sex trafficking.

Social and economic factors can create vulnerability for sex trafficking in both adults and children. Potential victims often have histories of trauma involving sexual, physical, and emotional abuse by parents or other caregivers. These vulnerabilities are realized by traffickers as they frequently target such individuals and manipulate them with threats of violence and other forms of control such as debt bondage and false promises of financial rewards or success in order to keep them involved in the sex trade. Consequently, victims of trafficking often suffer concurrent abuse, violence, and future exploitation (Walker-Rodriguez and Hill, 2011).

Who Are the Traffickers?

The global sex trade is one of the fastest growing areas of organized crime, and it generates the third highest revenue for organized crime groups after narcotics and guns (Deshpande & Nour, 2013). Perpetrators of human trafficking can be anyone, including U.S. citizens and foreign nationals; males and females; adults and minors; or strangers, family, friends, family members, or intimate partners; members of the victims' own ethnic or national background, and from diverse socioeconomic backgrounds. Trafficking networks are comprised of individuals, including pimps, neighbors, friends, relatives, intimate partners, international organization and diplomatic staff, and labor recruiters/brokers. These organized crime networks involve informal criminal operations, including family or extended family, pimp networks, and gangs. Traffickers typically engage in businesses (small or large), involving contractors and/or agents, and labor recruiters; these may be operating alongside legitimate businesses that may or may not be aware of the criminal enterprise.

Barriers to Victim Self-Identification

Given the critical nature of the sex trafficking issue in the United States and abroad, it is essential to identify and understand the barriers to victim self-identification in the context of successful identification of traffickers and their ultimate prosecution. Some of the more profound challenges based on the experiences of victims that have been identified by criminal justice and human services professionals include the nature of captivity and isolation, real or perceived threats of violence (including retaliation against loved ones), sense of loyalty toward the controller, and a general distrust or fear of authority (Jordan, Patel, & Rapp, 2013). Furthermore, law enforcement officials and service providers are quite aware that victims are frequently accompanied or guarded and may be significantly influenced by language and social barriers, shame, debt bondage, and a combination of drugs or alcohol (Kotrla, 2010). An additional barrier is that victims oftentimes have no documentation or personal identification.

While identified as barriers to report victimization, all of these factors are also used to explain the power and control used to attain abuse, coercion, and control by the traffickers. In conjunction with these variables, other indicators to identify victims of sex trafficking can be identified. Some observable characteristics of victimization may include obvious signs of physical abuse, not in control of own decisions, inconsistencies in story—claims of "just visiting" an area, restricted movement or ability to travel, the absence of personal possessions or records, a lack of insight as to present community or frequent movement, owing large debt that cannot be paid off, and an individual who is under the age of 18 who is providing commercial sex (Jordan et al., 2013; Polaris, 2014).

For youth specifically, some indicators of sexual exploitation may include an expressed interest in relationships with older men, involvement in Internet chat rooms, unexplained shopping trips, cell phones, jewelry, and clothing, certain types of language (e.g., referring to a boyfriend as "Daddy"), and late night outings or keeping unusual hours.

Case Study 2

Ratana P., who uses her Western name of "Crystal" when entertaining clients, is a very young-looking 19 year old who is originally from Laos. After failing to find steady work in her village, Ratana went to look for work in Pattaya when she was 14 years old. Many girls from her village had gone to Pattaya and Bangkok for work. A few years later, while working as a bar girl (i.e., prostitute) in a club owned by the Russian mafia, Ratana met an American man, Stan J.; Stan told her he would bring her to America where she could make a lot more money and live the "rich life that Americans live." Ratana quickly accepted, and Stan J. brought her to a hotel where he had documents for her and a plane ticket to New York City. When Ratana arrived in New York, she was met by a Thai woman, Pakpo, who had been living in America for over 20 years. Pakpo took Ratana to a small apartment with many other girls, mostly from Asia. Pakpo also told Ratana the "rules of the house"—Pakpo would keep Ratana's American documents (which were fake, but passed as legitimate at the customs stops), arrange Ratana's client schedule, and clients were to submit all payments to the controllers that would escort her to the designated client location. Ratana was told that she was to give the controllers any and all tips the clients may give her and that she was to be very careful because she could be put in prison or sent back to Laos if she did not follow the rules of the house. The other girls in the house bore the physical scars and bruises of other consequences for not following house rules. After about 10 days and approximately 50 clients, Ratana was not sure if this was the American life she had envisioned while working in Pattaya. There was no time to contemplate her choices, because she and three other girls were told to pack up their belongings and get in the back of one of the controller's vehicles. The girls were transported to Boston, where they stayed in an apartment similar to the one in New York. There was an older Thai woman, Anada, who ran the house much like Pakpo. This constant movement from city to city and working with no real pay became the routine for Ratana. As she waits with a frightened Ashley K. to enter the Beach Billionaire's massage room, Ratana's new dream is to escape this life.

Current State and Response through Policy

Sex trafficking in the United States exists within the broader transnational commercial sex trade, and often the incidence rates are larger than most people realize or understand. Similar to other crime categories, data collection of sex trafficking has been problematic. The reason for this mirrors that of other sex-related crimes: victims are reluctant to come forward. Based on currently available information, 2515 suspected incidents of human trafficking were investigated by federally funded task forces between 2008 and 2010, 82% of which were characterized as sex trafficking (Banks & Kyckelhahn, 2011).

Due to the fear experienced by victims of trafficking, Congress, with the passage of TVPA in 2000, has established "incentives" to encourage victims to come forward and assist in the prosecution of the traffickers, particularly, nonimmigrant classifications in the form of T- or U-Visas.* Furthermore, adult victims who are noncitizens of the United States may be offered certification (i.e., eligibility to receive federal benefits and services under refugee status). During the period of 2000–2009, between 1591 and 2078 T-Visas were issued to foreign nationals, and 2076 certifications were issued.

Estimates suggest that anywhere between 100,000 and 300,000 children may become victims of commercial sex exploitation each year in the United States, Canada, and Mexico (Estes & Weiner, 2001). The average age of entrance into prostitution in the United States is between 12 and 14 years. The Department of Justice (DOJ) has recently funded projects focused on assessing the number of youth in the United States who are involved in the commercial sex industry.

As with other crime data, there is a "dark figure" that pertains to the number of victims that never do come to the attention of law enforcement for various reasons. The human trafficking populations in the United States who are not represented in the preceding statistics include hidden victims, immigrant victims who elect to return to home countries rather than apply for the T-Visa, and adults who are U.S. citizens.

Emergence of International Policies

Given the more recent emergence of sex trafficking as a prevalent issue in the United States, it is important to study the legislative response to sex trafficking first through an international lens. The main international law addressing trafficking is the *United Nations Protocol to Prevent Suppress and Punish Trafficking in Persons, Especially Women and Children*, also known as the Palermo Protocol of 2000.

There are several international instruments founded prior to the Palermo Protocol of 2000 that are legally binding for United Nations Member States that have joined in the international efforts to combat human trafficking including the following:

- The Universal Declaration of Human Rights founded in 1948
- The International Labor Organizations (ILO) Convention Number 29 on Forced Labor, ratified on February 26, 1969

---

* "The T Nonimmigrant Status was created to provide protection to victims of severe forms of human trafficking. The U Nonimmigrant Status was designated for victims of certain crimes who had suffered mental or physical abuse and who were willing to assist in the investigation of human trafficking activity" (Banks and Kyckelhahn, 2011).

- The ILO Convention Number 105 on the Abolition of Forced Labor, ratified on December 2, 1969
- The Convention on the Elimination of All Forms of Discrimination against Women (CEDAW) founded in 1985
- The Convention on the Rights of the Child (1992)
- The International Covenant on Civil and Political Rights (CCPR) founded in 1996
- The International Covenant on Economic, Social and Cultural Rights (1999)
- Optional Protocol to the Convention on the Elimination of All Forms of Discrimination against Women (ratified on June 14, 2000)
- The ILO Convention Number 182 on the Worst Forms of Child Labor (2001)
- The International Convention on the Elimination of All Forms of Racial Discrimination (2003)

In addition, there are two regional declarations and two multilateral treaties (binding agreements) including the following:

- Association of Southeast Asian Nations (ASEAN) Declaration on Transnational Crime (signed in Manila on December 20, 1997)
- Bangkok Declaration on Irregular Migration (signed in April 1999 at the International Symposium on Migration in Bangkok)
- Convention on the Civil Aspects of International Child Abduction (2002)
- The Convention on Protection of Children and Co-operation in respect of Inter-Country Adoption (ratified on April 29, 2004)

A more recent development is Thailand's Anti-Trafficking in Persons Act (2008), which prohibits all forms of trafficking and imposes criminal penalties that may carry a sentence of 4–10 years of imprisonment. The act also provides for imperative services for victims, including compensation, health care, and shelter needs. Memorandums of Understanding (MoUs) have also been implemented by neighboring countries. MoUs are legal instruments that seek to strengthen the response to sexual and other forms of victimization, but also to encourage more effective collaboration among various agencies, states, and regions. It is also promising that 190 countries have initiated membership in the International Police Organization (Interpol), which promotes and facilitates international law enforcement collaboration (Martin, 2013).

In the United States, the primary legislative authority on trafficking is the TVPA of 2000 (which was reauthorized in 2003, 2005, 2008, and 2013). The Federal TVPA creates two categories: sex trafficking and labor trafficking. Under the statute, sex trafficking refers to

> The recruitment, harboring, transportation, providing or obtaining of a person for a commercial sex act, in which a commercial sex act is induced by force, fraud, or coercion, or in which the person induced to perform such an act has not attained 18 years of age.
>
> **Victims of Trafficking and Violence Protection Act of 2000**

As the subcategories within this definition reflect, the trafficking of children (under 18) need not involve force or fraud to meet the definition of sex trafficking. To determine whether the elements of the crime of severe forms of trafficking in persons are met, the

Actions–Means–Purpose (A–M–P) model has been utilized (National Human Trafficking Resource Center, 2012). Under the A–M–P model, for a case to be considered trafficking, at least one element from all three categories must be present. The categories are as follows: the trafficker induces, recruits, harbors, transports, provides, obtains (action) and employs force, fraud, coercion (means) for the purpose of compelling a victim to provide commercial sex acts (purpose). Examples of force include physical assault, sexual assault, confinement, and isolation. Fraud examples include false promises of legitimate employment and withholding wages. Coercion might involve threats to life, safety, and family deportation. Elements of physical restraint or kidnapping need not be present to meet the required elements of the crime of sex trafficking; means may also involve debt bondage, fear, and psychological manipulation. If a trafficked person consented before the abuse or was paid, it can still be trafficking; a victim cannot consent to be in a situation of sex trafficking.

Prior to the enactment of TVPA, trafficking was punishable under federal involuntary servitude statutes that required bodily harm as coercion. According to 2011 statistics from the U.S. Attorney's Office, there were 125 cases of human trafficking prosecuted under TVPA that year, resulting in 70 convictions. As of 2013, all 50 states had enacted laws against human trafficking; 49 of these had laws that specifically prohibited sex trafficking or sexual exploitation of minors. On the state level, charges related to sex trafficking may involve violations of other laws such as those pertaining to forcible rape, kidnapping, slavery, false imprisonment, assault, battery, fraud, and extortion.

Contemporary Legislation and Laws

There have been changes in legislation and enforcement as a direct consequence of legal decisions, media reports of high-profile incidents, and public awareness regarding trafficking in persons. Most of the high-profile incidents occurred during the early 2000s as a proactive national response to violence against women and policies that required law enforcement officials to discontinue the criminalization of victims who were forced to participate in illegal acts by their traffickers. For example, the 1997 *Cadena-Sosa* indictments raised public awareness of the extent of the sex trafficking problem in the United States, and subsequent legislation was enacted to address the already burgeoning problem (Butkus, 2007; Simmonsen, 2008). Further, because of *Cadena* and other publicized cases of sexual exploitation and related victimizations, state and federal initiatives requiring the apprehension and prosecutions of traffickers were initiated. Subsequently, a number of social research projects emerged to indicate the need for victims' rights advocacy and attention—particularly with regard to the more humane treatment of victims who are refugees.

Due largely to the strength and movement of advocacy groups and coalitions worldwide, there have been more recent legislative advancements. On the international front, new legislative provisions have been implemented so that traffickers could be criminally prosecuted; these include the Penal Code Amendment Act of 1997, the Money Laundering Control Act of 1999, the Criminal Procedure Amendment Act of 1999, the Child Protection Act of 2003, and the Protection of Witnesses in Criminal Cases Act of 2003 (Burke & Ducci, 2005). Unfortunately, weak law enforcement and police corruption in some areas have prevented successful enforcement of these laws. Several U.S. states have enacted legislation. One example is in Florida where "The Safe Harbor Act" was passed in 2013. This legislation provides protection for sexually exploited children, by placing them under the custody of the Department of Children and Families so they have a safe place to live while they receive services and as they move forward in the criminal justice process and anticipated prosecution of the traffickers.

Notwithstanding the developments in legislation, victims' services, education, data collection, and statistical research findings, one of the most salient challenges has been the lack of collaboration and enforcement of the laws designed to punish traffickers. As the preceding section illustrates, there have been legislative advancements; however, there are also numerous barriers to enforcement that should be understood. Like in the cases of drugs and weapons, sex trafficking is market driven. The primary reason why it is thriving can largely be attributed to the principles of supply and demand. Furthermore, from a rational choice or classical criminology perspective of crime and criminality, there have historically been huge incentives from the perspective of the trafficking networks and controllers. Particularly, traffickers realize there is relatively low risk for being identified and prosecuted, and there is an extremely high-profit potential. Exacerbating the problem is that in some countries, official indifference to sexual exploitation of others leads to official participation in these crimes, and because of profit potential, corruption is of major concern (Jordan et al., 2013; Kotrla, 2010). Consequently, successful prosecution of perpetrators, traffickers, or trafficking networks requires a legitimate law enforcement body and criminal justice institutions that advocate fully for victims of sexual violence and exploitation.

The most paramount issues from a criminal justice practitioner perspective relate to the lack of collaboration among agencies who are oftentimes dealing with the same victim(s) and perpetrators. Particularly, the message has been clear: the key to successful law enforcement and prosecution of the traffickers is in promoting cooperation among countries, states, and agents who are working in the field.

Summary

Efforts have continued to be made to raise awareness as to the incidence and prevalence of sex trafficking and, also, for the trauma experienced by adult and child victims. As with other types of victimization, there are collateral consequences experienced most profoundly by victims of sex trafficking. These consequences may include exposure to serious health risks such as HIV/AIDS and other sexually transmitted diseases and substance abuse or addiction. Federal antitrafficking efforts have included initiatives by agencies such as the Department of Health and Human Services, which has provided funding for victim services, research, and awareness; the DOJ, which has created a Child Exploitation and Observing section and a Civil Rights Division, which includes a Human Trafficking and Prosecution Unit; Federal Bureau of Investigation, which has implemented an Anti-Human Trafficking Task Force and has led several civil rights investigations pertaining to trafficking networks; and the Department of Homeland Security and its creation of a Human Smuggling and Trafficking Unit.

Based on a review of the literature and the statistics that indicate the extent to which sex trafficking has become a critical issue for the United States and abroad, policy implications to address the needs of victims more effectively must be forthcoming. These may include the need for governments to attain full and effective participation of communities and organizations in anti-trafficking bodies, including law enforcement and victim identification and services groups. Trafficking prevention campaigns and efforts should be targeted to at-risk communities, particularly youth who are segregated and socially excluded. All communities and individuals should have access to prevention and protection services for adults and children alike, which may include safe houses or shelters for victims and their children, legal and social services, and education or vocational assistance. Perhaps most importantly, law enforcement should recognize victims of sex trafficking as a particularly vulnerable group of individuals who should not be held criminally liable for crimes they were forced to commit (TIP Report, 2014).

Discussion Questions*

1. If child victims of sex trafficking were taken out of the commercial sex environment permanently, do you think that they could fully recover from the injustices and trauma that they have previously faced? Why? Why not?
2. Sexual exploitation of adults and children is a global problem, and no continent, country, or state is immune. What do you think is at the source of the high demand that fuels the commercial sex trade? Do you think the issues illustrated in the chapter are unique to sex trafficking, or are these worldwide issues? What can we do for kids who have not been presented with an opportunity to leave the brothels or massage parlors? What kind of programs can we implement to create sustainable change for all victims of sex trafficking?
3. What does it mean to have a right to education? What challenges do sexually exploited children face in claiming their right to education? Should the possibility of being HIV positive affect your right to an education? Should your economic or social status affect your right to an education? Should being the child of a sex worker take away that right? Explain your answers.

References

ABC News Internet Ventures. (2014). *Jeffery Epstein News*. Retrieved from http://abcnews.go.com/topics/news/jeffrey-epstein-sex-offender.htm

Banks, D., & Kyckelhahn, T. (2011). *Characteristics of suspected human trafficking incidents, 2008–2010*. Washington, DC: Bureau of Justice Statistics.

Burke, A., & Ducci, S. (2005). *Trafficking in minors for commercial sexual exploitation: Thailand*. Torino, Italy: United Nations Interregional Crime and Justice Research Institute.

Butkus, A. S. (2007). Ending modern-day slavery in Florida: Strengthening Florida's legislation in combating human trafficking. *Stetson Law Review, 37*, 297.

Deshpande, N. A., & Nour, N. M. (2013). Sex trafficking of women and girls. *Reviews in Obstetrics and Gynecology, 6*(1), e22–e27.

Estes, R. J., & Weiner, N. A. (2001). *The commercial sexual exploitation of children in the US, Canada and Mexico*. Philadelphia, PA: University of Pennsylvania, School of Social Work, Center for the Study of Youth Policy.

* Discussion questions borrowed and adapted from http://www.newwestinghouse.org/ourpages/auto/2012/3/30/47968548/Born%20Into%20Brothels%20Activity%20Guide.pdf.

Jordan, J., Patel, B., & Rapp, L. (2013). Domestic minor sex trafficking: A social work perspective on misidentification, victims, buyers, traffickers, treatment, and reform of current practice. *Journal of Human Behavior in the Social Environment, 23*(3), 356–369.

Kotrla, K. (2010). Domestic minor sex trafficking in the United States. *Social Work, 55*(2), 181–187.

Martin, G. (2013). *Understanding terrorism: Challenges, perspectives, and issues*, Los Angeles, CA: Sage Publications.

National Human Trafficking Resource Center. (2011, April 15). Comparison *chart of primary sex trafficking networks in the U.S.* Retrieved from http://act.polarisproject.org/o/5417/t/0/blast-Content.jsp?email_blast_KEY=1160584

National Human Trafficking Resource Center. (2012, January). *The actions means purpose (AMP) model.* Retrieved from http://www.traffickingresourcecenter.org/resources/actions-means-purpose-amp-model

National Human Trafficking Resource Center. (2013, January). *Fake massage businesses at a glance.* Retrieved from http://www.traffickingresourcecenter.org/sex-trafficking-venuesindustries/fake-massage-businesses

National Human Trafficking Resource Center. (n.d.). *Residential brothels.* Retrieved from http://www.traffickingresourcecenter.org/sex-trafficking-venuesindustries/residential-brothels

Ngwe, J. E., & Elechi, O. O. (2012). Human trafficking: The modern day slavery of the 21st century. *African Journal of Criminology & Justice Studies, 6*, 103–119.

Polaris. (2014, September). *Potential indicators of human trafficking.* Retrieved from http://www.traffickingresourcecenter.org/resources/potential-indicators-human-trafficking

Reddington, F. P., & Kreisel, B. W. (2009). *Sexual assault: The victims, the perpetrators, and the criminal justice system* (2nd ed.). Durham, NC: Carolina Academic Press.

Simmonsen, D. (2008, March 3). Human smuggling ring with Fort Pierce ties is back in court. *TC Palm.* Retrieved from http://www.tcpalm.com/

Types of trafficking cases in the U.S. (2010). Retrieved from Polaris Project, http://www.polarisproject.org/resources/resources-by-topic/human-trafficking

UN General Assembly. (2000, November 15). *Protocol to prevent, suppress and punish trafficking in persons, especially women and children, supplementing the United Nations convention against transnational organized crime.* Available at: http://www.refworld.org/docid/4720706c0.html (accessed October 2, 2014).

U.S. Department of State. (2014, June 20). *2014 Trafficking in persons report—United States of America.* Available at: http://www.refworld.org/docid/53aab98612.html (accessed October 2, 2014).

United States of America (2000). *Victims of Trafficking and Violence Protection Act of 2000* (United States of America, Public Law 106–386) [H.R. 3244]. Retrieved October 28, 2000 from http://www.refworld.org/docid/3ae6b6104.html (accessed October 2, 2014).

Walker-Rodriguez, A., & Hill, R. (2011). Human sex trafficking. *FBI Law Enforcement Bulletin, 80*(3), 1–9.

Cybercrime

7

CATHERINE D. MARCUM

Contents

The invention and evolution of technology has allowed individuals of all ages, sexes, races, and religious preferences to increase the speed of a task by the unimaginable. Legal documents can be sent, travel arrangements can be booked, and checks can be deposited in a matter of seconds. Twenty years ago, a computer in a classroom was reserved for the occasional game or typing practice. Today, public school children and undergraduates have constant access to laptops, pads, and other forms of technology to aid them in learning exercises and research.

The Internet in itself has revolutionized society and allows us to access information instantaneously. However, along with the constantly improving technology, the Internet has allowed a whole new class of criminality to breed and flourish. Cybercrime, or criminal behavior utilizing some form of technology, can be committed by any person having access to the Internet. While the skill required varies for each type, there is a litany of destructive behaviors that can be performed with a click of a mouse.

According to Wall (2010), cybercrime developed over the course of three notable generations. Illegal exploitations of computers and operating systems, generally for financial gain or to destroy information, are the first generation of cybercrime. These crimes are considered "low-end" or ordinary forms of crime. The second generation of cybercrime involved utilizing networks, such as hacking into systems for free services or information. Often considered "hybrid crimes," these are crimes that already existed in the offline world but have transitioned online (Wall, 2007). Last, the third generation of cybercrime is crimes that exist simply because of the Internet. Crimes such as digital piracy and malware are categorized in this manner (Wall, 2010).

While some crimes are dominated by a particular sex, male and female offenders alike have fueled the cybercrime surge. In fact, anyone who has computer access and necessary skills to participate in a particular crime is able to be a cybercriminal no matter sex. The same applies for victims as any user of some form of technology can be victimized at any time. This chapter will examine the various categories of cybercrime. The differentiating offending and victimization behaviors by the sexes (if any) will be discussed. However, what will be apparent is that cybercrime is not just a man's game.

History and Current State of Categories of Cybercrime

Child Pornography

Gone are the days of ordering dirty magazines with inappropriate pictures of children that arrive in discretely wrapped packages with the hope federal law enforcement does not catch on. However, since the birth of the Internet, it has become much easier to access this illegal material without apprehension (Wells, Finkelhor, Wolak, & Mitchell, 2007). Expert collectors and producers use specific codes and hidden locations online to distribute the material to make it more difficult for law enforcement to zero in on the perpetrators and their location.

The definition of a child can vary depending on the concept considered. Physical and psychological maturity varies, especially with regard to puberty, emotional maturity, and sexual behavior. However, with respect to participation in sexually explicit pictures or movies (aka pornography), the United States requires an individual be at least 18 years old (Gillespie, 2011). Specifically, United States Code, Chapter 110 defines the illegal act of the production of child pornography to constitute the following:

> advertises, promotes, presents, distributes, or solicits through the mails, or using any means or facility of interstate or foreign commerce or in or affecting interstate or foreign commerce by any means, including by computer, any material or purported material in a manner that reflects the belief, or that is intended to cause another to believe, that the material or purported material is, or contains—
>
> (i) an obscene visual depiction of a minor engaging in sexually explicit conduct; or
> (ii) a visual depiction of an actual minor engaging in sexually explicit conduct.

It has been difficult to solidify the legal definition of child pornography based on the debate centered in the Supreme Court (Marcum, Higgins, Ricketts, & Freiburger, 2011). Most notably are the cases *New York v. Ferber* (1982), stating that the material must contain sexual conduct by children and is not protected by the First Amendment, and *Ashcroft v. Free Speech Coalition* (2002), where the Court ruled that digitally created images could not be considered child pornography. In other words, only materials featuring actual live children are considered child pornography.

Child pornography–related offenses can be separated into three main categories: production, distribution, and possession. According to 18 U.S.C. §2251, production of child pornography can involve several different actions. First, it includes methods of inducing a minor to participate, or assist in sexual conduct. It also criminalizes parental permission that allows a child to be used in production of child pornography. Further, advertising material for distribution is also a criminal offense. However, based on 18 U.S.C. §2252, individuals can only be charged with production or possession of materials if they participate "knowingly," which means they must possess the *mens rea* to commit the crime

(*Harvard Law Review*, 2009). For instance, receipt of materials through unsolicited e-mails or viruses does not result in criminal charges if the recipient reports it immediately and can demonstrate it was not requested.

Possession of child pornography is defined by *United States v. Tucker* (305 F.3d 1193) as "having something as one's own, or in one's control" (2002, p. 1204). Access of child pornography with the intention to view is also a criminal activity as of 2008 [18 U.S.C. §2252A(a)(5)]. Further, simply deleting the material from a computer or technological device does not relieve control of child pornography. If an individual protests possession charges, he or she must demonstrate one of the following: (1) possession of three or less images; (2) good faith steps to destroy the image and report it to law enforcement; and (3) refusal of access of the material except to law enforcement (Marcum, 2013).

Last, individuals can be charged with distribution of child pornography if they knowingly transport the material in some way (e.g., U.S. mail, e-mail) [18 U.S.C. §2252A(a)(1)]. In addition, *United States v. Goff* [155 Fed.Appx. 773 (2005)] ruled that if an e-mail came from an offender's account, it did not have to be located on the computer hard drive for an individual to be charged with distribution. And finally, the United States Code also indicated that if material is considered inappropriate, it is termed dissemination.

At any time, up to 1 million images of child pornography can be available online at one time, with 200 new images posted daily. Perpetrators of child pornography offenses do not discriminate with regard to material online, as children of all races, ages, and sexes are present. Further, an online child pornography website can get up to one million hits in a month. The child pornography industry often operates in rings, rather than with individual producers. There are estimates between 50,000 and 100,000 operational rings in the world, with one-third of those being the United States alone (Wortley & Smallbone, 2012).

Case Study 1

On August 4, 2011, 50 members engaged in a child pornography ring who performed atrocious crimes against children ranging from infancy to age 12 were arrested. While the ring was based in the United States, participants spanned 5 continents and 14 different countries. Further, 72 members of online site that portrayed images from the ring, Dreamboard, were arrested after an intense investigation by federal law enforcement officers beginning in 2009 (otherwise known as Operation Delago). The lure of the website for users was a display of pictures that involved distress or pain experienced by the children as a result of the sexual activity (*Chicago Tribune*, 2011).

Cyberbullying

One of the more prevalent cybercrimes in the media spotlight recently has been that of cyberbullying, often because of the atrocious reactions by teenagers who are victimized in this way. Cyberbullying is the "willful and repeated harm inflicted through the use of computers, cell phones and electronic devices" (Hinduja & Patchin, 2008, 2009). This form of cybercrime can occur in several different ways:

1. Harassment—Repetitive, offensive messages
2. Outing—Unintended sharing of personal information, such as sexual preferences or telephone number

3. Flaming—A virtual argument, or exchange of insults
4. Denigration—Posting inappropriate and hurtful information about others
5. Exclusion—Isolation of the victim

These forms of cyberbullying can occur in multiple ways, but most often as posting on social networking sites, texts or e-mails (Beckstrom, 2008; Hinduja & Patchin, 2008, 2009; Kowalski, Limber, & Agatston, 2008).

Individuals who are cyberbullying offenders often have dominant, aggressive personalities with a short fuse (temper). They may show little remorse for their actions and compassion for victims (Camodeca & Gooseens, 2005; Hinduja & Patchin, 2007). Instead, they are proud of their behavior and feel as if abusing someone compensates for a wrong done to them. Hinduja and Patchin (2008) found that individuals who are computer proficient and spend longer amounts of time online also are more likely to commit cyberbullying acts, especially if their peers are also participating in the behavior.

The aforementioned characteristics could apply to males or females. However, we know from psychological literature that males more often participate in direct aggression while females tend to use indirect forms of aggression (Bjorkquist, Lagerspetz, & Osterman, 1992). In other words, males settle disputes with fists and violence, while females spread gossip and false statements. Due to these inherent traits of males and females, it would be reasonable to assume that females are more likely to participate in cyberbullying as there is no face-to-face contact. Studies have supported this assumption (Kowalski & Witte, 2006; Marcum, Higgins, Freiburger, & Ricketts, 2012), but more so in younger adolescents (i.e., middle and high school students) compared to undergraduates.

With regard to the victims of cyberbullying, it is assumed by many that offenders and victims are always minors, but that is not always the case. Adults and minors have both reported victimization in this manner. However, regardless of age or sex, victimization via cyberbullying can have devastating effects. Victims can become depressed or experience stress and anxiety (Ybarra & Mitchell, 2004). Their self-esteem can be challenged and they shrink back from social situations. Sadly, some cyberbullying victims turn to suicide to deal with the stress. Hinduja and Patchin (2010) found that cyberbullying victims were 1.9 times more likely to commit suicide compared to those who had not been cyberbullied. Media plagued cases such as Megan Meier, Amanda Todd, and Tyler Clementi are three of the many young people who took their own lives as a result of cyberbullying.

Cyberstalking

Much like cyberbullying, cyberstalking is similar in many ways to the physical version. Stalking involves intruding on another person to invoke fear or distress (McEwan, Mullen, MacKenzie, & Ogloff, 2009). Cyberstalking also uses various forms of harassment to intimidate and upset victims (e.g., sending hostile messages or threats), or gather and post personal information (Sheridan & Grant, 2007; Turmanis & Brown, 2006). Further, cyberstalkers can pretend to be a victim online and sign into social networking websites, post hurtful messages, or send inappropriate pictures. However, the benefit for cyberstalkers is that millions of victims are at easy disposal and choosing for offenders simply by having an e-mail address or social networking website profile. Offenders can change identity or be completely anonymous to the victims, giving more power to participate in stalking behaviors (Bocij, 2004). Victims of cyberstalkers are more likely to be females, mirroring the qualities of victims in the physical world. However, victims are cyberstalked more by acquaintances or strangers rather than intimate partners, which again is the benefit of using the Internet to perpetrate.

Bocij (2004) further confirms cyberstalking is a true criminal problem by disproving myths about the behavior. For instance, there is an assumption that cyberstalkers are obsessive as physical stalkers. This is not true as cyberstalkers can randomly select victims and may just enjoy making others they do not know uncomfortable. Also, there is an assumption that cyberstalkers cause less harm than offline stalkers, as victims can experience emotional, financial, and physical repercussions. Last, cyberstalking is not an offshoot of offline stalking. While some online stalkers do continue stalking a person offline, the behaviors used online can be completely different (Bocij, 2004).

Case Study 2

Kenna Haight, 27, a former student at the University of Missouri–Kansas City, pled guilty on August 14, 2014, to cyberstalking a faculty member. Haight repeatedly sent harassing and threatening e-mail messages between October and December 2013 to the faculty member, such as

- "I am having homicidal fantasies that keep me up at night about you."
- "I seriously want to hurt you, you know that?"
- "You may find yourself in your own bed begging for mercy."

Under Federal Statute, Haight is subject to a mandatory minimum of at least 1 year in prison plus a $250,000 fine (FBI, 2014).

Digital Piracy

Digital piracy is the illegal downloading of digital material, such as music, movies, and software. In order words, it is the theft of material without permission from the copyright holder (Gopal et al., 2004), and it is extremely prevalent in the world of cybercriminality. For example, between 2004 and 2009, 30 billion songs were illegally downloaded (Recording Industry Association of America, 2012). Software piracy rates are up 88% in Venezuela (Business Software Alliance, 2012). Further, the financial loss caused by pirated materials is devastating, despite the rationalization by many offenders that it is a victimless crime. The theft of copyrighted music has cost approximately $12.5 billion, $422 million in tax revenues, and 71,000 jobs (Siwek, 2007).

This particular cybercrime does not take a lot of computer skill, it is easy to do, and there is little planning required (Higgins & Marcum, 2011). Music and movies are generally stolen from peer-to-peer networks, which is accessible by any Internet user. Software piracy can be performed simply by installing multiple copies of licensed software, or sharing purchased software with friends for their own use. Further, the majority of digital pirates are under the age of 21, and therefore do not have advanced degrees (Higgins, 2005). Generally, piracy is a not a crime with a huge sex differential. While software piracy is typically committed by young males as they install software more than females (Business Software Alliance, 2012), music and movie piracy is performed by males and females alike.

Hacking

The conventional definition of hacking is unauthorized access of a computer system with criminal intention (Taylor, Fritsch, Liederbach, & Holt, 2010); in other words, the popular belief is that hacking is a crime. Hacking is associated with digital piracy, breaking into a computer system, using viruses, and committing fraud (Rogers, Smoak, & Liu, 2005). True hackers object to the assertion that hacking is only a crime, as to them it is an achievement earned through knowledge and skill. For example, skilled hackers assert that piracy is a separate crime as any unskilled computer user can pirate a song or movie.

The hacker subculture is a secretive community, so it is difficult to fully understand the organization of the participants. Research has indicated that there are various methods of categorizing hackers, generally by level of skill and activity online. One of the more popular ways of labeling hackers is simply as "old" and "new." Old hackers support information sharing and the open software movement (Best, 2003), while new hackers are interested in finding online security flaws and exposing them so they can be fixed. Hackers can also be categorized as "white hat" or "black hat." White hats are ethical hackers who seek to improve security system, but operate under the motto of "do no harm" (Holt, 2007). They may use their skills to notify companies of security issues, promote social change, or press for online safety of youth. Black hats, on the other hand, have the goal of exploiting and destroying. These individuals may destroy files or operating systems, stalk individuals, or participate in cyberterrorism. Even more destructive and dangerous are those hackers who participate in cyber warfare, which is the politically motivated hacking of one nation against another with the intention of destroying or disrupting national security (Clarke, 2010). For example, China has been accused of cyber warfare against the American, Russian, and Indiana governments.

Individuals who participate in destructive hacking may choose to use a form of malware to accomplish their goals. Trojan horses, viruses, and worms can infect computers and destroy files, or copy and transfer files without authorization. Spyware allows the offender to access passwords, e-mail accounts, and private websites (Furnell, 2010). In addition, those pesky pop-ups that occur during Internet surfing may be adware, which can infiltrate computers if clicked on by unsuspecting users.

Any individual of any demographic can be the victim of a hacker. Offender characteristics, however, are a bit different. Skinner and Fream (1997), along with other studies, have indicated that hackers are generally male. Specifically, educated males who are White or Asian are more likely to participate in hacking compared to any other group. In fact, the profile of a hacker is akin to a white collar criminal. However, the gender gap in hacker offender is not a result of intelligence, but lack of acceptance of females. A study of hacker chat rooms indicated that female hackers do not receive respect and are harassed by the male members (Holt & Bossler, 2009; Segan, 2000). Despite public forums and conventions available to hackers, females often shy away from participating as they are labeled "scene whores" and not respected as legitimate hackers (Segan, 2000).

Prostitution

Potentially one of the oldest forms of criminality, prostitution is constantly a controversial and debated topic. Is it a victimless crime? Should it be legalized and regulated for economic benefit? However, what is not up for debate is the fact that prostitution is a female-dominated crime and has the most negative repercussions and backlash on women. The development of the Internet has allowed these offenders to take their business to a new level with respect to finances, advertising, and safety.

Pre-Internet, prostitutes could simply advertise their services by wearing certain types of clothing and walking up and down streets. This type of advertisement by "street-walkers" generally occurred in unsafe areas of cities and often resulted in the assault of the women. Further, law enforcement apprehension is frequent and prostitution stings occur often. With the birth of the Internet, prostitutes could advertise their services online in a more discreet fashion. Eros.com was the first advertising site initiated in 1997 and allowed individuals to post information about their physical characteristics, willingness to travel, services provided, and costs (Cunningham & Kendall, 2011). In order to decrease the likelihood of law enforcement apprehension, prostitutes can use encrypted e-mail addresses (Holt & Blevins, 2007; Holt, Blevins, & Kuhns, 2008).

Online sites can also be used to rate and discuss the encounters between client and prostitute. Future clients can make informed choices based on the feedback from past clients. Message boards can include the date and time of the encounter, services offered, and the quality of the services. Further, if a prostitute has a long history of reviews, she is less likely to be law enforcement (Cunningham & Kendall, 2011).

Rating sites can also be beneficial for the safety of the prostitute, as the background of the client can be checked for previous assaults, hygiene issues, or problems with receipt of payment. Prostitutes also use e-mail services or blacklisting websites, such as the National Blacklist, to evaluate clients and search for "dirty Johns." They can even register with the National Blacklist to receive QuikAlerts via text message regarding any police activity in a specific area (Peppet, 2013). Last, identity verification services are funded by small fees paid by clients, which allows prostitutes to confirm the asserted information provided by a client.

Unfortunately, not all participation in prostitution is a victimless crime committed by free will. Adults and children are often victims of human trafficking for sex, defined by the Victims of Trafficking and Violence Protection Act (VTVPA) (2000) as "recruitment, harboring, transportation, provision, or obtaining of a person for the purpose of a commercial sex act" (p. 8). Human sex trafficking is an especially prevalent problem in the United States for minors, as over 100,000 children are victims of domestic minor sex trafficking (Smith, 2008). According to Kara (2009), there is a $91 billion profit associated with human sex trafficking and due to this extreme profit, the Internet Crimes Against Children Task Force has seen a 914% increase in child sex prostitution.

Scams and Cons

There are multiple ways that an individual can be scammed online. Potentially, the most popularly known form of online scam is identity theft, which is stealing an individual's personal information for the use of fraudulent activity (Moore, 2011). Essentially, identity theft can occur in two forms: theft of a person's physical identity or the more common version, theft of information for financial gain. Stolen Social Security numbers, names, birthdates, and other forms of personal information can be used to open up credit cards, take out loans, or make purchases online. Further, stolen login information and passwords can be used to make unauthorized posts or send e-mails, otherwise known as "virtual identity theft."

Identity theft can occur in a multitude of ways. *"Dumpster diving"* involves the theft of information from a person's garbage. For example, credit card applications and other paperwork are often thrown away without consideration that the information can be used in a fraudulent manner. This is extremely popular in university settings as students often toss their unwanted mail into a main trash can in the post office area. "Phishing" involves a person claiming to be a legitimate business or website to obtain personal information, such as e-mails from banks asking for a person's login and password. Last, another example is "shoulder surfing," which is simply watching an individual punch in a PIN or password and using it later for fraudulent activity.

There are multitudes of other forms of scams online in addition to identity theft. Product counterfeiting, Nigerian letter fraud, auction fraud, and other schemes are used to scam individuals from their money. This particular category of cybercrime does not have one particular type of participant as all demographics can offend or be victimized. Some research has indicated that victims of online scams are generally financially stable with some education past the high school level (Dolan, 2004), but there does not appear to be differential behavior between the sexes.

Sexting

One of the more recent controversial topics surrounding cybercrime is the debate of the legitimacy of sexting as an actual crime. Sexting is the sending or receiving of sexually suggestive and/or explicit images from one cell phone to another (Hinduja & Patchin, 2010; Judge, 2012; Mitchell, Finkelhor, Jones, & Wolak, 2012), and it is a prevalent behavior especially among adolescents. An early study by Lenhart (2009) found that 4% of youth between 12 and 17 years old had sent a sexually suggestive picture, and 15% reported receiving one. Hinduja and Patchin (2010) found slightly higher results with their sample of 11–18 years old, asserting that 7.7% of the sample has sent a message and 12.9% had received one. However, both studies did not find a distinct difference in these behaviors between males and females.

As time has passed, studies have found an increase in sexting behaviors, as high as over 30% of participating respondents (Dake, Price, & Maziarz, 2012; Temple et al., 2012). Of these studies, Strassberg, McKinnon, Sustaita, and Rullo's (2013) was the only one that indicated a difference in behaviors between the sexes, with males participating more than females. However, Temple et al. (2012) did find that girls who used or participated in risky behaviors, such as drug/alcohol use and promiscuous sex, were more likely to participate in sexting.

Many researchers have argued that sexting is a legitimate means of intimate expression between two consenting individuals (Lee, Crofts, Salter, Milivojevic, & McGovern, 2013; Shafron-Perez, 2009). However, there are a few contingencies with this assumption. First, not all recipients of sexting material are consenting. Second, even if the material is between two consenting adults, it is still considered a "risky" behavior as the images can be saved indefinitely, shared against their knowledge to other cell phone users, or posted on a social networking website without permission (Ling & Yttri, 2005; Wastler, 2010). This unapproved forwarding of the picture can result in emotional distress, bullying, and other forms of harassment from peers (Barkacs & Barkacs, 2010; Hinduja & Patchin, 2010; Strassberg et al., 2013).

However, potentially the biggest risk associated with sexting is the potential for involvement in child pornography. There have been several instances in which youth have been charged with possession and distribution of child pornography as a result of sexting (Barkacs & Barkacs, 2010; Hinduja & Patchin, 2010). Wolak, Finkelhor, and Mitchell (2012) found that between 2008 and 2009, almost 3500 cases of youth sexting were investigated and 18% of the investigations resulted in arrest. Although some of the charges are reduced to misdemeanors for adolescents who are charged, the danger is real (Lenhart, 2009). For instance, if a minor female sends a naked picture of herself to her boyfriend who is 18, he could be charged with possession of child pornography. Further, if the boyfriend forwards the picture to some of his adult friends, he could also be charged with distribution.

Case Study 3

A 16-year-old female in British Columbia is one of the first minors to be convicted of a child pornography charge related to sexting in Canada. The girl, who is unnamed due to her age, sexted pictures of her boyfriend's ex-girlfriend (a minor) to a few other cell phone users after discovering he was still in contact with her. In January 2014, a court found her guilty of the crime, as well as uttering threats against the ex-girlfriend. Crown Prosecutor Chandra Fisher hoped this conviction would prove to be a warning for other teenagers involved in the behavior. The convicted female is out on bail while awaiting sentencing (Conlon, 2014).

Sexual Solicitation

The availability of the Internet has increased the access of sexual predators to individuals of all ages. Sexual solicitation (the persuasion to talk about sex, do something sexual, or reveal personal sexual information) can be wanted or unwanted by the recipient (Mitchell, Finkelhor, & Wolak, 2007). However, sexual solicitation is most frequently associated with adults trying to lure minors into sexual activity online or offline, such as cybersex, masturbation, or viewing pornography (Bryce, 2010). These adult perpetrators are able to manipulate young people into participating in this activity through the grooming process, which begins with a nonsexual relationship. The adult earns the trust of the young person through trust-building conversations, much as normal relationships are formed between two adults. This relationship builds into an exchange of more personal information, telephone numbers, and even a proclamation of romantic feelings. The adult is taking advantage of the trusting nature of an adolescent, the desire to be loved, and naivety.

Early research using the first administration of the Youth Internet Safety Survey (YISS) data indicated that females were considered to be the main target of sexual solicitation online (Mitchell, Finkehor, & Wolak, 2003). The second administration of the YISS revealed similar findings, as females were more likely to report sexual solicitation. These female respondents were more likely to post personal information on blogs. Further, analysis of the data indicated that black females who had a past history of victimization were more likely to be asked to share pornographic photographs of themselves (Mitchell, Finkelhor, & Wolak, 2007; Mitchell, Wolak, & Finkehor, 2008). More recent studies using a dataset of college undergraduates found that females were more likely to be sexually solicited as high school seniors compared to males. However, the males in the study were more likely to report sexual solicitation as college freshmen compared to the females (Marcum, 2009).

There are studies that have further delved into the characteristics of participants of sexual solicitation. The YISS-2 found that aggressive sexual solicitors were most commonly male and 18 years old (Mitchell et al., 2007). On the other hand, recipients of sexual solicitation were more likely to be female and engage in conversation about sex with individuals online. Young recipients of sexual solicitation generally participate in risky behaviors online, such as disclosure of personal information, discussing sex, and harassing others (Marcum, Higgins, & Ricketts, 2010; Ybarra & Mitchell, 2007).

Unwanted sexual solicitation can have a variety of negative repercussions on its victims, as well as increase likelihood of victimization. The recipients may choose to remove personal information from their Facebook pages, or simply cancel the account. They may experience insecurities, uneasy feelings, a lack of safety, or anxiety. As a result, they may turn to alcohol or substance abuse, or criminal activity (Saunders, 2003). Further, teenagers with more advanced forms of mental illness are more likely to be sexually solicited as they often seek any form of attention (Schrock & Boyd, 2009).

Conclusion

Unlike other categories of crime, cybercrime is not dominated by one sex. While certain types of cybercrimes are more likely to a particular sex perpetrate the behavior, such as female offender participation in online prostitution or male offenders controlling the hacking world, overall it is an equal opportunity form of criminality. Further, policies and programs developed to combat cybercrime often target the environment of the behavior rather than the offender.

One of the classic, yet simple, methods of combating cybercrime is that of target hardening (CITE). In other words, target hardening is the creation of methods of protection online to make it more difficult for an individual to access information or websites. Based on Routine Activities Theory, it addresses the patterns of the user online that can often leave an individual wide open for victimization. For instance, many Internet users will use the same password for important accounts as it is easy to remember. This makes identity theft or hacking easy for offenders who steal the password. Simply changing your passwords regularly and not having the same password for your accounts, e-mail, and social networking websites will prevent this victimization. Further, individuals should not share their passwords with others to prevent unauthorized access.

Other forms of victimization are more difficult to prevent, and the legal repercussions have increased due to media coverage. Federal and state legislation has changed drastically to either include electronic language in bullying and stalking statutes, or create separate laws to prosecute and punish these cybercriminals. Computer usage and safe Internet use education programs are available online, as well as brought into schools and communities. One issue with regard to victimization is that young online users who are cyberbullied or cyberstalked often will not report their victimization for fear of having the technology taken away. They would rather continue to be harassed rather than lose computer or cell phone access. However, by educating youth on how to protect themselves and the importance of reporting, it is the hope that these reservations will go away.

There are certain government efforts aimed solely at apprehending and punishing offenders. One of the more popular efforts targeted at crimes against children (i.e., sexual solicitation, enticement, and child pornography) is the Internet Crimes Against Children

(ICAC) Task Force Program, which originated in 1998 with the Justice Appropriations Act. Continued funding was provided by the PROTECT and Recovery Acts. Since its inception in 1998, over 300,000 law enforcement officers and other professionals have been trained to investigate and prosecute related crimes. Further, over 30,000 arrests have been made from ICAC investigations (Office of Juvenile Justice and Delinquency Prevention, 2014). In addition, the National Center for Missing and Exploited Children sponsors the Child Victim Identification Program, which also assists in the identification of victims and arrests of child predators. Despite what efforts are taken, it is apparent that education of the general public is extremely important. Further, efforts do not need to be targeted specifically at males or females as both parties are participants and victims of the crimes on a fairly equal level.

Discussion Questions

1. What categories of cybercrime victimization do you feel would be particularly dangerous to females?
2. Is charging a young person with a child pornography offense with regard to sexting too harsh? Why/why not?
3. What online behaviors do you and your friends perform that could be placing you at risk for victimization?

References

Ashcroft v. Free Speech Coalition, 535 U.S. 234 (2002).

Barkacs, L., & Barkacs, C. (2010). Do you think I'm sexty? Minors and sexting: Teenage fad or child pornography? *Journal of Legal, Ethical and Regulatory Issues, 13*, 23–31.

Beckstrom, D. (2008). State legislation mandating school cyberbullying policies and the potential threat to students' free speech rights. *Vermont Law Review, 33*, 283–321.

Best, K. (2003). The hacker's challenge: Active access to information, visceral democracy and discursive practice. *Social Semiotics, 13*(3), 263–282.

Bjorkquist, K., Lagerspetz, K., & Kaukianini, A. (1992). Do girls manipulate and boys fight? Developmental trends in regard to direct and indirect aggression. *Aggressive Behavior, 18*, 117–127.

Bocij, P. (2004). *Cyberstalking: Harassment in the Internet age and how to protect your family.* Westport, CT: Praeger.

Bryce, J. (2010). Online sexual exploitation of children and young people. In Y. Jewkes & M. Yar (Eds.), *Handbook of Internet crime* (pp. 320–342). Devon, U.K.: Willan Publishing, xvii.

Business Software Alliance. (2012). *Shadow market: 2011 BSA global software piracy study.* Retrieved May 27, 2012 from http://portal.bsa.org/globalpiracy2011/downloads/study_pdf/2011_BSA_Piracy_Study-InBrief.pdf

Camodeca, M., & Goossens, F. (2005). Aggression, social cognitions, anger and sadness in sadness in bullies and victims. *Journal of Child Psychology & Psychiatry, 46*, 186–197.

Chicago Tribune. (2011). *72 charged in online global porn ring.* Retrieved August 19, 2014, from http://www.chicagotribune.com/entertainment/ktla-global-child-porn-ring-story.html

Clarke, R. (2010). *Cyber war.* New York: HarperCollins.

Conlon, K. (2014, January 10). Canadian teen convicted of sexting photos of boyfriend's ex. Retrieved August 19, 2014, from http://www.cnn.com/2014/01/10/world/americas/canada-sexting-teen/index.html?iref=storysearch

Cunningham, S., & Kendall, T. (2011). Prostitution 2.0: The changing face of sex work. *Journal of Urban Economics, 69*(2011), 273–287.

Dake, J. A., Price, J. H., & Maziarz, L. (2012). Prevalence and correlates of sexting behavior in adolescents. *American Journal of Sexuality Education, 7*, 1–15. Retrieved January 5, 2013 from http://dx.doi.org/10.1080/15546128.2012.650959

Dolan, K. (2004). Internet auction fraud: The silent victims. *Journal of Economic Crime Management, 2*, 1–22.

FBI gov. (2014). *Former student pleads guilty to cyberstalking University of Missouri-Kansas City instructor.* Retrieved August 18, 2014, from http://www.fbi.gov/kansascity/press-releases/2014/former-student-pleads-guilty-to-cyberstalking-university-of-missouri-kansas-city-instructor

Furnell, S. (2010). Hackers, viruses and malicious software. In T. Jewkes & M. Yar (Eds.), *Handbook of Internet crime* (pp. 173–193). Portland, OR: Willan Publishing.

Gillespie, A. (2011). *Child pornography: Law and policy.* New York: Routledge.

Gopal, R. D., Sanders, G. L., Bhattacharjee, S., Agrawal, M. S., & Wagner, S. C. (2004). A behavioral model of digital music piracy. *Journal of Organizational Computing and Electronic Commerce, 14*, 89–105.

Harvard Law Review. (2009). Child pornography, the Internet, and the challenge of updating statutory terms. *Harvard Law Review, 122*(8), 2206–2227.

Higgins, G. (2005). Can low self-control help with the understanding of the software piracy problem? *Deviant Behavior, 26*, 1–24.

Higgins, G., & Marcum, C. D. (2011). *Digital piracy: An integrated theoretical approach.* Durham, NC: Carolina Academic Press.

Hinduja, S., & Patchin, J. (2007). Offline consequences of online victimization: School violence and delinquency. *Journal of School Violence, 6*(3), 89–112.

Hinduja, S., & Patchin, J. (2008). Cyberbullying: An exploratory analysis of factors related to offending and victimization. *Deviant Behavior, 29*(2), 1–29.

Hinduja, S., & Patchin, J. (2009). *Bullying beyond the schoolyard: Preventing and responding to cyberbullying.* Thousand Oaks, CA: Sage Publications (Corwin Press).

Hinduja, S., & Patchin, J. W. (2010). Bullying, cyberbullying, and suicide. *Archives of Suicide Research, 14*(3), 206–221.

Holt, T., & Blevins, K. (2007). Examining sex work from the client's perspective: Assessing johns using online data. *Deviant Behavior, 28*, 333–354.

Holt, T., Blevins, K., & Kuhns, J. (2008). Examining the displacement practices of johns with online data. *Journal of Criminal Justice, 36*, 522–528.

Holt, T. J. (2007). Subcultural evolution? Examining the influence of on- and off-line experiences on deviant subcultures. *Deviant Behavior, 28*, 171–198.

Holt, T. J., & Bossler, A. M. (2009). Examining the applicability of lifestyle-routine activities theory for cybercrime victimization. *Deviant Behavior, 28*, 1–25.

Judge, A. M. (2012). "Sexting" among U.S. adolescents: Psychological and legal perspectives. *Harvard Review of Psychiatry, 20*, 86–96.

Kara, S. (2009, January 8). *The business of sex trafficking.* [Audio podcast]. Retrieved January 5, 2013 from http://www.wnyc.org/shows/lopate/episodes/2009/01/08/segments/120435

Kowalski, R., Limber, S., & Agatston, P. (2008). *Cyberbullying: Bullying in the digital age.* Maldon, MA: Blackwell Publishing.

Kowalski, R., & Witte, J. (2006). *Youth Internet survey.* Retrieved January 5, 2013 from http://www.camss.clemson.edu/KowalskiSurvey/servelet/Page1

Lee, M., Crofts, T., Salter, M., Milivojevic, S., & McGovern, A. (2013). 'Let's get sexting': Risk, power, sex and criminalisation in the moral domain. *International Journal for Crime and Justice, 2*, 35–49.

Lenhart, A. (2009). *Teens and sexting: How and why minor teens are sending sexually suggestive nude or nearly nude images via text messaging.* Washington, DC: Pew Internet & American Life Project.

Ling, R., & Yttri, B. (2005). Control, emancipation, and status: The mobile telephone in teen's parental and peer group control relationships. In: R. Kraut, M. Brynin, & S. Kiesler (Eds.), *New information technologies at home: The domestic impact of computing and telecommunications* (pp. 219–235). Oxford, U.K.: Oxford University Press.

Marcum, C. D. (2009). Identifying potential factors of adolescent online victimization in high school seniors. *International Journal of Cyber Criminology, 2*(2), 346–367.

Marcum, C. D. (2013). *Cyber crime.* New York: Wolters Kluwer Law & Business, Aspen College Series.

Marcum, C. D., Higgins, G. E., Freiburger, T. L., & Ricketts, M. L. (2012). Battle of the sexes: An examination of male and female cyberbullying. *International Journal of Cyber Criminology, 6*(1), 904–911.

Marcum, C. D., Higgins, G. E., & Ricketts, M. L. (2010). Potential factors of online victimization of youth: An examination of adolescent online behaviors utilizing Routine Activities Theory. *Deviant Behavior, 31*(5), 1–31.

Marcum, C. D., Higgins, G. E., Ricketts, M. L., & Freiburger, T. L. (2011). Investigation of the training and resources dedicated nationally to the investigation of production of child pornography. *Policing: A Journal of Policy and Practice, 5*(1), 23–32.

McEwan, T., Mullen, P., MacKenzie, P., & Ogloff, J. (2009). Violence in stalking situations. *Psychological Medicine, 39*, 1469–1478.

Mitchell, K. J., Finkelhor, D., Jones, L. M., & Wolak, J. (2012). Prevalence and characteristics of youth sexting: A national study. *Pediatrics, 129*, 13–20. doi:10.1542/peds.2011-1730.

Mitchell, K., Finkelhor, D., & Wolak, J. (2003). The exposure of youth to unwanted sexual material on the Internet: A national survey of risk, impact and prevention. *Youth & Society, 34*(3), 3300–3358.

Mitchell, K. J., Finkelhor, D., & Wolak, J. (2007). Online requests for sexual pictures from youth: Risk factors and incident characteristics. *Journal of Adolescent Health, 41,* 196–203.

Mitchell, K., Wolak, J., & Finkelhor, D. (2008). Are blogs putting youth at risk for online sexual solicitation or harassment? *Child Abuse and Neglect, 32*, 277–294.

Moore, R. (2011). *Cybercrime: Investigating high-technology computer crime* (2nd ed.). Philadelphia, PA: Anderson Publishing.

New York v. Ferber, 458 U.S. 747 (1982).

Office of Juvenile Justice and Delinquency Prevention. (2014). *Internet crimes against children task force.* Retrieved August 17, 2014, from http://www.ojjdp.gov/programs/progsummary.asp?pi=3#Resources

Peppet, S. (2013). Prostitution 3.0? *Iowa Law Review, 98*(5), 1989–2060.

Recording Industry Association of America. (2012). *Scope of the problem.* Retrieved August 16, 2014, from http://www.riaa.com/physicalpiracy.php?content_selector=piracy-online-scope-of-the-problem

Rogers, M., Smoak, N., & Liu, J. (2005). Self-reported deviant computer behavior: A big-5, moral choice, and manipulative exploitive behavior analysis. *Deviant Behavior, 27*, 245–268.

Saunders, B. (2003). Understanding children exposed to violence: Toward an integration of overlapping fields. *Journal of Interpersonal Violence, 18*(4), 356–376.

Schrock, S., & Boyd, D. (2009). *Online threats to youth: Solicitation, harassment, and problematic content: A review by the research advisory board of the Internet safety technical task force.* Retrieved July 2, 2009, from http://cyber.law.harvard.edu/research/isttf/RAB

Segan, S. (2000). Female hackers battle sexism to get ahead. *ABC News.* Retrieved May 1, 2012, from http://abcnews.go.com/Technology/story?id=99341&page=1

Shafron-Perez, S. (2009). Average teenager or sex offender? Solutions to the legal dilemma caused by sexting. *The John Marshall Journal of Computer & Information Law, 26*, 431–451.

Sheridan, L., & Grant, T. (2007). Is cyberstalking different? *Psychology, Crime & Law, 13*(6), 627–640.

Siwek, S. (2007). *The true cost of sound recording piracy to the U.S. economy.* Institute for Policy Innovation. Retrieved May 27, 2012, from http://www.ipi.org/IPI/IPIPublications.nsf/PublicationLookupExecutiveSummary/9631E78559D421458625733E0052D370

Skinner, W., & Fream, A. (1997). A social learning theory analysis of computer crime among college students. *Journal of Research in Crime and Delinquency, 34,* 495–518.

Smith, L. (2008, July). Keynote address. Delivered at Catholic Charities Anti-Human Trafficking Training. San Antonio, TX.

Strassberg, D. S., McKinnon, R. K., Sustaita, M. A., & Rullo, J. (2013). Sexting by high school students: An exploratory and descriptive study. *Archives of Sexual Behavior, 42,* 15–21.

Taylor, R. W., Fritsch, E. J., Liederbach, J., & Holt, T. J. (2010). *Digital crime and digital terrorism* (2nd ed.). Upper Saddle River, NJ: Pearson Prentice Hall.

Temple, J. R., Paul, J. A., van den Berg, P., Le, V., McElhany, A., & Temple, B. W. (2012). Teen sexting and its association with sexual behaviors. *Archives of Pediatrics and Adolescent Medicine, 166,* 828–833.

Turmanis, S., & Brown, R. (2006). The stalking and harassment behavior scale: Measuring the incidence, nature, and severity of stalking and relational harassment and their psychological effects. *Psychology and Psychotherapy: Theory, Research and Practice, 79,* 183–198.

United States v. Goff, 155 Fed.Appx. 773 (2005).

United States v. Tucker, 305 F.3d 1193 (2002).

Wall, D. S. (2007). Policing cybercrime: Situating the public police in networks of security in cyberspace. *Police Practice and Research: An International Journal, 8*(2), 183–205.

Wall, D. S. (2010). Micro-Frauds: Virtual robberies, stings and scams in the information age. In T. Holt & B. Schell (Eds.), *Corporate hacking and technology-driven crime: Social dynamics and implications* (pp. 68–85). Hershey, PA: IGI Global, Information Science Reference.

Wastler, S. (2010). The harm in 'sexting'?: Analyzing the constitutionality of child pornography statutes that prohibit the voluntary production, possession, and dissemination of sexually explicit images by teenagers. *Harvard Journal of Law and Gender, 33,* 687–702.

Wells, M., Finkelhor, D., Wolak, J., & Mitchell, K. (2007). Defining child pornography: Law enforcement dilemmas in investigations of Internet child pornography possession. *Police Practice & Research, 8*(3), 269–282.

Wolak, J., Finkelhor, D., & Mitchell, K. J. (2012). How often are teens arrested for sexting? Data from a national sample of police cases. *Pediatrics, 129,* 4–12.

Wortley, R., & Smallbone, S. (2012). *Child pornography on the Internet.* U.S. Department of Justice, Office of Community Oriented Policing Services, #2004-CK-WX-K002. Retrieved August 19, 2014, from http://www.cops.usdoj.gov/Publications/e04062000.pdf

Ybarra, M., & Mitchell, J. (2004). Online aggressor/targets, aggressors and targets: A comparison of associated youth characteristics. *Journal of Child Psychology and Psychiatry, 45,* 1308–1316.

Ybarra, M. L., & Mitchell, K. J. (2007). Prevalence and frequency of Internet harassment instigation: Implications for adolescent health. *Journal of Adolescent Health, 41,* 189–195.

Violent Women

8

TINA L. FREIBURGER

Contents

In Frida Adler's 1975 book, *Sisters in Crime*, she predicted an increase in female offending. This increase in female offending would be due to the emergence of a new female offender who would be equally as violent and brutal as her male criminal counterpart. Her emergence would be due to the liberation of females and the feminist movement bolstering women's status to that equal to men. According to Adler, women were not allowed to be violent prior to liberation due to the traditional female role of the passive and nonaggressive caretaker that was thrust upon them. With the liberation movement, however, opportunities for nontraditional roles in the workforce would become open to women. These roles would allow women to be more assertive. Adler believed that just as legitimate opportunities began to open up to women in the traditional workforce, additional illegitimate opportunities would also open up for women in the form of criminal behavior. Women being more assertive in society would then provide the opportunity for them to move from traditional female crimes such as petty theft and prostitution into more masculine crimes such as robbery and violence (Adler, 1975).

Although her theory became very popular at the time, many critics of Adler's ideas argue that her theory has not been supported as we did not experience the increase in female offending that she predicted (see Pollock, 1999; Pollock & Davis, 2004). Proponents of her theory, however, argued that this rise was never experienced because female's status in society stopped short of reaching equality to men. Had women achieved equality, the large increases in female offending predicted by Adler's ideas would have come to fruition.

Despite the fact that Alder's ideas have been largely debunked in research examining the differences in male and female rates of violent offending, they have held sentiment among the general public. The media has continued to perpetuate this idea, reporting that women have "gone wild" and are more violent than they were in the past. For example, an article in *Newsweek* published in 2005, "Bad Girls Go Wild," cites antidotal stories to

Table 8.1   Male and Female Involvement in Crime

	Males	Male (%)	Females	Female (%)
Murder and nonnegligent manslaughter	2,355	88.5	307	11.5
Forcible rape	4,979	98.8	59	1.2
Robbery	21,071	87.1	3,125	12.9
Aggravated assault	84,518	77.7	24,199	22.3
Violent crime	112,923	80.3	27,690	19.7
Other assaults	262,021	71.7	103,514	28.3
Prostitution and commercialized vice	2,280	39.2	3,539	60.8

argue that female violence is increasing. The article opens with the following story about a homicide that occurred when two girls were fighting over a pink rubber ball:

> When police arrived on the scene of a fatal stabbing last week in Brooklyn, N.Y., they were stunned by what they saw. The victim, an 11-year-old girl, lay crumpled on the floor, the front of her "Dora the Explorer" T shirt bloodied. The weapon, a steak knife, was in the kitchen sink. And the perpetrator, visibly upset and clinging to her mother, police say, was a little girl in a ponytail, only 9 years old. A few days later, she stood in white socks and shiny black dress shoes before a judge, listening as her lawyer entered a plea of not guilty.
>
> **Scelfo (2005, June 12)**

The article goes on to explain that the increase in female violent crime is due to the changing role of females in society and the availability of violent female role models in the media from which girls are able to model violent behavior. It further argues that girls are being raised the same as boys; therefore, we should expect equal levels of violence for them. The author also criticizes analytical investigations into the effect of changing policing practices to determine the extent to which the increase in female offending is real or due to changes in criminal justice practices. She argues these inquires deny the issue and delay societies response to combat girl violence (Scelfo, 2005, June 12).

Despite these reports in the media, rates of female perpetrated violence have still not come close to reaching the same rates as male violent offending. According to the Uniform Crime Reports (UCR), in 2012 males committed over 73% of the index-one crimes. Examination of specific violence offenses shows that men commit more crimes for every offenses examined, with men committing over 88% of murders, almost 99% of rapes, 87% of robberies, and almost 78% of aggravated assaults (see Table 8.1). Males also dominate the numbers for "other assaults," accounting for almost 72%. The only offense women committed more than men was prostitution and commercialized vice, with women making up almost 61% of the arrestees (Federal Bureau of Investigation [FBI], 2012a).

Changing Patterns of Female Crime and the Narrowing of the Gender Gap

When examining changes in arrests for violent offenses, however, a different picture emerges. From 2003 to 2012, the UCR shows that the number of women arrested for violent offenses has not decreased at a rate as great as that of men (see Table 8.2). During this time

Table 8.2   Changes in Crime Rate between 2003 and 2012

	Males	Females
Violent crime	−14.9	−2.8
Murder and nonnegligent manslaughter	−14.3	−8.3
Robbery	−7.1	+20.2
Aggravated assault	−16.1	−5.4
Other assaults	−7.1	+11.8

period, the number of men arrested for murder decreased over 14%; for females, the decrease was about 8%. The rate of robbery decreased for males by about 7%, but for females, arrests for robberies actually increased over 20%. Male rates of aggravated assault decreased by 16%, but female arrests for aggravated assault only decreased by about 5%. For other assaults, males experienced a 7% decrease in arrests while women experienced an increase of about 12% (Federal Bureau of Investigation [FBI], 2012b).

Case Study 1: The Barbie Bandits

Robbery is often referred to as the most "gendered" crime because males make up such a high proportion of incidences of robbery. Although rarer, cases involving female robbers often receive a greater deal of media attention than cases with a male perpetrator as the public seems especially intrigued by these cases. Take, for instance, the case of the "Barbie Bandits." In this case, 19-year-old Heather Johnston and Ashley Miller, also 19 at the time, robbed a bank located in a supermarket in Acworth, Georgia. Prior to the robbery, the girls worked as dancers at a strip club and lived a drug-infused party lifestyle. The idea of robbing a bank began as a joke but soon turned into a real plan.

On the day of the robbery, the girls walked into a Bank of America branch bank and passed the teller a threatening note demanding he hand over the money. A video camera at the bank recorded Miller and Johnston wearing sunglasses as disguises and laughing throughout the robbery. After making away with $11,000, the girls began a planned shopping spree and visited an upscale beauty salon. Media coverage of the robbery showed the video of Miller and Johnston all over the city, leading to many tips regarding the girls' whereabouts and their quick apprehension by police.

Ashley Miller was sentenced to 2 years of incarceration and an additional 8 years on probation for the robbery and for a drug possession charge. Heather Johnston was sentenced to 10 years of probation for the robbery. Benny Allen, the clerk at the bank who was later determined to be in on the robbery, was also found to be a co-conspirator in the crime. He was sentenced to 5 years of incarceration and an additional 5 years of probation. Their other co-conspirator, Michael Chastang, was sentenced to 10 years in prison (Joseph, 2007, July 9).

Some speculate that these increases and smaller decreases in females' rate of offending is a sign that the gap in violent crime is narrowing, and the "new female offender" that Adler predicted is emerging. Others, however, argue that women are not more violent. Instead, a change in arrest patterns is the cause of the increase in female arrests for violent crimes. For violent adult women, research has been conducted to determine which is the case, whether the increase in female violent offending is real or simply due to issues in using arrest data (specifically, UCR data). Lauritsen, Heimer, and Lynch (2009) examined whether the gender gap has changed over time using National Crime Survey (NCS) data and data from the National Criminal Victimization Survey (NCVS). For the victimization surveys, respondents are asked if they had been victims of certain crimes and the gender of their assailant. Therefore, victimization data are not affected by changes in the handling of certain offenses as are arrest statistics. Arrest statistics, on the other hand, are influenced by changes in the way police handle certain incidences. If police begin to view female crime as more serious, it may change the way they handle female cases. For example, it is possible that in the past when a police officer would encounter a female physically assaulting her boyfriend, the officer would decide not to arrest the female perpetrator or to arrest her for a lesser offenses, such as simple assault. Now that female violence is being taken more seriously, however, the officer might be more inclined to arrest her for aggravated assault. Although the actual criminal incident has not changed, the police handling of the cases have changed, making it appear that serious violent offending by females has actually increased.

In Lauritsen et al.'s (2009) study, they examined victimization data for the years 1973–2005 for simple assaults, aggravated assaults, and robberies to compare the number of offenses by a female perpetrator to the rate of offenses by a male perpetrator. Their results indicated that although males still committed more simple assaults, aggravated assaults, and robberies than females, the gender gap is in fact narrowing for these offenses. The results also suggest that this is not due to an increase in female offending but instead due to the fact that the number of these offenses committed by males has decreased at a higher rate than have female perpetrator offenses. In other words, females are not committing more simple assaults, aggravated assaults, and robberies, but men are committing fewer of these crimes.

Violent Girls

Similar to adult females, the gap between juvenile boys' and girls' violent offending appears to be narrowing. While violent offenses committed by juveniles has decreased overall, the number of girls being arrested for these offenses has increased or decreased at a lower rate than boys (Zahn et al., 2008). It is important to remember, however, that similar to adult females, the rate at which girls are being arrested is still much lower than the rate at which boys are being arrested. Girls only account for about 29% of total juveniles arrested; for violent index crimes, they account for 18%. Therefore, despite the increase in violent female offending, boys are still committing a larger number of violent offenses than girls (Zahn et al., 2010). Of these violent offenses, the highest percentage of girls (25%) is found for aggravated assault; females make up very small numbers of arrests for murder (9%), rape (2%), and robbery (9%). Looking at nonindex violent crimes, girls make up a larger proportion of minor violent offenses, accounting for 36% of simple assaults. Between the years 1996 and 2005, the rate of juvenile offending decreased for girls and boys for all offenses with the exception of simple assault. This decrease, however, was larger for boys than it was for girls. This is especially true for aggravated assault. The number of boys arrested for aggregated assault decreased 28%. For girls, the rate of aggravated assault only decreased by 5%. For simple assault, boys experienced a decrease during this period while girls experienced a 24% increase (Zahn et al., 2008).

The finding that the rate of minor female violent offending has increased and the rate at which girls commit aggravated assault has decreased at a rate much smaller than males has led research to ask whether girls are in fact more violent than they had been in past years or if the increase in violent girls is actually due to a change in the official response to female offending. This research has indicated that this is in fact the case; girls are not actually more violent than they used to be. The system, however, is more inclined to pursue violent charges against females for behaviors that were not considered violent in the past (Feld, 2009; Steffensmeier, Schwartz, Zhong, & Ackerman, 2005).

The juvenile court was developed to focus on treatment as opposed to punishment. Early in the juvenile court's history, status offenses were added to the list of offenses that were under the jurisdiction of the court. Status offenses are acts that are legal for adults to engage in but prohibited for juveniles, such as smoking, running away from home, or truancy. Although these offenses applied to all juveniles, the court was more concerned with girls who engaged in these behaviors than boys. For boys, the court was more concerned about involvement in criminal activities (Schlossman, 1977). This led to girls being detained more often for status and minor offenses (Platt, 1977; Schlossman, 1977). Concern over this practice was one of the motivations for the Juvenile Justice and Delinquency Prevention Act of 1974. Implementation of this Act led to the deinstitutionalization of status offenders, and had a much larger effect on girls than for boys, as they were being detained for status offenses at a much higher rate than boys.

The practice of detaining and incarcerating status offenders, however, was not completely eliminated by the JJDP Act. In 1980, an amendment was added to the Act allowing status offenders to be detained and incarcerated for violating procedural violations, even if these violations stemmed from status offenses. Therefore, a juvenile who is petitioned to the court for a status offense, such as running away, cannot be placed in a detention center for their offense. If the juvenile fails to follow a court order, however, they may be placed for that violation. Again, this disproportionately has affected females, with more girls being placed for violating probation or being found in contempt of court than boys (Bishop & Frazier, 1992). Others also expressed concern that the restrictions in placing a juvenile status offender would be circumvented by charging a juvenile with a delinquent act instead of a status offense (Handler & Zatz, 1982).

Steffensmeier et al. (2005) compared data from the Uniform Crime Reports (UCR) on girls' arrests for violent acts to the rates reported by the National Crime Victimization Survey and Monitoring the Future and National Youth Risk Behavior Survey (both self-report surveys). He found an increase in girls arrested for violent crimes but did not find an increase in victims' reporting female perpetrators or in girls self-reporting increased engagement in violent behaviors. This suggests that the rise in girls' violent offenses are likely due to police reclassifying female offenders who used to be considered status offenders as violent offenders. Feld (2009) further argues that the increase in simple and aggravated assaults is partially due to a change in the handling of female juvenile offenders. Girls are more likely than boys to commit acts of violence against family members, while boys are more likely to assault an acquaintance or a stranger. In the past, these girls who committed acts of violence against family members were processed as status offenders with charges of being incorrigible or unruly. With the get tough focus on domestic violence cases, however, these cases are now being treated as more serious offenses, resulting in charges of assault. Because girls are committing a larger number of these family-related offenses, they are disproportionately affected by this change.

Overall, there seems to be little evidence suggesting that the behaviors of girls have changed much over the last several years, despite the appearance of this being so in official arrest statistics. Instead, it appears that the increase in the arrest of violent girls is largely an artifact of changes within the system. It appears that violence perpetrated by girls and the offenses that girls typically commit are no longer being tolerated. This has resulted in more girls being labeled as violent and being eligible for confinement in the juvenile justice system.

Case Study 2: Violent Girls

Although girls only accounted for 9% of the juvenile arrests for murder and nonnegligent manslaughter, similar to murder cases with an adult female perpetrator, cases in which girls commit murder have received a great deal of media attention. Take, for instance, the case that occurred in Waukesha, WI, during the summer of 2014.

On May 30, 2014, two 12-year-old girls, Morgan Geyser and Anissa Weier, allegedly attempted to kill their friend, Payton Leutner, also 12, by stabbing her 19 times. It appears that the crime was not impulsive. Instead, it was well thought out and planned. From the girls' statements, it is also evident that the girls had many opportunities to back out of the plan, but chose not to on several occasions.

According to the criminal complaint in the case, Morgan and Anissa planned the murder since February. On May 19, the three girls had a sleepover and visited Skateland. After skating, Morgan and Anissa planned to slit Payton's throat when they returned to Morgan's home, cover her with a blanket, and then leave the house. Although the girls did not follow through with their plan that night, the next morning they devised a new one. The girls would visit a park and kill Payton in the park bathroom so the blood would flow down the drain, preventing a large mess. Once at the park, however, the girls could not agree on who would actually stab Payton. After this, the girls forced Payton into the nearby woods to play hide-and-seek. Once in the woods, Morgan took the knife and told Anissa that she would not "do it" until Anissa told her to. At this point, Anissa tells her to "Go ballistic. Go crazy." The girls then stabbed Payton 19 times. After the stabbing, the girls tell Payton that they will get help despite not having any intention to do so. After Morgan and Anissa left, Payton managed to crawl out of the woods where a bystander found her and called 911. Payton was rushed to the hospital and into surgery. Doctors reported that one of the stab wounds was less than a millimeter away from a major artery in Payton's heart. If this artery had been punctured, Payton would have likely suffered a heart attack and would have died within minutes. Luckily, Payton survived the attack despite her grave injuries.

When the police approached Morgan and Anissa 5 hours after Payton was found, the girls, covered in blood, were carrying backpacks containing some clothes, granola bars, bottles of water, and the knife they used to stab their friend. During police interviews, the girls told the police that they had wanted to kill Payton to please a fictional character they found on the Internet named Slenderman. Slenderman has been termed the modern day boogeyman of the digital age. He is a tall, slender, faceless figure with long limbs who lurks in the background and can often be found around children. Morgan and Anissa reported to police that they believed that by killing their friend they would prove that Slenderman was real and that he would take them into his woods to live with him in his mansion.

Under Wisconsin law, juveniles age 10 and older who commit murder are automatically waived into the adult court system; therefore, the girls are being treated as adults. Currently, the girls' attorneys have requested that the court move the case from adult court into juvenile court. If the girls are waived into the juvenile court, they will be released when they reach the age of 25. If they remain in the adult system, they face a possible 60-year sentence.

Female Violence in Intimate Relationships

Violence within intimate partner relationships is typically viewed as a male perpetrated act against a female victim. Self-report surveys, however, have indicated that women also use violence against their intimate partners. In her meta-analysis, Archer (2000) found that women were actually more likely than men to use violence against intimate partners. Her research was criticized, however, because it failed to include all types of abuse, arguing that female use of violence would not be greater for all types of abuse. Additional research conducted by Swan and Snow (2002) confirmed this argument, finding that women were about equally likely to use verbal abuse and more likely to use moderate violence than men. When it came to serious abuse (e.g., sexual violence or injury), however, men were more likely than women to be the perpetrators. Women were also more likely to sustain a serious injury from physical abuse (Archer, 2000; Muñoz-Rivas, Graña, O'Leary, & González, 2007). Similar to the other types of violence women engage in, female engagement in violence within an intimate relationship is related to a past history of violence. Females, who have been victims of emotional, physical, or sexual violence during childhood, have been found to be more likely to use violence in their relationships (Siegel, 2000; Swan & Snow, 2003).

Studies have also found that women's motivations for violence within intimate relations are different than men's. In particular, women are more likely to commit acts of violence against their partners out of fear of an assault, in self-defense (Swan & Snow, 2003), or in self-defense of children (Swan & Snow, 2006). When motivated by retribution, women are also more likely than men to be motivated by the desire to punish their partners for the abusive behavior their partners inflicted upon them (Hamberger, Lohr, Bonge, & Tolin, 1997). It appears, therefore, that female violence in an intimate relationship most often occurs when both partners are perpetrators of abusive behavior.

In some extreme cases, violence within an intimate partner relationship can escalate to murder. While men who murder most often kill other men, when women commit murder, their victims are more likely to be males. Most commonly, these male victims are their intimate partners. Take, for example, the case of Jodi Arias. Arias was convicted of first-degree murder in 2013 for the 2008 killing of her ex-boyfriend, Travis Alexander. Prior to the murder, Alexander and Arias shared an intimate relationship until he broke up with her. After the breakup, the two continued to see each other and continued a sexual relationship. According to Arias, the relationship was volatile and abusive. These claims, however, are disputed by Alexander's friends and family. After initial claims that Alexander was killed by someone who broke into the house, Arias admitted to stabbing him to death while he was in the shower but claimed it was in self-defense. Although Arias was found guilty of murder, the jury was deadlocked on whether to sentence her to death (Schwartz, 2014, October 21).

Similar patterns for juvenile girls who commit acts of extreme violence are found for juveniles as for adult women. Girls are more likely than boys to kill family members. In fact, 36% of the murders committed by girls had a victim who was a family member, and only 18% of the cases had a victim who was a stranger. For boys who commit murder, a stranger was the victim 38% of the time and a family member was a victim only 7% of the time (Snyder & Sickmund, 2006).

Female Serial Killers

Although we typically do not think of females when we think of serial killers, females make up approximately 15% of serial killers. According to Hickey (2002), there were only 62 female serial killers compared to 337 male serial killers between the years of 1825 and 1995. Of those 62 women, 68% acted alone and 32% acted with a partner. The majority of the female serial killers were Caucasian (74%); only 25% were African American and 1% was Asian. Lavinia Fisher is often reported to be the first female serial killer in the United States, although others argued that there were several before her. Fisher was born in 1793 and lived with her husband, John Fisher, in Charleston, South Caroline, where they owned a hotel. Along with her husband, Fisher is believed to have robbed and killed many male travelers who stopped at their hotel for lodging. Lavinia would serve the travelers poisoned tea, and once they were dead, she and her husband would rob them. When one of their victims escaped, the police found stolen property and the remains of many men in their residence. Both were convicted and hanged for their crimes (Orr, 2010).

Although it was first argued that the same typologies developed to explain male serial killers could be used to explain female serial killers, Kelleher and Kelleher (1998) argued that this was not the case and that separate typologies were needed to be developed to explain female serial killers. Their typology made distinctions between women who killed with a partner and those who killed alone and included the following categories: black widow, angel of death, sexual predator, revenge, profit of crime, team killer, question of sanity, unexplained, and unsolved.

The black widow murders multiple spouses, intimate partners, family members, or others with whom she has developed a close personal relationship. These offenders typically begin murdering their victims at about 30 years of age; they tend to be well organized and commit murders that are well planned. The most common motive for black widows is profit. Black widows do not typically draw a lot of attention to their activities and have a preference for poisoning their victims slowly over time. In the United States, black widows average six to eight victims and are often only caught after their victim count has become high enough to arouse suspicion (Kelleher & Kelleher, 1998).

An example of a black widow is Nannie Doss, born Nancy Hazel. Doss was known as the Giggling Grandma for her demeanor during her arrest, as she joked about dead husbands and about killing them. Nannie was an active serial killer from the 1920s to 1954, when she was finally caught and pled guilty. Her victims included four previous husbands, her mother, her sister, her grandson, and her mother-in-law. Nannie was motivated by money from life insurance policies and the assets she inherited from her murder victims. All her victims died of poisoning. She was only caught when an autopsy was performed on her last husband, revealing that he was killed by arsenic poisoning (Kelleher & Kelleher, 1998).

Female serial killers classified as angels of death are women who kill people who are in their care. Although their motivations may differ, female serial killers in this category victimize those who rely on them for some form of medical care. Angels of death are often motivated by ego and the need to dominate, picking victims who are the most vulnerable such as the elderly, children, or the very ill. These serial killers can include those who suffer from Munchausen by proxy, a psychological disorder in which a caretaker, typical a mother, exaggerates a child's symptoms or makes a child ill in order to generate sympathy and attention. When angels of death target adults they typically use lethal injections, when the victim is a child, they also use lethal injections or affixation. The murders often take place within their normal duties and work responsibilities (Kelleher & Kelleher, 1998).

Marybeth Tinning is an example of an angel of death. Mary Tinning had 10 children. All 10 children died. Marybeth's third child, Jennifer, was the first to die. This would be the only death that was not caused by Marybeth. Jennifer was born ill and died in the hospital of an infection. Seventeen days after Jennifer's death, Marybeth brought her 2-year-old son into the hospital reporting that he had a seizure. The boy was sent home after doctors failed to find anything wrong with him. Two hours later, Marybeth returned to the hospital with the boy, who was dead. Approximately 6 weeks after his death, Marybeth was back at the hospital with her daughter. Although doctors wanted to keep the girl for observation, Marybeth took the girl home, returning later with her unconscious daughter who died hours later. In 1973, Marybeth gave birth to her fourth child, who died 3 weeks later. Two years later, she gave birth to her fifth child, who died 5 months later. In 1978, Marybeth became pregnant with her sixth child; that same year she and her husband adopted a seventh child. In 1979, the child she bore also died. Marybeth again became pregnant, having another child that suddenly died. Many believed that Marybeth's children had died due to a rare genetic disorder, until 1981, when her adopted son also died. In 1985, Marybeth had her last child; that child would also die suddenly. At this point, those around Marybeth became very suspicious. Law enforcement began questioning her. After intense questioning, Marybeth confessed to smothering four of the nine children. Despite her confession, Marybeth was only convicted of second-degree murder for the killing of one of her children (Gado, n.d.).

The sexual predator commits murders that are sexual in nature. Not including women who committed sexually motivated crimes with a partner, the United States has only had one female serial killer who meets the requirements of this category—Aileen Wuornos (Kelleher & Kelleher, 1998). Aileen Wuornos's life and crimes have been presented in several documentaries and in the 2003 film, *Monster*, starring Charlize Theron. Wuornos was the victim of several sexual assaults as a child and became sexually active at a very young age. After birthing a child who she gave up for adoption, Wuornos left home at the age of 15 and became a prostitute. In 1989, at the age of 33 she murdered her first victim, Richard Mallory, and continued on to murder six additional men. Wuornos met all her victims through propositions of sex for money before shooting and robbing them. After being arrested, Wuornos confessed to the killing of six of the men, claiming self-defense for all the murders and that she shot the men after they tried to rape her. Despite her claims, Wuornos was found guilty of capital murder and was executed on October 9, 2002 (Macleod, n.d.).

The revenge female serial killer is motivated by retribution. Revenge serial killers are rare as it is uncommon for an individual to retain her feelings for retribution over the stagnant periods of time between several murders. Her most common targets are members of her own family. She is similar to the black widow in her preference for poison or suffocation as her means to kill. She is different from the black widow, however, in that she is motivated by emotion instead of profit, and her murders are not as well planned as those of the black widow (Kelleher & Kelleher, 1998). Kelleher and Kelleher (1998) only identify three female serial killers who fall into this category. One of which is Martha Ann Johnson. Johnson murdered her four children in fits of revenge to punish her husband for marital fights in which the two engaged.

Profit or crime murders target victims for monetary gain or in the commission of another crime. This serial killer is different than the black widow in that she does not target members of her family. Her crimes are typically well planned and organized. Her victims are often those for whom she provides care or individuals who she can easily control and manipulate (Kelleher & Kelleher, 1998). Anna Marie Hahn is an early example of a profit serial killer. Hahn murdered five elderly men and attempted to murder a sixth, all of whom she stole from while employed as a live-in attendant. After her crimes were detected, she became the first female to be executed via the electric chair in Ohio (Kelleher & Kelleher, 1998).

Women who murder with a partner or with several partners are classified as a team killer. These women can be motivated by a variety of factors. Their roles in the murders can also vary. In some situations, they may not be the dominate offender. In fact, it is possible that they participate in the murders, but do not actually commit any of them. In other situations, they may lead in the planning and execution of the murders. Kelleher and Kelleher identified three categories in which team killers can be placed. They include male/female teams, female teams, and family teams. Of the three, the male/female team killer is the most prevalent. The female team killer is younger on average than the women in the other categories. Her offending period is also relatively short, lasting only a year or two (Kelleher & Kelleher, 1998).

Karla Homolka and her husband, Paul Bernardo, are an example of a male/female serial killing team. Like most male/female teams, they were motivated by sexually dysfunctional desires. Karla and Paul met when she was just 17 and he was 23. They quickly started a sadomasochistic sexual relationship, with Paul as the master and Karla as the slave. Prior to the murders, Paul began to brutally rape female strangers with the approval of Karla. In an effort to please Paul, Karla agreed to allow him to rape her 15-year-old sister, Tammy, in an effort to make up for the fact that Kara was not a virgin when she met Paul. In 1990, Paul and Karla drugged Tammy and served her alcoholic drinks. After Tammy lost consciousness, Paul and Karla raped Tammy. Although they had not planned to kill her, Tammy became sick during the rape and died choking on her own vomit.

After Tammy's death, Karla and Paul drugged a young friend of Karla's. The couple brutally raped her while she was unconscious, but did not kill her. Their third sexual victim was Leslie Mahaffy, a young girl who Paul kidnapped. Karla and Paul kept the girl at their house for several days, brutally raping her. Then, they killed her, cut her body into pieces, and disposed of her remains in a lake. Their next victim was also a young girl whom the couple kidnapped. Again, the couple kept the girl at their home for several days, brutally raping her until they murdered her and dumped her body in a ditch.

After the third murder, Karla left Paul due to the physical abuse he began to inflict upon her. Later that year, forensic evidence from the earlier rapes led police to Paul. Knowing they would be caught, Karla then reported to police that Paul was a rapist and a murderer and quickly began negotiating a plea deal for her involvement. Her negotiations were successful, and Karla only received a 12-year sentence, with eligibility for parole after 3 years. Although Karla claimed she was also Paul's victim during the crimes, it became clear that Karla actively participated in the crimes and got enjoyment from the rapes after videotapes Paul and Karla had made of their crimes were reviewed. With the deal set, however, nothing could be done to lengthen Karla's sentence (CBC News Canada, 2010, June 17). Since her release in 2005, she has changed her name and remarried and is currently reported to live with her husband and their three children back in Quebec (Blatchford, 2014, October 17).

The question of sanity killer are those female serial killers who meet the M'Naughten test of sanity (Kelleher & Kelleher, 1998). The M'Naughten test stipulates that a person must be unaware of the impact of his or her actions and unable to distinguish right from wrong at the time of his or her crimes (Kaplan & Weisberg, 1991). Few serial killers are able to successfully prove insanity, making the question of sanity killer rare. At the time of the publication of their book, Kelleher and Kelleher (1998) only identified three serial killers who met this criterion. One such offender is Jane Toppan. Toppan became a private nurse after being fired from a hospital. She confessed to murdering 31 of her patients during her 20 years as a private nurse; although there is speculation that she may have murdered as many as 70 or even over 100 patients. Toppan was found to be insane and confined to a mental hospital (Kelleher & Kelleher, 1998).

The unexplained classification contains cases in which the motive is not known. Unsolved murders are those in which there is evidence that the perpetrator is female; however, their offender is not known (Kelleher & Kelleher, 1998). One example of an unknown motive serial killer is Christine Falling. Falling killed five children for whom she babysat and one elderly man. When she was arrested, Falling could not provide an explanation for why she committed the murders (Kelleher & Kelleher, 1998).

Female Gang Members

According to the National Gang Center (n.d.), law enforcement agencies commonly report that male gang members are much more prevalent than female gang members. In 2010, it was estimated that only 7.4% of all gang members were female. When examining self-report sources of gang involvement, however, the percentage of girls is much higher, with a reported 30% of 13-year-old gang members being female. At age 20, that number is reduced to about 15% of females (Pyrooz, 2014). Although females make up a small proportion of gang members, research has found that being affiliated with a gang results in a higher propensity toward violence for females (Deschenes & Esbensen, 1999; Fleisher & Krienert, 2004; Miller, 2001). The lives of gang girls also provide insight into this relationship.

In her book, Gini Sikes (1998) examines the lives of girls in the three U.S. cities of Los Angeles (California), San Antonio (Texas), and Milwaukee (Wisconsin). She found that girls typically held a lesser role in gangs than males. Girls who managed to gain respect and status in the gangs typically masculinized themselves. They would do this by dressing, acting, talking, and adopting the same demeanors as the boys. She further found that girls' involvement in gangs typically ended with motherhood. Once girls became pregnant, they often stopped being active members of the gang. However, many of them continued to live the lifestyle that accompanied gang involvement vicariously through their boyfriends and family members.

Research conducted by Fleisher and Krienert (2004) also found that women's engagement in gang behavior decreases when women become pregnant and have children. Their research focused on 74 female gang members in the North End, an all-black neighborhood with high levels of poverty and disorder located within Champaign, Illinois. All the girls studied were associated with one of the three largest gangs in the North End (Gangster Disciples, Vice Lords, and Black P-Stones). Fleisher and Krienert (2004) further found that the gang-involved girls had a higher rate of childhood victimization than other at-risk girls, with over 70% reporting such experiences. Most of the girls came from single-family households without a father present, had parents who had been arrested and incarcerated in the past, and had parents who used drugs and alcohol. The mean age for girls to join the gang was 14. This was the same mean age in which girls became sexually active and when girls became socially, economically, and emotionally independent from their households. When girls enter into the gangs at the age of 14, their gang associates were typically older men around 20 years of age. These older men exploited these young women, often coercing them into sexual acts and drug sales.

The sexual exploitation of females has been documented by other researchers as well. According to the Centre for Social Justice (2014), female gang members are often exploited. The report tells the story of a female gang member whose boyfriend forced her to engage in sexual activities with his fellow gang members by threatening to show others a videotape of the two having sex. The report states:

> From this moment on the 12-year-old girl's life descended into one of regular abuse and sexual exploitation. She was raped on a weekly basis, and many of these crimes were filmed and played back to her by her rapists.
>
> On one occasion she was forced to give oral sex to around 20 gang members as they stood around her in a circle and beat her. She became so desperate; she would have done anything to make it stop.

The Centre for Social Justice (2014, p. 8)

The girl was only able to escape the sexual violence by befriending other young girls and bringing them to the gang members to be raped (The Centre for Social Justice, 2014). In addition to being at greater risks for sexual victimization, through in-depth interviews and surveys, Miller (2001) also found that women who are involved with gangs were more likely to be physically assaulted than women who were at high risk for victimization but were not affiliated with gangs. In fact, the rate of physical victimization was 52% for gang-involved girls but only 26% for other at-risk girls.

With regard to the use of violence, Fleisher and Krienert (2004) found that gang girls most commonly engage in violence because of jealousy. This jealousy was typically directed at another girl or a past boyfriend, and stemmed from problems with a current or past boyfriend. Other times, girls engaged in violent fights with other girls at the request of male gang members (Fleisher & Krienert, 2004). The Centre for Social Justice also found this to be the case when talking to girls. The report details a female gang members experience with being asked to fight other girls. The report states:

> Whenever anyone in her gang had issues with another girl, they would call on Danielle to fight them. Danielle developed a fierce reputation for fighting and often defeated girls several years older than her. On one occasion, when she was 17 years old, she was called to help

a friend who was in an altercation with another girl. She agreed to help, borrowed a firearm from a fellow gang member and made her way down to the conflict. The situation was resolved without her discharging the weapon.

The Centre for Social Justice (2014, p. 9)

It seems, therefore, that female gang members appear to be more involved in violence than women who are not gang members. Similar to other violent females, they tend to have histories of abuse. Many who get involved with gangs are exploited for sex and violence. For most gang-involved women, the end to the gang life comes when they become pregnant and bear the responsibility of motherhood.

Theoretical Explanations for Violent Women and Girls

Because violence has long been viewed as a male phenomenon, theories to explain violent behaviors also historically focused on males. Lombroso was the first criminologist to focus on female criminality. In 1876, Lombroso published his book *The Criminal Man*. In this book, he argued that many criminals were atavists and were less evolved than normal man. In other words, criminals were born criminals due to biological factors outside their control. He had come to this conclusion while performing autopsies in a mental asylum when he noticed physically abnormalities in criminals and mental patients. Throughout his book, he describes those physical abnormalities and outlines the physical characteristics that are common among criminals (Lombroso, 2006).

Later, Lombroso and a colleague applied his theories to female offenders, and published a book in 1893 titled *The Female Offender* in which he described the physical abnormalities of the female criminal. Similar to his explanation for male criminals, Lombroso argued that female criminals were born criminals due to being atavists who were less evolved then their noncriminal counterparts. He also argued that women were biologically morally weaker and inferior to men. Therefore, even a normal female had the potential to engage in crime due to their inferiority to men. All women, even normal women, were semi-criminal, and shared many qualities with children such as being immature, jealous, and vengeful. The number of physical abnormalities female criminals exhibit were also fewer than men and less apparent. In fact, Lombroso argued that female criminals could exhibit no signs of physical abnormalities and look like normal women. Physical characteristics that female offenders could exhibit included such things as unaligned eyes, projecting ears, smaller proportion of arm span to height, skulls more similar to males, anomalous teeth, projecting cheekbones, and an oversized jaw.

Despite the fact that female criminals were rarer than male criminals, Lombroso believed they were more perverse than their male counterparts. When these females were violent, Lombroso argued that they were more violent and cruel than their violent male counterparts, taking pleasure in making their victims suffer. Although all women are naturally immoral and wicked, normal women are controlled by social entities such as religion, maternal desires, and sexual frigidity. For female criminals, however, these controls fail to suppress natural tendencies in female criminals. Without these controls to regulate their behaviors, female criminals act out in violence when motivated by such things as jealousy, revenge, and greed (Lombroso & Ferrero, 2004).

Although Lombroso's theories have been long debunked, biological theories are still used to explain differences in rates of violence for men and women. These theories suggest that biological differences such as testosterone levels and the greater muscle mass of men make men more inclined toward violent acts than women (see Pollock, 1999). Although it does not address the gender gap in male and female violent offending, mood and psychological change due to women's Premenstrual Syndrome (PMS) has also been used to explain female-perpetrated violence (Dalton, 1971). In 1991, Dr. Geraldine Richeter was the first defendant who successfully used PMS as a defense for her crimes. Richeter was pulled over by police for driving erratically while intoxicated with her three children in the car. During the stop, she cursed at the officer and tried to kick him in the groin (Successful PMS, 1991, June, 16). This case caused a great deal of controversy as many worried about the implications of excusing females' erratic behaviors on PMS.

Other theories have focused on why women are so much less likely to be violent than men. According to social learning theory, criminal behavior is learned the same as any other behavior is learned. Gender differences in rates of violence are due to differences in the types of behaviors that are learned and reinforced. Males are more likely than women to be exposed to violent role models from which they can imitate violent behaviors. As Pollock, Mullings, and Croch (2006) point out, this is consistent with research findings that girls who are victims of abuse are more likely to engage in violent behaviors as these girls are exposed to violent role models (i.e., their abuser).

Some research has attempted to develop a profile of a violent female offender to better understand the factors that correlate to her offending. Using face-to-face survey data collected from newly admitted female inmates in Texas, Pollock et al. (2006) examined differences between violent female inmates and nonviolent female inmates. They found that the violent inmates were more likely to be younger, African American, unemployed the year prior to incarceration, and had been living with children in the year prior to incarceration than the nonviolent women. Comparisons of prior involvement with the criminal justice system found no differences for violent and nonviolent women for times arrested, jailed or incarcerated, or placed on mandatory supervision. The violent inmates, however, were more likely to self-report criminal activity and began their criminal activities at a younger age than the nonviolent women.

Pollock et al. (2006) also found that the violent and nonviolent women differed in respect to their family histories. Violent females were more likely to be abused as children than the nonviolent women. They were also more likely to have been beaten or seriously physically hurt by an adult and more likely to have been sexually assaulted as children. No differences were found, however, in the number of violent and nonviolent women who grew up in one parent versus two parent households. However, violent women were more likely to have a parent with a substance abuse issue or a psychiatric problem than the nonviolent women. Multivariate analysis further showed that younger, African American women who experienced childhood physical and adult sexual abuse were significantly more likely to be violent. When the analysis was limited to only include violent women, it was found that having a history of physical abuse as a child was the strongest predictor of engagement in more violent behaviors. These findings provide support for social learning theory, suggesting that girls might learn violent behavior from their abusers and is similar to findings in other research (Fleisher & Krienert, 2004).

Treatment of Violent Females in the Criminal Justice System

One of the most consistent findings in the examination of punishment decisions is the more lenient treatment of female offenders than of their male counterparts. During all stages of court processing, females are found to fare better than males. This is true for charging decisions (Spohn & Spears, 1997), pretrial release decisions (Freiburger & Hilinski, 2010), the decision to incarcerate a defendant (Steffensmeier, Kramer, & Streifel, 1993), and in the sentence length decision for those incarcerated (Freiburger & Hilinski, 2013).

Theory has largely attributed this more lenient treatment of females to stereotypical images of females as less dangerous and blameworthy than males and as less able to serve time incarcerated (Steffensmeier et al., 1993). Chivalry theory further suggests that court actors feel the need to protect women from the criminal justice system as they are more childlike and fragile than males. The evil woman hypothesis, on the other hand, argues that this lenient treatment of females is only reserved for certain females. Specifically, only those who commit "female-like" crimes such as petty theft and prostitution are treated more leniently. Women who commit crimes that contradict their femininity are viewed even more harshly than the men who commit these crimes. As a result, females who commit more masculine offenses, such as violent crimes, will be subjected to harsher punishments than males because they have violated their traditional female roles. Although the evil woman hypothesis is largely cited and discussed, research on sentencing decisions find that women are treated more leniently than males regardless of their offense type. In fact, one of the most consistent findings in the sentencing literature is the more lenient treatment of females compared to males, with this finding holding across empirical examination in various states and counties (e.g., Freiburger & Hilinski, 2013; Spohn & Spears, 1997; Steffensmeier et al., 1993), as well as in an examination of federal sentencing decisions (e.g., Sorensen, Sarnikar, & Oaxaca, 2012).

In the case of juvenile girls, there is research that suggests the opposite of what is suggested by the evil woman hypothesis is actually true, and that girls who commit low-level offenses, such as status offenses, are treated more harshly than boys (see Freiburger & Burke, 2011). Girls who commit more serious offenses, on the other hand, are treated more leniently than boys (Bishop & Frazier, 1992). These findings are explained using a paternalistic explanation (Chesney-Lind, 1977; Johnson & Scheuble, 1991). According to this perspective, the court has an interest in controlling girls' sexuality. Court officials, therefore, are more inclined to process girls into the system in an attempt to protect them from promiscuous behavior and pregnancy.

In the case of the death penalty, fewer females are sentenced to death than males; according to the Death Penalty Information Center, in the past 100 years, only 40 women have been executed. Of those 40 executions, only 15 have taken place since 1976 when the death penalty was reinstated by the U.S. Supreme Court. During this time period, females only accounted for 1% of all executions (a total of 1389 executions during that time). In 2014, 59 women were on death row, 20 of whom are on death row in California. As of the writing of this book, the last female to be executed was Lisa Coleman on September 17, 2014, in Texas. Coleman was convicted of capital murder for killing her girlfriend's son by restraining and starving him (Berman, 2014, September 17).

Summary

Although men still commit the majority of violent crimes, the rates of females being arrested for violent crimes are either increasing or decreasing at a lower rate than men, resulting in a narrowing of the gender gap in violent arrests. It is not known for sure, however, whether the gap decrease is simply due to changes in the processing and handling of women or whether females are in fact committing more violent offenses. The same is true for girls. The gender gap appears to be narrowing as more girls are being processed through the juvenile system. Similar to adult women, many have questioned, however, whether this is also due to a systems change and not a behavior change. Despite making up a small portion of violent offenders, there are many cases in which women and girls have been capable of serious violent offenses, including offenses that are the result of gang violence, serial murders, and intimate partner violence. It seems that whenever females do engage in violent crimes they tend to garner a lot of media attention, especially the most violent of these offenses.

Theoretical explanations for females' engagement in violence range from biological explanations that point to inherent differences between men and women to social learning explanations that argue that females learn different behaviors than males. Regardless of the explanation used for explaining violence among girls and women, one cannot ignore the impact that past victimizations have on the lives of these girls and women. To combat female violence, it is essential that policies and programs address girls and women's histories to treat the traumas caused by past victimizations and to prevent subsequent victimizations.

Discussion Questions

1. Why do you think cases involving violent females generate more media attention than cases with a violent male perpetrator?
2. Is the differential treatment of male and female violent offenders justified? Why or why not?
3. Besides the theoretical explanations for female violence discussed in the chapter, what other criminological theories can explain female perpetrated violence?
4. Research examining the lives of violent girls and women consistently finds that violent women are more likely to have a history of being victimized. Do you think this should be considered in deciding appropriate treatments and punishments for female offenders?

References

Adler, F. (1975). *Sisters in crime: The rise of the new female criminal.* New York, NY: McGraw-Hill.
Archer, J. (2000). Sex differences in aggression between heterosexual partners: A meta-analytic review. *Psychological Bulletin, 126,* 651–680.
Berman, M. (2014, September 17). Texas carries out a rare occurrence: An execution of a woman. *The Washington Post.* Retrieved from http://www.washingtonpost.com/news/post-nation/wp/2014/09/17/texas-prepares-for-a-rare-occurrence-an-execution-of-a-woman/

Bishop. D.M., & Frazier, C. (1992). Gender bias in juvenile justice processing: Implications of the JJDP Act. *Journal of Criminal Law and Criminology, 82*, 1162–1186.

Blatchford, C. (2014, October 17). Jean Chretien's son, Karla Homolka's sister testify at Magnotta trial after being listed as "senders" of body part boxes. *National Post.* Retrieved from http://news.nationalpost.com/2014/10/17/jean-chretiens-son-karla-homolkas-sister-testify-at-magnotta-trial-after-being-listed-as-senders-of-body-part-boxes/

The Centre for Social Justice. (2014). *Girls and gangs.* Retrieved from http://www.centreforsocialjustice.org.uk/UserStorage/pdf/Pdf%20reports/Girls-and-Gangs-FINAL-VERSION.pdf

Chesney-Lind, M. (1977). Judicial paternalism and the female status offender: Training women to know their place. *Crime & Delinquency, 35*, 5–29.

Dalton, K. (1971). *The premenstrual syndrome.* Springfield, IL: Charles C. Thomas.

Deschenes, E.P., & Esbensen, F.A. (1999). Violence among girls: Does gang membership make a difference? In M. Chesney-Lind & J.M. Hagedorn (Eds.), *Female gangs in America* (pp. 277–294). Chicago, IL: Lake View Press.

Federal Bureau of Investigation [FBI]. (2012a). *Arrests by sex, 2012. Table 42.* Retrieved from http://www.fbi.gov/about-us/cjis/ucr/crime-in-the-u.s/2012/crime-in-the-u.s.-2012/tables/42tabledatadecoverviewpdf

Federal Bureau of Investigation [FBI]. (2012b). *Ten-year arrest trends by sex. Table 33.* Retrieved from http://www.fbi.gov/about-us/cjis/ucr/crime-in-the-u.s/2012/crime-in-the-u.s.-2012/tables/33tabledatadecoverviewpdf

Feld, B.C. (2009). Violent girls or relabeled status offenders? *Crime & Delinquency, 55*(2), 241–265.

Fleisher, M.S., & Krienert, J.L. (2004). Life-course events, social networks, and the emergence of violence among female gang members. *Journal of Community Psychology, 32*(5), 607–622.

Freiburger, T.L., & Burke, A.S. (2011). Status offenders in the juvenile court: The effects of gender, race, and ethnicity on the adjudication decision. *Youth Violence and Juvenile Justice, 9*(4), 352–365.

Freiburger, T.L., & Hilinski, C. (2010). The impact of race, gender, and age on the pretrial decision. *Criminal Justice Review, 35*(3), 318–334.

Freiburger, T.L., & Hilinski, C. (2013). The effects of race, gender and age on sentencing using a trichotomous dependent variable. *Crime & Delinquency, 59*(1), 69–86.

Gado, M. (n.d.) Baby killer. *Crime Library.* Retrieved September 23, 2014 from http://www.crimelibrary.com/notorious_murders/women/marybeth_tinning/index.html

Hamberger, L.K., Lohr, J.M., Bonge, D., & Tolin, D.F. (1997). An empirical classification of motivations for domestic violence. *Violence Against Women, 3*, 401–423.

Handler, J.F., & Zatz, J. (Eds.). (1982). *Neither angels nor thieves: Studies in deinstitutionalization of status offenders.* Washington, DC: National Academy Press.

Hickey, E.W. (2002). *Serial murders and their victims* (3rd ed.). Belmont, CA: Wadsworth/Thomson Learning.

Johnson, D.R., & Scheuble, L.K. (1991). Gender bias in the disposition of juvenile court referrals: The effects of time and location. *Criminology, 29*(4), 677–699.

Joseph, E. (2007, July 9). The fall of the 'Barbie Bandits'. *ABC News* Retrieved from http://abcnews.go.com/Primetime/story?id=3352813&page=1

Kaplan, J., & Weisberg, R. (1991). *Criminal law: Cases and materials* (2nd ed.). Boston, MA: Little, Brown.

Kelleher, M.D., & Kelleher, C.L. (1998). *Murder most rare: The female serial killer.* Westport, CT: Praeger.

Key events in the Bernardo/Homolka case. (2010, June 17). *CBC News* Retrieved from w.cbc.ca/news/canada/key-events-in-the-bernardo-homolka-case-1.933128

Lauritsen, J.L., Heimer, K., & Lynch, J.P. (2009). Trends in the gender gap in offending: New evidence from the National Crime Victimization Survey. *Criminology, 47*(2), 361–399.

Lombroso, C. (2006). *Criminal man: Translated with a new introduction by Mary Gibson and Nicole Hahn Rafter.* London, U.K.: Duke University Press.

Lombroso, C., & Ferrero, G. (2004). *Criminal women, the prostitute, and the normal women.* London, U.K.: Duke University Press.

Macleod, M. (n.d.). *Alieen Wuornos: Killer who preyed on truck drivers.* Retrieved from http://www. crimelibrary.com/notorious_murders/women/wuornos/1.html

Miller, J. (2001). *One of the boys: Girls, gangs, and gender.* New York: Oxford University Press.

Muñoz-Rivas, M.J, Graña, J.L., O'Leary, K.D., & González, M.S. (2007). Aggression in adolescent dating relationships: Prevalence, justification, and health consequences. *Journal of Adolescent Health, 40*(4), 298–304.

National Gang Center. (n.d.). *National youth gang survey analysis.* Retrieved August 15, 2014 from http://www.nationalgangcenter.gov/Survey-Analysis/Demographics

Orr, B. (2010). *Six miles to Charleston: The true story of John and Lavinia Fisher.* Charleston, SC: The History Press.

Platt, A.M. (1977). *The child-savers: The invention of delinquency.* Chicago, IL: University Chicago Press.

Pollock, J. (1999). *Criminal women.* Cincinnati, OH: Anderson.

Pollock, J., & Davis, S. (2004). The myth of the violent female criminal. *Criminal Justice Review, 30,* 5–26.

Pollock, J.M., Mullings, J.L., & Crouch, B.M. (2006). Violent women: Findings from the Texas inmates study. *Journal of Interpersonal Violence, 21*(4), 485–502.

Pyrooz, D.C. (2014). "From your first cigarette to your last dyin' day": The patterning of gang membership in the life-course. *Journal of Quantitative Criminology, 30,* 349–372.

Scelfo, J. (2005, June 12). *Bad girls go wild. Newsweek.* Retrieved from http://www.newsweek.com/ bad-girls-go-wild-119637

Schlossman, S.L. (1977). *Love and the American delinquent: The theory and practice of "progressive" juvenile justice 1825–1920.* Chicago, IL: University of Chicago Press.

Schwartz, D. (2014, October 21). *Arizona jury sworn in to consider death penalty for Jodi Arias. Yahoo! News.* Retrieved from https://news.yahoo.com/arizona-jury-consider-death-penalty-murderer-jodi-arias-102732365-sector.html

Siegel, J.A. (2000). Aggressive behavior among women sexually abused as children. *Violence and Victims, 15,* 235–255.

Sikes, G. (1998). *8 ball chicks: A year in the violent world of girl gangs.* New York, NY: Anchor.

Snyder, H.N., & Sickmund, M. (2006). *Juvenile offenders and victims: 2006 national report.* Washington, DC: U.S. Department of Justice, Office of Justice Programs, Office of Juvenile Justice and Delinquency Prevention.

Sorensen, T., Sarnikar, S., & Oaxaca, R.L. (2012). Race and gender differences under federal sentencing guidelines. *American Economic Review, 102*(3), 256–60.

Spohn, C.C., & Spears, J.W. (1997). Gender and case-processing decisions: A comparison of case outcomes for male and female defendants charged with violent felonies. *Women & Criminal Justice, 8,* 29–59.

Steffensmeier, D., Kramer, J., & Streifel C. (1993). Gender and imprisonment decisions. *Criminology, 31*(3), 411–446.

Steffensmeier, D., Schwartz, J., Zhong, S.H., & Ackerman, J. (2005). An assessment of recent trends in girls' violence using diverse longitudinal sources: Is the gender gap closing? *Criminology, 43,* 355–405.

Successful PMS defense in Virginia case revives debate. (1991, June 16). *Newsday* Retrieved from http://articles.baltimoresun.com/1991–06–16/news/1991167033_1_pms-richter-defense

Swan, S.C., & Snow, D.L. (2002). A typology of women's use of violence in intimate relationships. *Violence Against Women, 8,* 286–319.

Swan, S.C., & Snow, D.L. (2003). Behavioral and psychological differences among abused women who use violence in intimate relationships. *Violence Against Women, 9,* 75–109.

Swan, S.C., & Snow, D.L. (2006). The development of a theory of women's use of violence in intimate relationships. *Violence Against Women, 12*(11), 1026–1045.

Zahn, M.A., Agnew, R., Fishbein, D., Miller, S., Winn, D., Dakoff, G., … Chesney-Lind, M. (2010). *Causes and correlates of girls' delinquency.* Washington, DC: Office of Juvenile Justice and Delinquency Prevention, Office of Justice Programs, U.S. Department of Justice.

Zahn, M.A., Brumbaugh, S., Steffensmeier, D., Feld. B.C., Morash, M., Chesney-Lind, M., … Kruttschnitt, C. (2008). *Violence by teenage girls: trends and context.* Washington, DC: Office of Juvenile Justice and Delinquency Prevention, Office of Justice Programs, U.S. Department of Justice.

Role of Women in the War on Drugs

9

AMY POLAND

Contents

While there has been a great deal of coverage on the effect of the War on Drugs on men, especially minority men, it has been a War on Women as well. Twenty years ago, Tonry (1995) focused on the effect of the War on Drugs on black men because of the greater number of black men in the criminal justice system and the effect it had on their community. While many of our drug laws were a response to maintain social control of a minority population, the same laws have had many detrimental effects on women. The recent era of harsher drug laws has led to an increase in the incarceration of females and drug law initiatives targeted specifically toward women (using drugs while pregnant, for example) continue to spread throughout the country. While fewer women than men are incarcerated, the rate of incarceration of women has increased twice as fast as the rate of incarceration of men. Much of the dramatic increase can be attributed to the War on Drugs and incarceration of women for drug offenses. Minority females, single mothers, and other economically marginalized women are at a higher risk of being incarcerated for drug offenses.

Today, women represent 17% of all offenders under correctional sanction in the United States (Bloom, Owen, & Covington, 2004; Carson, 2014). Yet, as with almost every other criminal justice issue, much of the attention regarding the War on Drugs has been focused on men who are using, addicted to, and dealing drugs and their treatment in the criminal justice system. Little attention has been given to the unique ways in which the War on Drugs has affected and continues to affect women in the United States. The context of women's lives and realities of gender are ignored; women suffer as a result and are often punished disproportionately to the harm caused. This chapter will review the history of drug use and addiction by women in the United States, the War on Drug policies that have been passed and their effect on women, and the current state of the War on Drugs as it relates to women.

History of Women's Drug Use

Women have always had a unique interaction with drugs. Women's addiction to drugs is not a new phenomenon in the United States. In fact, some of the first drug addicts here in the United States were middle- and upper-class white women who used opiates and cocaine under a doctor's care or in the form of elixirs readily available and used to treat a wide array of *female* problems such as hysteria or menstrual cramps. Opium was originally used to treat insanity and then later seen as a cause of insanity. Heroin was prescribed to reduce coughing. Cocaine was in patent medications, cough drops, and beverages (such as Coca-Cola) and was used as a topical antiseptic.

Up until the 1800s, there was no distinction between medical and nonmedical use of opium and its derivatives (such as morphine). Even after regulations were put in place, recreational use of opiates continued; the only decline was in medical use. In fact, in the late 1700s, it was common practice for women of Nantucket Island to use opium every morning (Kandall, 1996). By the end of the nineteenth century, almost two thirds of the nation's opium and morphine addicts were women. They were self-medicating for women's ailments and child birth. Women who were deemed hysterical were self-administering morphine with a hypodermic needle to treat it; they became some of the nation's first opiate addicts. At the end of the nineteenth century, most of the nation's opiate addicts were white, middle-/upper-class housewives/socialites who were prescribed opium or morphine for masturbation, violent hiccoughs, or female problems.

While opiate and cocaine use among women was allowed in society, alcohol use by women was more restricted. During Colonial times, women were only allowed to drink at home or at social occasions. They were restricted from entering taverns; however, by the mid-1700s, most taverns were run by women. Alcohol was also consumed in the same patent medicines that contained cocaine and opiates. And while addiction to opiates and cocaine was tolerated, women who were drunk were thought to be promiscuous and fallen women; they could be sterilized for alcoholism.

Amid the increased regulations in the twentieth century, women's drug use changed rapidly. While heroin was the drug of choice for many of the first women addicted to drugs here in the United States, as drug laws were passed and over time, the drug of choice among women changed. When the War on Drugs was declared by Nixon, women were experiencing a resurgence of addiction to heroin with rates of addiction as high as 30%; however, they were also using, and becoming addicted to, cocaine in large amounts due to both its popularity among celebrities and athletes, and its ability to suppress appetite. The following decades introduced women to crack cocaine and synthetic club drugs found at raves (National Center on Addiction and Substance Abuse at Columbia University, 2006).

Contemporary Drug Use by Women

Flavin and Paltrow (2010) demonstrate the prevalent, regular drug use by women today, reporting that "Most women in the United States use some type of drug on a regular basis.

We use prescription and over-the-counter drugs to help us sleep, stay awake, alleviate pain, lose weight, cope with depression and anxiety, and so forth. We drink coffee and tea and eat chocolate, all substances that contain caffeine. We consume alcoholic beverages, and we smoke cigarettes" (p. 232). Before the twentieth century, smoking was predominantly male; after the Nineteenth Amendment, cigarettes became a symbol of women's freedom. Cigarette companies began to target women. While illegal drug use is relatively low among females, almost half of all females aged 12 years and older are current drinkers. In comparison, only 6.5% of females were currently using illegal drugs, including marijuana (5%). Just over 2% were illegally using prescription drugs. Approximately 6% of females reported substance abuse or dependence (Substance Abuse and Mental Health Services Administration, 2012).

According to the National Center on Addiction and Substance Abuse at Columbia University (2006), more than half of all women aged 18–25 have used illicit drugs at least once and more than 2.5 million women are dependent or abuse illicit drugs. One in five women smokes. Even if we consider only illegal drug use, the numbers demonstrate the need for attention to the unique relationship women have with substance abuse. Nine million women have used illegal drugs in the past year; 3.7 million women have taken prescription drugs illegally during the past year. Most women drug abusers use more than one drug. Almost half of all women aged 15–44 have used drugs at least once in their life; nearly 2 million have used cocaine and more than 6 million have used marijuana within the past year (National Institute of Drug Abuse, n.d.)

Even the pathways to substance abuse are unique for women as they become addicted at lower level of use and in shorter periods of time, but little attention is paid to female addicts, and 92% of women in need of treatment do not receive it. From 1941 to 1971, 15,000 women sought treatment at federal drug treatment facilities in Lexington, Kentucky. During his tenure as president, in the middle of increasing penalties for drugs, Kennedy recognized the need for drug treatment and initiated development of new drug treatment techniques—therapeutic communities, outpatient treatment, detoxification centers, correctional treatment programs, and methadone maintenance. However, all of these were male oriented and dominated in both their clients and their treatment approaches (Kandall, 1996).

Case Study 1

In 1973, the State of New York enacted harsh penalties for individuals convicted of possession or selling narcotic drugs. The law mandates minimum sentences without regard to prior criminal record and imposes the same sanction for selling a small or large amount of narcotics. The mandatory minimum of 15 years to life is the same as the mandatory minimum for murder and more severe than the sentence for rape, sexual abuse of a minor, or armed robbery.

Arlene O'Berg was a 22-year-old, divorced, single mother addicted to cocaine when she was arrested for selling cocaine. She had already given up her daughter to her ex-husband because of her addiction. She found out she was pregnant and wanted to get into a treatment program. She went to a friend to get money for treatment and was lured into a sting operation. She had no prior criminal history and was offered a plea bargain of 3 years to life; when she didn't take it, the district attorney increased the sentence with the plea bargain and she eventually went to trial thinking she had nothing to lose. She ended up convicted and sentenced to 20 years to life in prison. Her daughter was born while she was awaiting trial and was sent to live with her grandmother.

Cherie Gallipoli was physically and emotionally abused by her first husband and left her husband when she found out he was sexually abusing their 12-year-old daughter. She quickly remarried and later found out her new husband was a drug smuggler. She initially asked him to leave the drug trade but eventually helped him with his drug business. She and her husband traveled back to New York to help her son with a drug deal because she feared for her son who had also become involved in the drug trade. They were arrested, she pled guilty, and was sentenced to 15 years to life.

Leah Bundy was 21 years old when she was convicted of *constructive possession* because she was one of three people present when police entered the apartment of her boyfriend where drugs were present. Leah knew that her boyfriend was a drug dealer but was not involved with drugs herself. When the police showed up, she was in the bathroom; her boyfriend's brother, hearing the police, threw vials of crack out the window which was witnessed by other officers outside. She was sentenced to 15 years to life for her conviction, despite the fact that she has never been involved with drugs herself. Her conviction was upheld on appeal but she was granted clemency by the governor in 2000 after serving 10 years of her sentence (Gray, 2005; SenGupta & Peterson, 1999).

Drug Policies and Legislation

The War on Drugs has socially constructed certain drugs to be more harmful and more dangerous, and in an effort to protect society have made these drugs illegal. Specifically with regard to women, illegal drugs have been viewed as a threat to family and home life; the solution is to promote abstinence and prohibition (Boyd, 2004). This remains true today despite research that consistently shows that legal and socially acceptable drugs such as alcohol and nicotine are more dangerous and more harmful.

Young (1997) challenges us to consider the social, economic, and political environments that contribute to the historical and contemporary drug policies and laws in the United States. During Colonial times, punishment was restricted to those who overindulged, such as a public reprimand or punishment in the stocks for the alcoholic for his *self-indulgence*. As the nation grew and people began migrating west, not only did alcohol production and consumption grow but the migration allowed for the transportation of other mind-altering substances to places where they were not natively found. Initially, governments attempted to control the importation and exportation of psychoactive substances through the use of tariffs, which only resulted in those smuggling of substances.

Prior to the twentieth century, there were few restrictions on the importation and use of mind-altering substances (Chin, 2002). Both opium and cocaine use were quietly tolerated even in society upper classes. As detailed previously, both heroin and cocaine were widely available in tonics and even beverages, and physicians prescribed first opiates and later cocaine to treat a variety of female-specific syndromes. At the turn of the century, local laws directed at opium smoking led to federal drug laws aimed at fighting the *supply side* of the War on Drugs in this country. The laws were passed against drugs that were considered to be so dangerous they must be criminalized in an effort to protect the general public from drug traffickers, but most drug convictions were for possession, not trafficking. Further, most drug convictions were for marijuana, not cocaine or heroin.

Harrison Tax Act (1914)

By 1900, 1 in 200 Americans was addicted to cocaine and other narcotics. At the turn of the twentieth century, an international drug control treaty and the moral degradation caused by opiate use led to the passage of the Pure Food and Drug Act (1906) and the Harrison Narcotics Act (1914), which restricted the use and distribution of narcotics. The nonmedical use of narcotics was made illegal and prescriptions could not be provided for addicts to continue their addictions.

Within 6 weeks, sanatoriums and hospitals were filling up with addicts and others were committing crimes to get drugs. The Harrison Narcotic Act was upheld in a pair of Supreme Court cases 5 years later. *U.S. v. Doremus* (249 US 86) upheld the constitutionality of the act and that the law could restrict medical use of drugs. *Webb et al. v. U.S.* (249 US 96) restricted doctors from prescribing narcotics solely for addiction maintenance. There was a general decline in cocaine use in the years after the Harrison Act and Supreme Court decisions. Some female addicts, however, were still able to get narcotics from their doctors and rich women could still access drugs privately. There was an increase in the number of addicts, and the profile of the typical addict changed from middle- or upper-class white women to poor urban women who were dependent on male suppliers (Kandall, 1996; National Center on Addiction and Substance Abuse at Columbia University, 2006).

After the Harrison Narcotics Act, specific drugs were targeted for federal enforcement. The Eighteenth Amendment was passed in 1920 to prohibit the manufacturing and distribution (but not consumption) of alcohol in the United States. This was an extension of the Temperance Movement from the late 1800s and continued until the passing of the Twenty-First Amendment in 1937. Prohibition was unsuccessful in stopping the sale and distribution of alcohol; in fact, trafficking of alcohol across the country spurred the growth of organized crime in the United States. Two years later, the Narcotic Drugs Import and Export Act (1922) created the Federal Narcotics Control Board and eliminated the earlier exemption that still allowed opium smoking in opium dens, effectively creating the first nationwide ban on opium smoking in public.

The same year that prohibition was repealed, Congress passed the Marijuana Tax Act (1937), which required that anyone selling marijuana, cannabis, or hemp to register and pay a yearly tax. It did not specifically make marijuana illegal but did provide penalties for anyone selling marijuana without registering. The law was declared unconstitutional because it violated the Fifth Amendment provision against self-incrimination and was repealed in 1970.

Comprehensive Drug Abuse Prevention and Control Act (Controlled Substances Act; 1970)

In 1970, the Controlled Substances Act established a schedule of five levels of narcotic drugs according to both their risk for abuse and accepted medical use. The most restricted drugs, Schedule I drugs such as marijuana, heroin, or ecstasy, have no accepted medical use and are viewed as highly addictive; they are illegal to manufacture and distribute and no prescriptions can be written for their use. On the other end, Schedule V drugs have some limited possibility of dependence and are medically accepted; they require a prescription to obtain.

The act was amended in 1984 and 1988 to increase penalties for dealing near schools and allowed for civil forfeiture of property obtained with funds from drug manufacturing and distribution; previously only property used in illegal activity was subject to forfeiture. This provision affected women in relationships with men who were convicted of manufacturing and distributing drugs as they were at risk of losing property, money, and possessions, even if they were unaware of their partner's actions. In addition, the increase in penalties has been applied to women who are using drugs and has resulted in longer sentences for possession, even though the original target of the legislation is drug traffickers.

The Controlled Substances Act and the revisions of the act are the beginning of War on Drugs seen today. While Nixon had declared a War on Drugs, much of his policy focused on treatment rather than criminal punishment. Starting with Reagan and continuing with Bush, Clinton, Bush, and Obama, the administrations have waged a War on Drugs that emphasizes criminal penalties over treatment. Moreover, where previously drug control efforts had focused on crop reduction, interdiction at the borders, and major drug traffickers, laws and criminal sanctions were now being applied to low-level dealers and users (Mitchell, 2009).

Rockefeller Drug Laws and Anti-Drug Abuse Acts (1986 and 1988)

In 1973, the State of New York passed the strictest state laws regarding penalties for the sale and/or possession of drugs in the country. The penalty for selling 2 ounces or possessing 4 ounces of heroin, morphine, opium, cocaine, or cannabis was a minimum of 15 years in prison and up to 25 years to life in prison. This is the same as the penalty for first-degree murder; prior to the passing of the law, this sentence was imposed for possession of at least 16 ounces of a narcotic drug. The penalties were later reduced and the mandatory minimums were eventually removed, and individuals facing life sentences were allowed to apply for resentencing under the new laws. The revisions allowed judges to sentence people to drug treatment instead of jail or prison (Tinto, 2001).

The Rockefeller Drug Laws have led both to great increases in the prison population in New York (from 12,500 to 70,000) and an increase in the percentage of female inmates (from 3.5% to 5%; Tinto, 2001). The Rockefeller Drug Laws have also disallowed judges the ability to take individual circumstances into consideration at the time of sentencing; specifically many of the women convicted of drug offenses are in intimate relationships with men who use and/or sell drugs and their own drug use is only understood within the context of the relationship. Some women, in relationships with men involved with drugs, may use and/or sell drugs to support their partner; they may feel they cannot leave the relationship because of their addiction and need for narcotic drugs, because of domestic violence, or because of a desire to keep their family together (if they have children with their boyfriend/husband). Tinto (2001) argues that these women's relationship context should be taken into account at the time of sentencing, which was not allowed under the original Rockefeller Drug Laws and is not specifically provided for in the revisions.

At the federal level, the Anti-Drug Abuse Act of 1986 established the first sentencing guidelines for drug trafficking including mandatory minimums for specific drugs, mirroring the Rockefeller Drug Laws in New York. This act established the 100:1 disparity between sentences for crack cocaine and cocaine where the sentence for 1 g of crack is the same as the sentence for 100 g of cocaine. Originally, no mandatory minimums were established for methamphetamine; however, in the 1988 revision of the act, a 5-year mandatory minimum was established for 10 g of methamphetamine (Bush-Baskette & Smith, 2012). With regard to the effect of mandatory sentences on women drug offenders, judges are not allowed to consider the specific context of a woman's life and her children when they are restricted by mandatory sentencing guidelines. Further, these strict mandatory sentencing schemes have led to dramatic increases in the number of women in prison nationwide for drug offenses (Hagan & Coleman, 2001).

Disenfranchisement

One of the least understood areas of punishment is the disenfranchisement of ex-offenders upon return to the community. Disenfranchisement of female drug offenders can be seen as the real punishment even for women who are not sent to jail or prison. First-time offenders or minor offenders receive probation or suspended sentences even though long sentences are authorized by legislatures. The real sentence is the loss of rights as a convicted felon. Women who have been convicted of a drug offense, in addition to be unable to vote as a convicted felon, will face multiple bans as they try to put their lives back together and successfully integrate back into their community. They are often unable to qualify for state and federal aid as a result of their drug conviction. They will also not be able to take out federal student loans to help pay for college in an attempt to better their lives if they have been convicted of a drug crime. All of these bans make the transition to the community more difficult for women coming out of prison or jail and make it more difficult to find legitimate ways to be successful in society (Chin, 2002). The 1997 Adoption and Safe Families Act has taken away many, if not all, parental rights of incarcerated women in the name of finding permanent homes for their children while they are incarcerated. While most mothers who have been incarcerated intend to resume parental responsibilities upon release from prison, this act terminates their rights, thereby taking that decision and their relationship with their child(ren) away from them (Hagan & Coleman, 2001).

If they are in need of public housing, they may not be approved due to their drug conviction; if they have not been convicted of a drug crime but their partner and/or child's father is convicted of a drug crime, they will not be able to live together in public housing as he will be banned because of his conviction. Additionally, if a resident or guest in public housing is suspected of using or dealing drugs or any drug-related activity, the tenant can lose their apartment. Stemming from the Anti-Drug Abuse Act of 1988, the public housing ban is a civil, not criminal, matter and therefore a criminal conviction is not necessary for proof of drug-related activity. In 1994, the law was amended to include drug-related activities both in public housing and elsewhere and in 2002, in *Department of Housing and Urban Development v. Rucker*, the Supreme Court upheld the act giving public housing authorities the ability to evict tenants for their drug-related activities, their families, and their guests. Further, in an attempt to rid public housing of drug-related activity, eviction procedures in public housing have been streamlined and for tenants being evicted for suspected drug-related activity, all appellate procedures have been eliminated. These policies adversely affect single mothers who are most often in public housing, even when they do not engage in drug-related activities (Boyd, 2004; Chin, 2002).

Case Study 2

Dalanda Moses lived in public housing in Annapolis, Maryland, with her family for most of her life. At 19, she had a baby with James Alexander, who was on the banned list of the Housing Authority of the City of Annapolis (HACA) because of a juvenile drug arrest for which he was never prosecuted. The list bans more than 500 people from public housing property within the city; many are there even though they have never been charged or convicted of a crime, and of those with convictions, many are for minor offenses years ago. If they violate the ban they are arrested and prosecuted for trespassing and residents who allow them on the property are subject to eviction.

During her pregnancy, Dalanda suffered multiple health problems and complications but James was not allowed on the property to help Dalanda and even had to pick her up away from the property to be able to take her to medical appointments. Dalanda and her mother were told that they would be evicted if James was caught at the house.

After the baby was born, Dalanda remained in public housing with her mother where she tried to manage work, school, and motherhood. The ban forced her to either raise her child without a father or give up the help of family at a time when she needed it most. After appeals to the housing authority went unanswered, she decided to move out of public housing so that her family could be together and James could help care for their infant daughter.

The American Civil Liberties Union (ACLU) challenged the ban and in 2010 reached a settlement with HACA on behalf of the residents. The settlement put new policies and procedures in place that recognize that most of the people on the banned list are not a threat to the public housing community. The new policy allows for them to petition to be removed from the banned list. It also allows residents to designate banned individuals as *invited guests* with renewable passes. HACA will provide a list of banned individuals to residents so they will know if family and/or loved ones are on the list (ACLU, 2009, 2010; Migdal & Jeon, 2009).

Pregnancy and Substance Use

Regulation of women and subjugation to the home has occurred throughout history. Today the War on Drugs has converged with the regulation of reproductive rights and the resulting legislation has had detrimental consequences for women, especially women in the lower classes and women of color. Laws from around the country that criminalize drug use by pregnant women demonstrate the loss of control over a woman's own sexuality and reproduction; it is a war on all women (Boyd, 2004). These laws promote the idea that the fetus' rights outweigh the rights of the mother and actually identify the mother as an agent of harm (Gustavsson, 1991).

The laws also violate the due process rights of not only pregnant women but all women of childbearing ages. While possession of illegal drugs is a crime at the federal level and among the states, drug use and abuse is considered a public health, not criminal, concern. Similarly, alcohol possession and consumption is legal for adults over the age of 21 and alcohol abuse is a public health concern and not criminalized. However, pregnant women face discriminatory laws that criminalize their substance use and abuse. Gustavsson (1991) explains that these laws are based on the idea that pregnant women have a duty to protect their unborn child but that the idea fails to account for legal standards of intent. One of the most crucial stages of prenatal development is the first trimester (first 3 months of pregnancy); however, a woman may not know she is pregnant during this time due to stress, a poor environment, poor health, irregular menstrual cycles or other reasons. Therefore, it is impossible to establish intent (either knowing or reckless disregard) if the woman does not know she is pregnant at the time she is using alcohol or illegal drugs. The only way around this is to extend the duty to protect and therefore criminal liability for fetal harm to any woman of childbearing age who may believe she is pregnant, a change that is unprecedented here in the United States (Gustavsson, 1991).

The United States has experienced a rebirth in the past few years of moral panic over the effects of substance use on prenatal development and birth complications. In the last decades of the twentieth century, *crack babies* were said to have multiple and varied complications at birth and in their later development; however, those studies had many limitations including sample sizes as small as one, making it difficult to generalize the findings (Gustavsson, 1991). Legislatures across the nation passed laws to protect unborn children and criminalize the drug use of pregnant women. However, subsequent research showed that while babies who were exposed to cocaine in utero were more likely born premature, the complications they faced at birth were similar to all premature infants and they had normal development and met later developmental milestones.

Even with this information, today we are faced with a similar moral panic surrounding babies exposed to methamphetamine before birth. Even without evidence of harm to the fetus from methamphetamine use, states are again criminalizing drug use by pregnant women. Both of these legislative efforts have disproportionately punished low-income minority women in spite of statistics that show similar rates of both substance use and dependence among white, black, and Hispanic women (Flavin & Paltrow, 2010).

With all of the legal and public attention on pregnant women abusing crack cocaine, methamphetamine, and even alcohol, the most widely used and abused substance during pregnancy is tobacco. While approximately 3% of pregnant women use illegal substances or consume large amounts of alcohol during pregnancy, 17% of pregnant women smoke during pregnancy. Women abuse substances, both legal and illegal, during pregnancy for a variety of reasons. Some may not yet realize they are pregnant; others may not know or understand the risks of substance use and abuse on their pregnancy. Others still are unable to control their substance use and abuse as it is an escape from their reality of physical and sexual abuse and/or mental health problems (National Center on Addiction and Substance Abuse at Columbia University, 2006).

One of the unforeseen consequences of laws regarding substance use during pregnancy is the risk to the mother and fetus if a pregnant woman does not seek medical care out of fear of being prosecuted for her substance abuse. In their study of 36 pregnant women enrolled in a residential substance abuse treatment program during pregnancy, Jessup, Humphreys, Brindis, and Lee (2003) highlight many of the fears and barriers pregnant women face when seeking treatment, including the fear of losing custody of their infant child and being arrested and incarcerated for substance use during pregnancy. As a result of their concerns, many of the women interviewed avoided prenatal care during their pregnancies, an outcome predicted by previous research (Gustavsson, 1991). Moreover, medical and social service personnel threatened to remove the child from the home if the mother failed drug screenings, increasing the fear of the women and causing them to stop prenatal care. When referrals for prenatal substance abuse treatment were made, they were accompanied with threats about continued substance use and the removal of the child.

The pregnant women only sought substance abuse treatment when it was seen as necessary to maintain custody of their children or when they were transitioning out of jail and back into the community (Jessup et al., 2003).

Case Study 3

In 2012, Lacey Weld, 26 and in the final weeks of her pregnancy, was arrested after being caught on camera (worn by an undercover officer) visiting a meth lab for approximately 40 min. While there, she cooked and used methamphetamine. When her son was born, he tested positive for amphetamines and opiates and was drug dependent and suffered from withdrawal for about 6 weeks after birth. He experienced irritation, gastrointestinal problems, and a distended belly, all attributed to his mother's methamphetamine use when she was pregnant. A Department of Children's Services case manager testified that it was one of the worst cases she had seen. Her son is now 2 and according to her stepsister (the child's legal guardian) he suffers no adverse health conditions.

She later cooperated with law enforcement and testified against her codefendants. In 2014, she pled guilty to conspiracy to manufacture methamphetamine, punishable by up to 12 years in prison (and up to 24 years with the enhancement), though that would be reduced due to her cooperation with law enforcement. She was sentenced to 151 months (6.5 years) in prison and 5 years of supervised release after prison for conspiracy to manufacture methamphetamine and received an enhanced penalty of an additional 6 years for using methamphetamine while pregnant. This was a six-offense-level increase in her sentencing range for putting her unborn child at risk of substantial harm. However, methamphetamine use is not a crime at the state or federal level; possession is the crime and she was not convicted of possession of methamphetamine either. The additional sentence was administered for hurting her son, a crime for which she was not convicted.

Lacey Weld's case is not unique, according to McDonough (2014), as 413 women between 1973 and 2005 and an additional 350 women in the last decade have had their pregnancies become a factor in determining the charges against them, therefore depriving them of due process and basic legal rights because they are pregnant. The question here is whether women should be subject to separate, unequal, and harsher penalties simply because they are pregnant. This case sets a precedent that behavior that is not criminal for the general population would be considered criminal when committed by a pregnant woman (Associated Press, 2014; Gwynne, 2014; Marcotte, 2014; McDonough, 2014; National Association of Pregnant Women, 2014; Times Free Press, 2014).

Characteristics of Women in Prison for Drug Crimes

While women continue to make up approximately 7% of the state and federal prison population, the percentage of women imprisoned has increased at a higher rate (10%) than men (7%) in the past decade (2003–2013; Carson, 2014). When trends are examined from when prison populations first started to rise dramatically in 1980–2012, the number of women in prison has increased at more than twice the rate (756% vs. 347%) of men over the same time period (Carson & Golinelli, 2013).

U.S. Arrest Estimates as accessed through the Arrest Data Analysis Tool (Bureau of Justice Statistics, 2014) illustrates that more females are arrested and incarcerated for drug possession than for drug trafficking. When we break it down by race, white women are more likely to be jailed for trafficking while black women are more likely to be jailed for possession. The increase in the incarceration of females can be directly tied to the increase in the number and strictness of drug law initiatives since 1980 (Bureau of Justice Statistics, 2014; Carson, 2014; Carson & Golinelli, 2013).

Twenty-five percent of women are in prison for drug violations compared to 15% of men. They have little income, education, or job skills, which contributes to erratic employment histories. Women in the criminal justice system are more likely to have grown up in a single family home than women in the general population and are more likely than incarcerated men to have a family member who has been incarcerated. Forty percent of women in the criminal justice system had reported prior abuse (compared to 9% of men in the criminal justice system). Women offenders also report higher levels of substance use and abuse than men offenders and experience more health problems than men in jails and prisons (Bloom et al., 2004).

Mullings, Pollock, and Crouch (2002) examined 1200 female inmates in Texas and found that incarcerated women with drug problems were more likely to have parents with drug and/or mental health problems. They were also more likely to have been neglected as children and physically and/or sexually abused. As a result, they were also more likely to have run away from home, used illegal drugs before age 15, and become pregnant before age 15. These women continued to experience mental, physical, and sexual abuse as adults, as well as not having their basic needs (food, shelter, and safety) met. In addition to having higher rates of criminality, women in prison who had drug problems also reported higher levels of pimping, prostitution, and selling drugs to pay for their drug habit.

Women's experiences in prison as a result of drug convictions are affected by the patriarchal nature of society. Because women make up a small minority of the prison population, they often do not have access to adequate and appropriate programming to help them transition back into society upon release. As a result, they often do not have the work or life skills to be successful after reentry into the community (Mauer, Potler, & Wolf, 1999).

Treatment and Harm Reduction

Initially, substance abuse by women is seen as an individual moral failing and women who became addicted to alcohol or other substances were seen as reprehensible. Even after addiction was recognized as a medical problem, women were often deemed untreatable because they had been taught by society to hide their addiction. By the time they came for treatment, their addiction was seen as being too far advanced to be treated. Treatment centers for women, either as an add-on to an existing facility or a separate facility, became available at the turn of the twentieth century, recognizing the gender-specific needs of addicted women. One aim of the treatment centers was detoxification, either through immediate withdrawal of all narcotics or through the use of morphine or cocaine in gradually smaller doses over time. Both were unsuccessful until the middle of the twentieth century with the discovery of methadone, an opiate substitute, that helped to manage the symptoms of withdrawal during the detoxification process (Kandall, 1996; National Center on Addiction and Substance Abuse at Columbia University, 2006).

Even after this, women struggled to get treatment for addiction, especially for alcohol addiction. Women were excluded completely and later segregated in meetings of

Alcoholics Anonymous (AA) because of both misinformation about women's addiction to alcohol and fears of wives when large numbers of single and divorced women joined the group. Due again to the specific needs of women, including social isolation that was evidenced even in AA meetings, women's AA groups were formed separate from men's AA groups (National Center on Addiction and Substance Abuse at Columbia University, 2006).

Both residential and community-based treatment programs were developed to treat narcotic addictions, especially among women. Therapeutic communities started in California and spread throughout the country, offering a psychotherapeutic approach to overcoming addiction in a residential setting. Removing women from their homes, where drugs were readily available, was necessary to rid them of their addiction. The specific pathway of women to substance abuse, including potential physical, sexual, or emotional abuse in past relationships, was integrated into treatment programs. Methadone maintenance programs popped up around the country to keep women from abusing opiates. Inpatient and outpatient programs without methadone were also prevalent and correctional treatment programs for women grew as the female correctional population grew. Today, science has shown that addiction is a brain disease and many evidence-based treatments have been found to help women overcome their addiction (Kandall, 1996; National Center on Addiction and Substance Abuse at Columbia University, 2006).

Conclusion

The War on Drugs has been a War on Women as well. More than any other criminal justice policy, the War on Drugs has disproportionately affected women over the past four decades through drastically increasing jail and prison populations, discriminatory laws targeted specifically toward women (substance use during pregnancy), and policies that adversely affect even women not involved with drugs (asset forfeiture and housing bans). The very laws that were originally constructed to protect women from dangerous drugs have been used to control their behaviors.

Discussion Questions

1. How can sentencing of women for their drug crimes be more equitable and more sensitive to the needs of women and their children?
2. How would addressing substance abuse during pregnancy from a public health perspective rather than a criminal justice perspective change society's response?
3. How does the disenfranchisement of women convicted of drug offenses affect their successful reentry into their communities?

References

American Civil Liberties Union. (2009). *Stories of Annapolis residents challenging housing policy that tears families apart*. Retrieved August 4, 2014, from https://www.aclu.org/womens-rights/stories-annapolis-residents-challenging-housing-policy-tears-families-apart

American Civil Liberties Union. (2010). *Settlement reached in challenge to unlawful Annapolis public housing ban*. Retrieved August 4, 2014, from https://www.aclu.org/womens-rights/settlement-reached-challenge-unlawful-annapolis-public-housing-ban

Associated Press. (2014). *Attorney to appeal 12-year sentence of woman who was pregnant while helping cook, sample meth.* Retrieved October 19, 2014 from http://www.timesfreepress.com/news/2014/jul/17/attorney-to-appeal-12-year-sentence/

Bloom, B., Owen, B., & Covington, S. (2004). Women offenders and the gendered effects of public policy. *Review of Policy Research, 21*(1), 31–48.

Boyd, S. C. (2004). *From witches to crack moms: Women, drug law, and policy.* Durham, NC: Carolina Academic Press.

Bureau of Justice Statistics. (2014). *Arrest data analysis tool.* Retrieved October 23, 2014, from http://www.bjs.gov/index.cfm?ty=datool&surl=/arrests/index.cfm

Bush-Baskette, S. R., & Smith, V. C. (2012). Is meth the new crack for women in the war on drugs: Factors affecting sentencing outcomes for women and parallels between meth and crack. *Feminist Criminology, 7*(1), 48–69.

Carson, E. A. (2014). *Prisoners in 2013.* Washington, DC: Bureau of Justice Statistics.

Carson, E. A. & Golinelli, D. (2013). *Prisoners in 2012.* Washington, DC: Bureau of Justice Statistics.

Chin, G. J. (2002). Race, the war on drugs, and the collateral consequences of criminal conviction. *Journal of Gender, Race & Justice, 6*, 253–275.

Flavin, J., & Paltrow, L. M. (2010). Punishing pregnant drug-using women: Defying law, medicine, and common sense. *Journal of Addictive Diseases, 29*(2), 231–244.

Gray, G. (2005). *Drug felon finds that new laws don't mean quick release from prison.* Retrieved October 19, 2014, from http://www.nysun.com/new-york/drug-felon-finds-that-new-laws-dont-mean-quick/10664/

Gustavsson, N. S. (1991). Pregnant chemically dependent women: The new criminals. *Affilia, 6*(2), 61–73.

Gwynne, K. (2014). *A woman got six extra years in prison because she was pregnant.* Retrieved October 19, 2014, from http://www.vice.com/read/a-woman-got-six-extra-years-in-prison-because-she-was-pregnant-1010

Hagan, J., & Coleman, J. P. (2001). Returning captives of the American war on drugs: Issues of community and family reentry. *Crime & Delinquency, 47*, 352–367.

Jessup, M. A., Humphreys, J. C., Brindis, C. D., & Lee, K. A. (2003). Extrinsic barriers to substance abuse treatment among pregnant drug dependent women. *Journal of Drug Issues, 33*, 285–304.

Kandall, S.R. (1996). *Substance and shadow: Women and addiction in the United States.* Cambridge, MA: Harvard University Press.

Marcotte, A. (2014). *Tennessee sentenced a woman to six extra years in jail simply because she was pregnant.* Retrieved October 19, 2014, from http://www.slate.com/blogs/xx_factor/2014/10/13/lacey_weld_case_tennessee_woman_gets_six_extra_years_in_prison_for_being.html

Mauer, M., Potler, C., & Wolf, R. (1999). *Gender and justice: Women, drugs, and sentencing policy.* Washington, DC: The Sentencing Project.

McDonough, K. (2014). *Federal judge: Pregnancy can be grounds for enhanced criminal penalties.* Retrieved October 19, 2014, from http://www.salon.com/2014/07/15/tennessee_woman_may_face_a_double_prison_sentence_simply_because_she_was_pregnant/

Migdal, A., & Jeon, D. (2009). *Annapolis housing policy hurts families.* Retrieved August 4, 2104, from, http://articles.baltimoresun.com/2009-09-03/news/0909020048_1_public-housing-annapolis-housing-authority

Mitchell, O. (2009). Ineffectiveness, financial waste, and unfairness: The legacy of the war on drugs. *Journal of Crime and Justice, 32*(2), 1–19.

Mullings, J. L., Pollock, J., & Crouch, B. M. (2002). Drugs and criminality. *Women & Criminal Justice, 13*(4), 69–96.

National Association of Pregnant Women. (2014). *Nationwide coalition calls on Department of Justice to denounce enhanced sentence for pregnant woman* [Press Release]. Retrieved from http://www.legalvoice.org/news/documents/DOJLetterPressRelease.pdf

National Center on Addiction and Substance Abuse at Columbia University, The (2006). *Women under the influence.* Baltimore, MD: The Johns Hopkins University Press.

National Institute of Drug Abuse. (n.d.). *Women and drug abuse.* Retrieved October 23, 2014, from, http://archives.drugabuse.gov/WomenDrugs/Women-DrugAbuse.html

SenGupta, S., & Peterson, J. (1999). *Mandatory injustice: Case histories of women convicted under New York's Rockefeller Drug Laws* (A report of the women in prison project of the correctional association of New York). New York, NY: Correctional Association of New York.

Substance Abuse and Mental Health Services Administration. (2012). Results from the 2011 *National survey on drug use and health: Summary of national findings.* Rockville, MD: Substance Abuse and Mental Health Services Administration.

Times Free Press. (2014). *Woman gets 12-year prison term for making meth—While she's 9 months pregnant.* Retrieved October 19, 2014, from http://timesfreepress.com/news/2014/jul/15/woman-gets-12-year-prison-term-making-meth-while-s/

Tinto, E. K. (2001). The role of gender and relationship in reforming the Rockefeller Drug Laws. *NYU Law Review, 76,* 906–944.

Tonry, M. (1995). *Malign Neglect: Race, crime and punishment in America.* New York, NY: Oxford University Press.

Young, N. (1997). Alcohol and other drugs: The scope of the problem among pregnant and parenting women in California. *Journal of Psychoactive Drugs, 29*(1), 3–22.

The Female Thief

DOSHIE PIPER AND GEORGEN GUERRERO

10

Contents

Introduction

The simple act of theft or larceny is the taking of one's property without the owner's permission (Hagan, 2010). Larceny, as referred to under English common law, today has numerous legal definitions and varies by jurisdiction. The numerous forms of larceny consist of embezzlement, the receipt of stolen goods, shoplifting, burglary, robbery, check forgery, and auto theft (Hagan, 2010). This chapter will focus exclusively on the acts of larceny in which females are likely to engage.

Official statistics (Uniform Crime Report [UCR], National Crime Victim Survey [NCVS], and self-report studies) do not always categorize property crime in the same manner as do criminal justice scholars. Hagan (2010) includes any and all criminal acts, violent or not, committed against an individual, a structure/establishment, and an automobile as property crime. He also identifies vandalism, arson, identify theft, scams, and cons in his discussion of property crime. This chapter does not take such an inclusive approach but will include offenses of theft that are usually not considered larceny or theft by the nature of the crime.

Robbery and embezzlement are not classified as property crimes. Robbery usually gets classified as a violent crime (FBI, n.d.) and embezzlement as a white collar crime.

Nevertheless, when considering women who engage in theft, robbery and embezzlement must be included. Not including offenses where property was taken from individuals or organizations would paint an incomplete picture of the female thief.

Current State of Female Property Crime

Females have the reputation of committing crimes that are consistent with the stereotypical gender role of females as caretakers (Steffensmeier & Allan, 1996). These crimes include, but are not limited to, petty theft/shoplifting, writing bad checks, credit card fraud, and welfare fraud. There are many different explanations of why females commit property offenses. The gender inequality theory presents the most convincing account. According to Chesney-Lind (1997), women have consistently faced conditions of marginalization that keep them in low-paying, unrewarding, and unsecure occupations. A female's participation in property crime is thus a response to economic insecurity (Small, 2000).

On the other hand, Simon and Landis (1991) present a very different argument of why females commit more property crime than other offenses. They suggest that as a woman increases her occupation opportunities, her skill sets and social networks change and so will her chances to engage in criminality increase. Opportunity theory suggests that there are links between female criminality and changes in occupation opportunities.

Some women commit property crime to support their substance dependencies. Data clearly document a connection between property crime and women addicts. For example, Inciardi (1980) presents data from a study of women heroin users. This research examined the relationship between prostitution and drug use. Results revealed that only 15% of the sample reported prostitution as their first offense. The majority of the sample (55%) reported that their first criminal offense was a property offense: 5% burglary, 1% vehicle theft, 40% shoplifting, and 9% other theft (Inciardi, 1980).

Case Study 1: Jasmine Hernandez

In July 2013, a man left his car running as he dropped his children off in Phoenix, Arizona. Jasmine Hernandez, 19, jumped in the car and was revving up the engine, trying to steal the vehicle. When the owner came outside and ran to the car, he found her frantically stomping the pedals and pulling on the windshield wiper controls. The owner pulled her out of the car and held her captive until the police arrived at the scene to arrest her.

Important Legislation and Laws

It is well documented throughout the criminal justice literature that women navigate the underworld in order to support substance dependencies (Caputo & King, 2011; Inciardi, 1980; Steffensmeier, 1983). Inciardi (1980) gave a statistical account of women substance users who partake in property crime. Further, Caputo and King (2011) interviewed female substance abusers who shoplift to support their drug addictions. From the addicts' perspective, stealing is necessary to avoid being *dope sick*.

Society tends to view women who steal as *others* (Chesney-Lind, 2006; Jewkes, 2012). This perceived otherness is precisely the prevailing cultural ideology used to categorize criminal women. According to Jewkes (2012), deviant women will never be acceptable as a part of society. Take, for example, President George W. Bush's *Moral Values* campaign. President Bush used gender roles for his own political gain opposing gay and lesbian agendas, as well as abortion. His political agenda facilitated the criminalization of immoral behavior. Jewkes (2012) suggested that female crime is perceived as immoral and does not display the essence of a woman.

Offender Punishments

Russell (1978) recommends group therapy as a legal sanction for women who shoplift. The economic marginalization theory (Chesney-Lind, 1997) suggests that women who steal suffer from poverty, joblessness, and social isolation. Group therapy is a very useful technique that can facilitate the creation of support systems and begin to break down the social isolation and conditions of marginalization. This type of treatment was very popular from 1980 to 2000 (Kolman & Wasserman, 1991).

It is not uncommon for the criminal justice system to impose (court order) treatment as a response to criminality, especially when the offender does not have the resources to pay for private treatment. The Theft Program for Women is a criminal sanction for women who engage in property crime in Ramsey County, located in St. Paul, Minnesota. The Theft Program is a collaboration between the Wilder Community Assistance Program, the Wilder Foundation and the Ramsey County Community Corrections Department (Kolman & Wasserman, 1991). The program, which has been in existence for approximately 30 years, was intended to deliver a set of flexible, nonresidential services for adult offenders and their families. In addition to the theft groups for women offenders' program, they offer additional services such as property offenders' groups, women's domestic abuse programs, parenting programs for men and women, programs for children and adolescents from violent homes, custody and visitation dispute program, and support groups for women leaving prostitution (Kolman & Wasserman, 1991).

Kolman and Wasserman (1991) present information from their research "Theft Groups for Women: A Cry for Help" on how the nonprofessional shoplifters interpret theft programs. This research discusses the experiences of women in a group setting who engage in theft, through shoplifting. The goals of the theft program are outlined below:

> to talk in depth about their shoplifting offense and explore law-abiding alternatives to their shoplifting behavior and any other self-destructive behaviors which they may be exhibiting, to prevent further involvement in the court system, to get support from the other members of the group, to reduce the embarrassment and shame the women feel, to improve their problem-solving skills, to provide education and information about the court system, and to become aware of resources in the community to help the women deal with their problems and crises in the future.
>
> **Kolman and Wasserman (1991)**

This research surveyed 84% of the female clients that were sent to the program for shoplifting. The questions centered on attitudes and perceptions of treatment. The findings support Russell's (1978) recommendations for group therapy. The sample reported "(1) feeling remorseful about their crime (before and after counseling), (2) not understanding why they shoplifted (before counseling), and (3) citing frustration as a reason for their behavior (after counseling)" (Kolman & Wasserman, 1991).

Professional/Accomplice Theft

The role of women and men are very different when considering the professional criminal. Men are usually defined as "professionals" and women are more likely to be defined as "accomplices." In *Organizational Properties and Sex-Segregation in the Underworld*, Steffensmeier (1983) provides an explanation of why this is. Steffensmeier's (1983) research on organized crime observed that there was the existence of gender segregation and within the segregation women were either excluded or underrepresented in professional roles. Women's participation in professional crime is a breakdown of role allocation. Women are assigned specific tasks when partaking in professional theft. For example, women can be assigned roles of decoys, spies, or watchers. Again assisting by the opportunities offered through female role performance.

The existence of gender segregation limits female participation in theft crimes to a support role. Typically, the female role in theft crimes is as a cover for male criminal activity (Steffensmeier, 1983). A female who uses her femininity in a highly sexualized manner to exploit male masculinity during the commission of a crime is a sexual media. An example of "cover" will be provided under the discussion about robbery.

Robbery

Robbery and burglary are typically considered male offenses since men commit them more frequently than women. Data on female offenders who commit robbery and burglary just began to emerge in the past 60 years. Prior to the creation of the UCR and other forms of official statistics, reports of female robbery were scarce. However, some reports showed women in a support role as an accomplice, either a decoy or lookout (Pollack, 1978). There are, however, instances of woman who commit robbery. The female gang of bank robbers in Chicago is an exception to the rule. The Michigan Babies were a group of stick-up women who would target banks close to Lake Michigan and use their femininity to lure bank officials into their traps (Pollack, 1978). This abuse of the female gender role creates distractions, which lowers their detectability.

Case Study 2

In March 2008, Ashley Miller and Heather Johnston, aka the "Barbie Bandits," were sentenced for bank robbery in Acworth, Georgia. A bank video showed the two women laughing and joking with teller Benny Allen III, then handing him a hold up note. Apparently, the women who were dancers at an Atlanta-area strip club had made plans to split the $10,000 with Allen after the robbery. The women had met Allen through another convicted felon, who was also charged with participating in the robbery. The women led police in a car chase before their arrest, where marijuana and ecstasy were found in the car. Miller was sentenced to 10 years in prison and a fine, Johnston received 10 years' probation and a fine, and Allen received 10 years in prison with a fine.

Burglary

Similar to robbery, women who commit burglary are often working as accomplices (Pollack, 1978). The female burglar acts as a secret agent, a distraction, or a bystander. Historically, her goal has been to gain the confidence of any male property protector, and arrange a rendezvous to ensure that the property is unprotected when the professional male burglar arrives. This sounds old, but this continues to be the role of women in burglary today.

A study conducted by Mullins and Wright (2003) on gender and residential burglary showed that females were introduced to burglary by an intimate partner, usually a boyfriend. The males in the study typically were introduced to residential burglary through a same-gender peer; this was not the case for females (Miller & Wright, 2003). The findings use quotes from female participants who explained how they were initiated into residential burglary. One participant was quoted as saying:

> Okay, [on my first burglary] me and my boyfriend. my kids' father, we was together and he was way older than I was anyway. He was into breaking into houses and stuff so it was me, him and his brother.

Miller and Wright (2003, p. 820)

These findings are consistent with Steffensmeier's (1983) work on sex segregation and women thieves' role and relation in property offenses. He points out that the male thief perceives a woman as loyal, "if she's my woman, then she's safe" (Steffensmeier, 1983, p. 1013). Similarly, a woman will become a willing participant in the hustle if she perceives her participation as rewarding to the relationship.

Mullins and Wright (2003) sought to expand on the connection between gender, social networks, and residential burglary. They examined the gender structures of burglary networks and opportunities and means between men and women. This research examined 18 female and 36 male burglars. The interview questions centered around motivation, target selection, burglary commission, and desistence. The results of this data consistently show how women are constrained in their opportunities to commit burglary. Nevertheless, once the women successfully infiltrate residential burglary networks, the successful female offenders credited their success to gender-specific techniques (Mullins & Wright, 2003). For example, they may pose as a domestic worker (maid or housekeeper), through which they can obtain information on the layout, possible assets, accessibility, or inaccessibility.

Motor Vehicle

According to the UCR 10-year analysis between 2003 and 2012, arrests for motor vehicle theft have consistently decreased for males and females. For males, motor vehicle theft had the greatest percent decrease of all male crime categories with a 52.6% decrease in motor vehicle theft arrest. The actual number of arrests fell from 78,642 to 37,237. Female arrests for motor vehicle theft also decreased, dropping to 43.1%. The actual number of female arrests for motor vehicle theft fell from 15,531 in 2003 to 8833 in 2012. In their examination of motor vehicle theft victims, Steffensmeier and Allan (1996) found that women were responsible for 5% of the thefts (Steffensmeier & Allan, 1996).

Motor vehicle theft is the criminal act of stealing or attempting to steal an automobile and is often referred to as grand theft auto. Each year, nearly 1 million vehicles are stolen

(1 out of every 267 registered motor vehicles) (UCR, 2009). There are various forms of motor vehicle theft including *carjacking, alert opposition theft, active search*, and *master key and cousin keys theft* (Copes & Cherbonneau, 2006). *Carjacking* involves taking a car with brute force and is the least used of all the types of motor vehicle thefts (Copes & Cherbonneau, 2006). *Alert opposition theft* is the theft of an automobile by a perpetrator who has no intention of stealing an automobile, but just happened to have an opportunity to steal an automobile (Copes & Cherbonneau, 2006). *Active search* theft is the intentional searching for an available automobile or the keys of an automobile for the purposes of stealing the car (Copes & Cherbonneau, 2006). *Using master keys* is simply the use of a master key from a dealership that can start several vehicles in a particular make of auto- mobiles or a *close-cousin key* that is manufactured by trimming or shaving an existing key of another automobile (Copes & Cherbonneau, 2006).

Motor vehicle theft is generally a male-dominated crime and is generally studied as such. The research literature reveals only a handful of studies that include females in their examinations of auto theft. Females that engage in crimes of theft will generally avoid crimes that may lead to violence or that may involve police chases such as motor vehicle thefts (Mullins & Cherbonneau, 2011). Even males who engage in auto theft will avoid hav- ing females in their crews because of a fear that they will rat out their male counterparts when they are caught (Mullins & Cherbonneau, 2011). Women are viewed as not being fast enough to outrun the police, not being able to handle police pressure when caught, and if they are included in a crew they are generally relegated to the role of lookouts (Mullins & Cherbonneau, 2011).

Occasional/Conventional Theft

Occasional property criminals steal items on an irregular basis (Hagan, 2010). These thieves are generally considered noncareer criminals. These offenders possess the characteristics to maintain some conventional norms and blend in with what some scholars call the upper- world or legitimate world (Steffensmeier, 1983). The upperworld is the opposite of the under- world that is considered to be a "culture, setting, or social organization associated with criminal activities and more general rule-violating behavior" (Steffensmeier, 1983, p. 1011).

The conventional thief commits crime on a more regular and frequent basis (Hagan, 2010). These are women who maintain their livelihood from theft/larceny and burglary. Although they exhibit some characteristics of the professional/career criminals, these women remain at the lower end of the career continuum. These women usually maintain their legitimate status as wives or mothers.

Shoplifting

In *Shoplifting: Work, Agency, and Gender*, Caputo and King (2011) write about women who participate in shoplifting as economically motivated and view theft as work. The authors situate shoplifting as work for female offenders and "examine its occupational dimensions" (p. 159). They discuss shoplifting as work committed for income represent- ing similar structures of conventional occupations. For example, deviant workers have to complete tasks, manage stress, and socialize inside and outside of the job much like conventional workers.

Information is provided on the means in which women obtain shoplifting work. Caputo and King (2011) debunk the gendering of shoplifting as institutionalized sexism. This suggests that women who engage in shoplifting do so because men make it possible. Despite the suggestion that men only involve women when making their criminal work more profitable, this article suggests otherwise. Men have been known for providing transportation to and from retail centers and they provide a customer base. However, this is not always true. In fact, this notion is far from true when it comes to the women who shoplift.

Caputo's (2008) writings on substance-dependent women show females that employ criminal activity as their primary economic resource and cultivate community systems that make it profitable. They know who and where to sell their stolen goods, namely, "customers, best friends, social acquaintances, even strangers" (Caputo & King, 2011, p. 167). These females establish a customer base over a period of time just as suppliers do in the legitimate business world. Customers range from individuals to businesses. Having dependable customers makes shoplifting profitable. A shoplifter targets particular products and steals in an effort to keep her products moving and her customers happy.

A significant amount of detail is discussed by Caputo and King about the organizational and technical extents that go into to shoplifting as work. It is important to note that all of the participants in this study talked about it in occupational terms, using descriptive terms like: *career, profession, sales, customers, income,* and *technology* (Caputo & King, 2011). The organizational dimensions of shoplifting involve some dependence on others for transportation or a cover while in a retail store. The *drivers* or *hacks* are typically men. The women in the study discussed this organizational relationship in professional terms:

> Carmela keeps hacks competing for her business because she maintains relationships with them. "You have to take care of your driver," Francine similarly remarked, because they will take care of you in return in their loyalty and going out of their way to keep your business. To take care of hacks can mean keeping the drug-using hack high
>
> **Caputo and King (2011, p. 166)**

On the other hand, the technical dimension of shoplifting has three components that determine the success or failure of the crime. The three technical parts of shoplifting are planning, shoplifting, and minimizing risk (Caputo & King, 2011). The planning stage is the most critical. Plans range from very simple to extremely complicated. This includes decisions about where to shoplift, the number of stores to target, the amount of time to devote to one or more stores, and what to wear.

> Preparation also means gearing up to take on the criminal risk. For shoplifters, steering clear of incapacitation means they need to worry about apprehension by store security, deal with limits imposed by retailers who ban them from stores, and avoid incarceration. Shoplifting specialists must accept that each time they enter into the crime, they face apprehension, a "fifty-fifty chance" many of them reasoned. A common mechanism the women employ to get ready to take on this risk is to use drugs to take the edge off, to get ready.
>
> **Caputo and King (2011, p. 169)**

Women who steal view their actions as much more than just a way to earn money, but as their occupation or career. From this point of view, shoplifting can be considered any other type of illegal work (loan sharking, prostitution, and gambling). What sets this type of illegal work apart from others is the various degrees of gender and agency (Caputo & King, 2011). That is, the way in which women and men think, walk, and talk are gendered. Women who partake in shoplifting do not view themselves as feminine or masculine, but they do take part in gender dualism that recommends that the female thief has agency (Caputo & King, 2011).

Larceny

Larceny is the theft of money, goods, or services of another without permission. In the United States, larceny can be divided into two subcategories: grand larceny and petty (petit) larceny. Grand larceny is generally defined as the theft of any item of value over a certain dollar amount; however, dollar amounts vary across jurisdictions. In Texas, for example, grand larceny is the theft of any item over $500.00, while in Vermont it is the theft of any item over $900.00. In Virginia, it is the theft of any item over $200.00.

Petty larceny, on the other hand, is generally defined as the theft of items of lessor value; generally under $200.00. One who shoplifts $80.00 of clothing from the local department store is engaging in petty larceny. One who steals a brand new automobile from the local car dealer is engaging in grand larceny. Petty larceny has always been one of the highest arresting crimes for females. For example, a study of females that were committed to the California Youth Authority in 1960 found that half of them were committed for property offenses (Warren & Rosenbaum, 1986).

Even though larceny theft is viewed as one of the more female-dominated crimes, it still trails the male arrest rate for this crime. Males are arrested for shoplifting at a (3:1) ratio over females (Chesney-Lind & Shelden, 1992). When larceny theft is combined with running away (a predominately female status offense), these two offenses account for half of female crimes since 1965 (Chesney-Lind & Shelden, 1992). As a result of numerous biological, attitudinal, and situational differences, males and females generally commit crimes in different contexts. Females will generally have different styles, approaches, and attitudes to committing certain types of offenses. However, in the context of juvenile crimes, males and females were found to have no significant differences in their context of committing larceny theft (Triplett & Myers, 1995). If we pay attention to female criminality, we can start to see small patterns emerging. The strongest correlation between females and larceny appears to be with unemployment rates—larceny rates rise as female unemployment rises (Warner, 2012).

Fraud

Fraud is the intentional deceit or misrepresentation of self or fact to deprive another of property, money, goods, or services. Females have traditionally been the targets of fraud, but have started to be the perpetrators of such crimes because of political, social, technological, and economic changes in the recent decades (Gottschalk, 2012). In the business sector, female fraud has generally been found in self-acting-type fraud and avoided in more complex tax and securities frauds (Daly, 1989). As women are moving into higher company positions, their willingness to engage in fraud appears to equal to that of men (Steffensmeier, Schwartz, & Roche, 2013). However, females engage in business-related fraud for different reasons. Women engage in corporate fraud to protect their families or valued relationships; while males engage in fraud to protect their business or corporation (Cressey, 1953; Zeitz, 1981).

According to the UCR (2013), arrests for fraud have been decreasing for both males and females, despite being a category that includes welfare fraud. In the 10 years from 2003 to 2012, arrest for fraud was the second greatest declining category of arrest for males, second only behind motor vehicle theft. Fraud fell 47.8%, while motor vehicle theft fell 52.6%. However, fraud arrests had the greatest single change in all offense categories for females. With a 57.8% decrease in the number of fraud arrests, fraud surpassed even curfew and loitering violations, which had a 51.0% drop in the number of arrests. The 57.8% change was attributed to a drop from 101,513 arrests for female fraud in 2003 to 42,809 in 2012 (UCR, 2013). Furthermore, when women do engage in fraud schemes, they profit less than their male counterparts (Daly, 1989).

White Collar Theft

Women's increased presence in the labor force has had a significant impact on female criminality. Occasional and conventional theft has offered women a dramatic increase in the opportunity to engage in fraud, embezzlement, and forgery. Changes in the labor force have changed drastically over recent years. The more females occupy positions of power, status, and control in the economy, the greater opportunity exists for white collar crimes. As Rita J. Simon accurately predicted in her *Women in Crime* book some 40 years ago, that women's level of fraud, embezzlement, larceny, and forgery will all increase as women enter the workforce (Simon, 1975). Simon and Landis (1991) argued that not only would female embezzlement, larceny, and fraud increase as they enter the workforce but also as they acquire new skills and knowledge in these positions. Haantz (2002) found that one in four individuals imprisoned for federal white collar crime convictions for forgery, counterfeiting, fraud, and embezzlement were females (as cited in Warner, 2012). Furthermore, women appear to engage in these crimes for different reasons than men. Explanations of male offenders tend to focus on issues of wealth, self, status, and greed; while women appear to focus on issues of family, survival, and need.

Embezzlement

Embezzlement is the withholding of assets that one has been entrusted with for the purposes of conversion into a different area, usually for the perpetrators personal use. A review of the literature for the crime of embezzlement reveals that women may not have as many opportunities to engage in embezzlement, but it appears that women are more likely to engage in the crime of embezzlement when given an opportunity (Warner, 2012). Similar to male offending, upper-level corporate embezzlement is a rare offense for females (Steffensmeier & Allan, 1996). Its rarity develops due to the lack of opportunity of individuals in society to engage in such a crime. Embezzlement generally is restricted to those in power who have access to large sums of money. As women enter the labor market and continue to break through the glass ceiling and overcome traditional gender barriers, their opportunities for crimes such as embezzlement continue to rise.

Even though embezzlement is generally restricted to those in class and power and women have started to break through those traditional barriers, traditionally there have been opportunities for females to offend in the workplace. Female embezzlement has been found in lower-level administrative assistant or secretarial positions (Dodge, 2009). Additionally, Daly (1989) found that the highest levels of embezzlement were found in bank embezzlement, where women had nearly identical rates of embezzlement as men. Female bank embezzlers traditionally worked as bank tellers and stole by manipulating accounts or taking money and had high rates of convictions due in large part to having a higher degree of surveillance and regular financial audits. Common explanations for embezzlement include greed and in some cases need (Haantz, 2002). However, that may be too simplistic an explanation (Haantz, 2002). The real question becomes, why steal just a little if you are in that rare position to steal a lot more (Dodge, 2009)?

Female justifications for embezzlement in some cases mirror that of males. These females want to live lavish lifestyles, have excess money to spend, and even, like their male counterparts, have gambling addictions. However, females may also engage in embezzlement for any number of altruistic reasons (Dodge, 2009). Females increasingly carry the economic responsibilities in households, have to care for children and their significant others (Haantz, 2002), and need money for survival (Warner, 2012), or for day-to-day existence. Historically, women engage in nonconfrontational property crimes such as theft, fraud, and embezzlement and avoid crimes that may involve physical resistance, physical confrontation, and police chases such as robbery and burglary (Warner, 2012). Additionally, a pattern has started to emerge of females engaging in embezzling in groups (Dodge, 2009).

Just like for males female embezzlement has been steadily falling over the past decade. In 2003, the UCR reported 6426 arrests for female embezzlement and that number dropped to 5376 in 2012 for a net change of 16.3%. During the same time frame, male embezzlement dropped 11% from 6301 offenses in 2003 to 5605 in 2012. An examination of these numbers clearly shows that female arrest for the crime of embezzlement matches the rate of arrest for males. In 2009, female offending actually surpassed male offending with 6013 arrests for females and 5743 arrests for males, a rarity for any crime (Warner, 2012). It could easily be argued that female offending is currently exceeding male offending, but females may still be avoiding punishment through the criminal justice system. Women in top executive positions may be prosecuted to the fullest extent of the law, but females in mid-level administrative positions may be simply asked to resign from their positions or may be terminated in lieu of criminal prosecution.

Check Fraud

Like their male counterparts, forgery offenses for females have been falling over the past 10 years. According to the UCR, in 2003, males accounted for 45,818 crimes of forgery and counterfeiting; while females accounted for 31,184 crimes of forgery and counterfeiting. However, both of those numbers were drastically reduced by 2012. Male arrests for forgery and counterfeiting fell to 28,225 arrests, accounting for a 38.4% decrease, while numbers for female arrests for forgery and counterfeiting were nearly cut in half, falling to 16,823 arrests, accounting for a net change of 46.1%.

Check fraud is a type of embezzlement that takes various forms. It is generally defined as the cashing, withdrawing, or the borrowing of funds through the use of a check, from an account that does not have the funds available. Check fraud is considered to be one of the easiest and simplest forms of any major crime to commit (Lemert, 1953).

Check fraud can take various forms: check kiting, paper hanging, hot check writing, and check forgery.

Check kiting is one of the more common forms of check fraud that involves the cashing or writing of a personal check from an account that does not have sufficient funds to cover the expense (Waite, 2013). The kited check is covered with a deposit (in some cases, days later) into the account prior to the check arriving at the financial institution (Turner & Albrecht, 1993). Many individuals will kite a check for groceries on the last days of a month with full knowledge that they will have their employment check automatically deposited at their bank the next business day, generally on the first day of the next month. However, when weekends and holidays are taken into considerations or combined, such as having a holiday on a Monday, the kited check can float for, sometimes, 3 or 4 days until it clears. In most cases, the funds will arrive in time to cover and clear the check.

Hot check writing involves the cashing or writing of a personal check from an account that does not have sufficient funds. However, unlike a kited check, the fraudulent individual has no intention of depositing the funds needed to cover the bad check. Another form of *hot check writing* would include depositing a bad check into an account and then withdrawing the funds from the account prior to the financial institution discovering that the check was bad.

Check forgery takes on various forms. It can result from simply stealing a legitimate check from someone and then cashing it. It could also be the *counterfeiting* of a self-manufactured check (Slotter, 1996). A subtype of check forgery known as *check altering* is the altering of a legitimate check by inscribing a different dollar amount than the check was originally written for by raising the value of the dollar amount on the check (Waite, 2013).

Theoretical Considerations

Critical criminology should be examined when considering the female thief. Feminist criminology is a component of critical criminology. The main premise of most accounts of feminist criminology is that many theories express an androcentric bias. Feminist theories attempt to define criminology and criminal justice based upon the experiences, understanding, and view of the world as perceived by women. The feminist perspective attempts to counter most theories of criminology that have been developed, tested, and applied by men to men, which have only incorporated women as an afterthought. Chesney-Lind (2006) calls this "add women and stir."

Feminist theories focus on three prominent areas of study: victimization of women, gender differences in crime, and gendered differences in the administration of justice. There are different types of feminist theories from liberal feminists who believe in the liberation thesis. This thesis proposed that female crime would increase as women assumed more assertive positions in society. The other types are the critical/radical feminists whose major theme is patriarchy. These theories view patriarchy as the male power and domination in society as an influence on female criminality. The feminist theorists view male aggression and control of female sexuality as the basis of patriarchy and the subordination of women.

Small (2000) provided a 35-year account of female offending, applying four theoretical perspectives to female offending. The article "Female Crime in the United States, 1963–1998" summarized the masculinity theory, the opportunity theory, the economic marginalization theory, and the chivalry theory in their application to female offending. Then (Small, 2000) presented what she calls a middle ground theory that is a gendered theory acknowledging the organization of gender and opportunity. The results showed that women overall are committing crime at a steady rate but, on the other hand, the data showed that women commit more property offense than men. Women seem to commit embezzlement, fraud, forgery, and larceny according to the middle ground theory (Small, 2000). Steffensmeier and Allan's (1996) middle ground gender theory suggests that women can and do approach criminal activities as occupations. Females see the utility in property crimes as their primary means of income, cultivating systems to make the crimes profitable.

Steffensmeier and Allan (1996) critique information on what they identify as the so-called gender equality hypothesis that argues that as the gender gap closes, offending patterns become similar. They suggest a unified theoretical framework to explain gender differences for female criminality (Steffensmeier & Allan, 1996). Key elements of a gendered approach include (1) explaining both male and female criminality, (2) accounting for differences in the context of offending, (3) considering females' paths to crime and how they differ from men, and (4) exploring social, historical, cultural, biological, and reproductive differences (Steffensmeier & Allan, 1996).

Conclusion/Summary

To conclude, a lot has been said about females who engage in property crime. Property crime has been loosely defined as an offense of taking money or property that does not involve force or physical injury to the individual. This includes offenses such as burglary, larceny or theft, motor vehicle theft, and fraud and forgery. Women are some of the most prevalent perpetrators of property crimes. Women are more likely to engage in embezzlement now than in the past. The data is clear that women who participate in acts of theft, and are caught, are more likely to be arrested and prosecuted for the nonviolent property offense than male property offenders (Steffensmeier, 1983). Male property offenders typically engage in robbery and burglary.

Overall, female crime has been described as less serious than male crime. The female thief does shoplift and commit acts of fraud and embezzlement (Caupto, 2006). This is attributed to the lack of confrontation these particular offences pose. Despite antitheft and group therapy programs for women to get involved in post conviction, they are still going to prison. According to BJS (n.d), women's incarceration rates are outpacing men's arrest rates for property and public order offenses. Chesney-Lind's (2006) recommendations point to the over- or underpunishment of female criminal behavior as the reason behind the criminal justice system's response to women offending.

Discussion Questions

1. What do the author(s) suggest would be a successful strategy for responding to female property offenders? What offense?
2. How do poverty and patriarchy impact women that engage in theft and justice?
3. Do you believe females have an unbiased role in property crime? Can their input contribute to our understanding of professional and accomplice theft? If so, how? If not, why?

References

Bureau of Justice Statistics (BJS) (n.d.). *Bureau of Justice Statistics (BJS)*, n.p. Retrieved August 6, 2014, from http://www.bjs.gov/index.cfm?ty=pbdetail&iid=568

Caputo, G. A. (2008). *Out in the storm: Drug-addicted women living as shoplifters and sex workers*. Boston, MA: Northeastern University Press.

Caputo, G. A., & King, A. (2011). Shoplifting: Work, agency, and gender. *Feminist Criminology, 6*(3), 159–177.

Chesney-Lind, M. (1997). *The female offender: Girls, women, and crime*. Thousand Oaks, CA: Sage Publications.

Chesney-Lind, M. (2006). Patriarchy, crime, and justice: Feminist criminology in an era of backlash. *Feminist Criminology, 1*(1), 6–26.

Chesney-Lind, M., & Shelden, R. G. (1992). *Girls, delinquency and juvenile justice*. Pacific Grove, CA: Brooks/Cole in Belknap, J. *The invisible woman: Gender, crime, and justice* (2nd ed.). Belmont, CA: Wadsworth/Thomson Learning.

Copes, H., & Cherbonneau, M. (2006). The key to auto theft: Emerging methods of auto theft from the offenders' perspective. *British Journal of Criminology, 46*(5), 917–934.

Cressey, D. (1953). *Other people's money*. Montclair, NJ: Patterson Smith in Steffensmeier, D. J., Schwartz, J., & Roche, M. (2013). Gender and twenty-first-century corporate crime: Female involvement and the gender gap in Enron-era corporate frauds. *American Sociological Review, 78*(3), 448–476.

Daly, K. (1989). Gender and varieties of white collar crime. *Criminology, 27*, 769–794 in Steffensmeier, D. J., Schwartz, J., & Roche, M. (2013). Gender and twenty-first-century corporate crime: Female involvement and the gender gap in Enron-era corporate frauds. *American Sociological Review, 78*(3), 448–476.

Dodge, M. (2009). *Women and white-collar crime*. Upper Saddle River, NJ: Prentice Hall.

Federal Bureau of Investigation (FBI). (2011, July 25). *FBI*. Retrieved August 5, 2014, from http://www.fbi.gov/about-us/cjis/ucr/crime-in-the-u.s/2011/crime-in-the-u.s.-2011/aboutucrmain

Gottschalk, P. (2012). Gender and white-collar crime: Only four percent female criminals. *Journal of Money Laundering Control, 15*(3), 362–373.

Haantz, S. (2002, October). *Women and white collar crime*. Washington, DC: National White Collar Crime Center.

Hagan, F. E. (2010). *Crime types and criminals*. Thousand Oaks, CA: Sage Publications.

Inciardi, J. (1980). Women, heroin, and property crime. In *Women, crime, and justice* (1st ed., pp. 215–222). New York, NY: Oxford University Press.

Jewkes, Y. (2012). *Media & crime: Key approaches to criminology*. London, U.K.: SAGE.

Kolman, A., & Wasserman, C. (1991). Theft groups for women: A cry for help. *Federal Probation, 55*(1), 48.

Lemert, E. (1953). An isolation and closure theory of naïve check forgery. *Journal of Criminal Law, Criminology & Police Science, 44*(3), 296–307.

Mullins, C. W., & Cherbonneau, M. G. (2011). Establishing connections: Gender, motor vehicle theft, and disposal networks. *Justice Quarterly, 28*(2), 278–302. doi:10.1080/074188525.2010.499877.

Mullins, C., & Wright, R. (2003). Gender, social networks, and residential burglary. *Criminology, 41*(3), 813–840.

Pollak, O. (1978). *The criminality of women*. Philadelphia, PA: University of Pennsylvania Press. (Original work published 1950).

Russell, M. (1978). Groups for women who shoplift. *Canadian Journal of Criminology, 20*, 73–74.

Simon, R. J. (1975). *Women and crime*. Lexington, MA: Lexington Books.

Simon, R. J., & Landis, J. (1991). *The crimes women commit: The punishments they receive*. Lexington, MA: Lexington Books.

Slotter, K. (1996). Check fraud. *FBI Law Enforcement Bulletin, 65*(8), 1.

Small, K. (2000). Female crime in the United States, 1963–1998: An update. *Gender Issues, 18*(3), 75–90.

Steffensmeier, D. (1983). Organizational properties and sex-segregation in the underworld: Building a sociological theory of sex differences in crime. *Social Forces, 61*, 1010–1032.

Steffensmeier, D., & Allan, E. (1996). Gender and crime: Toward a gendered theory of female offending. *Annual Review of Sociology, 22*(1), 459–487.

Steffensmeier, D. J., Schwartz, J., & Roche, M. (2013). Gender and twenty-first-century corporate Crime: Female involvement and the gender gap in Enron-era corporate frauds. *American Sociological Review, 78*(3), 448–476.

Triplett, R., & Laura B. M. (1995). Evaluating contextual patterns of delinquency: Gender-based differences. *Justice Quarterly, 12*(1), 59–84 in Belknap, J. *The invisible woman: Gender, crime, and justice* (2nd ed.) by Belmont, CA: Wadsworth/Thomson Learning.

Turner, J. S., & Albrecht, W. S. (1993). Check kiting: Detection, prosecution and prevention. *FBI Law Enforcement Bulletin, 62*(11), 12.

Uniform Crime Report. (UCR, 2009). *Uniform Crime Report: Crime in the United States, 2008.* Washington, DC: U.S. Department of Justice.

Uniform Crime Reports. (UCR, 2013). The Federal Bureau of Investigation (FBI). Retrieved August 14, 2014, from http://www.fbi.gov/about-us/cjis/ucr/ucr

Waite, M. (2013). Check fraud and the common law: At the intersection of negligence and the uniform commercial code. *Boston College Law Review, 54*(5), 2205–2243.

Warner, J. A. (2012). *Women and crime: A reference handbook.* Santa Barbara, CA: ABC-CLIO, LLC.

Warren, M. Q., & Rosenbaum, J. L. 1986. Criminal careers of female offenders. *Criminal Justice and Behavior, 13*, 393–418 in *The invisible woman: Gender, crime, and justice* (2nd ed.) by J. Belknap (Ed.). Belmont, CA: Wadsworth/Thomson Learning.

Zeitz, D. (1981). *Women who embezzle or defraud.* New York, NY: Praeger in Steffensmeier, D. J., Schwartz, J., & Roche, M. (2013). Gender and twenty-first-century corporate crime: Female involvement and the gender gap in Enron-era corporate frauds. *American Sociological Review, 78*(3), 448–476.

Prostitution

11

KATHERINE WINHAM AND
GEORGE E. HIGGINS

Contents

The focus of this chapter is introducing students to the historical and current legal context of prostitution and sex work in the United States, highlighting current legislation and contemporary punishments for this crime. This text also provides a contextual description of the sellers and buyers of sex today, highlighting significant issues and debates around violence against women and children, mental health issues and substance use, public health, legalization, globalization, and researching those who sell sex.

Defining Prostitution and Sex Work

The definition of prostitution is highly debated. The debate stems from a number of ideological lenses in viewing prostitution (Edlund & Korn, 2002). One of these ways is to become married solely to have a home and livelihood. While others suggest that prostitution is a practice of nonmarital sexual activity absent any emotional connection between partners. In addition, Edlund and Korn (2002) suggested that promiscuity needs to be included in the definition. The problem with these components was that emotional connection and the idea of promiscuity are terms that were difficult to clearly define. For instance, the idea of an emotional connection seems to differ across individuals and partners. Further, defining the proper number of partners to accurately capture promiscuity is difficult as well. Another way to define prostitution is to refer to *it* as the "world's oldest profession," the practice of selling sex is a deeply embedded cultural practice in nearly every major society over human history (Sanders, O'Neill, & Pitcher, 2009). Prostitution, a practice which spans sociological, criminological, economic, and sometimes moral contexts, generally refers to the consensual engagement in sexual activity for a fee; it is an inherently social behavior, requiring at least two participants (Sanders et al., 2009). The central elements to this definition are the exchange of money and sexual contact. The National Institute of Justice defines prostitution as "the offering of something of value in exchange for sexual activity" (Moses, 2006). This term also indicates a commodification of women's sexual activity as a commercial product (Moses, 2006).

While this may seem closer to a definition of prostitution, others suggest that prostitution needs to have some form of social and moral deviance components (Ditmore, 2006). From this perspective, prostitution may be viewed as an undesirable trade. The lack of desirability suggests that the prostitute is performing an act that is risky. The high risk, with assumed undesirability, suggests that the behavior is immoral. The lack of morality, in this context, suggests that prostitutes are not behaving in a morally acceptable manner; prostitution is often viewed as a threat to the moral fabric of society. As such, prostitutes carry a stigmatization that their work is socially unjust and morally incorrect. This led to much of the legislation that criminalized prostitution (Ditmore, 2006).

Feminists and other social activists provide two different views of prostitution. First, liberal feminists see prostitution as legitimate work or a profession. From this view, prostitutes enter their profession willingly (Jenness, 1990). As will be discussed later, this view suggests that the term "prostitution" does not adequately capture their decision to freely enter this profession, and it needs to be referred to as "sex workers." The term "sex worker" provides a sense of professionalism that will remove the sense of degradation that comes from the term "prostitute" (Ditmore, 2006).

Second, radical feminists view prostitution as a violent act. They see prostitution as violence whether it was forced or voluntary. Under this view, prostitution is an act that is inherently traumatic to the person being prostituted (Farley & Kelly, 2000). A key part of this view is whether prostitution is forced or voluntary. Many that engage in prostitution, under this view, tend to make prostitution normal because they see the prostitutes as participating voluntarily (Farley & Kelly, 2000).

Helping students to develop an understanding of prostitution includes introducing them to the complexities of language around the sale of sex and their implications for the enduring sociological, criminological, and feminist debates (Sanders et al., 2009). Language is a complex part of the discussion of prostitution, and many scholars today use the words prostitution and sex work interchangeably, however, in a legal sense, prostitution is the name of the crime. While legal definitions of prostitution vary by state, generally, in a legal sense, a person commits the crime of prostitution when they knowingly "(1) offer to engage, agree to engage, or engage in sexual conduct for a fee or (2) solicit another in a public place to engage with the person in sexual conduct for hire" (Code, Sept. 1, 1994; example from the Texas Penal Code). Many find the term "prostitute" to be demeaning, preferring other terms including sex worker or the lengthier modifier "prostitution involved woman/man" (Klein, 2000; Sallman, 2010; Sanders et al., 2009). The term sex worker refers to "anyone who exchanges sexual intercourse (including oral sex) for money or some other material good" (Murphy & Venkatesh, 2006). Sexual acts may be exchanged for a number of items of value including money, drugs, or other desired objects.

This chapter primarily focuses on prostitution involving women and will generally refer to this population as simply "prostitutes" for two major reasons: (1) evidence suggests that in the United States female prostitutes greatly outnumber male prostitutes in all types of sex work* (MacKinnon, 2011), (2) female prostitutes are more frequently targeted for arrest than male prostitutes (Johnson, 2014; Weitzer, 2000), and finally (3) much of the cultural and legal history of prostitution has focused on women, and the traditional image of prostitution remains that of a woman (Goffman, 1963; Moses, 2006; Pheterson, 1996). Male prostitution is an important issue that certainly warrants its own investigation, some of which is discussed later in this chapter.

Across the millennia, prostitution is a topic which often elicited views from scholars, government officials, religious groups, and people in society, often leading to the stigmatization of the prostitute as a member of an outsider group (Goffman, 1963; Pheterson, 1996). The majority of Americans consider the practice of prostitution to be immoral (Weitzer, 2000), a factor that has implications for public opinion and policy. Mutual consent on the part of both the sex seller and the customer led many to refer to prostitution as a "victimless crime." But many have questioned whether prostitution can truly be victimless when (1) the vast majority of women who engage in prostitution have histories of childhood or adult abuse, (2) violence is often part of the job, and (3) the vast majority of women report wishing they could leave prostitution.

We introduce a brief history of prostitution in Western Civilization and in the United States, highlighting legal efforts over time to increasingly regulate or eliminate prostitution. Arguments for and against prostitution have been largely relegated to a dichotomous explanation concerning whether women engaged in prostitution are being exploited or exercising their choice to engage in prostitution. Over time, the discourses have shifted from one of sin and morality to labor laws, human rights, and acknowledging the issues of violence and exploitation of women, men, and young people working in the sex industry. We ask readers to keep these ongoing debates in mind as they review the history and legislation related to this crime.

History of Prostitution and Legal Work

Ancient History

The earliest records date from the Sumerians in 2400 BC and describe prostitution within the temples as an occupation and act of worship undertaken by women (Lerner, 1986). Ancient Greek traditions included visiting a prostitute as a method of worshiping a goddess; in fact one of the earliest known goddesses was Inanna, a female prostitute (Bassermann, 1993). During this time, prostitution was not seen as deviant behavior.

---

* The ratio of male to female prostitutes cannot be accurately estimated and is bound to change over time.

A number of "cults" of Venus were centered around goddess worship, and throughout ancient history temple prostitution was a part of worship for peoples of Ancient Greece, Mesopotamia, and the Near East (Lerner, 1986; Ringdal, 2005). Prostitution during this time existed in several forms with different associated social statuses, ranging from temple prostitutes to brothel slaves (Lerner, 1986). Women with greater status, such as temple prostitutes and courtesans, were allowed a level of autonomy, and education, but were required to follow codes of dress which distinguished them from other "respectable" women (Henriquez, 1962; Roberts, 1992).

The first resistance to prostitution began around 1200 BC when ancient Israel condemned erotic religious practices in surrounding societies (Eisler, 1995) and continued through 350 AD when Christians successfully prohibited temple prostitution in Rome. Since that time, the systematic denigration of sexuality, especially female sexuality, has led to increasingly intolerant attitudes toward prostitutes, and since that time, sex workers have fought back for their rights and staged resistance to the oppression that they faced (Sanders et al., 2009). The historical construction of "the prostitute" is a prototype of the stigmatized woman, who is defined by her in chastity, and characterized as a "whore" (Goffman, 1963; Pheterson, 1996). This is contrasted with the idea of the "Madonna," the sacred and holy women who portrays the image of pure femininity. The "Madonna/ whore" dichotomy depicts the prostitute as the example of failed womanhood, defined by her immoral sexual behaviors as someone to be avoided (Pheterson, 1993). This dichotomy would follow women throughout the Middle Ages (Karras, 1996a), and the stigma associated with prostitution is enduring for sex workers today (Sallman, 2010).

Prostitution during the Middle Ages

During medieval times, in Western Europe, while prostitution was largely thought of as a "sin," the practice was for the most part tolerated, institutionalized, and taxed (Karras, 1996b). The commonly held belief during that time was that young men would seek out sexual relations regardless of their options, and prostitutes were seen as a means to meet that need and avoid the seduction or even rape of "respectable" women (Bullough, 1982). Ruth Mazo Karras, a contemporary expert on prostitution during the Middle Ages remarks that houses of prostitution, commonly known as brothels, were common during this time, and thought of as a "necessary evil." This belief system is best summarized by the theologian Augustine's remarks (Karras, 1989). Culpability for the "sin" of fornication or lust as placed upon women, and women's sexuality, immorality, and shrewishness were common themes for medieval sermons with iconography depicted the sin of "lust" as a woman (Karras, 1989).

Following the Black Death epidemic in 1348, which caused an imbalanced sex ratio with few men and labor opportunities for the large numbers of female survivors, prostitution was seen as one of a range of opportunities available to women without dowries (Karras, 1989, 1996b). Bullough (1982) describes the regulations during this time required prostitutes to dress in certain clothes, for example, in Florence, Italy, prostitutes were required to wear hats and gloves with bells on them, and if found on the street out of this attire by a citizen, they could be forced to strip. Some government officials especially in Italy recognized the opportunity to make money and set up municipal brothels, which had certain regulations including taking a cut of the prostitute's earnings but also limiting the number of clients she could see in a day and restricting brothel owners from beating prostitutes (Karras, 1996b). Those who were against prostitution blamed its existence on poverty, lust, greed, and even astrological origins (Bullough, 1982). A number of "Magdalene" homes sprung up across Europe during this time as monastic communities which were designed to rescue and rehabilitate prostitutes from this lifestyle (Karras, 1989). Later, in 1586, Pope Sixtus V declared that the death penalty be imposed for prostitution and all "sins against nature"; few death sentences were actually imposed (Ringdal, 2005). Where prostitution was regulated during much of the Middle Ages, the practice would be abolished in England by Henry VIII in 1546, and brothels would be closed in France by Charles IX in 1560.

Prostitution in Colonial America

Similarly in the United States, the sale of sex was ubiquitous in colonial America and thrived in part due to the fact that men vastly outnumbered women (Butler, 1987; Johnson, 2014). In early America, prostitution was entirely legal; however, it was often seen as a specific sort of vagrancy. Prostitutes were sometimes punished as sexual deviants under laws against adultery, fornication, or for being "common nightwalkers," a term used for women who walked the streets at night for immoral purposes (Miller, Romenesko, & Wondolkowski, 1993). For example, Massachusetts, in its colonial assembly, enacted a law against nightwalking in 1699, which was reenacted by the state legislature in 1787; however, prostitution would not become a crime in that state until 1917. Despite public condemnation, prostitution thrived as an occupation from the eighteenth into the nineteenth century.

Prostitution in the United States in the Nineteenth Century

With the Industrial Revolution, many young American and immigrant women who were excluded from the manufacturing sector found work as prostitutes in cities (Johnson, 2014). In response to the number of women immigrating to the United States who ended up working as prostitutes, Congress passed the Page Act of 1875 (1875 Page Law, Session II, Chapt. 141, Stat. 477, 1875), which outlawed the importation of women to the United States for the purposes of prostitution. The U.S. Supreme Court would later rule in *Keller v. United States* in 1909 that deporting an alien resident who became a prostitute after coming to the United States was a violation of the Tenth Amendment.

During this time, brothels were especially common in urban areas and along the coasts, eventually spreading to the interior, more rural areas of the United States. The Gold Rush which began with gold discoveries in California in 1842 would spread to the Klondike River by the 1880s, which led to the creation of boomtowns in the Western United States with flourishing communities of prostitutes and dance hall women (Butler, 1987; Johnson, 2014). Prostitution thrived as an occupation, and prostitution was not legally defined as a crime in most states during this time.

Local governments began to enact criminal laws prohibiting prostitution. An example was an ordinance passed in the city of St. Louis, Missouri, where in 1870, the Social Evil Ordinance was passed, allowing the Board of Health to require brothels to become licensed and prostitutes to register and undergo medical exams (Sneddeker, 1990). The medical examiners were paid through fees collected from prostitutes, who were referred to as "social evilists" and madams. This ordinance was nullified by the Missouri state legislature in 1974 (Sneddeker, 1990). As governments found their efforts to prevent prostitution to be unsuccessful, they began confining prostitution to certain geographic areas, which were known as "red light districts." In 1857, New Orleans would pass its first prostitution ordinance, which prohibited prostitution on the first floor of buildings, but was soon declared unconstitutional (Long, 2004). Following the Civil War, in 1865, regulations led to the creation of the famed red light district, Storyville, in 1987. This red light district would stay open until concerns over health risks to U.S. soldiers who would be fighting in World War I forced it to close in 1917 (Long, 2004).

The Twentieth Century: Shift from Sin to Social Evil

During the Victorian era, prostitution was seen as "the great social evil" (Diduck & Winson, 1977) as cultural attitudes framed prostitution as a crime against morality, a foundation which organizes our perceptions and regulations of prostitution today (Sanders et al., 2009). Cultural values during this era were based upon the growth of Christianity and Protestantism, which epitomized the ideal of social purity and morality as contrasting between the good wife and mother and the bad girl and sinner (Sanders et al., 2009). Prostitutes during this time were frequently working-class and lower-class women living in cities in dire economic poverty (Kishtainy, 1982; Walkowitz, 1980).

A shift had begun where prostitution began to be seen as a social problem, needing state regulation (Lubove, 1962). The police and the judiciary worked to organize the regulation of prostitution during this time as attempting to meet three main social needs in need of protection: (1) public morality, (2) male prosperity, and (3) the nation's health from sexually transmitted diseases (Lubove, 1962). As prostitution was seen as a problem of women, the state sought to regulate women's bodies, which were objectified as associated with images of rot, disease, death and tied to meeting the instinctive needs of upper-class males (Corbin, 1990).

A major federal effort to curtail prostitution came in the 1910 with the White Slave Traffic Act, which was more commonly known as the Mann Act, named after Illinois representative James Robert Mann (White Slave Traffic Act, aka the Mann Act, 36 Stats., Vol. 1, p. 825, CHAP. 395., 1910). The Mann Act created a federal law against "prostitution or debauchery, or for any other immoral purpose." The law made the transportation of a woman across state lines for prostitution illegal and outlawed forced prostitution as well as harboring of immigrant prostitutes. In 1913, the U.S. Supreme Court ruled in *Hoke v. United States* (1913) that states were responsible for regulating prostitution within state boundaries with one exception: Congress could regulate interstate travel for purposes of prostitution or immoral purposes. In 1913, the Bureau of Social Hygiene formed after being incorporated by John D. Rockefeller, which was followed by the American Social Hygiene Association that same year (Connelly, 1980; Luker, 1998). Both organizations sought to eliminate prostitution and sexually transmitted diseases, and part of their techniques included researching delinquent women and encouraging the recruitment and use of a female police force. Within 15 years of the Mann Act passing into law, prostitution would be made illegal through laws passed in every state.

During World War I, the Chamberlain-Kahn Act of 1918 (Chamberlain-Kahn Act, 1918) was enacted to prevent the spread of uncontrolled venereal diseases among soldiers. Under this law, the government could quarantine and examine any woman suspected of having venereal disease for the protection of the military and naval forces of the

United States. If a women was discovered to have a venereal disease upon examination, this could be used a proof that she had engaged in prostitution (Connelly, 1980). By this time, prostitution was illegal in every state, and these laws would remain in place, largely unchanged through the 1970s and to the present.

1970s to Present

By 1971, the State of Nevada began to formally regulate prostitution giving rural counties the option to license brothels, and to this day, prostitution is illegal in every other state (Symanski, 1974). The first prostitute's rights group, COYOTE (Call Off Your Old Tired Ethics), formed in 1973 in San Francisco by Margo St. James, which was followed by several other similar groups forming across the country (Jenness, 1990). Later, in 1981, AIDS would emerge for the first time in the Centers for Disease Control's weekly report (Centers for Disease Control and Prevention, 1981); this disease would impact the health and safety of sex workers and increase the social stigma associated with prostitution.

Contemporary Legislation

Prostitution and Solicitation of Prostitution

Prostitution and solicitation of prostitution remains illegal in every state, with the exception of a few rural counties in Nevada (Bartol, 2002; Johnson, 2014). In most states, prostitution is considered a public order crime, which disrupts the order of a community, and is a misdemeanor offense (Bartol, 2002). In other states, prostitution is considered a form a disorderly conduct. In most cases, the crime of prostitution includes offering, agreeing to, or actually engaging in a sexual act in exchange for money. Statutes typically describe the sexual acts in vague terms, often using the term "lewd acts" to describe intimate physical contact of some type. The laws require that the defendant receive compensation, directly or through a third party, in exchange for that contact.

In many states, the government must only prove that the prostitute offered or agreed to engage in sexual activity, without jest, regardless of whether he or she intended to follow through with the offer or agreement. In other states, the prosecution must prove the defendant specifically intended to engage in the sexual act in exchange for money. In these states, the defendant must have engaged in some act showing that she or he intended to follow through on the offer or agreement (e.g., touching the patron's genital area after offering sex). In states where prostitution is illegal, the intentions of the would-be client are irrelevant, and the alleged prostitute can be convicted even if the client does not agree to or intend to engage in sexual contact.

Several rural counties in Nevada are the only places where prostitution is legal in the United States (NRS, 201.354). Within these counties, a client may legally buy sex acts from a licensed brothel. Per Nevada state law, all prostitutes must use *condoms when engaging in sexual acts*, and must be tested weekly for sexually transmitted diseases (STDs) and monthly for HIV (NRS, 201.354). Brothel owners and prostitutes are required to be licensed and registered, and to pass a background check. Street prostitution remains illegal in Nevada.

Offender Punishments for Prostitution and Solicitation of Prostitution

Penalties for prostitution and solicitation of prostitution vary by state and are often different based upon whether it is a first-time or repeated offense. See Table 11.1 for a list of penalties by state for prostitution and solicitation of prostitution. Among the stiffer penalties are Alabama's prostitution charge which is a Class A misdemeanor and carries up to 1 year sentence and/or $6000 fine (ALA,13A-12-110-122). The first time charge of prostitution in Hawaii, by contrast, is a petty misdemeanor which has a 30-day sentence and/or $500 fine. In some states, repeated offenses carry stiffer penalties and may lead to felony charges. For example, in Illinois, a second prostitution charge is a Class 4 felony, while in Arizona, four or more charges are considered a Class 5 felony.

In most states, the crime classification and penalties for solicitation of prostitution are the same as those for prostitution. In a few states, the penalties tend to be slightly more lenient for solicitation as compared to prostitution itself, mirroring the historical context of holding the prostitute more culpable than her client (Johnson, 2014). For example, in Delaware, the sentence for the crime of prostitution is up to 6 months with a $1150 fine, while the sentence for solicitation is up to 30 days with a mandatory fine of $500. New York, by contrast, has imposed stiffer penalties for solicitation (Class A misdemeanor, up to 1 year sentence and/or $1000) than for prostitution (Class B misdemeanor, up to 3 months sentence and/or $500). These penalties are similar to those in Sweden, where only those who solicit prostitution are charged with a crime (Thompson, 2013, December 11).

Pimping and Pandering

A "pimp" is important to understand in prostitution. The term "pimp" is difficult to define. Some write that a pimp is someone that controls the actions and lives off of the proceeds of one or more women who work in prostitution (Williamson & Cluse-Tolar, 2002). This definition does not make clear who a pimp is. Some see that pimping and trafficking are the same things. The United Nations (2002) defined trafficking as, "the threat or use of force, coercion, abduction, fraud, deception, abuse of power or vulnerability, or giving payments or benefits to a person in control of the victim is present" (2000, p. 2). Rather than rely on this definition, others define a pimp as an individual(s) that earns money through facilitation or provision of sex work transactions (O'Connell Davidson, 1998).

While little is known about being a pimp, an Urban Institute report suggests that becoming a pimp may be due to a number of different influences. For instance, the term pimp may have cultural connotations for many. The glorification of being a pimp is something that is common in rap music. Kubrin (2005) writes that the misogamy that occurs in rap music may influence many to participate in different types of acts.

Pimping may be a product of family socialization. For instance, some argue that many pimps has a family experience of this behavior. Beyond family or parental socialization, pimping appears to have some environmental components, specifically, neighborhood context. The neighborhood context provides a socially acceptable environment that allows the individuals to become pimps.

One of the activities of a pimp is to bring individuals into prostitution. This is typically known as "pandering." Pandering is defined as enticing, procuring, forcing, or coercing a person to become a prostitute.

Table 11.1 Prostitution Laws by State

	State	Penalty for Prostitutes (Crime Classification)	Penalty for Customers (Crime Classification)
1.	Alabama	Up to 1 year and/or $6000 (Class A misdemeanor)	Up to 1 year and/or $6000 (Class A misdemeanor)
2.	Alaska	Up to 90 days and/or $2000 (Class B misdemeanor)	Up to 90 days and/or $2000 (Class B misdemeanor)
3.	Arizona	First offense 15 days, 2nd 30 days, 3rd 60 days, 4+ offenses 180 days–1.5 years (First offense Class 1 misdemeanor, 4 or more offenses are a Class 5 felony)	Up to 30 days and/or $500 (Class 3 misdemeanor)
4.	Arkansas	Up to 90 days and/or $500, then up to 1 year and/or $1000 (First offense Class B misdemeanor, subsequent offense Class A misdemeanor)	Up to 90 days and/or $500, then up to 1 year and/or $1000 (First offense Class B misdemeanor, subsequent offense Class A misdemeanor)
5.	California	Up to 1 year and/or $1000 (Misdemeanor)	Up to 1 year and/or $1000 (Misdemeanor)
6.	Colorado	Up to 6 months and/or $50–$750 (Class 3 misdemeanor)	Up 6 months and/or $500, then 6–18 months and/or $500–$5000 (First offense Class 1 petty offense, 3+ offenses Class 1 misdemeanor)
7.	Connecticut	Up to 1 year and/or $2000 (Class A misdemeanor)	Up to 1 year and/or $2000 (Class A misdemeanor)
8.	Delaware	Up to 6 months and/or $1150 (Class B misdemeanor)	Up to 30 days and a minimum mandatory fine of $500 (Misdemeanor)
9.	District of Columbia	First offense 1–90 days and $500, 2nd 1–135 days and $750, 3+ 1–180 days and $1000	First offense 1–90 days and $500, 2nd 1–135 days and $750, 3+ 1–180 days and $1000
10.	Florida	First offense 2nd degree misdemeanor, 2nd offense 1 misdemeanor, 3+ offenses 3 felony	2nd degree misdemeanor, 3 felony $500 fine
11.	Georgia	Up to 1 year and/or $1000 (Misdemeanor)	Up to 1 year and/or $1000 (Misdemeanor)
12.	Hawaii	30 days and/or $500 (Petty misdemeanor)	30 days and/or $500 (Petty misdemeanor)
13.	Idaho	1–6 months and/or $500, then 1–5 years (First offense misdemeanor, 3+ offenses are a felony)	1–6 months and/or $500, then 1–5 years (First offense misdemeanor, 3+ offenses are a felony)
14.	Illinois	Up to 1 year and/or $2500 then 1–3 years and/or $25,000 (First offense Class A misdemeanor, subsequent convictions are a 4 felony)	Up to 1 year and/or $2500 then 1–3 years and/or $25,000 (First offense Class A misdemeanor, subsequent convictions are a 4 felony)
15.	Indiana	Up to 1 year and/or $5000, then 6 months–3 years and/or $10,000 (First offense Class A misdemeanor, 3+ convictions are a D felony)	Up to 1 year and/or $5000, then 6 months–3 years and/or $10,000 (First offense Class A misdemeanor, 3+ convictions are a D felony)
16.	Iowa	Up to 2 years and/or $500–$5000 (Aggravated misdemeanor)	Up to 2 years and/or $500–$5000 (Aggravated misdemeanor)

(Continued)

Table 11.1 (*Continued*)   Prostitution Laws by State

	State	Penalty for Prostitutes (Crime Classification)	Penalty for Customers (Crime Classification)
17.	Kansas	Up to 6 months and/or $1000 (Class B nonperson misdemeanor)	Up to 1 month and/or $500 (Class C misdemeanor)
18.	Kentucky	Up to 90 days and/or $250 (Class B misdemeanor)	Up to 90 days and/or $250 (Class B misdemeanor)
19.	Louisiana	First offense up to 6 months and/or $500, 2nd offense up to 2 years and/or $250–$2000, 3+ convictions 2–4 years and $500–$4000	Up to 6 months and/or $500
20.	Maine	Up to 6 months and/or $1000 then up to 1 year and/or $2000 (First offense Class E crime, then consequent offenses Class D crime)	Up to 6 months and/or $1000 then up to 1 year and/or $2000 (First offense Class E crime, then consequent offenses Class D crime)
21.	Maryland	Up to 1 year and/or $500 (Misdemeanor)	Up to 1 year and/or $500 (Misdemeanor)
22.	Massachusetts	Up to 1 year and/or $500	Up to 1 year and/or $500
23.	Michigan	First offense up to 93 days and/or $500, 2nd offense up to 1 year and/or $1000, 3+ convictions up to 2 years and/or $2000 (1–2 offenses misdemeanor, 3rd offense felony)	First offense up to 93 days and/or $500, 2nd offense up to 1 year and/or $1000, 3+ convictions up to 2 years and/or $2000 (1–2 offenses misdemeanor, 3rd offense felony)
24.	Minnesota	First offense is up to 90 days and/or $1000, consequence offense is up to 1 year and/or $3000	First offense is up to 90 days and/or $500–$1000, consequence offense is up to 1 year and/or $1500–$3000
25.	Mississippi	6 months and/or $200	6 months and/or $200
26.	Missouri	30 days–6 months and/or $500 (Class B misdemeanor)	30 days–6 months and/or $500 (Class B misdemeanor)
27.	Montana	6 months and/or $500	First offense up to 1 year and/or $1000, consequence offense up to 5 years and/or $10,000
28.	Nebraska	Up to 1 year and/or $1000 (Class I misdemeanor)	First offense at least $200, consequent convictions at least $500 (First offense Class I misdemeanor, subsequent offenses Class IV felony)
29.	Nevada See Section III below for legal prostitution	Up to 6 months and/or $1000 (Misdemeanor)	Up to 6 months and/or $1000 (Misdemeanor)
30.	New Hampshire	Up to 1 year and $2000 (Misdemeanor)	Up to 1 year and $2000 (Misdemeanor)
31.	New Jersey	First offense up to 6 months and/or fine, consequent convictions up to 18 months and/or fine (First disorderly persons offense, subsequent offenses crime of the 4th degree)	First offense up to 6 months and/or fine, consequent convictions up to 18 months and/or fine (First disorderly persons offense, subsequent offenses crime of the 4th degree)
32.	New Mexico	First offense up to 6 months in a county jail and/or $500, subsequent offenses up to 1 year in a county jail and/or $1000 (First offense petty misdemeanor, subsequent offenses misdemeanor)	First offense up to 6 months in a county jail and/or $500, subsequent offenses up to 1 year in a county jail and/or $1000 (First offense petty misdemeanor, subsequent offenses misdemeanor)

(Continued)

Table 11.1 (*Continued*)   Prostitution Laws by State

	State	Penalty for Prostitutes (Crime Classification)	Penalty for Customers (Crime Classification)
33.	New York	Up to 3 months and/or $500 (Class B misdemeanor)	Up to 1 year and/or $1000 (Class A misdemeanor)
34.	North Carolina	Up to 45 days and a fine (Class 1 misdemeanor)	Up to 45 days and a fine (Class 1 misdemeanor)
35.	North Dakota	Up to 30 days and/or $1000 (Class B misdemeanor)	Up to 30 days and/or $1000 (Class B misdemeanor)
36.	Ohio	Up to 60 days and/or $500 (3rd degree misdemeanor)	Up to 60 days and/or $500 (3rd degree misdemeanor)
37.	Oklahoma	First offense 30 days–1 year or up to $2500, 2nd offense 30 days–1 year or up to $5000, consequent offenses 30 days–1 year or up to $7500 (Misdemeanor)	First offense 30 days–1 year or up to $2500, 2nd offense 30 days–1 year or up to $5000, consequent offenses 30 days–1 year or up to $7500 (Misdemeanor)
38.	Oregon	Up to 1 year and/or $6250 (Class A misdemeanor)	Up to 1 year and/or $6250 (Class A misdemeanor)
39.	Pennsylvania	First two offenses up to 1 year, 3rd offense up to 2 years, and subsequent offenses up to 5 years (1st and 2nd offense a 3rd degree misdemeanor, 3rd offense a 2nd degree misdemeanor, 4+ offenses 1st degree misdemeanor)	First two offenses up to 1 year, 3rd offense up to 2 years, and subsequent offenses up to 5 years (1st and 2nd offense a 3rd degree misdemeanor, 3rd offense a 2nd degree misdemeanor, 4+ offenses 1st degree misdemeanor)
40.	Rhode Island	Up to 6 months and/or $250–$1000, subsequent convictions up to 1 year and/or $500–$1000 (Misdemeanor)	Up to 1 year and/or $250–$1000, subsequent convictions up to 1 year and/or $500–$1000 (Misdemeanor) Up to 6 months and/or $500–$1000, subsequent convictions up to 1 year and/or $750–$1000 (Only applies to soliciting from motor vehicles)
41.	South Carolina	First offense up to 30 days or $200, 2nd offense up to 6 months and $1000, 3+ at least 1 year and/or up to $3000	First offense up to 30 days or $200, 2nd offense up to 6 months and $1000, 3+ at least 1 year and/or up to $3000
42.	South Dakota	Up to 1 year in county jail and/or $2000 (Class 1 misdemeanor)	Up to 1 year in county jail and/or $2000 (Class 1 misdemeanor)
43.	Tennessee	Up to 6 months and/or $500 (Class B misdemeanor)	Up to 6 months and/or $500 (Class B misdemeanor)
44.	Texas	First offense up to 180 days and/or $2000, 2nd up to 1 year and/or $4000, 3+ 180 days–2 years and/or $10,000 (First offense is a Class B misdemeanor, 2nd a Class A misdemeanor, 3+ is a state jail felony)	First offense up to 180 days and/or $2000, 2nd up to 1 year and/or $4000, 3+ 180 days–2 years and/or $10,000 (First offense is a Class B misdemeanor, 2nd a Class A misdemeanor, 3+ is a state jail felony)
45.	Utah	First offense up to 6 months and/or $1000, subsequent offenses up to 1 year and/or $2500 (First offense Class B misdemeanor, subsequent offenses are Class A misdemeanors)	Up to 6 months and/or $1000 (Class B misdemeanor)

(Continued)

Table 11.1 (*Continued*) Prostitution Laws by State

	State	Penalty for Prostitutes (Crime Classification)	Penalty for Customers (Crime Classification)
46.	Vermont	First offense up to 1 year or $100, 2nd offense up to 3 years	First offense up to 1 year or $100, 2nd offense up to 3 years
47.	Virginia	Up to 1 year and/or $2500 (Class 1 misdemeanor)	Up to 1 year and/or $2500 (Class 1 misdemeanor)
48.	Washington	Up to 90 days and/or $1000 (Misdemeanor)	Up to 90 days and/or $1000 (Misdemeanor)
49.	West Virginia	60 days–6 months and $50–$100	First offense 60 days–6 months and $50–$100, 2nd offense 6 months–1 year and $100–$200, consequent offenses 1–3 years
50.	Wisconsin	Up to 9 months and/or $10,000 (Class A misdemeanor)	Up to 9 months and/or $10,000 (Class A misdemeanor)
51.	Wyoming	Up to 6 months and/or $750 (Misdemeanor)	Up to 6 months and/or $750 (Misdemeanor)

Source: Procon.org, Prostitution Laws by State, 2015, Retrieved from http://prostitution.procon.org/view. resource.php?resourceID=000119.

Case Study 1

Two dozen suspected gang members from San Diego were indicted on Wednesday for their alleged involvement in a cross-country sex trafficking ring that officials said included "branding" prostitutes with tattoos.

According to U.S. attorney Laura E. Duffy, the suspected sex trafficking operation spanned 46 cities across 23 states and involved underage girls and women.

The defendants recruited girls from El Cajon Boulevard and social media sites by showing them glamorous rap videos on YouTube and promising them a lavish life, as depicted in those videos.

Once they became prostitutes, the suspects allegedly branded the women by tattooing them with gang signs, bar codes, or a pimp's name, officials said. The suspects would then trade and gift these women among themselves.

Officials from the FBI, Homeland Security, and the District Attorney's office revealed sordid details of the sex trafficking ring at a press conference on Wednesday in San Diego following a warrant sweeps operation tied to busting the ring wide open.

On Wednesday, 17 arrests were made across San Diego, Arizona, and New Jersey as part of a year-long investigation by multiple law enforcement agencies.

The alleged street gang members were also arrested for murder, kidnapping, robbery, and drug-related crimes.

According to the federal grand jury indictment, an organization known as "BMS"—made up of several street gangs hailing from San Diego's North Park community—lured underage girls and women to work as prostitutes, promising them a glamorous life if they joined the ring.

In some instances, the gang members allegedly forced many of their victims into prostitution through threats of violence, according to the indictment.

There were approximately 60 victims from San Diego and officials said at least 11 of those victims were underage.

"Some of the underage girls were kids who lived at home with their parents or
guardians. They are kids who went to school, socialized with their friends and
over the Internet just like regular teens," Duffy explained.

The indictment alleges that the local suspects involved in this sex trafficking ring
ranged in age from 22 to 36 years old.

According to court documents, some of the defendants attended parties in San
Diego or around the country known as "Players' Balls," invitation-only gather-
ing for pimps. One defendant—33-year-old Robert Banks—even received an
award at one of these parties.

A photo posted to social media from one of these gatherings in Las Vegas showed
Banks posing with a "pimp cup" and "pimp stick," flanked by a woman on each
arm. Court documents said one of these women in the photo is a known prostitute.

According to court documents, it's common for pimps to carry highly-adorned
chalices known as "pimp cups" as a symbol of their status. Some pimps also
have dental "grills"—dental add-ons made of gold that can be worth thousands
of dollars.

In the indictment, the government is seeking to forfeit these items from the defendants, as well as other items allegedly purchased with proceeds from the sex
trafficking ring.

Officials said that during Wednesday's search warrants, detectives seized two
firearms, 20–30 marijuana plants, six luxury cars, flat-screen televisions,
thousands of dollars in cash, pimp cups, pimp sticks, and more than 50 pairs
of Air Jordan shoes.

If convicted on the racketeering conspiracy charges, the suspects in this case
could face up to 20 years in jail and a fine of $250,000.

The defendants will make their first appearance in federal court on Thursday.

Officials said the female victims of the sex trafficking ring are being offered
resources to help them start a new life. (Tevrizian, Garske, & Wood, 2014)

This activity is closely related to sex trafficking. The activities of pandering and trafficking
are similar in that they involve coercion and forcing someone into prostitution. Dank et al.
(2014) write:

Under the United States penal code, sex trafficking is a "severe form of trafficking"
under which "a commercial sex act is induced by force, fraud, or coercion" or the individual involved in the commercial sex act is under 18 years old (Title 22 §7102). Sex trafficking
can also occur when "recruitment, harboring, transportation, provision, or obtaining of a
person" occurs for the purpose of commercial sex.

Pandering is illegal in every state. Given the close connection between pandering and
trafficking, the activity of coercing someone into prostitution appears to be illegal at the
federal level as well; thus, one of the main activities of recruiting individuals into prostitution is illegal at all levels of government.

Other Crimes Related to Prostitution

Beyond pimping and pandering, several prostitution-related crimes involve third parties
and prohibit certain categories of behavior that foster prostitution. These behaviors include

keeping or residing in a house of prostitution, leasing a house for prostitution, procuring a person to travel for purposes of prostitution, bringing a person to a place kept for prostitution, sending a minor to or permitting a minor to enter a house of prostitution, and taking a person against his or her will for prostitution.

Victim and Offender Characteristics

Sex work is traditionally seen as a female occupation, and the vast majority of research and policy reports focus on girls and women in the sex industry, paying particular attention to street-based sex workers who have criminal justice involvement (Sanders et al., 2009). This perception excludes the number of men who engage in sex work, as well as obscures the fact that the vast majority of sex workers, male and female, are not street based, and instead work indoors (Perkins & Lovejoy, 2007; Sanders, 2005). Additionally, emerging research is examining transgendered persons who engage in the sex industry (Klein, 2000). Evidence increasingly demonstrates that the sex trade takes on many forms and contexts that shape what sex trading looks like among various individuals and subpopulations. Sex workers historically and currently are stigmatized as a deviant group, who are characterized as diseased, representing a social evil, a public nuisance, or as victims needing to be "rescued' from their current circumstance (Pheterson, 1996; Sallman, 2010; Sanders, 2005). We believe it is important to recognize that their selling of sex is one part of their lives, and not a single, defining characteristic (Sanders et al., 2009). They are individuals and rational agents, occupying roles including as son, daughter, sister, brother, parent, and friend in their families and communities (Dank et al., 2014).

To our knowledge, no reliable studies have estimated the number of people working in the sex industry in the United States today, and that the underground commercial sex economy brings in an estimated $39.9 to $290.0 million per year in eight major U.S. cities alone (Dank et al., 2014). The vast majority of studies indicate that most sex workers began working in the industry when they were under the age of 18; however, many individuals began this work as adults (Dank et al., 2014; MacKinnon, 2011).

Case Study 2: Underage Prostitution

Operation underground railroad has been on this case for months now and tonight, with the sting about to happen, the danger is real and the stakes are high. A group of Americans hoping to catch pimps trafficking underage girls. Will it work?

Once again tonight, here's ABC's David Wright. Hola! Reporter: In Colombia, the bachelor party is on.

A parade of pretty young girls ready to work. Thirty girls in all. Many of them are very young.

The alleged traffickers, true to their word. You're the king, man. Reporter: But this isn't your typical bachelor party.

Upstairs, Colombian authorities are quietly waiting for just the right moment to drop the hammer. Tim Ballard plays the part of the rowdy best man, buying girls for sex.

But really, he's in on the sting. He's the leader of a team of Americans who have been setting this up. They go by the name operation underground railroad.

And they work with local authorities to catch sex traffickers and pimps who sell underage girls for sex. Worldwide, over 1 million children are trafficked each year.

Many of them sold into sexual slavery. May I ask, your name is Andrea? That's what we call you.

Reporter: Andrea disguised her face for this interview. Her parents have no idea she's a prostitute. She's 17.

And she's been working for six years. So, you started at age 11. This is very young.

Do the men pay more for young girls? Especially under 14. How much more?

Almost twice the price. Andrea says she wishes she didn't do this. Why do you have to do this now?

Reporter: At the operation underground railroad party—You brought like 100 girls. I'm missing three, they're right. He got 100 girls.

Reporter: Some of the girls are just 14 years old. You can tell they're a minor though, right?

Of course, of course, absolutely. They're giving eyes out, right? You know, like, trying to flirt with guys.

Yeah, so sad. Reporter: Marcus talks up one girl in particular. She's nice.

How old? 14. She's here?

Yeah, she's beautiful. Reporter: Legally, it's not enough just to have brought them. In order to prosecute, there has to be no doubt why.

A clear quid pro quo. She's 14? Yes.

Okay, so—here's the thing. Does she do everything? I'll talk to her.

I told her anything crazy that he wants, if she wants more money, she better ask. Not going to be any problems? Reporter: And money has to change hands.

In Colombia, it's legal to have consensual sex with a 14 year old. But paying for sex with a minor is a crime. Money time.

This is the good part. These are the two. Okay, let me see.

Reporter: Cold, hard cash. Right there on the table. This is the crucial moment investigators need to seal the deal.

The 14 year old—Do they know what's going on? No, the parents don't know. Reporter: The man on the left there is an undercover investigator for the CTI, Colombia's equivalent of the FBI.

He gives the code word, agreed in advance. Calling for wine to celebrate. The bust is on.

Whoa. What the heck? Reporter: Federal police to arrest the five alleged traffickers.

Social workers to attend to the girls. Tim is still playing his part. Who called the cops, man?

Reporter: Demanding to see his lawyer as if he's being arrested, too. For us, a chance to talk to Marcus before he's carted away. Is it worth it?

Worth what, sir? Reporter: To bring underage girls—There's no underage girls here. Reporter: You told him there's a girl that's 14 years old.

I lied to them about that. Reporter: He tells me that all of the girls are of legal age. He insists it's all just a misunderstanding.

So, were you lying then or now? I was lying because I wanted him to be happy with the girls that I found, okay, but no, I did not—there's not a single girl here that's underage, I promise you that. Reporter: Marcus tells me he has a daughter back in the statements who is 15.

How could you do this if you have a daughter that's 15 years old? I don't get it. I'm not looking for young girls.

Reporter: Do you think this is just a total mistake? Yes. It's a total mistake.

You know why, sir? Reporter: Why? I did not look for young girls.

Reporter: You brought some. Those are the girls that look young, sir. Please, check their I.

D.S. I promise—Jimmy: I think they' Reporter: I think they will check more than their I.

D.S. I hope they do.

Reporter: Out by the pum, the social workers are one by one checking I. D. S.

No idea. It's okay. Reporter: Many of the girls are afraid they're being arrested.

This is their livelihoods. For some of them, their main concern is not to be rescued, but to get paid for a night's work. When they first showed up, some of them looked really terrified.

I talked to a few of them and asked them how old they were and some were 12, some were 13, most were 14. One of the girls came and embraced me and started to cry and then I started to cry. It's a very Reporter: Your heart goes out to them, huh?

For these girls, it's a long road ahead. Over the next few days, social services did interviews with the girls, their families and the traffickers. In all, 17 of the girls were under 18.

Their I.D.s, fake or nonexistence.

What makes me sad is that, yes, we got four traffickers and I hope they fry, but what makes me sad is that I think so many of these little girls, they don't know any different. Reporter: End up back out on the street. Yeah.

Reporter: You think they did some good tonight? I know they did. But so much more needs to be done.

Reporter: Any underage girl will be taken to a certified foster care program, dedicated to making sure they get the care they need. How do you feel at the end of all this? I mean, you must be elated, but on the other hand—It's bittersweet.

I want to celebrate, but I don't, because it's—it's so horrific. So horrific. I see my own children in this.

Reporter: But anyone of age is free to go. In so many cases, even the youngest girls return to what they know best. The streets.

Sure enough, later that night, we saw some of the same girls from the party, the ones who could prove they were over 18, back out on the streets, making up for lost time. Tonight's raid, just an inconvenient ordeal. I'm David Wright for *Nightline* in Cartagena, Colombia. (Wright, 2014)

People enter the sex industry for a number of reasons including wanting to earn money and having few other options for income, being introduced to the industry by a friend, deciding independently to start working, and a history of abuse or exploitation as a young person (Sanders et al., 2009). Despite the vast diversity among sex workers, they share a commonality in that sex work is indeed "work" for them, and not an expression of their sexuality or sexual desires (Perkins & Lovejoy, 2007).

Female Sex Workers

A number of women in the United States engage in some form of prostitution today. An estimated 300 licensed prostitutes work in 20–30 Nevada brothels (Warnick, 2008). Women represent an especially diverse group in terms of their age, background, personal relationships, and sexuality as well as where and how they do sex work (Sanders et al., 2009). Female sex workers can identify as heterosexual, bisexual, or lesbian. Almost all research indicates that women enter prostitution for economic reasons, which some see as a signal that prostitution always arises from inequality and exploitation, and that no one would choose prostitution if they had other employment options (Farley, 2004; Farley & Kelly, 2000). However, other research indicates that women sometimes choose prostitution because they can make more money in fewer hours as compared to other forms of work (Sanders et al., 2009).

The majority of women in the sex industry today work indoors, and street-based sex work seems to be declining (Dank et al., 2014). Findings suggest that female street-based sex workers are more likely to have entered sex work before age 18, and they are more likely than indoor workers to use drugs, especially crack cocaine and heroin (Galatowicz, Pitcher, & Woolley, 2005; Linton, Celentano, Kirk, & Mehta, 2013; May, Harocopos, & Turnbull, 2001). Homelessness and debt are other issues among street-based women. It should be noted that certainly not all women who are street based are addicted to drugs or enter sex work as minors. Some women prefer the independence of working on the street to indoor settings (O'Connell Davidson, 1998; Pitcher, Campbell, Hubbard, O'Neill, & Scoular, 2006). Indoor workers, by contrast, can be found in such settings as licensed or unlicensed brothels, saunas, and massage parlors; private rented apartments or houses, alone or with others; working in windows; working as escorts (independently or with an agency); working from their own homes; or working as lap dancers, strippers "hospitality workers" in clubs and bars (Dank et al., 2014). Given the lack of public attention that indoor sex workers receive, less police attention is directed at them (Bungay, Halpin, Atchison, & Johnston, 2011). Women who work indoors are likely to be slightly older than women who work on the street (Sanders, 2006). A number of migrant women work in the sex industry in certain U.S. regions, and in some areas, they may represent the majority of indoor workers in that area (Sanders et al., 2009). Little research currently exists distinguishing migrant and trafficked sex workers, and a considerable grey area exists (Yea, 2012). In theory, migrant sex workers make the choice to work in the sex industry over other low-paid and sometimes abusive forms of labor, whereas trafficked women are coerced into sex work; however, in actuality exploitation and coercion are part of the experience for nearly all migrant sex workers (MacKinnon, 2011; Vijeyarasa, 2010).

In terms of brothel work, where women pay a fee to the brothel manager who provides the women with a room, women report that they work in these settings for the additional security and assistance facilitating sex worker/client exchanges. Often there are fixed rates in these settings but a sex worker and client often negotiate over the rate (Dank et al., 2014). Other women prefer to work in an independent setting, often at home or through escort services. Women who work independently on their own property are often in a much better place economically and are able to assert greater choice and control over their sex work (O'Connell Davidson, 1998; Sanders, 2005). Exotic dance tends to be viewed very differently than other forms of sex work (Mavin & Grandy, 2013); dancers are often able to set boundaries regarding the amount of physical contact they have with customers, but this depends upon the type of club in which they work (Sloan & Wahab, 2004).

Male Sex Workers

Far less attention has been paid to male sex workers than female sex workers; less literature exists describing these populations (Kaye, 2014; Minichiello, Scott, & Callander, 2013). Findings suggest that male sex workers may be classified into: escorts, independent workers, and street workers (Connell & Hart, 2003; Sanders et al., 2009). Findings also suggest that men are more likely to engage in indoor-based sex work than street based, with the exception of known outdoor spaces for public sex. Many male sex workers identify as gay or bisexual; however, a number of male sex workers identify as heterosexual and have female clients. Findings regarding female sex tourism indicate that a number of affluent heterosexual women purchase sex from men or boys in certain counties (O'Connell Davidson, 1998). Male street-based workers represent the minority of male sex workers, and they often find clients in the centers of large cities, "cruising" on foot in busy areas with bars and cafes for potential clients (Gaffney, 2007). Sexual transactions often take place in clients' cars or homes, saunas, or quiet outdoor areas, like parks (Connell & Hart, 2003; Wolff, Grov, Smith, Koken, & Parsons, 2014). Violence is greater for street-based workers, which is partially attributed to homophobia (Argento et al., 2014; Marlow, 2006), as is contraction of sexually transmitted infections and HIV, which is attributed to greater drug use among this population (Connell & Hart, 2003; Kaye, 2007; Wolff et al., 2014). In fact, sex is often sold for drugs among this population, often to mitigate the effects of drug withdrawal from stimulants. Sex sold for drugs is thought to carry a higher risk for HIV/STI contraction since it is less likely to involve condom use (Semple, Strathdee, Zians, & Patterson, 2010). Indoor-based male sex workers sell sex in brothels, bars, apartments, or as escorts (either independently or via agency), and on the Internet (Gaffney, 2007). Many men involved in sex work are migrant workers, which likely reflects economic vulnerability among this population (Sanders et al., 2009).

Transgendered Sex Workers

Relatively little is known regarding transgendered sex workers, however, microcommunities have emerged in certain settings (Sanders et al., 2009). Research has suggested that transgendered adolescents are more likely not to have support from their families, which leads them to drop out of school, leave home, use drugs, and engage in prostitution (Klein, 2000; Ryan & Futterman, 1998).

Other Relevant Information

A number of other issues are important to understand about prostitution. Issues in this section will include methodological problems in prostitution and how they have importance for understanding the major correlates of prostitution. Then comes the idea of violence and prostitution. This is followed by a brief discussion of the globalization of prostitution and how technology has importance in the behavior.

Correlates of Prostitution

Methodologically sound research on prostitution is difficult to produce. Two major limitations are sampling and access. These issues generally place the focus of research on the lower echelon prostitute rather than the high-end prostitute. Given the limited samples that researchers, often, use to examine prostitution, research tends to come from convenience samples, including jail, prison, and treatment facilities. While methodology is often difficult, the consistent study of these issues provides consistent patterns of these issues, and some of these patterns will be discussed next.

The most consistent rationale for prostitution, especially for women, is economic. Economic markets usually rely on strong gender and class, and racial hierarchies tend to be closed to individuals, especially women, with limited skills. Prostitution becomes a reasonable alternative because it provides otherwise unskilled women an opportunity to earn a viable income. This is not a phenomenon that is unique to the United States, but one that occurs globally. It is instructive to note women that engage in prostitution do not do so for their entire adulthood, but will hold often legitimate jobs throughout their adulthood.

Economic issues are not the only reasons women become involved in prostitution. One reason for this activity is childhood violence, neglect, or abuse. Researchers show that prostitution is more likely to occur when childhood abuse, including sexual abuse, takes place (Kramer & Berg, 2003; Raphael & Shapiro, 2002; Widom & Kuhns, 1996). This underscores the importance of childhood sexual abuse and the deleterious effects that it can have. While childhood sexual abuse is not the only cause of later prostitution, it is a consistent correlate of this behavior.

Running away from home is another important correlate of prostitution. To be clear, when someone successfully runs away from home, they are homeless. Often the homeless nature interacts with low levels of economics. Researchers show that this occurs among girls that successfully run away from home (Nadon, Koverola, & Schludermann, 1998; Weber et al., 2004). A deeper inspection reveals that the age of onset homeless (i.e., the age that someone becomes homeless) is an important correlate to girls becoming a prostitute.

Another important correlate of prostitution is drugs. The connection between drugs and prostitution has a bit of controversy. Some show that drugs precede prostitution, but others show that drugs do not precede prostitution (Maher, 1997). Regardless of how drugs precede engaging in prostitution, few will deny that drug use is a major correlate with prostitution. Researchers consistently show that women engage in prostitution in order to fund their drug use or addictions.

Violence against Prostitutes

While a number of correlates are present that may push women to engage in prostitution, another correlate reveals the dangerous nature of this type of work—violence. Women that are engaged in prostitution are constantly at risk of physical and sexual violence. High rates of rape—either by clients or pimps—and physical abuse by pimps are routinely reported in the literature (Miller, Romenesko, & Wondolkowski, 1993; Raphael & Shapiro, 2002; Silbert & Pines, 1982). Their exposure to clients and pimps constantly keeps prostitutes in danger.

The nature of "street" prostitution increases the likelihood of violence. Prostitutes are consistently attempting to avoid the police. This means that prostitutes are likely to work in areas that are not well protected by police or law enforcement. Inherently, prostitution is illegal in most states—in the United States—so prostitutes will work in areas that will provide them a means of anonymity and confidentiality. This type of situation may also put prostitutes at risk because they will make poor decisions about the clients that they take. Miller, Romenesko, and Wondolkowski (1993) write that street prostitutes will quickly enter a car and take someone as a client to avoid being apprehended by the police.

Police avoidance is not the only behavior that increases the likelihood of violence. Violence is increased by public perception and attitudes toward their work. For instance, violence against prostitutes in the media (i.e., movies and television) is often glorified, which has the tendency to desensitize or dehumanize those involved in prostitution. This lack of sensitivity contributes to the violence that takes place against prostitutes.

Globalization and Technology in Sex Work

Globalization refers to increased mobility, or connectivity of labor, capital, goods and services, technology, communication, and flows of people throughout the world. The sex industry has globalized with the growth of consumer capitalism and the opening of adult entertainment markets (Brysk, 2011). The global sex industry involves the movement of people and capital across national boundaries, a process which has been referred to as "transnational sex work." At the present time, the lines between migration, which is the willful migration to another country for sex work, and trafficking, which refers to the forced or coerced travel for sexual reasons, are often blurred, making efforts to reduce trafficking additionally challenging (Sanders et al., 2009).

The extent of sex work is not completely known, but some estimates are available. In 2007, the sex work industry generated between $39.9 and $290 million. This amount of income may suggest that there is some overlap between weapons trafficking. A National Institute of Justice report indicated that this was not the case. The report did indicate that sex work did overlap with drug trafficking. To clarify, pimps were not only in control of their sex workers, but also engaged in dealing drugs. The connection with drug trafficking adds to the globalization of sex work making it a lucrative business.

The lucrative nature of sex work has come from the acquisition and delivery of services. The Internet provides the easiest medium for soliciting and acquiring sex work services. Websites (e.g., Craigslist, Backpage, or Eros) provide an opportunity for a pimp or prostitute to advertise these services. These advertisements generally suggest prices for the transference of services. For instance, some websites indicate that sex work may be between $600 and $1000 per hour. Further, these websites provide an opportunity for anonymous and, seemingly, confidential contact in the transaction.

The Internet is also a medium for the transference of sex workers. For instance, a pimp may be able to utilize social networks to acquire or trade sex workers. This is a common phenomenon. Dank et al. (2014) indicated that a large number of women and girls that are involved in sex work were from Eastern European countries. In these Eastern European countries, sex work appears to be connected to a transnational organized crime network. Because the networks are highly organized, the ability to reduce their influence is low.

Conclusion

In general, prostitution is a complex and lucrative business. In most of the United States, prostitution is illegal. The behavior, however, does persist. Fewer women are participating in prostitution as a street occupation, but are participating using different mediums that include the Internet. Because of economics, childhood sexual abuse, and drugs, girls and women from around the world are engaging in this behavior. Men, who may also be prostitutes, are generally pimps that create a number of additional issues that keep women involved in prostitution. Researchers consistently show that pimps physically and sexually abuse prostitutes to further their life in this occupation. Unfortunately, as prostitution continues to become more global, the behavior will continue to spur into stronger organized networks resulting in higher trafficking issues.

Discussion Questions

1. How are drugs related to prostitution?
2. What medium is used to acquire prostitution?
3. Are there any ways to reduce instances of prostitution?

References

1875 Page Law, Session II, Chapt. 141, Stat. 477 (1875).

Argento, E., Muldoon, K. A., Duff, P., Simo, A., Deering, K. N., & Shannon, K. (2014). High prevalence and partner correlates of physical and sexual violence by intimate partners among street and off-street sex workers. *PLoS One, 9*, 1–7. doi:10.1371/journal.pone.0102129

Bartol, C. (2002). *Criminal behavior: A psychosocial approach* (6th ed.). Englewood Cliffs, NJ: Prentice Hall.

Bassermann, L. (1993). *The oldest profession: A history of prostitution.* New York, NY: Dorset Press.

Brysk, A. (2011). Sex as slavery? Understanding private wrongs. *Human Rights Review, 12*, 259–270. doi:10.1007/s12142-010-0182-7

Bullough, V. L. (1982). *Prostitution in the later Middle Ages.* Buffalo, NY: Prometheus Books.

Bungay, V., Halpin, M., Atchison, C., & Johnston, C. (2011). Structure and agency: Reflections from an exploratory study of Vancouver indoor sex workers. *Culture, Health & Sexuality, 13*, 15–29. doi:10.1080/13691058.2010.517324

Butler, A. M. (1987). *Daughters of joy, sisters of misery: Prostitutes in the American West 1865–90.* Champaign, IL: University of Illinois Press.

Centers for Disease Control and Prevention. (June 5, 1981). Pneumocystis Pneumonia—Los Angeles. *Morbidity and Mortality Weekly Report, 30*(21), 1–3.

Chamberlain-Kahn Act (1918). 73rd Leg. (September 1, 1994).

Connell, J., & Hart, G. (2003, June). An overview of male sex work in Edinburgh and Glasgow: The male sex work perspective. In O. P. MRC Social and Public Health Sciences Unit (Ed.). *MRC Social and Public Health Sciences Unit* (Occasional Paper).

Connelly, M. T. (1980). *The response to prostitution in the progressive era.* Chapel Hill, NC: University of North Carolina Press.

Corbin, A. (1990). *Women for hire: Prostitution and sexuality in France after 1850.* Cambridge, MA: Harvard University Press.

Dank, M., Khan, B., Downey, P. M., Kotonias, C., Mayer, C., Owens, C., … Yu, L. (2014). *Estimating the size and structure of the underground commercial sex economy in eight major US cities.* Washington, DC: The Urban Institute.

Diduck, A., & Winson, W. (1977). Prostitutes and persons. *The Journal of Law and Society, 24,* 504–525.

Ditmore, M. H. (2006). *Encyclopedia of prostitution and sex work.* Westport: Greenwood Press.

Edlund, L., & Korn, E. (2002). A theory of prostitution. *Journal of Political Economy, 110*(1), 181–214.

Eisler, R. (1995). *Sacred pleasure: Sex, myth, and the politics of the body.* London, U.K.: Harper Collins.

Engagement in prostitution or solicitation for prostitution: Penalty; exception NRS 201.354 (2013, 2430).

Farley, M. (2004). "Bad for the body, bad for the heart": Prostitution harms women even if legalized or decriminalized. *Violence Against Women, 10,* 1087–1125.

Farley, M., & Kelly, V. (2000). Prostitution: A critical review of the medical and social sciences literature. *Women & Criminal Justice, 11,* 29–64.

Gaffney, J. (2007). A coordinated prostitution strategy and response to *Paying the Price*—But what about the men? *Community Safety Journal, 6,* 27–33.

Galatowicz, L., Pitcher, J., & Woolley, A. (2005). *Report of the community-led research project focusing on drug and alcohol use of women sex workers and access to services.* Coventry, U.K.: Terrence Higgins Trust, for University of Central Lancashire and Department of Health.

Goffman, E. (1963). *Stigma: Notes on the management of spoiled identity.* Englewood Cliffs, NJ: Prentice Hall.

Henriquez, F. (1962). *Prostitution and society.* London, U.K.: MacGibbon and Kee.

Hoke v. United States, No. 308, 227 (U.S. Supreme Court 1913).

Jenness, V. (1990). From sex as sin to sex as work: COYOTE and the reorganization of prostitution as a social problem. *Social Problems, 37,* 403–420. doi:10.1525/sp.1990.37.3.03a00090

Johnson, E. M. (2014). Buyers without remorse: Ending the discriminatory enforcement of prostitution laws. *Texas Law Review, 92,* 717–748.

Karras, R. M. (1989). The regulations of brothels in later medieval England. *Signs, 14,* 399–433.

Karras, R. M. (1996a). *Common women: Prostitution and sexuality in Medieval England.* Oxford, U.K.: Oxford University Press.

Karras, R. M. (1996b). *Prostitution in Medieval Europe.* New York, NY: Garland Publishing.

Kaye, K. (2007). Sex and the unspoken in male street prostitution. *Journal of Homosexuality, 53,* 37–73.

Kaye, K. (2014). Male sex work in modern times. In V. Minichiello & J. Scott (Eds.), *Male sex work and society* (pp. 34–49). New York: Harrington Park Press.

Keller v. United States, No. 138, 213 (U.S. Supreme Court 1909).

Kishtainy, K. (1982). *The prostitute in progressive literature.* London, U.K.: Allison and Busby.

Klein, R. (2000). Group work practice with transgendered male to female sex workers. *Journal of Gay and Lesbian Social Services, 10,* 95–109. doi:10.1300/J041v10n03_07

Kramer, L. A., & Berg, E. C. (2003). A survival analysis of timing of entry into prostitution: The differential impact of race, educational level, and childhood/adolescent risk factors. *Sociological Inquiry, 73*(4), 511–528.

Kubrin, C. (2005). Gangstas, thugs, and hustlas: Identity and the code of the street in rap music. *Social Problems, 52*(3), 360–378.

Lerner, G. (1986). The origin of prostitution in ancient Mesopotamia. *Signs, 11,* 236–254.

Linton, S. L., Celentano, D. D., Kirk, G. D., & Mehta, S. H. (2013). The longitudinal association between homelessness, injection drug use, and injection-related risk behavior among persons with a history of injection drug use in Baltimore, MD. *Drug and Alcohol Dependence, 132,* 457–465. doi:10.1016/j.drugalcdep.2013.03.009

Long, A. P. (2004). *The great southern Babylon: Sex, race, and respectability in New Orleans, 1865–1920.* Baton Rouge, LA: Louisiana State University Press.

Lubove, R. (1962). The progressives and the prostitute. *The Historian, 24,* 308–330.

Luker, K. (1998). Sex, social hygiene, and the state: The double-edged sword of social reform. *Theory and Society, 27,* 601–634.

MacKinnon, C. A. (2011). Trafficking, prostitution, and inequality. *Harvard Civil Rights–Civil Liberties Law Review, 46,* 271–309.

Maher, L. (1997). *Sexed work: Gender, race, and resistance in a Brooklyn drug market.* Oxford University Press.

Marlow, J. (2006). *Thinking outside the box: Men in the sex industry.* Stanford, CA: Stanford University Press.

Mavin, S., & Grandy, G. (2013). Doing gender well and differently in dirty work: The case of exotic dancing. *Gender, Work and Organization, 20,* 232–251. doi:10.1111/j.1468-0432.2011.00567.x

May, T., Harocopos, A., & Turnbull, P. (2001). *Selling sex in the city: An valuation of a targeted arrest referral scheme for sex workers in Kings Cross.* London, U.K.: Home Office.

Miller, E. M., Romenesko, K., & Wondolkowski, L. (1993). *The United States.* London, U.K.: Greenwood.

Minichiello, V., Scott, J., & Callander, D. (2013). New pleasures and old dangers: Reinventing male sex work. *Journal of Sex Research, 50,* 263–275. doi:10.1080/00224499.2012.760189

Moses, M. C. (2006). Understanding and applying research on prostitution. *National Institute of Justice Journal, 55,* 22–25.

Murphy, A. K., & Venkatesh, S. A. (2006). Vice Careers: The changing contours of sex work in New York City. *Qualitative Sociology, 29,* 129–154.

Nadon, S. M., Koverola, C., & Schludermann, E. H. (1998). Antecedents to prostitution childhood victimization. *Journal of Interpersonal Violence, 13*(2), 206–221.

O'Connell Davidson, J. (1998). *Prostitution, power and freedom.* Cambridge, MA: Polity.

Perkins, R., & Lovejoy, F. (2007). *Call girls: Private sex workers in Australia.* Crawley, Western Australia: University of Western Australia Press.

Pheterson, G. (1993). The whore stigma. *Social Text, 37,* 37–64.

Pheterson, G. (1996). *The whore stigma.* Amsterdam, the Netherlands: Amsterdam University Press.

Pitcher, J., Campbell, R., Hubbard, P., O'Neill, M., & Scoular, J. (2006). *Living and working in areas of street sex work: From conflict to coexistence.* Bristol, U.K.: The Policy Press.

Prostitution Defined (13A-12-110-122).

Raphael, J., & Shapiro, D. L. (2002). *Sisters speak out: The lives and needs of prostituted women in Chicago.* Chicago, IL: Center for Impact Research.

Ringdal, N. J. (2005). *Love for sale: A world history of prostitution.* New York, NY: Grove Press.

Roberts, N. (1992). *Whores in history: Prostitution in western society.* London, U.K.: Harper Collins.

Ryan, C., & Futterman, D. (1998). *Lesbian and gay youth: Care and counseling.* New York, NY: Columbia University Press.

Sallman, J. (2010). Living with stigma: Women's experiences of prostitution and substance use. *AFFILIA: Journal of Women and Social Work, 25,* 146–159.

Sanders, T. (2005). *Sex work: A risky business.* Cullompton, U.K.: Willan.

Sanders, T. (2006). *Behind the personal ads: The indoor sex markets in Britain.* Cullompton, U.K.: Willan.

Sanders, T., O'Neill, M., & Pitcher, J. (2009). *Prostitution: Sex work, policy, and politics.* London, U.K.: Sage.

Semple, S. J., Strathdee, S. A., Zians, J., & Patterson, T. L. (2010). Social and behavioral characteristics of HIV-positive MSM who trade sex for methamphetamine. *American Journal of Drug and Alcohol Abuse, 36,* 325–331. doi:10.3109/00952990.2010.505273

Silbert, M. H., & Pines, A. M. (1982). Entrance into prostitution. *Youth and Society, 13*(4), 471–500.

Sloan, L., & Wahab, S. (2004). Four categories of women who work as topless dancers. *Sexuality & Culture, 8,* 18–43.

Sneddeker, D. (Fall 1990). Regulating vice: Prostitution and the St. Louis social evil ordinance, 1870–1874. *Gateway Heritage, 10,* 20–47.

Symanski, R. (1974). Prostitution in Nevada. *Annals of the Association of American Geographers, 64,* 357–377.

Tevrizian, M., Garske, M., & Wood, M. (2014). Feds: Alleged pimps branded prostitutes with tattoos. *NBC News.* Retrieved From http://www.nbcsandiego.com/news/local/police-warrants-sex-trafficking-bomb-squad-239304771.html

Thompson, H. (2013, December 11). Prostitution: Why Swedes believe they got it right. *The Guardian.* Retrieved from http://www.theguardian.com/global-development/2013/dec/11/prostitution-sweden-model-reform-men-pay-sex

Vijeyarasa, R. (2010). Exploitation or expectations: Moving beyond consent. *Women's Policy Journal of Harvard, 7,* 11–22.

Walkowitz, J. (1980). *Prostitution and Victorian society.* Cambridge, U.K.: Cambridge University Press.

Warnick, A. (2008). *Sex without romance: The political economy of prostitution.* In E. Lopez (Ed.) *Law without romance: Public choice and legal institutions* (Forthcoming Publication) Retrieved from http://ssrn.com/abstract=1081624

Weber, E. U., Shafir, S., & Blais, A. R. (2004). Predicting risk sensitivity in humans and lower animals: Risk as variance or coefficient of variation. *Psychological Review,* 430–445.

Weitzer, R. (2000). *Sex for sale: Prostitution, pornography, and the sex industry.* New York, NY: Routledge.

White Slave Traffic Act, aka the Mann Act, 36 Stats., Vol. 1, p. 825, Chap. 395. § 2421 (1910).

Widom, C. S., & Kuhns, J. B. (1996). Childhood victimization and subsequent risk for promiscuity, prostitution, and teenage pregnancy: A prospective study. *American Journal of Public Health,* 1607–1612.

Williamson, C., & Cluse-Tolar, T. (2002). Pimp-controlled prostitution still an intergral part of street life. *Violence Against Women, 8*(9), 1074–1092.

Wolff, M. M., Grov, C., Smith, M. D., Koken, J. A., & Parsons, J. T. (2014). Male clients' behaviours with and perspectives about their last male escort encounter: Comparing repeat versus first-time hires. *Culture, Health & Sexuality, 16,* 850–863. doi:10.1080/13691058.2014.919408

Wright, D. (2014). Undercover for alleged underage prostitution raid at Colombia villa. *ABC News.* Retrieved from http://abcnews.go.com/Nightline/video/undercover-alleged-underage-prostitution-raid-colombia-villa-26205014

Yea, S. (2012). "Shades of grey": Spaces in and beyond trafficking for Thai women involved in commercial sexual labour in Sydney and Singapore. *Gender, Place & Culture: A Journal of Feminist Geography, 19,* 42–60. doi:10.1080/0966369X.2011.617906

Mothers Who Kill

12

KIMBERLY D. DODSON AND LEANN N. CABAGE

Contents

Filicide is the killing of one or more children by a parent, stepparent, or guardian. Included within filicide are two subcategories: infanticide and neonaticide, which are differentiated based on the child victim's age. Infanticide refers to the killing of a child less than 1 year old. Neonaticide, or the killing of a newborn with 24 hours of birth, is a specific type of infanticide (Resnick, 1969). Filicide is a serious problem in the United States. For example, 94,146 (approximately 15%) homicides were classified as filicides in the period 1976–2007. Arrest data from the Federal Bureau of Investigation's (FBI) Supplementary Homicide Reports (SHR) indicate that an average of 2942 filicides occurred annually from 1976 to 2007. There was a peak in filicides between 1991 and 1995, with an average of 3233 filicides each year. The yearly average of filicides declined between 2001 and 2005 to 2668. Among developed countries, the United States ranks as one of the highest in rates of filicide (Ferguson, Miller-Stratton, Heinrich, Fritz, & Smith, 2007).

Few crimes cause greater public reaction than that of a mother who murders her child. In the United States, the cases of Casey Anthony, Andrea Yates, and Susan Smith elicit reactions ranging from compassion and sympathy to rage and anger. The media hype undoubtedly contributes to our morbid curiosity about these cases and we are often mesmerized by the news accounts as the details emerge. As a result, many may have the perception that mothers kill their children more frequently than fathers because the media disproportionately covers cases involving mothers (Levéillée, Marleau, & Dubé, 2007). In reality, mothers are only the perpetrators of child murder in a little over 40% of the cases (Mariano, Chan, & Myers, 2014). However, these cases still leave us wondering what would drive a mother to kill her child.

Case Study 1: Infanticide—The Case of Ka Yang

Ka Yang, 30, of Sacramento, California, was arrested on April 21, 2011, for the murder with special circumstances of her 6-week-old daughter, Mirabelle Thao-Lo. On March 17, 2011, Yang called 911 to report that her daughter was dead. Emergency medical personnel and police responded to her residence and found that Mirabelle had suffered serious burns from head-to-toe but that the infant's clothes were not burned nor was her hair singed. Authorities could not immediately locate the source of the burns after their arrival but sometime later discovered a pacifier in the microwave. Yang initially told investigators she fainted while working at her computer with Mirabelle in her arms. Yang said that when she woke up Mirabelle was lying next to a space heater and the infant had apparently suffered severe burns. She later admitted that she lied and claimed she might have a "split personality." The Sacramento County Coroner determined Mirabelle died of "extensive thermal injuries." At the time of the crime, Yang was living with her husband and three young sons. Her sons were placed with relatives after her arrest. She has not been to trial.

Source: Associated Press (2011, October 26).

In this chapter, we will discuss the history of filicide and notable cases of filicide in the United States. We also will discuss legal issues regarding the prosecution and defense of filicide cases. The characteristics of both the victims and offenders of filicide will be presented and we will explore victim–offender relationships. Finally, we discuss why mothers kill their children.

History of Filicide

Filicides have occurred for centuries and have been documented in practically every society, from advanced, industrialized countries to indigenous groups (McKee, 2006). Historically, infanticide was encouraged as a means of population control and, therefore, often handled with ambivalence. The earliest recorded history of infanticide occurred in ancient Rome. Disabled newborns were frequently the victims of infanticide and they were killed almost exclusively by their fathers (Meyer and Oberman, 2001). The killing of a child was considered a private family matter. Roman law gave fathers absolute legal authority and thus the father could decide the fate of an infant child without any repercussions.

In early Islamic nations, mothers often killed their female infants to prevent them from living a life of absolute domination. Families who felt they could not offer a proper dowry when their daughter came of age to marry also used it. However, with the introduction of Islamic law came a call for the abolition of the practice, but there is little indication it ceased (Spinelli, 2003). Traditional Chinese cultures faced a similar battle. Many argued the worth of a female child was far less than that of a male child because the female could not carry on the family name and honor her family in the same way a male could. Additionally, the one child per family practice implemented in 1979 resulted in an increase of infanticide. The practice continues today.

Infanticide also was used in Medieval Judeo-Christian Societies to hide the birth of illegitimate children. During this time, the link between illegitimacy and infanticide was so prevalent, infanticide was considered a crime committed exclusively by unmarried women (Meyer and Oberman, 2001; Spinelli, 2003). Therefore, some of the first criminal laws associated with infanticide referred to the crime as "bastardy infanticide." Punishment for bastardy infanticide ranged from burying alive to drowning and decapitation (Moseley, 1986). In Christian societies, the crime was often associated with witchcraft; therefore, the punishments often corresponded with those given to women suspected of being witches (Trexler, 1973).

Notable Past Cases of Filicide in the United States

Marybeth Tinning

The story of Marybeth Tinning spans more than a decade. Tinning's third child, Jennifer, was the first of her children to die, but the death was not under suspicious circumstances. Jennifer was sick at birth and never left the hospital. However, the deaths of Marybeth's next seven biological children and one adoptive son were questionable. From 1972 until 1985, eight of Tinning's children would die. Until the death of her adopted son, many suggested there was perhaps some type of genetic disorder linked to the deaths of the children.

The circumstances surrounding the death of each child were similar. She would rush the child to the hospital to report she had found the child unconscious and not breathing. For the first child to die under her care, Tinning reported the child was having seizure-like symptoms, but doctors were unable to find anything and sent the child home. Within hours, the child was back at the hospital, but this time he was dead, reportedly from becoming entangled in his sheets while sleeping. Tinning reported the second child had gone into convulsions, but refused to let doctors monitor the child overnight. Once again, the story is the same; within hours, she was back at the hospital with the unconscious child. As with the first child, the cause of death was unknown and no one seemed suspicious. Tinning took the third child to the hospital reporting she had found the child lifeless in his crib. This time the cause of death was listed as sudden infant death syndrome (SIDS). Within a month of the death of her third child, she brought her fourth child to the hospital complaining of seizure-like symptoms. The doctors released the child but within hours Tinning was back at the hospital but this time the child was dead.

The fifth child was taken to the hospital where Tinning reported she was driving with the child when she noticed he had stopped breathing. He was pronounced dead at the hospital. The story for the sixth child was similar to the others; Tinning had found the child unconscious and did not know why. Once again, the cause of death was listed as SIDS. The seventh child was very similar, taken to the hospital unconscious for unknown reasons. Revived the first time, but later brought back to the hospital unconscious where he was pronounced brain dead. Her adopted son would become the next victim. This time Tinning took the unconscious child to her pediatrician's office. The eighth and final child, Tinning reported, was found entangled in a blanket. The exception to this case was instead of taking the child to the hospital or doctor, Tinning called a friend. When the friend arrived, she reported the child was lying on a changing table and was purple; unable to determine why the child was struggling, she called for EMS assistance. The child was pronounced dead upon arrival at the emergency room.

Eight of Tinning's children were now dead. Until the death of her adopted son, many had suggested there must be some type of genetic defect causing the deaths of the children. However, concern mounted after the death of the eighth child and Tinning's actions immediately following his death. After the child's funeral, Tinning had people over for brunch where it was reported she was smiling and interacting in a manner that did not indicate distress or sadness. These actions combined with growing concern led police to question Tinning. When police arrived to question Tinning she indicated she knew they were there to arrest her and take her to jail (Egginton, 1989). The police interpreted her statement as an admission of guilt or at least a guilty conscience. However, there was a lack of evidence and additional information was needed for a successful prosecution. To obtain the additional information, Schenectady police detective Bob Imfeld and state police investigator Joseph Karas asked Tinning to come to police headquarters for questioning. During the interview, Tinning denied hurting her children repeatedly. However, after hours of interrogation, she admitted to playing a role in the deaths of three of her children. She admitted to smothering each of the three children with a pillow because she felt inadequate as a mother. This admission to police and a later conversation with her husband in which she stated she killed one of the children, her daughter, Tami, ultimately led to her arrest and indictment.

At trial, Tinning reported she agreed to questioning by the police because she felt obligated. She also denied being provided the Miranda warning. Additionally, she argued she felt intimidated by the police. The arguments were dismissed and Tinning was found guilty of second-degree murder of her daughter, Tami. She received a sentence of 20 years to life. Indictments were later issued for the other two children, but charges were dismissed because of lack of evidence (Gado, n.d.).

Susan Smith

On October 25, 1994, in Union, South Carolina, Susan Smith drove to John D. Long Lake. She parked her car in the middle of the boat ramp with her two young sons, Michael (3 years old) and Alex (14 months old) asleep in the back. She placed the car in neutral permitting it to roll a few yards before braking. She then pulled the emergency brake, got out of the car, and stood on the boat ramp reportedly thinking of suicide. Then thoughts of her sons suffering entered her head. She did not want her sons to suffer, so she believed killing her sons and then committing suicide would create less suffering for the two young boys. She released the emergency brake, shut the driver's side door, and permitted the car to roll into the lake with her two sons strapped into their car seats and asleep in the back seat. Smith watched as the car sank into the lake before running to a nearby residence to call for help.

The story Smith would tell on that October night would capture the nation's attention for days before she finally confessed to her actions. Smith reported to police she had been carjacked by a black man who had drove away with her sons still in the car. Over the 9-day period, she appeared on national television pleading for any information that would lead to the rescue and return of her two children. Police would launch an intensive investigation including a nationwide search for the vehicle and the suspect. During the investigation, detectives noticed discrepancies in Smith's story and results of polygraph exams came back inconclusive. Smith had become a suspect in the case of her two missing children.

On Thursday, November 3, 1994, Susan Smith admitted to driving to the lake and rolling the car into the lake with her two children still inside. Smith was arrested that afternoon and charged with two counts of murder in connection with the deaths. On January 16, 1995, the state filed a notice of intention to seek the death penalty against Smith. After multiple psychiatric evaluations, Smith was ruled mentally competent to stand trial on July 11, 1995. Opening statements for the trial began on July 19, 1995.

Smith's confession to the murder of her two sons left her defense team with two options. The first was to have Smith plead not guilty by reason of insanity and the second was to have her plead guilty, but mentally ill. However, Smith was not insane or mentally ill. The defense was left with arguing Smith was suffering from severe mental depression and the murders were a failed suicide in which Smith also planned to drown herself. After deliberating for 2.5 hours, the jury returned a guilty verdict for two counts of murder. At the conclusion of the sentencing phase, the jury took the same amount of time to reject the death penalty and instead recommend a life sentence. Judge Howard sentenced Smith to 30 years to life in prison. Smith will be eligible for parole in 2025 after completing 30 years of her sentence.

Ultimately, Smith was upset that her boyfriend, Tom Findley, had ended their relationship because he did not want children. In an attempt to win Findley back, Smith concocted the plan of rolling her car into the lake and then telling officials she had been carjacked in hopes of getting away with the murders.

Andrea Yates

On June 20, 2001, Yates called the Houston Police to report she had drowned her four boys and infant daughter in the bathtub. Yates filled the tub with water after her husband left for work. Beginning with Paul, Yates systematically drowned her three youngest sons, placed them on her bed, and covered them. Next, she drowned Mary who she left floating in the tub. Still alive, her 7-year-old son Noah asked his mother what was wrong with his sister, then turned and ran away. Yates caught up with her son, dragged him back to the tub, and forced him in next to his siblings floating body. After Noah succumbed to the drowning, Yates took Mary to the bed and placed her in the arms of her brothers. During her confession, Yates stated her children were not developing correctly and it was her fault because she was not a good mother.

Yates's trial lasted a short 3 weeks. On March 12, 2002, the jury rejected Yates's insanity defense and convicted Yates of capital murder in the deaths of Noah, John, and Mary. During the sentencing phase, the jury elected for a sentence of life in prison instead of the death penalty. On April 30, 2004, Yates's attorney, George Parnham, filed an appeal.

During Yates's trial, four mental health experts testified that the defendant did not know right from wrong, was incapable of knowing what she did was wrong, or believed that her acts were right. The State's lone mental health expert, Dr. Park Dietz, testified that the defendant knew her actions were wrong although she was psychotic at the time of the murders. The expert testified that Yates had watched an episode of the television show *Law and Order* in which a woman with postpartum depression drowned her children in the bathtub and was found not guilty by reason of insanity. Dietz also testified that because Yates indicated her thoughts were coming from Satan, she must have known they were wrong. The defense team ultimately discovered there was no such episode of *Law and Order* and moved for a mistrial, but the motion was denied. The trial court did grant the request for the stipulation of the false testimony to be admitted into evidence and read to the jury.

The Court of Appeals considered whether the State knew the testimony of Dietz was false, whether the State used the false information, and whether or not the information was material to the guilty verdict. The Appellate Court ruled the case did not involve the State's knowing use of perjured testimony. The Appellate Court continued stating if a witness has testified to material, inculpatory facts against a defendant and, after the verdict but before a motion for a new trial has been ruled upon, the witness makes an affidavit that he testified falsely, a new trial should be granted (*State of Texas v. Yates*, 2005). Further, the record indicated the State used Dr. Dietz's testimony on two occasions. First, the State used the testimony in a cross-examination. Second, the State juxtaposed Yates's depression her dark thoughts, watching *Law and Order*, and seeing a way out. Therefore, the State used Dietz's false testimony to suggest to the jury that Yates patterned her actions after the television episode. In conclusion, the Court of Appeals state there was a reasonable likelihood that Dietz's false testimony could have affected the judgment of the jury and the false testimony substantially affected the rights of Yates. Therefore, the trial court abused its discretion in denying the motion for mistrial (*State of Texas v. Yates*, 2005). The Court reversed the trial court's decision and remanded the case for further proceedings.

Yates who had battled with depression for years would again face trial for the murder of her children. This time the jury would hear evidence of Yates's psychiatric past, her development of postpartum psychosis and schizophrenia. The outcome this time would find Yates not guilty by reason of insanity. After the verdict, Yates was transferred to Vernon State Hospital, a maximum-security state mental health facility where she will likely spend the rest of her life.

Casey Anthony

Although Anthony was not convicted of the murder of her daughter, Caylee Anthony, many still question her involvement in her child's death. On June 15, 2008, Anthony and her mother, Cindy, argued over photographs of Anthony at a party. Cindy questioned whether Anthony was a fit mother and threatened to sue for custody of Caylee. The next day, Anthony left her parents' home with Caylee telling her parents she was traveling to Tampa to work at Universal Studios.

Over the next month, Cindy called to check on Caylee, each time being told the child was with a babysitter, Zenaida "Zanny" Fernandez-Gonzalez. On July 13, 2008, Anthony's parents received a letter stating Anthony's car was being held in a tow yard. When her father, George, retrieved the car, he found Casey's purse along with Caylee's car seat and toys. He also noticed a strong smell of decomposing organic matter coming from the trunk. Casey was located at the home of her boyfriend and told her mother and brother she had left Caylee with the nanny on June 16, and that Gonzalez had kidnapped the child.

On July 15th, Cindy Anthony reported Caylee missing to the Orange County Sheriff's Office. Detectives questioned Casey Anthony and found discrepancies in a signed statement she made about the disappearance. It was later discovered there was no nanny and that Anthony had lied about working at Universal Studios. Anthony was arrested on July 16.

On December 11, 2008, a meter reader found a plastic bag of human remains in a wooded area near the Anthony's home. On December 19, the remains were confirmed to be those of Caylee Anthony. Three years after the disappearance of her daughter, the trial of Casey Anthony began in May 2011.

Anthony was portrayed by the prosecution as a promiscuous party girl who was unconcerned with her missing daughter. Trial testimony indicated that Google searches about chloroform had been discovered on the Anthony's home computer. This was significant because chloroform was found in the trunk of Anthony's car. The prosecution presented evidence that they believed showed that Anthony used the chloroform to murder Caylee. However, the defense painted a different picture. They presented testimony that Caylee had drowned in the family's pool on June 16, 2008, and that George Anthony had helped cover up the death.

On July 5, 2011, the jury found Anthony not guilty of first-degree murder, aggravated manslaughter, and aggravated child abuse. She was however found guilty of four counts of providing false information to a law enforcement officer and sentenced to four years in jail and a $1,000 fine for each count. She received credit for time served and was released on July 17, 2011.

Legislation on Filicide

The legal ramifications associated with filicide are as varied as the background of each case. In England and Canada, the individual is prosecuted under statutes that specifically address infanticide (Walker, 2006). Prosecution under these statutes often results in a lenient sentence (Oberman, 1996). Austria, Colombia, Finland, Greece, India, Italy, Korea, New Zealand, New South Wales, the Philippines, Tasmania, Turkey, and Western Australia have implemented similar statutes. However, the United States has fallen drastically behind in the implementation of statutes designed specifically for the prosecution of filicide and often rely on existing murder statutes.

Legislative History of Filicide

The British legal history details the lax view taken toward infanticide. Parliament passed a law in 1623 making it a capital offense to conceal the birth of an illegitimate child (Hoffer & Hull, 1981). The law required the defendant to produce a witness to testify the child was stillborn; otherwise she was to be found guilty of murder (Oberman, 1996). The law put the women at a disadvantage because a woman hiding her illegitimate pregnancy was extremely unlikely to have a witness to the birth. Therefore, the law resulted in innocent women being sentenced to death because they could not provide a witness to testify that the child was stillborn. The unfairness associated with the law led juries to refuse a conviction of the woman if she could provide an acceptable defense that she was preparing for the birth of the child (Hoffer & Hull, 1981; Rapaport, 2005). This eventually led to the passage of a new infanticide statute by the Parliament in 1830. The new statute required the prosecution to prove the child was born alive (Spinelli, 2003). If the prosecution could not prove their case, the woman could receive a maximum 2-year sentence for concealing the birth of an illegitimate child; however, if the prosecution could provide proof of a live birth, the sentence was death. Juries quickly came to prefer the lesser offense even when the evidence suggested otherwise (Backhouse, 1984). The jurors' attitudes and the push from psychiatrists to recognize infanticide as a correlate of pregnancy and mental illness led to the passage of the British Infanticide Act of 1922. The act was amended and expanded in 1938. Twenty-two additional nations have adopted similar statutes (Oberman, 1996). The British Infanticide Act of 1922 recognized postpartum disturbance as a partial defense to infanticide and reduces the charge from murder to manslaughter (Rapaport, 2005).

The 1938 amendment set the limit of the laws application to children under a year old (Rapaport, 2005). The 1938 statute is often interpreted as permitting virtually any woman charged with infanticide to have the benefit of the partial defense regardless of mental condition (Rapaport, 2005). Punishment under the law requires the mother to undergo treatment versus prison time (Oberman, 1996; Rapaport, 2005). Since the amendment of the act in 1938, Britain has made additional attempts to further the medicalization of maternal infanticide. An attempt was made by reformers in the 1970s to amend the law to recognize social stressors of motherhood; however, these attempts failed (Rapaport, 2005).

BRITISH INFANTICIDE ACT 1938

Offence of infanticide.

(1) Where a woman by any wilful act or omission causes the death of her child being a child under the age of twelve months, but at the time of the act or omission the balance of her mind was disturbed by reason of her not having fully recovered from the effect of giving birth to the child or by reason of the effect of lactation consequent upon the birth of the child, then, notwithstanding that the circumstances were such that but for this Act the offence would have amounted to murder, she shall be guilty of felony, to wit of infanticide, and may for such offence be dealt with and punished as if she had been guilty of the offence of manslaughter of her child.

(2) Where upon the trial of a woman for the murder of her child, being a child under the age of twelve months, the jury are of opinion that she by any wilful act or omission caused its death, but that at the time of the act or omission the balance of her mind was disturbed by reason of her not having fully recovered from the effect of giving birth to the child or by reason of the effect of lactation consequent upon the birth of the child, then the jury may, notwithstanding that the circumstances were such that but for the provisions of this Act they might have returned a verdict of murder, return in lieu thereof a verdict of infanticide.

Canada passed similar legislation in 1948. The Canadian Infanticide Act states

A female person commits infanticide when by a wilful act or omission she causes the death of her newly born child, if at the time of the act or omission she is not fully recovered from the effects of giving birth to the child and by reason thereof or of the effect of lactation consequent on the birth of the child her mind is then disturbed.

Similar to outcomes in Britain, the punishments are lax. The maximum sentence received for mothers who commit infanticide has been no more than 5 years (Walker, 2006).

Beyond providing a statute specific to infanticide, the Canadian Act does not require a mental disorder diagnosis. The burden of proof in such cases is placed on the Crown and they therefore must prove the mother has fully recovered from the effects of birth at the time of the crime (Walker, 2006).

The British and Canadian approach is drastically different from the approach taken by the legal system in the United States. Currently, there is no federal statute addressing the crimes of filicide, infanticide, or neonaticide in the United States. Individuals charged with murdering their children are prosecuted under existing homicide or manslaughter statutes and may use an affirmative defense (i.e., insanity, involuntary act, or diminished capacity) to suggest they were suffering from a mental defect at the time of the crime. The success of an affirmative defense lies solely on the defense, which must prove their client was suffering from some type of mental illness at the time of the crime. If the defense is successful in their argument, the individual may receive an acquittal, conviction of a lesser offense, a verdict of not guilty by reason of insanity, or guilty but mentally ill.

Current Legal State of Filicide in the United States

Prosecution and Defense of Filicide

As noted above, the United States has failed to take approaches such as those taken by England, Canada, and others to recognize infanticide specifically as a separate crime from murder. Rather than recognizing filicide including infanticide and neonaticide as distinct crimes, the United States prosecutes cases under current homicide and manslaughter statutes. The statutes and the sentencing guidelines associated with them do not take into consideration the medical or mental condition of the offender. Instead, the legislation is designed to prosecute individuals who are fully capable of understanding the intent and consequences of their actions. For mothers who kill their children, the legal system provides a set of minimal options. The defense team may argue their client's case does not meet the elements of a specific crime and have the charges reduced, or the defense may use one of the three affirmative defenses, making it the responsibility of the defense team to prove their client meets the guidelines for such defense.

If a charged individual invokes the insanity defense, depending on the jurisdiction, their mental state will be evaluated using either the M'Naghten Test or the Model Penal Code (MPC). The M'Naghten Test was established by an English case in 1843 and is often referred to as the "right and wrong test." For a successful insanity defense under M'Naghten, the defense must clearly prove

> at the time of the committing of the act, the party accused was laboring under such a defect of reason, from disease of the mind, as not to know the nature and quality of the act he was doing; or, if he did know it, that he did not know he was doing what was wrong. (*Queen v. M'Naghten*, 1843)

In other words, the prosecution must establish the defendant knew right from wrong when the act was committed and the individual was capable of understanding the nature and quality of their actions.

Some states have rejected the M'Naghten Test in favor of the irresistible impulse test. For example, in Tennessee the irresistible impulse test "relieve[s] criminal responsibility when his mental condition is such as to deprive him of his will power to resist the impulse to commit the crime" (*Graham v. State*, 1977). In the federal court of appeals and several states, the MPC is used to determine a person's mental state. The MPC states,

> [a] person is not responsible for criminal conduct if at the time of such conduct as a result of mental disease or defect he lacks substantial capacity either to appreciate the criminality [wrongfulness] of his conduct or to conform his conduct to the requirements of law. (Model Penal Code, 1985)

Therefore, the test has two prongs: the cognitive aspect of the behavior and the volitional aspect of the behavior. The cognitive aspect of the test may be satisfied if the defense can provide evidence that at the time of the crime, a mental defect caused the defendant to lack the capacity to understand their actions were wrong. The volitional element is satisfied if the defense can provide proof the mental illness prevented the defendant from conforming their conduct to the law. If the defense can meet either element of the test, they have grounds for invoking an insanity defense. For a successful defense using either test, it is essential the defense be able to prove the defendant suffered from a medically recognized mental disorder at the time of committing the crime.

Defendants also may argue their commission of the crime was the result of an involuntary act. Meaning at the time the crime was committed the defendant was incapable of controlling their actions because of a physical or mental disability. In other words, because of a disability the defendant was unable to control the actions of their body. The specifics of the defense differs across jurisdictions, but Robinson (1984) summarizes the Model Penal Code (1985) this way: "An actor is excused for his conduct constituting an offense if, as a result of (1) any mental or physical disability, and (2) the conduct is not a product of the actor's effort or determination" (p. 260). For example, the defense may be used when someone commits a murder involuntary while sleepwalking. The involuntary act defense is recognized in most jurisdictions if the defense can prove the defendant suffered from a disability that caused the individual to lose control and commit the crime involuntarily.

The final defense that may be used by a defendant is diminished capacity. This defense is used to argue a mental illness negates the *mens rea* (i.e., mental intent) of the crime. In other words, the defendant's mental illness prevented her from formulating or possessing the mental state required for a conviction under the charged statute. The diminished capacity defense is often used to gain a lesser but included offense conviction versus conviction of the charged crime.

A successful defense under either of the aforementioned has the potential to result in one of four options: (1) an acquittal, (2) conviction of a lesser-included offense, (3) a verdict of not guilty by reason of insanity, and (4) a verdict of guilty but mentally ill. However, the lack of federal and/or state laws results in cases being reviewed on a case-by-case basis. The failure to provide standardization results in varying charges, convictions, and sentences across jurisdictions.

Safe Haven Laws

Safe haven laws were first introduced in Texas in 1999. Safe haven laws give mothers in crisis the opportunity to relinquish their babies safely to a designated location where the infant receives protection and medical care until a permanent home is found (Child Welfare

Information Gateway, 2013). Currently, safe haven legislation has been enacted in all 50 states, the District of Columbia, and Puerto Rico. The period in which infants may be surrendered to a safe haven ranges from within 72 hours of birth to 1 month after birth (Child Welfare Information Gateway, 2013). Additionally, the person permitted to surrender the child varies by jurisdiction.

Safe haven laws were enacted to ensure relinquished infants are left with a person(s) who can provide the care needed for their safety and well-being. Locations in which the infant may be surrendered include hospitals, emergency medical service providers, health care facilities, fire stations, law enforcement agencies, emergency medical personnel responding to 911 calls, and churches; however, the permissible locations vary by state. Safe haven providers must provide emergency protective custody and any immediate medical care the infant may require. Some states attempt to obtain family and medical history information for the infant being surrendered. States may also provide the individual surrendering the child with information pertaining to legal repercussions of leaving the infant as well as providing information obtaining to referral services. In regards to anonymity, express anonymity is only guaranteed in 13 states and the District of Columbia; while 26 states and Puerto Rico cannot force the parent to provide any identifying information (Child Welfare Information Gateway, 2013). The remaining states do not provide specific provisions for anonymity. Additionally, 14 states provide confidentiality for any information volunteered by the parent (Child Welfare Information Gateway, 2013). Beyond the anonymity protection, most states provide protection from criminal liability for parents who safely relinquish their infants; compared to parents who may decide to abandon their child in a location that is not a safe haven or commit an act of filicide in which the parent may face criminal charges.

When the parent relinquishes the child to a safe haven, the child welfare department assumes custody of the child. The department then has the responsibility of placing the infant in a preadoptive home and petitioning the court for termination of the birth parents' parental rights. Before these actions are taken, 14 states and the District of Columbia, require the child welfare department to inquire whether the baby has been reported as a missing child through local law enforcement (Child Welfare Information Gateway, 2013). States also may have procedures in place to allow the parent to reclaim the infant within a specified period or to allow a nonrelinquishing father to petition for custody.

Although safe haven laws are not directly affiliated with infanticide, they do offer an alternative for the parent. Instead of abandoning the child in a location where they will not receive care and will likely die, mothers have the option of leaving their infant at a safe haven where the child will receive the necessary medical care and be provided with a safe and secure home. Leaving the child at a safe haven location also protects the mother from criminal prosecution in most jurisdictions. In other jurisdictions, the safe relinquishment of an infant is an affirmative defense for charges such as abandonment, neglect, or child endangerment.

Offender Punishment

Punishments for filicide vary widely from country to country and across jurisdictions in the United States. Despite the "get tough" rhetoric that these cases often generate, some juries and judges are rather lenient with mothers who kill their children, especially in cases involving neonaticide (Oberman, 2003). In the United States, investigators often choose not to file charges or file charges that are significantly reduced from that of murder. For example, in California, a mother who commits filicide can be charged with child endangerment rather than murder. Many mothers who are charged are frequently sentenced to probation and avoid prison (Meyer and Oberman, 2001). Throughout the many different countries (e.g., Finland, Great Britain, Scotland, and Wales), infanticide laws specify that manslaughter is the greatest charge that can be brought against maternal filicide offenders (Meyer and Oberman; 2001; Oberman, 1996). A sentence of probation accompanied by mandatory counseling is the most common response in other countries (Fazio & Comito, 1999; Oberman, 2003).

Although some mothers escape harsh punishment, others do not. In some U.S. jurisdictions, there is a push to try teenage mothers who commit neonaticide as adults. Judges have the authority to decide whether cases involving juveniles will be transferred to adult court or whether these cases will be handled in juvenile court. Some argue that because of the cognitive immaturity of teenagers, these cases should be tried in juvenile courts (Brink, 2004). In addition, juvenile courts are focused on the rehabilitation with the ultimate goal of reintegrating the offender back into society. Even so, it seems that teenage mothers who commit neonaticide are more often tried as adults (Fazio & Comito, 1999; Meyer and Oberman, 2001).

When teen mothers are tried as adults for neonaticide, younger defendants seem to fare better than older defendants in terms of sentence length. For example, Schwartz and Isser (2006) reviewed the cases of 44 teens sentenced for neonaticide in the United States. In their sample, 22 were above the age of 19, and 22 were younger. Of the mothers in the older category, 15 received sentences of 5 or more years. In contrast, only 10 mothers in the younger category received sentences of 5 years or more.

Schwartz and Isser (2006) also studied neonaticide cases to determine whether there were geographic variations in sentencing trends. They examined 10 cases out of California, but they only had information on the dispositions of five cases. California seemed to have the most consistent sentencing (one was 14 years to life, two were 15 years to life, and two were 25 years to life). They reviewed the sentences of two cases from Louisiana and Pennsylvania and found that these states had rather harsh sentences (e.g., 45 years and life, respectively). Illinois had the widest range of imposed sentences (i.e., 90 days through 58 years). New York had the most lenient sentences (i.e., 8 months through 1.75 years) (Schwartz & Isser, 2006).

Currently, fathers often face harsher penalties than mothers for killing their children. One reason for this discrepancy may be attributed partly to legal systems like those in Europe that have infanticide laws, which significantly reduce the penalties for mothers for filicidal deaths (Oberman, 1996). Penalties in the United States for fathers who murder their children are greater for several reasons. First, there is empirical evidence that indicates judges, juries, and criminal investigators perceive women to be less culpable than men who commit infanticide (Oberman, 2003). Second, men are more likely to use a firearm in the commission of killing their children and the use of firearm in the furtherance of a felony often enhances the criminal penalties (e.g., requires a mandatory minimum sentence). Third, women are more successful in using an insanity defense to avoid criminal responsibility (Cirincione, Steadman, & McGreevy, 1995). Finally, men are more likely to kill multiple children and their spouses during a filicidal event (Harris, Hilton, Rice, & Eke, 2007; West, Friedman, & Resnick, 2009).

Characteristics of Filicide Victims and Offenders

Mariano et al. (2014) conducted the most comprehensive study of filicide in the United States. They analyzed arrest data from the FBI's SHR for a 32-year period (1976–2007). The SHR database included offender demographic information, victim characteristics, and circumstances surrounding homicides. A total of 632,017 individuals were arrested for homicides between 1976 and 2007, of those cases, 94,146 (14.9%) were classified as filicides (Mariano et al., 2014). In the next section, we discuss the demographics of both victims and offenders of filicide and the relationship between the victims and offenders.

Victim Demographics

White children (including Hispanics) are the mostly likely to be murdered across all age categories (62.3% of infant victims, 58.1% child/adolescent victims, and 57% of adult victims). Black or African American children are the next most frequently killed (38.2%). Among black or African American children, infants are the least likely to be filicide victims (35.2% of infant victims, 39.1% child/adolescent victims, and 41.5% of adult victims). Less than 2.5% of the victims are from other races (e.g., American Indian, Asian, and Pacific Islander) (Mariano et al., 2014).

Infants, those below 1 year of age, represent the largest victim group and account for about one-third of all filicidal deaths. Children between the ages of 1 and 6 represent about two-fifths of all filicides. The remainder of victims accounts for less than 10% of filicides and range in age from 7 to 69 years old (Mariano et al., 2014). In the infant and child/adolescent groupings, male children are more likely than female children to be killed (58.3%). However, the rates are significantly higher for males above the age of 18, with approximately 75% of the victims being adult males (Mariano et al., 2014).

Offender Demographics

White offenders commit most filicides in the United States. Specifically, white offenders are responsible for about 59.5% of filicidal deaths. Black or African American offenders come in second and they are significantly overrepresented in filicidal deaths based on mean population averages. That is, blacks commit about 37.9% of filicides but they represent about 12% of the U.S. population. Offenders from other races are responsible for the remainder (less than 3%) of child murders.

Historically, fathers have not been the primary perpetrators in filicide cases (West, 2007). However, recent estimates show that more than half of filicide offenders are fathers (57.4%) and they tend to kill children who are over the age of 1. Comparatively, females are more likely to commit neonaticide (41%) than males (29%). Fathers are especially likely to kill adult children, which accounts for about 78.3% of these cases (Mariano et al., 2014).

In filicide cases, female offenders tend to be significantly younger (mean age of 27.2 years) than male offenders (mean age of 34.8 years). The mean age of offenders increases across victim categories. For example, the mean age of offenders who killed infant victims is 24.14 years, 29.52 years for child/adolescent victims, and 50.95 years for adult victims (Mariano et al., 2014).

Case Study 2: Multiple Neonaticide—The Case of Megan Huntsman

Megan Huntsman, 39, of Pleasant Grove, Utah, was arrested on April 13, 2014. She is accused of killing six of her infants over a 10-year period from 1996 to 2006. On April 12, 2014, her estranged husband, Darren West, discovered the body of one of the infants while cleaning out the garage with another family member. He promptly notified police and they recovered the remains of the other six infants. DNA tests indicate that West is the father of all of the infants. Huntsman admitted to killing six of the seven infants, claiming that one was stillborn. She told police she either strangled or suffocated the infants immediately after they were born. She wrapped their bodies in a towel or shirt, put them in plastic bags, packed them inside boxes, and then stored them in her garage. Huntsman also told police that she was suffering from a severe meth addiction and, as a result, she could not properly care for them. At the time of her arrest, she was living in the house with three of her daughters—one teenager and two adults. She has been charged with six counts of murder and is being held on $6 million bond.

Source: McCombs (2014, April 13).

Victim–Offender Relationship

Almost 90% of filicidal victims are the biological children of the offenders (i.e., 51.6% are biological sons and 37.9% are biological daughters). Fathers are more likely to kill biological sons (29.5%) in filicidal events than mothers (22.1%). Mothers are slightly more likely to kill biological daughters in filicidal events (19.7%) than fathers (18.1%). This pattern of killing held across all age groups of victims with the exception of cases involving infant victims, in which mother–son and father–son killings were relatively equal (Mariano et al., 2014).

The remainder of the child victims (10.6%) are stepchildren of offenders (i.e., 6.7% stepsons and 3.9% stepdaughters). Filicides committed by stepparents look very different from filicides committed by biological parents. Specifically, the majority of stepparent killings are perpetrated by stepfathers against stepsons, followed by stepfathers killing stepdaughters. Stepfathers are the offenders in approximately 92% of the cases. Thus, according to the research, stepmothers rarely kill their stepchildren (Mariano et al., 2014).

Classification of Filicide: Identifying Why Mothers Kill Their Children

Phillip Resnick, a forensic psychiatrist from the United States, was the first to create a classification system of filicide. The classification system or typology that he developed was based on the "apparent motive" of the perpetrator (Resnick, 1969, p. 325). Resnick's typology was developed by examining cases involving maternal and paternal filicide. He conducted a comprehensive review of the worldwide literature on child homicide from 1751 to 1967 and found relevant articles written in 13 languages. Resnick examined 155 cases including 131 filicides and 24 neonaticides, the latter of which were committed solely by mothers. After studying the filicide cases, Resnick (1969) classified filicide into five distinct categories: altruistic, acutely psychotic, unwanted child, accidental, and spouse revenge.

According to Resnick (1969), some parents kill their children out of a sense of altruism or out of love. Altruistic filicide is broken down into two subcategories: filicide associated with suicide and filicide to relieve suffering. In the first subcategory, parents who left suicide notes stated that they killed their children because they could not stand the thought of abandoning them. In the second subcategory, the filicide is the result of euthanasia to relieve the real or imagined suffering of a child. For example, a parent may decide to suffocate a child instead of watching the child slowly die of cancer. Acutely psychotic filicide occurs when parents kill while under the influence of hallucinations, epilepsy, or delirium. In some cases, parents kill a child because he or she was unwanted. Unwanted children include those who are conceived illegitimately or represent an impediment to a new relationship. Accidental filicide refers to unintentional deaths that occur as a result of physical abuse or neglect by a parent. Last, Resnick's research shows that some parents kill their child out of revenge or in an attempt to make a spouse suffer.

In 1973, Scott, a British forensic psychiatrist, also developed a typology of parental filicide, like Resnick, that was not specific to women. Scott proposed five categories of filicide: elimination of an unwanted child (by physical abuse or neglect), mercy killing, gross mental pathology, stimulus outside the victim (e.g., revenge), and the victim creating the stimulus (e.g., frustration or exasperation). Although the works of Resnick and Scott represent significant contributions to our understanding of why parents kill, their studies fail to examine maternal filicide independently (Meyer and Oberman, 2001). In response, d'Orban (1979), another British forensic psychiatrist, reviewed the cases of 89 women admitted to the Holloway Prison in Great Britain during a 6-year period who were charged with killing or attempting to kill their children. He conducted an extensive examination of available records including psychiatric histories, police, probation, and relative reports, and court dispositions. In addition, he personally conducted psychiatric evaluations on 41 of the 89 women in the sample.

From d'Orban's (1979) study, six types of maternal filicide emerged: mothers who batter, mentally ill mothers, those who kill unwanted children, retaliating mothers, mothers who commit neonaticide, and those who commit mercy killings. d'Orban (1979) described filicides of battering mothers as arising from acts precipitated by the victim in which the mother lost her temper, and in a moment of impulse, she killed the child. Mothers with mental illness included those who suffered from depression, psychosis, and personality disorders. Retaliating mothers were those who decided to kill the child or children as a way to inflict suffering or emotional pain on a spouse. Neonaticides were the result of maternal rejection of the child or unwanted pregnancy. Unwanted children were killed by their mothers during overt physical abuse and passive neglect. Mercy killings were carried out by mothers whose children were actually suffering from some type of illness and the mother killed the child out of a sense of love and compassion. Filicides classified as mercy killings excluded cases in which the mother received some kind of secondary gain (e.g., receiving insurance benefits).

In 1991, Baker conducted a comprehensive review of all the cases of suspected filicide in Victoria, Australia, between 1978 and 1988. Her sample included 46 men and 25 women. Baker identified six major motives for filicide including altruism, spouse revenge, jealousy and rejection, unwanted child, discipline-related events, and self-defense. Alder and Baker (1997) conducted a follow-up study using Baker's original data and extended it to include maternal filicide cases through 1991. There were a total of 32 maternal filicide cases reported during this time period. They divided the cases into three groups: filicide and suicide, neonaticide, and fatal assaults. Mothers who committed filicide and suicide expressed in their suicide notes an inability to cope with their difficult circumstances and that the child or children were better off dead. Women in the neonaticide group never accepted or feared the consequences of their pregnancies. Those in the fatal assault group indicated that they did not intend to kill the child; however, many of these cases involved prior reports of child abuse. Alder and Baker (1997) also found that women in this category experienced several difficulties that contributed to the death of a child. Specifically, filicidal women faced "financial problems, inadequate housing, dislike of the child, health problems, exhaustion, frustration, depression, isolation and lack of practical support" (Alder & Baker, 1997, p. 33).

McKee and Shea (1998) wanted to investigate whether the typologies of maternal filicide identified by researchers from other countries was similar to that of maternal filicide in the United States. They conducted a cross-national comparison of data samples from international (Resnick, 1969), English (d'Orban, 1979), and Canadian (Bourget & Bradford, 1990) filicidal women. The researchers included a retrospective case review of 20 adult women from the United States who were charged with killing their children between 1986 and 1995. The women in the sample were required to undergo a pretrial evaluation of their mental state at the time of the offense and competency to stand trial. McKee and Shea (1998) identified four filicide classifications including pathological filicide (mental illness, homicide–suicide/altruistic), accidental (battered child), retaliating filicide (spouse), and neonaticide. They found that their classifications were consistent with the classifications of Resnick (1969), Bourget and Bradford (1990), and d'Orban (1979) and that no new categories of maternal filicide emerged.

Meyer and Oberman (2001) set out to develop a typology relevant to maternal filicide cases in the United States. Their typology was based on an examination of 219 cases of filicide located through a search of the Nexis database that maintains full text articles from regional and local newspapers, newsmagazines, trade magazines, transcripts of television and radio broadcasts, and abstracts. From this review, Meyer and Oberman (2001) identified five classifications of maternal filicide including filicide related to an ignored pregnancy, purposeful filicide, abuse-related filicide, filicide due to neglect, assisted/coerced filicide, and filicide in which the mother acted alone.

Mothers who fall into the ignored pregnancy category deny they are pregnant often right up to the birth of a child. These mothers are most likely to commit neonaticide (i.e., kill their children within 24 hours of giving birth). Mothers in denial fear the potential repercussions of their pregnancies and this prompts them to kill their newborns. For example, a pregnant teenager may kill her infant to avoid the disapproval of her family or friends. In some cases, mothers act deliberately to kill their children. Mothers who have recently suffered a romantic breakup that leaves them depressed are among this group. They may also experience significant financial stressors that precipitate the filicidal event. Interestingly, in this category, mothers tend to kill multiple children.

Case Study 3: Spouse Revenge and Murder–Suicide—The Case of Lisette Bamenga

On July 5, 2012, Lisette Bamenga, 29, and her 5-year-old son, Trevor Noel, Jr., and daughter, 4-month-old Violet Lily Noel, were found unresponsive in Bamenga's Bronx, New York, apartment. Police were called to investigate a gas leak at the apartment complex that was called in by a neighbor. Shortly before midnight, police officers entered the apartment and they found Bamenga with her wrists slit and the children dead in an adjacent room. Bamenga was rushed to the hospital and recovered from her injuries. She told investigators that she was distraught over the discovery that her husband, an NYPD cop, Trevor Noel, had fathered a child with another woman. In response, she said she decided to kill their children. Bamenga also told investigators that she conducted Internet research on how to poison her children. She admitted that she gave the children grape juice laced with two tablespoons of deicing fluid. However, when the children did not die, she drowned them in the bathtub. She then turned on the gas and slit her own wrists. She was charged with two counts of murder. She has not been to trial.

Source: Glynn (2012, July 9).

Filicides that are the result of neglect usually occur because of an act of omission or commission. Acts of omission include fires that broke out when the child or children were left unattended, automobile suffocation, bathtub drowning, suffocation while cosleeping, failure to maintain the child's nutritional needs, and an inattention to safety needs. Acts of commission consist of indirect and direct actions on the part of the mother. Mothers may kill their child indirectly by placing a plastic bag or blanket over the infant's head or place baby wipes or tissues in their mouths to muffle the sound of their crying. Children also may die as a result of their mother's direct actions such as shaking the baby, throwing the child across the room or out of a window, and slamming the child's head into a stationary object. Instances of direct neglect usually happen when the mother feels overwhelmed, and impulsively, she overreacts to the situation and kills the child.

Unlike cases of neglect that end in the unintentional death of a child, Meyer and Oberman (2001) point out that deaths that occur as a result of abuse are often intentional and there has been a pattern of abuse in the home. However, some women report they unintentionally killed the child while punishing them for misbehavior. Assisted or coerced filicide happens when a women's spouse or romantic partner facilitates or actively encourages the abuse of a child that results in his or her death. There are also mothers who act alone in killing their children.

Case Study 4: Assisted Filicide—The Case of Jessica Dutro and Brian Canady

Jessica Dutro, 25, of Tigard, Oregon, was arrested August 14, 2012, for the murder of her 3-year-old son, Zachary Dutro-Boggess. At the time of the crime, Dutro and her boyfriend, Brian Canady, were living in a Tigard homeless shelter. Dutro wrote in a Facebook message to Canady that she was mad because she thought her son was going to be gay. She wrote that "he walks like it and talks like it ugh" and that Canady needed to "work on" him "big time." Dutro's 7-year-old daughter testified that she saw the couple repeatedly "kick and punch" her little brother throughout the day. She also testified that "They knew his was sick [but] they didn't tell anybody." The abuse happened on August 12, 2014, and on August 14, 2014, Zachary fell unconscious and Dutro called 911. Zachary was taken via ambulance to a local hospital but died later that day after being removed from life support. On March 4, 2014, Canady pleaded guilty to first-degree manslaughter and second-degree assault. Dutro was found guilty of murder, murder by abuse, and second-degree assault on April 3, 2014. She received a life sentence.

Source: Smith (2014, March 26).

How Do Mothers Kill Their Children?

Murder Weapons Used in Filicide

There are five distinct categories of murder weapons that are used in filicidal incidents: (1) personal weapon (killing with hands, feet, strangulation, beating, asphyxiation, drowning, and defenestration (throwing the child out the window); (2) contact weapon (blunt object); (3) edged weapon (knife); (4) firearm (handgun, rifle, shotgun, and other guns); and (5) other weapons (drugs, poison, fire, and explosives) (Mariano et al., 2014). The types of weapons used by mothers and fathers to kill their children differed significantly. Personal weapons were more likely to be used by mothers (54.1%) versus fathers (45.5%). Firearms were the next most frequently used murder weapon by both mothers and fathers but fathers were three times as likely to use a firearm as mothers (32.8% and 10.9%, respectively). Mothers were twice as likely to use other weapons like drugs, poison, and fire as fathers (23.7% compared to 10.7%). Mothers and fathers infrequently used contact or edged weapons in filicidal events (Mariano et al., 2014).

Conclusions

Filicide is a serious issue in the United States with about 3,000 cases reported annually. Of those cases, mothers are the perpetrators in just over 40% of the cases. Several countries have implemented filicide and infanticide statutes in an effort to deal with the offenders in a more effective way, many of them choosing rehabilitation over retribution. Thus far, the United States continues to prosecute offenders under existing jurisdictional homicide statutes.

Research shows that fathers are more likely than mothers to commit filicide. However, mothers are disproportionately the perpetrators of neonaticide. Fathers and mothers are more likely to kill their sons than daughters. In addition, filicides tend to be committed by whites rather than blacks. Children under the age of 5 are at an increased risk of becoming victims, with infants being the most at-risk group.

Filicide typologies help us to understand why mothers kill their children. We know that many mothers suffer from mental illness (e.g., postpartum depression). We also know that there are other contributing factors including financial stressors, health-related problems, and inadequate social support, all of which lead to an increased risk of mothers killing their children. If we are able to identify the risk factors, then maybe we can reduce the number of filicides in the United States.

Discussion Questions

1. Define the terms filicide, infanticide, and neonaticide. How many filicides are committed in the United States annually? How many of those filicides are committed by mothers?
2. Pick one of the following cases: Marybeth Tinning, Susan Smith, Andrea Yates, or Casey Anthony. Discuss the facts of the case and the punishment the mother received. Do you agree with the punishment? Why or why not? If you were the judge, how would you sentence the mother?

3. What is the significance of the British Infanticide Act of 1938? Why do you think other countries like England and Canada have enacted infanticide laws and the United States has not? What is the M'Naghten Test? What is the Model Penal Code? Which one do you think should be applied in filicide cases? Defend your answer.

4. Offender punishment in maternal filicide is both lenient and harsh. Which type of punishment do you support? Explain your answer. Mothers receive more lenient sentences than fathers who commit filicide. Why do they receive disparate sentences? Do you think this is fair? Why or why not?

5. What are the characteristics of the typical filicide victim? What are the characteristics of the typical filicide offender?

6. Describe Resnick's typology or classification of filicide. Compare and contrast it with one of the other typologies. Which typology do you think best describes why mothers kill their children? Defend your answer.

References

Alder, C., & Baker, J. M. (1997). Maternal filicide: More than one story to be told. *Women and Criminal Justice, 9*(2), 15–39.

Associated Press. (2011, October 26). Ka Yang microwave baby death: Investigators seek more evidence. *Huffington Post*. Retrieved from http://www.huffingtonpost.com/2011/08/26/ka-yang-microwave-baby-death_n_938338.html

Backhouse, C. B. (1984). Desperate women and compassionate courts: Infanticide in nineteenth-century Canada. *University of Toronto Law Journal, 34*(4), 447–478.

Baker, J. M. (1991). *You can't let your children cry: Filicide in Victoria 1978–1988* (Master's thesis). Retrieved from the University of Melbourne. http://cat.lib.unimelb.edu.au/

Bourget, D., & Bradford, J. M. W. (1990). Homicidal parents. *Canadian Journal of Psychiatry, 35*(3), 233–238.

Brink, D. (2004). Immaturity, normative competence, and juvenile transfer: How (not) to punish minors for major crimes. *Texas Law Review, 82*, 1554–1585.

Child Welfare Information Gateway. (2013). *Infant safe haven laws*. Washington, DC: U.S. Department of Health and Human Services, Children's Bureau.

Cirincione, C., Steadman, H. J., & McGreevy, M. A. (1995). Rates of insanity acquittals and the factors associated with successful insanity please. *The Bulletin of the American Academy of Psychiatry and the Law, 23*, 399–409.

d'Orban, P. T. (1979). Women who kill their children. *British Journal of Psychiatry, 134*, 560–571.

Egginton, J. (1989). *From cradle to grave*. New York, NY: Jove Books.

Fazio, C. A., & Comito, J. L. (1999). Rethinking the tough sentencing of teenage neonaticide offenders in the United States. *Fordham Law Review, 67*(6), 3109–3168.

Ferguson, C. J., Miller-Stratton, H., Heinrich, E., Fritz, S., & Smith, S. (2007). Judgments of culpability in a filicide scenario. *International Journal of Law & Psychiatry, 31*(1), 41–50. doi:10.1016/j.ijlp.2007.11.007

Gado, M., (n.d.). *Baby killer*. Retrieved from http://www.crimelibrary.com/notorious_murders/women/marybeth_tinning/index.html

Glynn, C. (2012, July 9). Lisette Bamenga, NYC mother, arrested for allegedly poisoning 2 kids in a double murder-suicide, police say. *CBS News*. Retrieved from http://www.cbsnews.com/news/lisette-bamenga-nyc-mother-arrested-for-allegedly-poisoning-2-kids-in-double-murder-attempted-suicide-police-say/

Graham v. State, 547 S.W.2d 531 (1977).

Harris, G. T., Hilton, N. Z., Rice, M. E., & Eke, A. W. (2007). Children killed by genetic parents versus stepparents. *Evolution and Human Behavior, 28*, 85–95.

Hoffer, P. C., & Hull, N. E. H. (1981). *Murdering mothers: Infanticide in England and New England, 1558–1803*. New York, NY: New York University Press.

Levéillée, S., Marleau, J., & Dubé, M. (2007). Filicide: A comparison by sex and presence and absence of self-destructive behavior. Journal of Family Violence, 22(5), 287–295. doi:10.1007/s10896-007-9081-3

Mariano, T. Y., Chan, H. C. O., & Myers, W. C. (2014). Toward a more holistic understanding of filicide: A multidisciplinary analysis of 2 years of U.S. arrest data. *Forensic Science International, 236*, 46–53. doi:10.1016/j/forsciint.2013.12.019

McCombs, B. (2014, April 13). Megan Huntsman arrested after 7 dead babies found in Utah garage. *Huffington Post*. Retrieved from http://www.huffingtonpost.com/2014/04/13/megan-huntsman-arrested_n_5144126.html

McKee, G. R. (2006). *Why mothers kill: A forensic psychologist's casebook*. New York, NY: Oxford University Press.

McKee, G. R., & Shea, S. J. (1998). Maternal filicide: A cross-national comparison. *Journal of Clinical Psychology, 54*(5), 679–687.

Mental Disease or Defect Excluding Responsibility, 4 MPC § 1 (1985).

Meyer, C. L., & Oberman, M. (with White, K., Rone, M., Batra, P., & Proano, T. C.) (2001). *Mothers who kill their children: Understanding the acts of moms from Susan Smith to the "Prom Mom"*. New York, NY: New York University Press.

Moseley, K. L. (1986). The history of infanticide in Western society. *Issues in Law & Medicine, 1*(5), 345–361.

Oberman, M. (1996). Mothers who kill: Coming to terms with modern American infanticide. *American Criminal Law Review, 34*, 2–109.

Oberman, M. (2003). Understanding infanticide in context: Mothers who kill, 1870–1930 and today. *The Journal of Criminal Law & Criminology, 92*(3–4), 707–737.

Queen v. M'Naghten, 8 ER 718 (1843).

Rapaport, E. (2005). Mad women and desperate girls: Infanticide and child murder in law and myth. *Fordham Urban Law Journal, 33*(2), 101–142.

Resnick, P. J. (1969). Child murder by parents: A psychiatric review of filicide. *American Journal of Psychiatry, 126*(3), 325–334.

Robinson, P. H. (1984). *Criminal law defenses* (Vols. 1–2). St. Paul, MN: West Publishing Co.

Schwartz, L. L., & Isser, N. (2006). *Child homicide: Parents who kill*. Boca Raton, FL: CRC Press, Taylor & Francis Group.

Scott, P. D. (1973). Parents who kill their children. *Medicine, Science, and the Law, 13*(2), 120–126.

Smith, E. (2014, March 26). Jessica Dutro murder trial: Daughter, 7, told police mom assaulted Tigard 4-year-old. *The Oregonian*. Retrieved from http://www.oregonlive.com/tigard/index.ssf/2014/03/jessica_dutro_murder_trial_daughter.html

Spinelli, M. G. (2003). *Infanticide: Psychosocial and legal perspectives on mothers who kill*. Washington, DC: American Psychiatric Publishing.

State of Texas v. Yates, 171 S.W.3d 215, 218 (Tx. Ct. App., 2005).

Trexler, R. (1973). The founding of Florence, 1395–1455. *The History of Childhood Quarterly, 1*(4), 259–275.

Walker, A. J. (2006). Application of the insanity defense to postpartum disorder-driven infanticide in the United States: A look toward the enactment of an infanticide act. *University of Maryland Law Journal of Race, Religion, Gender, and Class, 6*(1), 197–222.

West, S. G. (2007). An overview of filicide. *Psychiatry, 2007*, 48–57.

West, S. G., Friedman, S. H., & Resnick, P. J. (2009). Fathers who kill their children: An analysis of the literature. *Journal of Forensic Sciences, 54*, 463–468.

Incarcerated Women in the United States

13

SUSAN MARCUS-MENDOZA

Contents

In a country where liberty is one of the founding ideals of our government, it is astonishing that we have had the highest incarceration rate in the world for over a decade (Tsai & Scommegna, 2012). In such a system, to deprive someone of their liberty is a very harsh sentence. Of course, it is necessary to incarcerate people to protect the public in some cases. It is hopeful to note that the number of prison admissions from 2009 to 2012 has been less than the number of releases, and therefore, the prison population in the United States has decreased every year from 2009 to 2012 (Carson & Golinelli, 2013). However, we are still number one in incarceration. This mass incarceration has created many problems for those incarcerated, their families and communities, and is not the best solution to the problems that cause people to be incarcerated, especially women. This chapter looks at the women incarcerated in the United States, past and present: who they are, why they are in prison, and the challenges they face during and after incarceration.

History of Women in Prison

The history of women's incarceration was, and still is, the complex history of women's personal, political, and social problems spanning the history of the United States. Women's incarceration has long been linked with gender-role stereotypes and social control. In medieval Europe, women who committed adultery could be executed, and in the seventeenth century, unmarried mothers in England were imprisoned or shipped to the colonial United States (Feinman, 1980; Freedman, 1981). These punishments were exacted for failing to meet the gender-role expectations of being married, being faithful to their husbands, and having children only within the confines of marriage. Having children to further both the name and property line was one of the primary duties of women during this period. These practices continued in Europe and in the colonies through the beginning of the eighteenth century, most notable in Salem, Massachusetts, where women were executed for being "witches," a practice that spilled over from Europe.

In the United States during the nineteenth century, women were arrested for moral crimes, including prostitution (Freedman, 1981). Later in that century, there was an increase in arrests of women for crimes such as vagrancy and drunkenness, and women were more likely to be incarcerated than men. There were a growing number of women who turned to prostitution as a means of supporting their families during the Civil War, as there were few jobs for women at that time. With increasing urban growth and industrialization in the nineteenth century came a further increase in prostitution. Female prostitutes, who were mostly in their teens and early 20s, were frequently homeless and illiterate. Immigrant women, who came to the United States seeking a better life, resorted to prostitution due to the lack of job opportunities for women who were still constrained by gender roles. The irony of this is that prostitutes were generally sought after by successful men, the same men who would have nothing to do with such women in "polite society," further decreasing the chances that these women could find better lives.

The early nineteenth century saw the creation of the prison reform movement (Freedman, 1981). By the 1820s, the northern states had begun using prison as a means of punishment and decreasing crime, and a significant number of women were being incarcerated. Also at this time, women were becoming more social conscious and involved in reform movements. Therefore, middle-class women activists became concerned about the increasing number of their sisters behind bars. What they found was that women's crimes at the time were not serious or violent, but were personal crimes against social order, such as drunkenness and vagrancy. As there continued to be fewer job opportunities and lower salaries for women, women were still economically marginalized, and therefore resorted to crime. According to Freedman (1981), the increase of women in prison between 1815 and 1860 was partly due to the stricter moral codes for women, which led to a higher incarceration rate for women than men for such crimes. It is not surprising then that during this period women and minorities were overrepresented in prison, a trend that continues today, along with the economic marginalization of women. In prison, women convicted of crimes were taught skills that were "appropriate" for women, such as cooking and cleaning (Freedman, 1981). The stigma attached to being an incarcerated "fallen woman" meant that they were neglected and subject to abuse and overcrowding. Once out of prison, the stigma of being a fallen woman made it difficult for them to get jobs or marry, making it hard to them to create better lives.

Theories of women's crime in this era began to shift. William Sanger's research with 2000 women incarcerated with venereal disease found that most of the women were teenagers and unskilled immigrants, many of whom were single mothers, widows, or had been deserted by men (Sanger, 1921). The median age of the women interviewed was 15. However, there were also women who were not economically disadvantaged and did have job skills, who said they were attracted to the easy money. Unfortunately, although prostitution was more lucrative than many of the jobs available to women, Sanger projected that the average life span of a prostitute was only 4 years after they started working.

In the late nineteenth century, Emile Durkheim maintained the idea that religious values that held societies together which when violated led to punishment (Clear & Dammer, 2000), thus continuing the "fallen woman" explanation of crime and the need for punishment. However, he also wrote about anomie, the lack of necessary social regulations in a time of great change. After the Civil War, the United States saw great growth in technology as steamships and railroads allowed for faster transportation. These factors, according to Durkheim, led to crimes by women.

In the twentieth century, some theorists looked to biological causes for women's crimes. Lombroso and Ferrero (1990) posited the idea of the "born criminal," a woman who was less evolved and had masculine traits (Rafter, 1997). These women even looked different, with dark features and misshaped skulls, and were more evil than male criminals. Such biological theories were similar to the earlier dualistic theories that saw women as either good or bad, depending on their adherence to gender roles. They did not believe that social factors led to women's crime. W. I. Thomas, who acknowledged that society might play a role in women's crime, believed that psychological factors, such as the need for love, led to promiscuity. Judge Marcus Kavanaugh's work posited that women were more evil than men, were the driving force behind men's crime, and that the natural order had been disrupted by giving women the right to vote (Dodge, 2002). Otto Pollak put forth the idea that women were just as prone to crime as men, but were deceitful and cunning, and used these skills to both hide their crimes and to secure leniency if caught. Frances Kellor's research on how economic factors were associated with women's crime began to challenge the notion of biological determinism (Rafter, 1997). Her research revealed that most incarcerated women came from poverty, and did not have the education and skills to take care of themselves. The only work they could find was low-paying jobs. Rather than discipline and punishment, feminist reformers suggested that education and job skills would help women support themselves upon release, whereas opponents of this idea said that giving women education and job training would only lead to more crime. Unfortunately, the reformers ideas were not largely espoused by society or those who governed the prisons, although the reformers continued to work toward change.

As the reform movement continued, other models emerged to counter the biological models (Simon & Ahn-Redding, 2005). Freda Adler's masculinity thesis posits that women in taking on roles and jobs previously held by men also took on male characteristics. This theory revisits the idea of the "fallen woman." The opportunity thesis states that women's and men's crimes become similar as women are gain access to jobs traditionally held by men. However, others theorists say that this thesis is not upheld by crime statistics. The marginalization thesis suggests the opposite of the opportunity thesis—that women commit crimes because they do not have the same career opportunities, and therefore the same wages, as men. Opponents of this theory say if it were true, women's crime would decrease as women gain access to job traditionally held by men, which has not happened. The chivalry thesis blames the women's advocacy movements for the increase in convictions of women and incarceration for women, stating that campaigning for equal rights led to equality in the form of harsher sentences for women.

Currently, the feminist pathway model is one of the most prevalent theories. It looks at the various pathways for women into the crime and the criminal justice system. Feminist pathway models attempt to chronicle the progression of women offenders' lives from childhood to prison, focusing on how the psychological consequences of events lead to the crimes for which women are incarcerated (Chesney-Lind & Pasko, 2013; Girshick, 1999; Morash & Schram, 2002; Owen, 1998; Quina & Brown, 2007; Wattanaporn & Holtfreter, 2014). Consistent with feminist psychological theory (Brown, 2010), feminist pathway models ground this sequence of events in the context (or multiple social locations) in which women lives occur, such as ethnicity, race, education, nationality, violence and abuse, and socioeconomic status. Kruttschnitt and Macmillan (2006) suggest a life course perspective that takes into account women's individual experiences as well as their relationships with others, how behaviors and events are linked throughout women's lives, and the sociohistorical context in which they live. Their research findings highlight the different frequencies of violence (isolated versus ongoing), the different abusers (family versus nonfamily), and stresses the need for more research on the connection between childhood violence and violence experienced as an adult.

Feminist pathway models have become more complex as research supports the importance of context and issues that continue across the lifespan, and acknowledges that diversity plays a role in determining a women's trajectory into prison. Richie (1996) described six pathways, each of which defines a unique pathway into illegal activity for black women who have been battered. She stresses the importance of such contextual variables as personal history, culture, and economic circumstances. In her book, *Arrested Justice: Black Women, Violence, and America's Prison Nation*, Richie (2012) further illustrates, through cases, how society's response to black women who have been marginalized and victimize results in the incarceration of those women. Another example is a study of traumatic events experienced by incarcerated women prior to incarceration by Cook, Smith, Tusher, and Raiford (2005). This study also revealed differences in experiences of trauma among women by race, age, and marital status, but found that the variable that accounted for the biggest difference in experiences of violence was homelessness. Women who had been homeless prior to incarceration were 5.6 times more likely to have been sexually abused as children, and they had also experienced more of the 21 traumatic events Cook et al. asked about in their study. Although this research did not examine the sequence of events, the association is noteworthy. In another study, Brennan, Breitenbach, Dieterich, Salibury, and Van Voorhis (2012) surveyed a large group of soon-to-be-released inmates in California and identified eight distinct pathways for women who habitually offend. Such studies as these are providing valuable and more specific information about how women become offenders.

Women's prisons in the United States have reflected the dominant thinking of the era. Starting at the beginning of the nineteenth century, prisons became a means of punishment and reform. However, women's prisons were focused on helping women conform to gender-role stereotypes, and did not teach them how to take care of themselves once released. As women criminals were thought to be depraved, they were considered beyond help and largely ignored, and in some cases, sexually abused. As the reform movement gained momentum and the first women's prison opened in 1873, feminists such as Susan B. Anthony helped shift the emphasis away from the fallen woman concept to looking at the social and economic plight of women (Freedman, 1981). Some prisons focused on reformation instead of punishment, and along with domesticity religion, they were offered education and job training focused on being a domestic servant.

As the dominate theories moved away from biological determinism in the twentieth century, prison programs expanded to include clerical training, recreation, and gardening on the prison grounds. However, women's prisons soon became overcrowded due to the emphasis on social control, which led to more incarceration of women. Prisons were also not equipped to treat the myriad of physical and mental health problems of these women, who came from impoverished homes or were homeless, had histories of abuse, and had been exposed to various illnesses such as venereal diseases, which had gone untreated. Gradually, women's prisons have evolved to include more training, education, and psychological and health services, although they still struggle with having sufficient resources to meet all the women's needs, and programming, in many cases, still reflects gender stereotypes.

Women in Prison in the Twenty-First Century

Trends in crime and punishment in the twentieth century have continued into the twenty-first century, and women in prison are still a marginalized population about which we hear very little. Television shows portray women whose crimes viewers will find exciting, but these series are created to entertain rather than to inform the viewer, and do not give us an accurate description of the women incarcerated in the United States.

According to the Bureau of Justice Statistics (Carson & Golinelli, 2013), 108,772 women were in prison in the United States in December 2012, down from 111,407 in 2011. Of those, 14,049 were in federal prisons, and 94,723 were in state prisons. The vast majority of women incarcerated in 2011 were under the age of 45. Black and Hispanic women are disproportionally represented in the prison populations. In 2011, black women were three times more likely to be incarcerated than white women in the 18–19 age group, and Hispanic women were twice as likely to be imprisoned than white women. This disparity continues, at differing rates, throughout the spectrum of ages. In 2011, 18% of women sentenced to prison committed violent crimes, the majority of which were assault or robbery (Carson & Golinelli, 2013). Property crimes comprised 36% of crime, with fraud being the largest category. Drug offenses, fueled by the war on drugs, were 32.5% of crimes for which women were incarcerated, and public order offenses (including drunk driving, weapons, and vice) made up 12% of the crimes for which women were sentenced in 2011. Only 40% of incarcerated women were employed prior to their incarceration, and most came from poverty (Van Wormer, 2010).

Overall, there has been an increase in the total crime rate of women, from 16% in 1980 to 26% in 2011 (Van Gundy, 2014), but that number has just started to decrease in recent years. Although incarceration of women has risen steadily over the years, from 85,044 women incarcerated in the United States in 2000 to 105,197 in 2009, between 2011 and 2012, there was an overall decrease in the number of women given a sentence of incarceration. The total of women sentenced to incarceration in a state or federal facility for a year or more decreased 2.3% overall, and 2.8% for state facilities, but there was an increase of 1.4% of women sentenced to federal facilities (Carson & Golinelli, 2013). In 2013, 35 states enacted legislation to reduce prison populations and associated costs, expand or strengthen community-based sanctions, implement need and risk assessments to determine the needs of offenders, support offender reentry into the community, and make better informed policies and laws (Van Gundy, 2014). This hopefully signals a shift in ideas, a willingness to consider community sanctions as opposed to the more costly alternative of incarceration, and an interest in reducing reincarceration by strengthening reentry support. Even though these changes may be due to a need to reduce costs more than a real shift in ideology, it is a positive trend.

Mothers in prison face many concerns with regard to their children as they can do little to help them from behind bars. More than 70% of women in prison are mothers of minor children, and they were often the only parent living with the child. Incarceration of mothers can have very negative effects on their children (Arditti, 2012; Eddy & Poehlmann, 2010). Children of incarcerated mothers face multiple traumas including seeing their mother being arrested, and moving between family members or being in foster care. Such events have been linked to PTSD, especially if there was violence during the arrest, or any sort of abuse occurs in their new home. Adults, likely in an effort to protect children, do not adequately explain the events the children have witnessed, leaving them to feel confused and to develop inaccurate scenarios of their own. Children are uncertain about their future, including if they will see their mother again, and during visits, they may see emotional scenes that may create further stress. Children separated from their mother may feel shame, anger, resentment, loneliness, and worry, and may have interpersonal problems at school. These children are at an increased risk for mental and physical health problems, substance abuse, and offending, and are more likely to earn failing grades and drop out of school. Having an incarcerated mother has also led to lower college graduation rates (Hagan & Foster, 2012). The caregivers who they live with while their mothers are in prison may experience stress, adding to the difficulties of the child and incarcerated mother. Mothers in prison have little control over these issues, or ways to make changes for their children, and it is a source of great worry for them.

Many women in prison have experienced violence and trauma as children and adults. Research with women prisoners reveals that they have a higher rate of mental health diagnoses, substance abuse, and childhood sexual victimization than either men prisoners or nonincarcerated women (Belknap & Holsinger, 2006; Marcus-Mendoza, Sargent, & Chong Ho, 1994; Mumola, 1999; Quina & Brown, 2007; Zlotnick, 2002). The majority of women prisoners have been victims of one or more types of violence, both as children and adults, and many were in violent relationships before their arrests (Cook et al., 2005; Marcus-Mendoza et al., 1994; Owen, 1998; Sharp, 2005; Sharp & Marcus-Mendoza, 2001). A qualitative life history study by Chesney-Lind and Rodriguez (2013) confirms these ideas, finding that the women's histories of sexual victimization and violence were interlaced throughout their lives with involvement in the criminal justice system from an early age, and much of the violence and victimization was perpetrated by family members. DeHart, Lynch, Belknap, Dass-Brailsford, and Green (2014) conducted a five-state jail study and found a difference in offending patterns by types of violence and abuse, for example, intimate partner violence was associated with an increased risk of committing property crimes, drug offending, and commercial sex work. These relationships between violence, abuse, trauma, substance abuse, mental illness, and offending have been the focus of research that tries to illuminate the complexity of pathways into crime.

Incarcerated women suffer from many of the same health issues as other women, but with a higher frequency and greater severity. They have health problems related to substance abuse, sex work, and violence, as well as mental health issues, chronic health conditions, and sexual and reproductive health concerns (Arriola, Braithewaite, & Newkirk, 2006). There is also an overpresentation of low-income women in prisons, resulting in a population of incarcerated women who have had little or no access to quality health care, and limited ability to pay for needed treatment. It is not a surprise then that incarcerated women are in worse health than nonincarcerated men and women, and incarcerated men. Incarcerated women have high rates of infectious diseases, headaches, ear infections, musculoskeletal diseases, respiratory conditions, digestive conditions, skin diseases, and genitourinary disorders (Arriola et al., 2006). In prison, many of these diseases, which are exacerbated by stress, become worse due the shortage or absence of effective mental health care, and the strain of being in prison and all that it entails, such as separation from family and friends.

An important question is whether women's physical and mental health concerns are being met. Two studies looking at the female inmates' satisfaction with health services found that women were dissatisfied with access to health care, quality of care, and policies that lead to poor health outcomes (Morgan, 2013; Tanguay, Trestman, & Weiskopf, 2014).

These studies were each conducted in one prison only but may indicate a pervasive problem. It is also important to examine health needs of specific subgroups. For instance, the treatment of eating disorders is predicated on the woman being able to have control over her thoughts and emotions, which is hard to manage in a setting where women have little control over their lives (Farber, 2013). A similar issue exists with doing feminist therapy with survivors of violence, as the prison structure recreates abusive dynamics if the same individuals are both therapists and correctional officers, and it can be difficult to help women feel empowered in a setting where advocating for oneself can lead to punishment (Marcus-Mendoza, 2004; Marcus-Mendoza, Klein-Saffran, & Lutze, 1998). Leigey and Hodge (2012) reveal that the interests of another group, older female inmates, has also not been adequately addressed. The findings of their research reveals that older female inmates have more physical and mental health needs than older male inmates, but are less likely to report receiving treatment than male inmates. As the inmate population ages, women prisoners' needs for treatment, and attention to such activities as smoking and exercise, are increasingly important.

Case Studies 1 and 2

To show how all these factors come together in the lives of women offenders, it is important to look at case studies. A good illustration of the pathways model is the case of Amber (Carr & Hanks, 2013). Amber, a pseudonym given by the authors, is a white woman who grew up in rural Alabama. At the time of her interview with the authors, she was 36 and incarcerated for possession of a controlled substance, receiving stolen property and a probation violation. Amber's father died when she was young, and she lived with her mother, who had been sexually assaulted by her own father as a child. Amber was sexual assaulted by her brother and other male relatives over many years, starting when she was 6 years old. Her mother accused her of lying when Amber told her what was happening, and reprimanded her for trying to get attention. She was put in a secure juvenile facility at 13 for stealing, and had already started drinking. When Amber started acting out at age 14, her mother thought that she was on drugs but Amber said it was from the rage and pain of the sexual abuse, which by then she realized should not have happened. Amber was married twice, at the ages of 17 and 27, and had two children. Her first marriage was abusive, and she worked overtime to save money so she and her daughter could move out. Amber's second marriage was to a man who was in jail for 1½ years before she bonded him out, and they were married. She did sex work and took drugs during her second marriage, and her husband beat her with numerous items including bottles, a table leg, a brick, and a fire extinguisher. Amber reached out for help, going to a shelter for battered women three times, and even writing to the district attorney for assistance. She used crack to numb herself to the pain of her life.

Richie (1996) provides case studies of black women's pathways into to the legal system. One pathway she describes is women arrested for the death of their children. These are battered women whose children were killed by the batterer, but the women are charged as codefendants, conspirators, or with homicide. Richie relates the case of Sebina, a 32-year-old woman arrested for homicide for the death of her 4-year-old son. Sebina's husband was jealous of the son, and when the son tried to help his mother during a beating, both the mother and son were beaten. The husband would tie the mother up, and then abuse the child, and would threaten to call child welfare to say she was abusing the child if she called the police. Sebina rarely left the house and lost her welfare assistance because she was so badly beaten, she would not go to her required meeting. Sebina did not have money, was being beaten daily, and she did not think the police would help. One day, when her son was crying from hunger, the husband tied him up, put him under the bed, and made Sebina have sex with him. When she could get free, she found her son was not breathing. For the next few days, her husband moved the body of Sebina's son to different rooms and continued to beat Sebina. They eventually went to her grandmother's house, where he beat both Sebina and her grandmother. When he took the body out to bury it, they went to the police but Sebina said her son was missing. The police arrested her and charged her with failure to protect her son, despite her obvious injuries.

Both case studies show somewhat similar pathways into the legal system. The women in these cases were severely abused mothers, and the abuse escalated over time. There was an intergenerational pattern of abuse in Amber's family, and her trajectory started as a young child. According to Richie (1996), Sebina came from a family background in which she learned her adult family life would be a sense of pride, and the abuse and subsequent isolation of feeling like a hostage in her own home were disorienting. However, their entry into the legal system separated them from their children, classifies them as felons rather than helping them deal with the multiple issues that led them there, ended employment, and makes it harder for them to support themselves with a prison record.

Programming for Women in Prison

Given the histories of women in prison, it is imperative to offer programming that meets their unique needs. However, too often in prisons, programming that is gender appropriate and trauma informed is not offered. Researchers have responded by pointing out the inherent difficulties of not taking into account these factors, and advocating for gender-responsive programs in prison (Bloom, Owen, & Covington, 2002; Bruns & Lesko, 1999; Marcus-Mendoza et al., 1998; Richie, 2000). Such programming should provide treatment strategies that are appropriate for women with histories of trauma, substance abuse, illness, and other such factors, and should be offered in an environment conducive to therapy. However, this can present quite a challenge in a prison as the environment is punitive and does not allow for inmates to control their lives, and feminist, trauma-informed therapy advocates for empowerment and resistance to oppressive societal structures (Bruns & Lesko, 1999; Marcus-Mendoza, 2011; Marcus-Mendoza et al., 1998). According to Maidment (2006), prison programming does not take into account the important contexts in which women live and offend, so they cannot succeed in helping women. Much prison programming has relied on cognitive–behavioral models that try to fix faulty thinking that correctional programs assume is causal to women's crime, and do not meet the unique needs of these women.

Research has been done to look at how these characteristics of women offenders relate to such desired outcomes as adjustment in prison, and treatment in prison. Wright, Van Voorhis, Salisbury, and Bauman (2012), in their article, "Gender-Responsive Lessons

Learned and Policy Implications for Women in Prison," provide a summary of research and echo the previous work in concluding that such factors as victimization, substance abuse, and mental health problems do relate to maladjustment to prison and prison rule violations. They reiterate the need for an environment conducive to change, and programming that is trauma informed and developed for women in prison. Programs should address such topics as relationships, substance abuse, parenting, violence and abuse, job and life skills, and should generally focus on treatment and rehabilitation instead of punishment. Many such programs exist and are being used in prisons, but not widely enough.

Texts and research focusing on gender-responsive programming for women help make such programs available, and further advocate for treatment and activities specifically designed for women in prison (Quina & Brown, 2007; Sharp, 2003; Van Wormer, 2010; Zaplin, 2008). Many creative modalities have been created and implemented to assist women in prison. For instance, animal-assisted therapy in a women's prison in Utah helped decreased anxiety and depressive symptoms in women (Jasperson, 2010). A study looking at the needs of older women found that religion or participation in religious activities was particularly important to older women doing life in prison (Aday, Krabill, & Deaton-Owens, 2014). A qualitative project in England found many benefits to having sports and physical activities in women's prisons, including increased wellness and self-esteem, weight management, healthier life styles, and better relationships with staff (Meek & Lewis, 2014). Bibliotherapy, using books about disorders such as depression, has also been found to be effective with women in prison (Pardini et al., 2014). However, having such programs is just one part of the task. The other is having enough qualified service providers working in prisons to provide the programs to every woman who needs them, which is a chronic problem in prison settings.

Challenges Faced Once Released from Prison

Cobbina and Bender (2012), in their qualitative study of incarcerated women, found that many women were optimistic about their chances of being successful after release, and that they felt they were more likely to succeed than the average inmate. Incarcerated mothers especially had a change in mentality, often due to concern about their children, as they saw that their criminal behavior was not compatible with being a mother. This finding shows the importance of mothers staying in contact with their children. Cobbina and Bender (2012) also found that there were a number of women who were uncertain about their success. These women seemed unsure that they could overcome the circumstances that brought them into prison, particularly if they had been using drugs before prison. The women were concerned that they might start using drugs again. The authors point to the need for effective substance abuse treatment, as the likelihood of reoffending increases when drug abuse is not treated in prison, and they also suggest follow-up treatment upon release.

Formerly incarcerated women face many of the same challenges that they were experiencing before prison, in addition to new problems created by being a convicted felon and by the prison experience. Upon release, many are trying to rebuild their lives from the ground up. However, they lack vocational skills, recent job references, and need to find basics such as housing and a job (Van Wormer, 2010). As the majority of women do not reoffend and go back to prison, supportive programs upon release are critical to assisting women make a successful transition, and may also reduce the rate of recidivism.

According to Spjeldnes, Jung, and Yamatani's (2014) study, both women and men released from jail have less education, lower income, fewer job skills, are more likely to be chemically dependent, and have more mental and physical health issues than the general population. Porter (2014) found that former inmates, male and female, were more likely to consume fast-food and smoke cigarettes, which was associated with financial stress and lower social standing. Spejldnes et al. (2014) found that women released from prison have more mental health, physical health, and chemical dependency treatment needs than men who have just been released. They also found that these women were more likely to have been living with their children before they were incarcerated, and were much more likely to have requested treatment while in prison, which is consistent with Cobbina and Bender's (2012) results, that mothers were concerned about changing their lifestyle so that they could be good mothers upon release.

Relationships are also important to women's success after incarceration. Bui and Morash (2010) conducted a qualitative study of successful parolees and found that women's social networks facilitated their criminal activities prior to incarceration, and the separation that occurs during incarceration, in combination with prison programming and the desire to change, helps women develop supportive social networks. These successful parolees had also been able to obtain jobs, many for more than the minimum wage, as nearly all had at least a high school diploma, and some had taken college courses. Employment led to a sense of confidence, competence, and autonomy. Only four women in their study, who were disabled, had not found employment. The women in the study did note that their success in finding jobs and otherwise being successful was due to their social networks, and not their parole contacts. These findings echo similar results of other research (McDonald & Arlinghaus, 2014; O'Brien, 2001), pointing to the crucial importance of programming and social networks for women, both during incarceration and upon release.

As women try to reform their families, they face many barriers to living with their children. Mapson (2013) reviewed the obstacles that incarcerated mothers face. According to Mapson, the majority of incarcerated women lived with their children prior to incarceration, but less than half received visits from their children while incarcerated, often due to the distance between the prison and where their children lived. The majority of children lived with grandparents, usually maternal, which may not always be the safest placement, as many of the women were physically or sexually abused as children, and their children could now be at risk as they are living in the same environment that their mother had been in when she was abused (Sharp, Marcus-Mendoza, Bentley, Simpson, & Love, 1999). Mapson also reports that jail and prison policies can negatively impact the ability of children to visit, especially when children are in foster care. Upon release, there are many conditions that offenders have to meet, such as housing and employment, and they may find themselves back in familiar, dysfunctional patterns, and will therefore be unable to get their children back in their custody. Legal barriers are numerous, including laws that do not allow drug offenders to get aid for food and housing, and laws meant to allow for permanent homes for children that lead to increased termination of parental rights and inadequate time for former inmates to be reunited with their children. Mapson suggests more services for women upon release to help them meet the conditions that will enable them to be reunited with their children.

Conclusion

Women in prison have been facing the same challenges for centuries. Many incarcerated women are marginalized before coming to prison, either by poverty, race, lack of education, or by not adhering to acceptable social norms for women. A substantial group have health problems that have not been adequately treated, and in many cases, the health problems stem from sex work, violence, substance abuse, and lack of health care prior to going to prison. Incarcerated women have mental health problems, many of which have been untreated, and also stem from violence and multiple traumas. They have lacked the income to take care of their families, and many of the crimes they commit are property offenses to get the resources to care for their children. Once in prison, they are separated from family and friends, and their children are also suffering. There is inadequate health care, and programming offered in prisons has often not been developed with the needs of this group of women in mind. Where programming is available, there are often not enough spots in programs for all the women who need it. Prison itself can be traumatic, as women may be further subjected to violence, and they have little control over their lives.

Upon release, incarcerated women may face similar problems to those they faced before, but this time, with the stigma of having been in prison, and the handicap of having a felony record, which denies them access to aid such as housing assistance and food stamps, although as mentioned previously, many states are changing these laws. After prison, they are still in need of medical care and psychological services, which may be no more accessible than it was before their incarceration. Many formerly incarcerated women also struggle to find jobs. Even if they receive a high school diploma, vocational training, or take some college classes and are more prepared for work, they still have to find someone who is willing to hire them. Finding work is often a precondition for having their children come live with them, so it is critical that they find employment that allows them to support themselves and their children. Of course, reuniting with children and other family members can be very difficult after the stress and disruption caused by the former criminal activity, and the stress of the legal process and incarceration.

Given all of the issues that women and their children face while women are in prison and after reentry, community sanctions, treatment, and correctional options that do not require incarceration can be a better alternative for women (Chesney-Lind & Pasko, 2013). Community sanctions potentially allow women to stay employed, keep their children, receive better medical and psychological services than in prison, and avoid the traumas associated with incarceration. Van Gundy and Baumann-Grau (2013), in examining the lives of women in prison, posit that many of the experiences women face can be construed as human rights violations, and rightfully so. Looking at the prison experience as a human rights violation, community sanctions certainly seem to be the most humane solution for women offenders.

Discussion Questions

1. Why does the author believe that most women offenders could benefit from community sentencing? What problems might be avoided by keeping women in the community?

2. If it was your job to lower the incarceration rate in your state by opening a nonprofit designed to keep women out of the prison system, what services would it include and why? What challenges might you face in the areas of funding, politics, and recruiting clients?

3. Two trends consistent in this country over centuries are the economic marginalization of women and the overrepresentation of women in prison. What keeps these trends going?

4. How does incarceration of mothers harm their children, and how could these problems be minimized or eliminated?

5. What was your opinion of women prisoners and former prisoners before taking this course? How did the information and case studies in this chapter change your ideas about women in prison?

References

Aday, R. H., Krabill, J. J., & Deaton-Owens, D. (2014). Religion in the lives of older women serving life in prison. *Journal of Women & Aging, 26,* 238–256.

Arditti, J. A. (2012). *Parental incarceration and the family: Psychological and social effects of imprisonment on children, parents, and caregivers.* New York, NY: New York University Press.

Arriola, K. J., Braithewaite, R. L., & Newkirk, C. (2006). An overview of incarcerated women's health. In R. L. Braithwite, K. J. Arriola, & C. Newkirk (Eds.), *Health issues among incarcerated women* (pp. 3–17). New Brunswick, NJ: Rutgers University Press.

Belknap, J., & Holsinger, K. (2006). The gendered nature of risk factors for delinquency. *Feminist Criminology, 1*(1), 48–71.

Bloom, B., Owen, B., & Covington, S. (2002). *Gender-responsive strategies: A summary of research, practice, and guiding principles for women offenders.* Washington, DC: National Institute of Corrections.

Brennan, T., Maurkus, B., Dietrich, W., Salibury, E. J., & Van Voorhis, P. (2012). Women's pathways to serious and habitual crime: A person-centered analysis incorporating gender responsive factors. *Criminal Justice & Behavior, 36*(11), 1481–1508.

Brown, L. S. (2010). *Feminist therapy.* Washington, DC: American Psychological Association.

Bruns, C. M., & Lesko, T. M. (1999). In the belly of the beast. *Women & Therapy, 22*(2), 69–85.

Bui, H. N., & Morash, M. (2010). The impact of network relationships, prison experiences, and internal transformation on women's success after prison release. *Journal of Offender Rehabilitation, 49,* 1–22.

Carr, N. T., & Hanks, R. S. (2013). "Everything I've done I've done for men": One women's deployment of femininities and her pathway to crime. *Sociological Spectrum, 33,* 433–452.

Carson, E. A., & Golinelli, D. (2013). *Prisoners in 2012 trends in admissions and releases 1991–2012* (NCJ 243920). Washington, DC: U.S. Department of Justice.

Chesney-Lind, M., & Pasko, L. (2013). *The female offender: Girls, women, and crime* (3rd ed.). Thousand Oaks, CA: Sage Publications.

Chesney-Lind, M., & Rodriguez, N. (2013). Women under lock and key: A view from the inside. In M. Chesney-Lind & L. Pasko (Eds.), *The female offender: Girls, women, and crime* (3rd ed., pp. 187–198). Thousand Oaks, CA: Sage Publications.

Clear, T. R., & Dammer, H. R. (2000). *The offender in the community.* Belmont, CA: Wadsworth.

Cobbina, J. E., & Bender, K. A. (2012). Predicting the future: Incarcerated women's views of reentry success. *Journal of Offender Rehabilitation, 51,* 275–294.

Cook, S. L., Smith, S. G., Tusher, C. P., & Raiford, J. (2005). Self-reports of traumatic events in a random sample of incarcerated women. *Women & Criminal Justice, 16*(1/2), 107–126.

DeHart, D., Lynch, S., Belknap, J., Dass-Brailsford, P., & Green, B. (2014). Life history models of female offending: The roles of serious mental illness and trauma in women's pathways to jail. *Psychology of Women Quarterly, 3*(1), 138–151.

Dodge, L. M. (2002). *Whores and thieves of the worst kind: A study of women, crime, and prisons.* DeKalb, IL: Northern Illinois Press.

Eddy, M., & Poehlmann, J. (Eds.). (2010). *Children of incarcerated parents: A handbook for researchers and practitioners.* Washington, DC: The Urban Institute.

Farber, S. (2013). Eating disorders in women's prisons: An under-report phenomenon? *Advances in Eating Disorders: Theory, Research and Practice, 1*(1), 39–50.

Feinman, C. (1980). *Women in the criminal justice system.* New York, NY: Praeger.

Freedman, E. B. (1981). *Their sisters' keepers.* Ann Arbor, MI: University of Michigan Press.

Girshick, L. B. (1999). *No safe haven: Stories of women in prison.* Boston, MA: Northeastern University Press.

Hagan, J., & Foster, H. (2012). Children of the American prison generation: Student and school spill-over effects of incarcerating mothers. *Law & Society, 46*(1), 37–69.

Jasperson, R. A. (2010). Animal-assisted therapy with female inmates with mental illness: A case example from a pilot program. *Journal of Offender Rehabilitation, 49,* 417–433.

Kruttschnitt, C., & Macmillan, R. (2006). The violent victimization of women: A life course perspective. In K. Heimer and C. Kruttschnitt (Eds.), *Gender and crime: Patterns in victimization and offending* (pp. 278–334). New York, NY: New York University Press.

Leigey, M. E., & Hodge, J. P. (2012). Gray matters: Gender differences in the physical and mental health of older inmates. *Women & Criminal Justice, 22,* 489–408.

Lombroso, C., & Ferrero, W. (1900). *The female offender.* New York, NY: Appleton.

Maidment, M. R. (2006). "We're not all that criminal": Getting beyond the pathologizing and individualizing of women's crime. *Women & Therapy, 29*(3/4), 35–56.

Mapson, A. (2013). From parenting to prison. *Journal of Human Behavior in the Social Environment, 23,* 171–177.

Marcus-Mendoza, S. T. (2004). Feminist therapy behind bars. *Women's Studies Quarterly, 32*(3/4), 49–60.

Marcus-Mendoza, S. T. (2011). Feminist therapy with incarcerated women: Practicing subversion in prison. Women & Therapy, 34(1&2), 77–92.

Marcus-Mendoza, S. T., Klein-Saffran, J., & Lutze, F. (1998). A feminist examination of boot camp prison programs for women. *Women & Therapy, 21*(1), 173–185.

Marcus-Mendoza, S. T., Sargent, E., & Chong Ho, Y. (1994). Changing perceptions of the etiology of crime: The relationship between abuse and female criminality. *Journal of the Oklahoma Criminal Justice Research Consortium, 1,* 13–23.

McDonald, D., & Arlinghaus, S. L. (2014). The role of intensive case management services in reentry: The northern Kentucky female offender reentry project. *Women & Criminal Justice, 24,* 229–251.

Meek, R., & Lewis G. E. (2014). Promoting well-being and desistance through sport and physical activity: The opportunities and barrier experienced by women in English prisons. *Women & Criminal Justice, 24,* 151–172.

Morash, M., & Schram, P. (2002). *The prison experience: Special issues of women in prison.* Long Grove, IL: Waveland Press.

Morgan, K. (2013). Issues in female inmate health: Results from a southeastern state. *Women & Criminal Justice, 23,* 141–142.

Mumola, C. (1999). *Substance abuse treatment: State and federal prisoners, 1997* (NCJ 172871). Washington, DC: U.S. Department of Justice.

O'Brien, P. (2001). "Just like baking a cake": Women describe the necessary ingredients for successful reentry after incarceration. *Families in Society: The Journal of Contemporary Human Services, 82*(3), 287–295.

Owen, B. (1998). *"In the mix": Struggle and survival in a women's prison.* Albany, NY: State University of New York Press.

Pardini, J., Scogin, F., Schriver, J., Domino, M., Wilson, D., & LaRocca, M. (2014). *Psychological Services, 11*(20), 141–152.

Porter, L. C. (2014). Incarceration and post-release health behavior. *Journal of Health and Social Behavior, 55*(2), 234–249.

Quina, K., & Brown, L. S. (Eds.). (2007). *Trauma and dissociation in convicted offenders.* Binghamton, NY: The Haworth Press.

Rafter, N. H. (1997). *Creating born criminals.* Urbana, IL: University of Chicago Press.

Richie, B. E. (1996). *Compelled to crime: The gender entrapment of battered black women.* New York, NY: Routledge.

Richie, B. E. (2000). Exploring the link between violence against women and women's involvement in illegal activity. In B. Ritchie, K. Tsenin, & C. Widom (Eds.), *Research on women and girls in the justice system, research forum* (pp. 1–13). Washington, DC: National Institute of Justice.

Richie, B. E. (2012). *Arrested justice: Black women, violence, and America's prison nation.* New York, NY: New York University Press.

Sanger, W. (1921). *The history of prostitution: Its extent, causes and effects throughout the world.* New York, NY: Medical Publishing Company.

Sharp, S. F. (Ed.). (2003). *The incarcerated woman: Rehabilitative programming in women's prisons.* Upper Saddle River, NJ: Prentice Hall.

Sharp, S. F. (2005). *Oklahoma study of incarcerated mothers and their children: Phase III.* Oklahoma City, OK: Oklahoma Commission on Children and Youth.

Sharp, S. F., & Marcus-Mendoza, S. T. (2001). It's a family affair: Incarcerated women and their families. *Women & Criminal Justice, 12*(4), 21–49.

Sharp, S. F., Marcus-Mendoza, S. T., Bentley, R., Simpson, D., & Love, S. (1999). Gender differences in the impact of incarceration on the children and families of drug offenders. In K. Train & M. Corsianos (Eds.), *Interrogating social justice: Politics, culture and identity* (pp. 217–246). Toronto, Ontario, Canada: Canadian Scholars Press.

Simon, R. J., & Ahn-Redding, H. (2005). *The crimes women commit, the punishments they receive* (3rd ed.). Lexington, MA: Lexington Books.

Spjeldnes, S., Jung, H., & Yamatani, H. (2014). Gender differences in jail populations: Factors to consider in reentry strategies. *Journal of Offender Rehabilitation, 53*, 75–94.

Tanguay, S., Trestman, R., & Weiskopf, C. (2014). Patient health satisfaction survey in Connecticut correctional facilities. *Journal of Correction Health Care, 20*(2), 127–134.

Tsai, T., & Scommegna, P. (2012). *U.S. has world's highest incarceration rate.* Washington, DC: Population Reference Bureau.

Van Gundy, A. (2014). *Feminist theory, crime and social justice.* Waltham, MA: Anderson Publishing.

Van Gundy, A., & Baumann-Grau, A. (2013). *Women, incarceration, and human rights violations: Feminist criminology and corrections.* Farnham, U.K.: Ashgate Publishing Limited.Van Wormer, K. (2010). *Working with female offenders.* Hoboken, NJ: John Wiley & Sons.

Wattanaporn, K. A., & Holtfreter, K. (2014). The impact of feminist pathways research on gender-responsive policy and practice. *Feminist Criminology, 9*(3), 191–207.

Wright, E. M., Van Voorhis, P., Salisbury, E. J., & Bauman, A. (2012). Gender-responsive lessons learned and policy implications for women in prison. *Criminal Justice and Behavior, 39*(12), 1612–1632.

Zaplin, R. T. (Ed.). (2008). *Female offenders: Critical perspectives and effective interventions* (2nd ed.). Sudbury, MA: Jones & Barlett.

Zlotnick, C. (2002). *Treatment of incarcerated women with substance abuse and posttraumatic stress disorder, final report.* Rockville, MD: National Criminal Justice Referencing Service.

Women in Law Enforcement

14

WENDY PERKINS

Contents

Women have had a role in American policing since at least the 1800s when they began serving as volunteer matrons in prisons and jails. While there are still far fewer women in policing than there are men, women have made great strides in the policing profession. This chapter discusses female police officers, focusing primarily on female officers in America. It begins with a history of women in policing and is followed by a discussion about the current representation of women in policing. This chapter also discusses potential barriers to the recruitment and retention of female officers, and examines the on-the-job performance and experiences of female officers. The movement of women officers into high-level administrative positions is also discussed. Finally, a brief comparison is made between women police in the United States and women police in other countries.

History of Women in Policing

This chapter divides the history of women in the policing profession into three time periods. From the mid-1800s to approximately 1900, women primarily served as matrons for prisons and city jails and took care of women who had been arrested or were incarcerated. Around the late nineteenth century, women began to engage in police work that largely focused on protecting women from sexual immorality and children from delinquency. From about 1920 to the 1950s, women still largely remained in the roles they had been relegated to in previous years but began to make strides in being accepted as legitimate police officers among their peers and the public. From the 1960s until the present, women have been engaging in what can be considered modern patrol work. For our purposes, we will discuss female police officers in terms of the roles they have played in the policing field, which largely coincides with the time periods described.

Matrons

The movement of women into policing began with efforts of religious and civic organizations to reform the treatment of women within the penal system in the 1800s. Prior to the 1830s, female prisoners were housed alongside their male counterparts and supervised by male police officers (Schulz, 1995). Concerned with rehabilitating female inmates into good Christians, Quaker women in Philadelphia were some of the first volunteers to visit other women who were in prison or jail during the 1820s (Schulz, 1995; Wells & Alt, 2005). The Women's Christian Temperance Union (WCTU) also sent visitors to jails and prisons to provide education and skills training for imprisoned women (Owings, 1969; Schulz, 1995). The conditions observed by the volunteers spurred the movement to hire paid matrons to care for women who were in prison or jail. There was valid concern that female prisoners were being abused by male officers and by male prisoners (Schulz, 1995; Segrave, 2014). In addition, the upper-middle class women who were volunteering were convinced that men were ill equipped to address the problems that female lawbreakers faced, such as pregnancy (Schulz, 1995).

Eventually, paid matrons replaced or supplemented the volunteer visitors and were tasked with taking care of female prisoners. The hiring of matrons was often at the behest of external pressure placed on jails, prisons, and police departments by the same civic organizations that supplied volunteers. Despite opposition from male administrators and ridicule from newspaper editors and political cartoonists, paid jail matrons became a fixture in many American cities (Duffin, 2010). New York City began using jail matrons in 1845 after pressure from the American Female Reform Society. The city hired six women to be matrons in the city jail and on Blackwell's Island (Duffin, 2010; Owings, 1969). Indiana was the first state to have an all-female penitentiary with an all-female staff in 1873 (Schulz, 1995). Sherborn, Massachusetts, opened an all-female facility in 1877, which housed approximately 355 inmates, many of them illiterate. Some women gave birth in The Women's Prison, which had a nursery so mothers could stay with their children until the children were 18 months old (Segrave, 2014).

City police departments and police departments in the southern states were much slower to hire matrons. Similar to the movement to place matrons in prisons, there was opposition from police administration to hire women to work in the policing environment. In 1891, the New York City Police Department hired its first matrons to assist with women who had been arrested in despite concerns that women would not be able to control drunken and disorderly prisoners (Schulz, 1995). Other cities that hired matrons in the late 1800s include Boston, Massachusetts; Chicago, Illinois; Cleveland, Ohio; and Denver, Colorado (Owings, 1969). Notably, the State of Massachusetts passed a law in 1888 that required the police departments in all cities populated with 20,000 citizens or more to have matrons (Owings, 1969). While some cities did not follow this law, the law did indicate that lawmakers felt the issue was important enough to warrant legislation.

Paid matrons had a variety of duties that set the stage for the subsequent hiring of paid policewomen, but all of these duties revolved around caring for female prisoners. The women belonging to organizations that lobbied for paid matrons had no desire to encroach upon traditional police work that they believed was better left to men. Instead, they wanted to focus on the needs of female prisoners such as supervising the mentally ill or those women who needed medical assistance (Owings, 1969; Schulz, 1995). Schulz (1995) argues that these women aptly used the doctrine of women's sphere to gain entry into a profession that was dominated by men. The doctrine of women's sphere states that women are best cared for by other women.

Compared to male police officers, the matrons' pay was paltry and their working hours tended to be around the clock as opposed to fixed shifts. These earliest matrons were better educated than the male officers and many were social workers by profession. Sometimes matron positions were eliminated by administrators who did not want them to exist in the first place. Despite these poor working conditions and the challenges of keeping their positions, matrons made significant progress in securing a place for women in policing. Unfortunately, as women began to move into police positions the status of the matron position declined. Eventually, the matrons who were hired were older and less educated than the women who were hired to act as policewomen. This led to animosity between women who occupied these positions, with policewomen viewing themselves as better than matrons (Schulz, 1995).

Policewomen

The position of policewoman was a natural outgrowth of the matron movement. The WCTU and other civic organizations maintained their stance that male police officers were not well suited to handle problems involving women and girls (Duffin, 2010). For some of the earliest policewomen, their primary goal was still rehabilitating wayward women and children. For others, however, their goals expanded to include the regulation of behavior that contributed to their delinquency such as monitoring gambling halls. Essentially, one primary function of the earliest policewomen was crime prevention.

Because record keeping and sharing of information was haphazard at the time, new discoveries are always being made about the earliest appointed policewomen. Marie (or Mary) Owens is generally cited as being the first sworn policewoman in America. She was given sworn police powers in 1893, several years after her police officer husband died. As part of her duties she helped officers with cases involving women and children and visited the courts (Owings, 1969; Schulz, 1995). She earned praise from city officials for her ability to build relationships with businesses (Segrave, 2014). Other women have been identified who were policewomen at approximately the same time as Marie Owens, including Mrs. Edwin T. Root of St. Paul, Minnesota; Florence Klotz of Allegheny, Pennsylvania; and Helen Wilder of Hawaii (Segrave, 2014).

Other early policewomen of note are Lola Baldwin and Alice Stebbins Wells. Lola Baldwin was charged with overseeing the safety of women and girls during the 1905 Lewis and Clark Exposition that was held in Portland, Oregon (Owings, 1969). Subsequently, she was sworn in as a police officer and appointed as commander of the Department of Public

Safety for the Protection of Young Girls and Women (Duffin, 2010). Alice Stebbins Wells has the most notoriety as being one of the earliest policewomen, successfully lobbying for an appointment to the Los Angeles Police Department in 1910. She was one of the founders of the International Association of Policewomen and spent much of her time on the public-speaking circuit (Duffin, 2010; Schulz, 1995).

Policewomen had several duties for which they were responsible. One early description of these duties is provided by Eleanor Hutzel (1929), deputy commissioner of police in the Detroit Police Department. Hutzel divided the duties of early policewomen into the categories of protective patrol and complaints. Protective patrol including the regulation of speakeasies, gaming rooms, and dance halls. Policewomen addressed complaints about juvenile delinquency, child abuse, and missing persons/runaways. They also took care of complaints of crimes committed by females and drug and alcohol problems of women.

In essence, early policewomen were "morals police," concerned with keeping the virtue of society's women intact and with preventing juveniles from being delinquent. Some of this morals work coincided with World War I and military encampments near American cities. Policewomen became very focused on keeping young girls and women from getting pregnant and on the prevention of sexually transmitted diseases (Owings, 1969; Schulz, 1995). The concern with maintaining public morals was so important that some policewomen were charged with insuring that women wore proper attire when at the beach. They were also charged with protecting women from sexual harassment by "mashers" and with regulating the activity of dance halls, which promoted sexualized dancing (Duffin, 2010).

It is important to note that early policewomen did not desire to do the jobs of the male police officers. Many of them did not want to carry weapons or wear uniforms and badges and refused to bear the title of police officer (Schulz, 1995). Despite their dedication to their jobs, policewomen were paid less than their male counterparts. They were better educated than the male police officers, but this did little to curtail criticism of their presence in policing and the firing of officers at the discretion of police administrators (Duffin, 2010). As time progressed, more departments began hiring women as officers and created women's bureaus to organize them (Schulz, 1995). Police departments also began providing weapons and self-defense training. In some departments, women assisted male officers with drug and prostitution investigations, with policewomen sometimes going undercover (Segrave, 2014). World War II brought some new opportunities for women as many male officers joined the military. While they did not have full police powers and the positions were temporary, female auxiliary officers filled the roles of dispatcher, parking patrol, and traffic control (Schulz, 1995).

Policewomen still faced challenges. Promotional opportunities were virtually nonexistent, and after WWII male police officers began to take over crime prevention duties, something that had before been within the female sphere (Schulz, 1995). Print media was also generally unsupportive, publishing many patronizing articles that profiled the "gals" in policing (Segrave, 2014). However, the 1950s and 1960s were decades of accomplishment for women in policing. Women became more involved with undercover investigations, began wearing uniforms, and became partners with the male officers (Schulz, 1995). Women also began patrolling in police cars during this time period. Betty Blankenship and Elizabeth Coffal were the first female–female police partnership to engage in vehicle patrol in the country (see Case Study 1) and Officer Mary Conforti in Warren, Michigan, was put on patrol duty in a single officer car in 1965 (Duffin, 2010).

Case Study 1: Car 47

Betty Blankenship and Elizabeth Coffal of the Indianapolis Police Department were the first female partners to engage in vehicle patrol on their own. After discussing this possibility with Winston Churchill (not of England) while they were attending the police academy, he promised that if he were ever in the position to put the women on patrol together he would do so. Churchill kept his word when he was appointed as chief of police of the Indianapolis Police Department and on September 10, 1968, Car 47 took to the streets.

There was some resistance from the department to having two women on patrol. They were sometimes passed over for calls or were sent to calls that were unlikely to place them in dangerous situations. Snow's (2010) interview with Betty Blankenship's daughter revealed that the policewomen had to work around their uniforms of short skirts and purses when pursuing suspects. This interview also revealed that the partners figured out early on in their careers how to use each other's strengths to insure they did their job well. Both Blankenship and Coffal have since passed away but their impact on the role of women in policing still resonates today.

Today, female police officers assume the same roles as male officers. They conduct general patrol and crime response work, are part of special units such as SWAT and K-9, and are detectives. Some women have achieved the rank of chief of police, an accomplishment that was only a dream when women first began working within police departments. The brief history provided in this chapter provides only a cursory look at the challenges faced by early matrons and policewomen and their accomplishments despite the odds being stacked against them. The following sections of this chapter focus on more current issues related to women in policing and discuss the current representation of women in policing, the performance and experiences of women in policing, and the status of women in administrative police positions.

Current Representation of Women in Policing

The total estimated percentage of female officers with arrest powers in the United States varies across studies due to differing methodology in reporting, but generally hovers between 11% and 20%. The Uniform Crime Report (UCR) reported that in 2012, there was a total of 670,439 sworn officers, 88.1% ($n = 590,656$) of whom were male and 11.9% ($n = 79,782$) of whom were female (Federal Bureau of Investigation, 2013). Langton (2010) examined trends of women in policing for the time period of 1987–2008. She estimated that approximately 20% ($n = 100,000$) of police officers were women. Methodology is likely the reason for the differing estimates. The UCR includes data that are collected from city and county agencies, whereas Langton's data included federal and state agencies. Federal agencies have higher percentages of women employed as sworn officers compared to city and county agencies (Langton, 2010). To provide a more detailed view of the representation of women in policing, specific information about female representation in federal, state, and local law enforcement agencies is presented next.

Federal Agencies

There are many federal agencies that employ sworn female officers including the FBI, the Central Intelligence Agency (CIA), and the Internal Revenue Service (IRS). From 1998 to 2008, the number of female officers employed at the federal level increased from 14% to 15.25%. As of 2008, the Office of Inspectors General employs the most female officers, with 25% of its officers being female. Also in 2008, the FBI employed 2428 female agents, or 19% of its total, and females were 32% ($n = 835$) of the sworn officers employed by the IRS (Langton, 2010).

City and County Agencies

Over a 20-year period, the percentage of female officers employed in American city and county police agencies increased from approximately 7.6% in 1987 to approximately 12% in 2007 (Langton, 2010). Women working in agencies with between 100 and 999 sworn officers comprise approximately 10% of the workforce in city agencies and 13% of the workforce in county agencies (Schuck, 2014). Smaller city and county sheriff's departments employ far fewer female officers compared to their larger counterparts. It is important to note that sheriff's departments that have jail duties employ more sworn female officers than sheriff's offices that do not have jail duties (Schuck, 2014). This suggests that women employed in county agencies where they have arrest powers may have duties that are more similar to that of matrons as discussed earlier in the history section of this chapter, such as supervising female prisoners.

State Agencies

From 1987 to 2007, the percentage of women employed as sworn officers has increased from 3.8% to 6.5% (Langton, 2010). Based upon the most recent UCR (2010) data, the California Highway Patrol employs the highest number of female sworn officers ($n = 565$), which is approximately 5% of its total of 10,885 officers. The South Dakota Highway Patrol employs only three female officers out of 157 total sworn personnel. Based upon this information, it can be concluded that state police agencies lag behind their city and county counterparts in hiring women as sworn officers. However, little information is known about why this is the case.

Recruitment, Selection, and Retention of Female Police Officers

Given the small proportion of women in policing, it becomes necessary to examine the factors related to the recruitment, selection, and retention of female police officers. This is particularly important since police departments are encouraged to staff its agency with officers that are representative of the people it serves (Raganella & White, 2004). As mentioned in the earlier section discussing the history of women in law enforcement, it was relatively uncommon for women to be employed as sworn officers until the 1980s. This section discusses the barriers to and facilitators for women to become police officers.

Barriers

Aside from general resistance by male administrators, city officials, and officers to the hiring of women, one early barrier that served to keep women out of the policing profession was physical fitness testing and physical stature. Departments often had minimum height and weight requirements that women could not attain (Birzer and Craig, 1996). While some of these requirements have been eliminated, there has been little overall progress in insuring that the physical testing required for hire is consistent with the actual work that is performed (Jordan, Fridell, Faggiani, & Kubu, 2009). In an analysis of recent police employment data, Schuck (2014) found that departments mandating a physical fitness test have fewer female officers. Current female officers and police chiefs indicate that the physical fitness test often eliminates female candidates from the job pool (Cordner & Cordner, 2011). The argument could be made that if females cannot meet the physical fitness test requirements then they would not be able to properly perform the job of police officer. However, departments often do not mandate physical fitness requirements after an officer has been hired, seemingly making the entry requirements moot. Female officers and police chiefs in Cordner and Cordner's (2011) study identified other potential barriers for women to enter the policing profession. Among the identified barriers for recruiting are better/more attractive employment options and the perception that policing is not female-friendly. The culture of policing and its relationship to the acceptance and treatment of female officers is discussed in the "Performance and Experience of Female Officers on the Job" section.

Facilitators

In general, city agencies with a Commission on Accreditation for Law Enforcement Agencies (CALEA) certification, and that support community–oriented policing employ higher percentages of female officers. Sheriff's offices with education requirements also tend to employ higher percentages of female officers. While better salaries and benefits are also associated with higher percentages of female officers (Schuck, 2014), a major factor contributing to the increase in women in law enforcement over the past three decades is affirmative action.

In the 1980s, several police departments were mandated by court orders and consent decrees to make their departments more representative of the populations of their jurisdictions (Doerner, 1995; Martin, 1991). Departments were ordered to recruit more minority males and more white and minority females. Martin (1991) specifically examined the impact of affirmative action and consent decrees upon the hiring of female law enforcement officers in the early 1980s. At the end of 1986, agencies that were under consent decrees or court orders had a higher percentage of sworn female officers than agencies that were not under these orders.

Overall, there is little information about the recruitment and retention of female police officers who are part of an ethnic or racial minority. Women in minorities may not pursue careers in policing because the challenges they will face because of their sex may also be exacerbated by their race or ethnicity (Greene, 2000). Larger police departments appear to hire more minority women than smaller departments. In addition, police departments operating in a jurisdiction with an overall larger population and a high percentage of minority citizens tend to employ more minority female officers. Police departments with formal programs designed to recruit minority females also tend to have more black female officers. Female officers of all races are more likely to be employed at departments that have a history of hiring female of the same race. For example, black women may be more likely to be recruited into police departments that already have a history of hiring black female officers. This suggests that large departments may offer the best opportunities for all women to become police officers because there is a precedence for their hiring (Zhao, Herbst, & Lovrich, 2001).

Retention

Women become police officers for the same reasons as their male counterparts. They want to help their community, have secure jobs with good benefits, an opportunity for advancement, and a job that is exciting (Raganella & White, 2004). What differs between male and female officers, however, are the reasons for leaving the policing profession.

Women leave the policing at higher rates than men, and black females are even more likely to leave the profession than other officers (Doerner, 1995). While most female officers intend to stay in policing (Schuck, 2014), those who have left indicated that the job did not meet their expectations, they had a bad field training experience, and that there was a lack of support in the police academy (Haarr, 2005), or that policies were not family friendly for men or for women (Cordner & Cordner, 2011).

It is clear that differences exist between agencies in the employment of sworn female police officers. One thing that has remained consistent over at least the past three decades is that larger police departments employ more women as sworn officers than smaller departments (Cordner & Cordner, 2011; Langton, 2010; Schuck, 2014; Zhao, Herbst, & Lovrich, 2001). Agencies that employ targeted marketing may have more success in recruiting women than agencies who engage in general recruitment (Jordan et al., 2009). Women enter policing for similar reasons as their male counterparts, making a discussion of their experiences and performance on the job an important component of this chapter.

Performance and Experience of Female Officers on the Job

As mentioned previously, the resistance to hiring women to be police officers was due to a lack of confidence in their abilities to perform police functions as well as male officers. One area of concern was whether women would be able to use physical force in situations when citizens were uncooperative (Schulz, 1995). It must be pointed out that most police encounters with citizens do not involve the use of physical force such as hitting, holding, or use of an object to gain compliance (Durose & Langton, 2013; Greenfeld, Langan, & Smith, 1997). However, the masculine culture of policing perpetuates the stance that only males should be employed as police officers because sometimes physical force is necessary and women are incapable of using force. This section describes the experiences and performance of female officers on the job.

Academy and Street Performance

The history of women in policing often discusses the issue of training. Some female officers received formal training before assuming their duties, but many did not. As women began to enter patrol and have more traditional policing duties, they also began to have the same training as male officers. Some recent research has examined the performance of recruits in the police academy, including women. While these studies are not directly focused on sex differences in performances, they do provide insight on any differences that may exist between male and female police recruits. There is evidence that women perform just as well as men in the police academy and in some cases perform better than male recruits (Henson, Reyns, Klahm, & Frank, 2010; White, 2008). Despite their success, evidence exists that illustrates women have negative experiences during police academy training that emphasizes to female recruits they do not belong in policing (Prokos & Padavic, 2002).

Much of the controversy surrounding women in the policing profession is related to the use of force. There are many factors that are related to officer use of force. Regardless of officer sex, physical force is more likely to be used against citizen suspects when they have a poor demeanor, and when they resist arrest (Garner, Maxwell, & Heraux, 2002). Research has demonstrated that women officers perform at parity with their male counterparts with regard to the use of force (Hoffman & Hickey, 2005; Paoline & Terrill, 2004), and that suspects were less likely to be injured when interacting with a female officer using force (Hoffman & Hickey, 2005). There is some indication that female officers use force less often than male officers (Schuck & Rabe-Hemp, 2005). This is not necessarily a bad thing. Many times situations can be resolved without making an arrest and it is possible that women have better conflict resolution skills than men. However, because policing's culture and reputation is that of law enforcement, not using force may be construed as a weakness instead of being construed as a strength (Hunt, 1985).

In addition to examining the performance of recruits in the police academy, Henson et al. (2010) examined the performance of recruits once they assumed full police duties. They suggest that the evaluation system is biased against female officers based upon their findings that female officers received lower evaluations when compared to men. They point out that police evaluations are often numbers-based (i.e., the number of traffic stops or arrests). If female officers are able to use conflict resolution skills to avoid making arrests, then it stands to reason that their arrest numbers would be lower (Henson et al., 2010). The researchers also report that the female officers received fewer citizen complaints against them. It stands to reason that if police departments desire to reduce the likelihood of complaints against their officers, they should consider targeting their recruiting efforts toward females.

Personal Experiences of Female Officers

The culture of policing is dominated by male beliefs and masculine orientations that value authority, physical strength, and the willingness to use deadly force if necessary to fulfill the role of law enforcer (Rabe-Hemp, 2007). Even when females had no police powers and were relegated to the role of matron, there were concerns about whether or not women could handle the demands of police work given the situations they would encounter (Duffin, 2010; Wells & Alt, 2005). In sum, male officers did not believe women would make good cops.

Resistance to having female officers within the ranks of fully sworn police officers often begins in police academy training and spills over into field training. Anastasia Prokos engaged in participant observation to gather data about the female experience in the police academy. She observed that the "hidden curriculum" was unconsciously taught to police officers. The hidden curriculum teaches officers that male characteristics are desirable and female characteristics are undesirable in policing. She cited numerous examples of women being marginalized in the academy or overly targeted by training instructors (Prokos & Padavic, 2002). Officers in Rabe-Hemp's (2007) study describe incidents of being humiliated with sexual remarks in front of classmates during academy training and experiencing overt hostility from field training officers. They also described being passed over for promotion once they were on the streets because of their sex. Female police officers may feel pressure to fit in with the men rather than the men adapting to their new coworkers. Hunt's (1985) groundbreaking study emphasizes that female officers feel the need to demonstrate their worth and ability to do the job of law enforcer through the use of force. In addition, Hunt's study illustrated that acceptance of female officers by their male peers occurred after use of force incidents. Rabe-Hemp (2007) also reports that one way female officers describe gaining acceptance in their departments is through the use of force.

Female officers are sometimes targets of sexual harassment and discrimination. Examples of sexual harassment experienced by female officers include sexual innuendos, inappropriate sexual advances, and sexual assaults (Chaiyavej & Morash, 2009; Rabe-Hemp, 2007). Many times female officers who experience sexual harassment do not report the incident to their superiors and some become resigned to such actions being part of the job or to believe it is not serious behavior (Chaiyavej & Morash, 2009). Accepting such behavior as being part of their job may reflect female officers being socialized into the male-dominated culture.

While some female officers have negative experiences in the academy and on the street, others feel they have proven themselves and are accepted among their peers (Rabe-Hemp, 2007). Women are confident in their abilities to do the job of policing (Kakar, 2002) even if their male counterparts express doubt. Some women believe they have had unique opportunities because female officers are few in number (Rabe-Hemp, 2007). Sometimes, these opportunities present themselves in the forms of advancing up the ranks to higher administration. This is the topic of the next section.

Case Study 2: Being a Modern-Day Female Police Officer

Unlike some of my predecessors in policing, I (the author of this chapter) had a very positive experience at my department. Shortly after my 21st birthday in 1995, I was sworn in as the first female police officer hired in the history of the Rising Sun, Indiana Police Department. The chief, Tom McKay, knew that women could be effective police officers and made it a point to seek out female candidates for the job. His belief that women could be competent police officers helped shape my experience. The other officers were willing to teach me and maybe even more importantly were willing to let me make mistakes that did not endanger me, them, or the public. Chief McKay encouraged me to follow my own path and did not make me feel obligated to only focus on policing tasks that were traditionally associated with female officers, such as child abuse investigations. With only five officers at the time of my hire, I was on patrol alone some days. The public was a little wary at first—I was a novelty. However, with a little time and some good people skills I was able to become a part of the community I served. There were a few marriage proposals from people I arrested, some people really liked to call me disparaging names, but in all everyone—even if they were going to jail—was very respectful. Generally, the people who were hostile to me were hostile to the male officers as well—we were all treated the same. I never felt pressure to fit in by becoming "one of the guys." I discovered I could be a woman and be a police officer at the same time. My experiences at the academy were, for the most part, very positive. I did meet some male cadets who were not happy with the presence of females. More than one told me he did not believe women should be police officers because women were not strong enough to do the job. Even though I left the policing profession, I am still in touch with many of my comrades and now have lifelong friendships. My experience as a police officer shaped my entire career and I am grateful for the opportunity Chief McKay and the Rising Sun Police Department provided me.

Women in Administrative Positions

While the proportion of women in policing has remained between 11% and 20% of the total officers in America, the proportion of women in administrative policing positions remains low (National Center for Women in Policing, 2001). There are several barriers that women identify as impeding their advancement. One reason is an unwillingness to outdo their male peers. Female officers who are working in patrol may have gained acceptance among their peers but achieving a promotion would put them in a position of power over the men with whom they have forged relationships. Female officers also may be reluctant to seek promotions because it may require returning to shift work or street work, which could disrupt their family lives (Wertsch, 1998). Other female officers indicate they are interested in seeking supervisory positions but without administrative support, the "glass ceiling" effect limits the upward mobility of female officers (Rabe-Hemp, 2007). To achieve higher ranking positions, female officers sometimes find they have to relocate (Schulz, 2003). This complicates family relationships and responsibilities which have also been cited as barriers to advancement (Rabe-Hemp, 2007). Despite these difficulties to advance, women continue to make strides in leadership positions in America and around the world. The next section briefly discusses female police officers in other countries.

Female Officers: An International Perspective

In many countries, the entry of women into the policing profession has mirrored that of the United States. Civic and religious organizations pressured the government and police administrators to hire women as officers so they could attend to female offenders and victims. Like the United States, this was largely motivated by the desire to monitor the behavior of women and keep them from sexual activity outside of marriage. Women officers in other countries also monitored saloons, gambling halls, and other establishments where they perceived wayward women might be led astray. In England, female monitors were responsible for watching over women in the areas of military encampments in World War I for the same reasons as their counterparts in America (Owings, 1969; Segrave, 2014).

A recent report on the status of women in policing indicates that there is very little information about female police officers in non-English-speaking countries, so it is difficult to draw direct comparisons between countries (Prenzler & Sinclair, 2013). In some countries, such as England, the rate of growth for women in policing is similar to that of the United States. However, several countries appear to have higher overall percentages of female officers based upon the available data. Female officers comprise approximately 25% of Australia's police force and 24% of South Africa's police agencies. Women were 30% of the total commissioned officers in South Africa (Prenzler & Sinclair, 2013).

Female officers in other countries may differ from their American peers in attitudes about policing. For example, female officers in Thailand are more likely to support aggressive police patrol and less likely to support selective enforcement of the law than female officers in the United States (Sun & Chu, 2008). Women in other countries sometimes have negative experiences similar to that of their American counterparts, such as sexual harassment (Burke & Mikkelsen, 2005). Unfortunately, there is little comparative research from which to draw conclusions about differences and similarities between female officers in America and female officers in other countries.

Conclusion

This chapter has presented a brief overview of female police officers in America. Despite being involved in policing for almost two centuries, women still experience barriers to joining the policing profession. A male-dominated culture that values physical strength over feminine qualities presents challenges to the recruitment and retention of female officers, and also has an impact on their on-the-job experiences. While some police departments have made efforts to recruit more female officers, smaller departments often do not have female officers in their employ. Targeted recruitment and administrative support of hiring females are likely key to successfully recruiting females for open police positions. Equal opportunity for advancement is important to insure that women are represented among the rank system, but many female officers face barriers to promotion. There is much work to be completed before female officers will be at parity with their male counterparts. This chapter has provided an overview of the key issues facing female officers and offered an opportunity for you to think about the experience of the female officer.

Discussion Questions

1. Women have faced many barriers to their recruitment, selection, and retention in the policing profession. How have these barriers been addressed? Is it necessary to continue efforts to make policing a more positive experience for women?
2. It is sometimes necessary for police officers to use physical force as part of their job. However, the use of physical force is relatively rare compared to other activities in which the police engage. Given this, should physical entrance examinations be modified to reflect the actuality of police work, or should they focus on ensuring that officers are prepared to handle the extreme circumstance of using force?
3. Compared to the proportion of women working street patrol, there are relatively few women in police administration. What barriers might women face as they make the decision to pursue administrative positions, and how can these barriers be reduced?
4. One concern expressed by male officers about women in policing is that women are unable to perform the functions of a police officer properly. Given the reality of policing (i.e., use of force is relatively rare), assess the validity of this concern.

References

Birzer, M. L., & Craig, D. E. (1996). Gender differences in police physical ability test performance. *American Journal of Police, 15*(2), 93–108.

Burke, R. J., & Mikkelsen, A. (2005). Gender differences in policing: Signs of progress? *Employee Relations, 27*(4), 425–436.

Chaiyavej, S., & Morash, M. (2009). Reasons for policewomen's assertive and passive reactions to sexual harassment. *Police Quarterly, 12*(1), 63–85.

Cordner, G., & Cordner, A. (2011). Stuck on a plateau? Obstacles to recruitment, selection, and retention of women police. *Police Quarterly, 14*(3), 207–226.

Doerner, W. G. (1995). Officer retention patterns: An affirmative action concern for police agencies? *American Journal of Police, 14*(3/4), 197–210.

Duffin, A. T. (2010). *History in blue: 160 years of women police, sheriffs, detectives, and state troopers.* New York, NY: Kaplan Publishing.

Durose, M., & Langton, L. (2013). *Police behavior during traffic and street stops, 2011* (NCJ 242937). Washington, DC: United States Bureau of Justice.

Federal Bureau of Investigation. (2013). *Crime in the United States 2012.* Washington, DC: U.S. Department of Justice.

Garner, J. H., Maxwell, C. D., & Heraux, C. G. (2002). Characteristics associated with the prevalence and severity of force used by the police. *Justice Quarterly, 19,* 705–746.

Greene, H. T. (2000). Black females in law enforcement. *Journal of Contemporary Criminal Justice, 16*(2), 230–239.

Greenfeld, L. A., Langan, P. A., & Smith, S. K. (1997). *Police use of force: Collection of national data* (NCJ 165040). Washington, DC: United States Bureau of Justice.

Haarr, R. N. (2005). Factors affecting the decision of police recruits to "drop out" of police work. *Police Quarterly, 8*(4), 431–453.

Henson, B., Reyns, B. W., Klahm, C. F., and Frank, J. (2010). Do good recruits make good cops? Problems predicting and measuring academy and street-level success. *Police Quarterly, 13,* 5–26.

Hoffman, P. B., & Hickey, E. R. (2005). Use of force by female police officers. *Journal of Criminal Justice, 33,* 145–151.

Hunt, J. (1985). Police accounts of normal force. *Journal of Contemporary Ethnography, 13,* 315–341.

Hutzel, E. L. (1929). The policewoman. *Annals of the American Academy of Political and Social Science, 146*(Nov), 104–114.

Jordan, W. T., Fridell, L., Faggiani, D., & Kubu, B. (2009). Attracting females and racial/ethnic minorities to law enforcement. *Journal of Criminal Justice, 37,* 333–341.

Kakar, S. (2002). Gender and police officers' perceptions of their job performance: An analysis of the relationship between gender and perceptions of job performance. *Criminal Justice Policy Review, 13,* 238–256.

Langton, L. (2010). *Women in law enforcement, 1987–2008* (NCJ 230521). Washington, DC: United States Bureau of Justice Statistics.

Martin, S. E. (1991). The effectiveness of affirmative action: The case of women in policing. *Justice Quarterly, 8*(4), 489–504.

National Center for Women in Policing (2001). *Equality denied: The status of women in policing: 2001.* Arlington, VA: National Center for Women in Policing.

Owings, C. (1969). *Women police: A study of the development and status of the women police movement.* Montclair, NJ: Patterson Smith.

Paoline, E. A. III, & Terrill, W. (2004). Women police officers and the use of coercion. *Women and Criminal Justice, 15*(3/4), 97–119.

Prenzler, T., & Sinclair, G. (2013). The status of women police officers: An international review. *International Journal of Law, Crime and Justice, 41*(2013), 115–131.

Prokos, A., & Padavic, I. (2002). 'There oughtta be a law against bitches': Masculinity lessons in police academy training. *Gender, Work and Organization, 9*(4), 439–459.

Rabe-Hemp, C. (2007). Survival in an "all boys club": Policewomen and their fight for acceptance. *Policing: An International Journal of Police Strategies and Management, 31*(2), 251–270.

Raganella, A. J., & White, M. D. (2004). Race, gender, and motivation for becoming a police officer: Implications for building a representative police department. *Journal of Criminal Justice, 32,* 501–513.

Schuck, A. M. (2014). Female representation in law enforcement: The influence of screening, unions, incentives, community policing, CALEA, and size. *Police Quarterly, 17*(1), 54–78.

Schuck, A. M., & Rabe-Hemp, C. (2005). Women police: The use of force by and against female officers. *Women and Criminal Justice, 16*(4), 91–117.

Schulz, D. M. (1995). *From social worker to crimefighter: Women in United States municipal policing.* Westport, CT: Praeger.

Schulz, D. M. (2003). Women police chiefs: A statistical profile. *Police Quarterly, 6,* 330–345.

Segrave, K. (2014). *Policewomen: A history.* Jefferson, NC: McFarland and Company.

Snow, R. L. (2010). *Policewomen who made history.* Lanham, MD: Rowman and Littlefield.

Sun, I. Y., & Chu, D. C. (2008). A cross-national analysis of female police offices' attitudes in the United States and Taiwan. *International Criminal Justice Review, 18*(1), 5–23.

Wells, S. K., & Alt, B. L. (2005). *Police women: Life with the badge.* Westport, CT: Praeger.

Wertsch, T. L. (1998). Walking the thin blue line: Policewomen and tokenism today. *Women and Criminal Justice, 9*(3), 23–61.

White, M. D. (2008). Identifying good cops early: Predicting recruit performance in the academy. *Police Quarterly, 11*(1), 27–49.

Zhao, J., Herbst, L., & Lovrich, N. (2001). Race, ethnicity and the female cop: Differential patterns of representation. *Journal of Urban Affairs, 23*(3–4), 243–257.

Women in the Judicial System 15

STEPHANE J. KIRVEN

Contents

Women have been members of the legal profession for over a century. In recent years, the legal profession has undergone significant changes, with rapidly rising numbers of women entering the legal profession (ABA, 2011). Today, women comprise about one-third of the total number of law students in the country and constitute almost 30% of the profession (ABA, 2011). Women have made far more advances in the legal profession than in other criminal justice fields (Van Wormer & Bartollas, 2013). Despite the significant progress of women in the law, however, a legacy of discrimination and gender bias remains. For underneath this façade of progress and seeming equality, women continue to experience discrimination in compensation, responsibilities, and advancement (ABA, 2011). This chapter will trace the historical integration of women in the legal profession and survey current issues of gender inequities.

Historical Overview

> You can't be shining lights at the Bar because you are too kind. You can never be corporation lawyers because you are not cold-blooded. You have not a high grade of intellect. I doubt you could ever make a living.
>
> **—Clarence Darrow to a group of women lawyers (Morello, 1984)**

This message by Clarence Darrow in the 1800s echoed the sentiment of the times when law was considered too "coarse" of a profession for the dainty female creature. Historically, women were barred from the practice of law on the notion they had inferior minds and body and an inability to be discreet (Weeisber, 1982). The perception was that women were best "suited for the home" (Weisberg, 1982). Males who oversaw the entrance of persons into law argued that law was a "hard nosed, male profession, which could impugn the delicacy of a female's biological character" (Bernat, 1997, p. 53). Similar to the pioneering women in policing and corrections, objections to women practicing law came from their male colleagues who perceived women as innately unsuited to practice law because of their emotional and sentimental nature (Pollock-Byrne & Ramirez, 1995, p. 80).

In the early days, the only avenues for women to pursue a legal education were through a clerkship with their husbands or fathers who were practicing attorneys. Margaret Brent was the first practicing female lawyer in North America and was selected by the Governor of Maryland to be the executor of his estate. Brent litigated over 124 cases on behalf of the Governor's estate. She was so powerful in her day that the Colonists called her "Gentlemen Brent" (Feinman, 1994). However, little else is known about women practicing law until the mid-1800s except that they were prohibited from attending law school or qualifying to take the Bar exam (Belknap, 2007). It is possible that a few women appeared in court on their own behalf and others practiced law in the frontier areas; however, few pursued legal careers (Bernat, 1992).

In 1869, Arabella Babb Mansfield became the first woman to be recognized as a lawyer in the United States, admitted by the Iowa State Bar. Many married women who were legally permitted to practice were restricted by society and their husbands. In addition to their strong likelihood of having fathers and husbands as lawyers, these women also came from wealthy families (Belknap, 2007; Feinman, 1994). Many chose the legal profession because of their early contact and influence with family members who were lawyers, while others joined the legal profession as a byproduct of the need to manage large inheritances (Feinman, 1994).

The first female to graduate from a law school in the United States was Ada Kepley who graduated from the University of Chicago in 1870. According to the U.S. census in 1870, there were five woman lawyers in the United States (Belknap, 2007). In 1872, Charlotte E. Ray became the first African American woman admitted to the bar. These women were the exceptions, whereas in other jurisdictions women applicants were denied membership (Belknap, 2007).

As to be expected, some of the pioneering women in law were dedicated to fighting different aspects of discrimination including women's issues and advocating for the poor, Native American Indians, African Americans, and immigrants (Morello, 1986). One such woman was Belva Lockwood. In the late 1800s, after countless denials to appear before the federal courts solely because she was a woman, Belva Lockwood was finally granted the opportunity to be the first woman lawyer to argue a case before the U.S. Supreme Court (Barteau, 1997). There, she succeeded in obtaining a $5 million settlement for the Cherokee Nation from the U.S. government (Morello, 1986). This was remarkable, given Lockwood was initially denied admission to numerous law schools, as it was felt that she would distract her male classmates. Her male classmates were not supportive and threatened to boycott graduation if she was awarded a law degree (Barteau, 1997). Throughout her career, Lockwood encouraged women to join the legal profession and to fight back against the discriminatory treatment of women seeking careers in the law.

"Laws forbidding women to enter into contracts also stymied their ability to practice law" (Belknap, 2007, p. 442). A case in point was that of Myra Bradwell who in 1873 was denied admittance by the Illinois State Supreme Court despite her argument to the court that her marital status did not matter. The court in *Bradwell v. Illinois* barred married women from practicing law. Justice Bradley, concurring with the opinion of the court and not concerned with discrimination against married or unmarried woman, wrote:

> It is true that many women are unmarried and not affected by any of the duties, complications, and incapacities arising out of the married state, but these are exceptions to the rule. The Paramount destiny and mission of women are to fulfill the noble and benign offices of wife and mother. This is the law of the Creator. And the rules of civil society must be adapted to the general Constitution of things and cannot be based upon exceptional cases. (Justice Bradley in *Bradwell v. Illinois*, 1873)

Belknap (2007, p. 443)

Bradwell appealed to the U.S. Supreme Court claiming that her rights under the Equal Protection Clause had been violated. The Supreme Court denied her appeal stating,

> The natural and proper timidity and delicacy that belongs to the female sex evidently unfits it for the practice of law... Additionally a woman has no legal existence separate from her husband.

Martin and Jurik (2007, p. 109)

The Supreme Court denied Bradwell not only on the basis of gender but also as a married woman because she could not sign contracts on behalf of her clients, a requirement for any lawyer. "While denial of the rights of married women to be members of the bar or to practice before a specific court was based on common law precedent, the denial of the rights of single women was based on the additional belief that women were not to be encouraged to remain single or to become educated professionals or to have equal careers with men" (Feinman, 1994, p. 133). The Court's decision in Bradwell to exclude women from the bar meant women had to challenge their exclusion state by state to gain the right to practice law (Belknap, 2007).

In the 1830s and 1840s, two historical events served to open the door to women's entry into the legal profession: America's westward expansion and the Civil War (Morello, 1986). Interestingly, women found greater freedom in the west as they moved away from the staid and Victorian norms of northeastern society (Morello, 1986). One reason for less resistance in Western states was the expanded role of women that had characterized the westward expansion of the 1800s (Feinman, 1994). The images of frail and dainty women were inconsistent with the realities of the rugged west where women had worked side by side with the men (Morello, 1986). As a result, the first law schools to open to women were in the west (Morello, 1986). Also, with men engaged in the Civil War, women had the opportunity to fill vacant slots in law schools and in some legal positions.

In 1888, the women's international bar association was established, and in 1899 the National Association of Women Lawyers was organized in New York (Feinman, 1994). Through the efforts of these groups women gained admittance to law schools and to state bars, courts and used their access to improve the legal status of women in the profession (Feinman, 1994, p. 134). However, it was not until 1918 that the American Bar Association (ABA) began accepting women. In 1920, 51 years after the first woman became a lawyer, women were allowed to practice law before the courts in every state (Feinman, 1994). Eventually, every state legislature struck down the barriers to female practice. In 1920, women made up 1.1% of all lawyers in the United States. In the 1960s, almost a century since Iowa granted a law license to Arabella Babb Mansfield, women were only 4.7% of all practicing attorneys in the United States (Sarver, Keheny, & Azmer, 2008). American lawyers as a professional group maintained strict entrance requirements to join the profession.

Women in Law School

For many years, the male-dominated legal profession controlled its membership by limiting women's enrollment in law school. Until the 1900s, the common route to the legal profession was through an apprenticeship. However, the professionalization of the legal practice led to an increase of lawyers following the academic route. The access to legal education was very limited and many law schools denied admittance to women altogether. Rejection from most law schools led women to create their own law programs. For example, the Women's Legal Education Society set up the women's law class of New York University in 1890 (Feinman, 1994). Its purpose was to educate women about their rights so that they could protect themselves and other women (Feinman, 1994). In the late 1920s, the Ivy League schools began to open their doors to women applicants and women quickly learned that admission was not in and of itself acceptance. Once in law schools women were faced with discrimination in the classroom as male students refused to associate with them and sometimes stamped their feet when they tried to recite (Morello, 1986). In 1950, Harvard Law School became the last of the Ivy League schools to accept woman. For the most part, it was not until the passage of Title IX of the 1972 Educational Amendment Act prohibiting sex discrimination in all public institutions of higher learning receiving federal monies including major universities and their law schools, did women enjoy equal access to a legal education (Belknap, 2007). "Facing denial of federal funds if they continued to discriminate, law schools began admitting women applicants in unprecedented numbers and continue to do so today" (Van Wormer & Bartollas, 2013, p. 334). "The number of women enrolled in law schools tripled between 1969–70 and 1974–75 and increased tenfold from 1966 (2,600) to 1975 (26,000)" (Feinman, 1994, p. 127).

As late as the 1970s, women were admitted to law schools only after being questioned about their personal life plans, such as marriage, children, and career goals. They were asked if they planned to practice law or look for a husband (Feinman, 1984). They were often told that they were taking places in the law school that should go to men and that they did not belong. Both faculty and male students made the environment hostile and unwelcoming to women. Despite the fact that women's representation in law schools greatly increased in decades following the passage of Title IX of the Higher Education Act in 1972, recent research revealed significant differences in the way women and men experience law school. In a study of female students at the University of Pennsylvania in the 1990s by Lani Guinier entitled "Becoming Gentlemen: Women Experience at one Ivy League law School," researchers found that many of the women expressed feelings of alienation and reported that they received lower grades and were selected for fewer honors and awards than their male peers. The research also revealed:

> Although there were no gender differences in the law school entry level credentials, by the end of the first year of law school "men are three times more likely than women to be in the top 10% of their law school class." The women in the first year class are far more critical of

their social status quo, their legal education, and themselves then the first year man, but by the third year have become less critical than their third year male peers.

Guinier et al. (1994, p. 3)

In a more recent study on current experiences of women students in law school, Jackson (2007) echoes Guinier's findings and reveals that certain elements of the law school curriculum continue to be problematic for women. The traditional and rigorous educational approach of the Socratic method is found to be counter to how women learn best (Merlo & Pollock, 1995). Research shows that female students "tends to shrink back from aggressive professors and take critical interaction more personally," whereas the male students confront the professors head on and treat such interactions impersonally (Merlo & Pollock, 1995, p. 84). Women were found to participate less in class and often felt insecure and uncertain of their abilities, and their comments were more likely to be overlooked and devalued (ABA, 2011). Furthermore, law students study case law from the male point of view, and mainly only men's opinions are cited. Legal issues that are important to women, such as domestic violence, rape, sexual discrimination, and harassment, are often dealt with superficially and maybe trivialized (Belknap, 2007). Many of the women lawyers report that being trained to "think and act like man" was distressing to them (Guinier, 1990, p. 3).

Law Professor Lani Guinier of Harvard Law School has been instrumental in introducing a more women-friendly approach to teaching law. "The new teaching method is built on teamwork and role-playing: the purpose is to redesign the classroom experience so that people with different learning styles can thrive" (Van Wormer & Bartollas, 2013, p. 339). The influence of female faculty like Lani Guinier and female administrators is helping to create a more inclusive academic environment. Findings show that women tend to perform better when they have female role models and mentors (ABA, 2011; Martin & Jurik, 2007). Women in legal education and administration today are underrepresented and they also face issues of alienation and gender bias (ABA, 2011; Martin & Jurik, 2007). Although more women now hold faculty and administrative positions, they are often relegated to teaching "women's issues" and are placed in lower echelon positions with less power and authority. As of the 2004–2005 school year, women comprised 35% of law school faculty but only 25% of tenured faculty (Martin & Jurik, 2007). They also represented only 19% of law school deans (ABA, 2006). In order to fully serve the needs of its female population and offer a gender-neutral and nurturing environment, law schools will have to implement a more inclusive curricular as well as commit to actively recruiting and retaining female faculty and administrators.

Not surprisingly, research has also shown that the difference in the way men and women experience law school is also carried over into the profession as women move from law school to legal practice.

Women Lawyers

At the turn of the twentieth century, women accounted for almost a third of the nation's lawyers, and for the first time women constituted a majority of entering law students. Over the last decades, the number of women law partners, general counsels, and federal judges has doubled (ABA, 2011). Despite this numerical gain, women in the legal profession remain underrepresented in positions of the greatest status, influence, and economic reward (ABA, 2011). In power and status position such as federal judgeships and partnerships, women make up only 15% (ABA, 2011). When women are hired, they are often offered opportunities in specialty areas deemed suitable and appropriate for women such as family law and probate. "Women lawyers' median salary for full time work is around 75% of men's and significant income disparities persist even between similar qualifications, experience and positions" (ABA, 2011, p. 5). Research has determined that women holding the same positions as men, with the same types of responsibilities, the same number of years of experience, the same class rank working at similar types of firms earned substantially less than their male counterparts (ABA, 2011; Martin & Jurik, 2007). This income differential often starts in the first year of practice and with the passage of time men increase their income lead.

More than 80% of women lawyers believe that the "glass ceiling" for women still exists in the workplace (Gaffney, 2011). In every area of practice in the legal profession, there are key disparities in women's experiences as compared to their male counterparts. Though the data find significant inequalities in pay and promotion, only about a quarter of female lawyers and only 3% of male lawyers believed that the prospect for women's advancement was greater for men than women (ABA, 2000, Journal Poll). This lack of consensus by both men and women "that there are problems further compounds the problems" (ABA, 2011, p. 5). The overall research shows women's opportunities are limited by such factors as "unconscious stereotypes, inadequate access to support networks, inflexible workplace structures, sexual harassment and gender bias in the justice system" (ABA, 2011, p. 5).

Discrimination

Reminiscent of the gendered law school culture, women looking to be hired find themselves outsiders to the "good old boy network subject to gender stereotypes and discrimination." They find the legal professional landscape riddled with "double standards" in the areas of hiring, compensation, promotion, and expectations. The historical overview of women lawyers reveals a strong resistance to women in the legal profession. "Historically, objections offered to restrict women from practicing law included accusations that women had inferior minds and bodies, an inability to be discreet and a role conflict between career and wife and motherhood" (Belknap, 2007, p. 441, citing Weisberg, 1982). Similar to women in policing and corrections most of the opposition in women practicing law came from males in the profession (Belknap, 2007). The reasons for the resistance to women in law can never be fully explained, perhaps it is because of law's close relationship to power in society (Martin & Jurik, 2007) and men want to hold on to the power. "Perhaps it is because the law is viewed as inherently masculine" (Van Womer & Bartollas, 2013, p. 340). Both male and female lawyers feel that the adversarial nature of the law speaks to masculine traits. The law is based on an Anglo-American format and is born of conflict and strife (Van Wormer & Bartollas, 2010). The Anglo-American adversarial system is warlike in nature with a "winner takes it all ethos" (Van Wormer & Bartollas, 2013, p. 340). It is often presumed that successful lawyers must have a "fighting disposition and that disposition is often attributed to men" (Van Womer & Bartollass, 2010, p. 340). "He must be able to find 'creative solutions to problems and persuade clients to take them, a willingness to take risks but knowing when to pull back and compromise. He must have 'quick mastery of the facts,' sharp attention to details and unusual self-confidence'" (Van Wormer & Bartollas, 2013, p. 340). These qualifications are often *not* associated with women. The character traits traditionally associated with women run counter to the character traits associated with successful lawyers. However, this argument is inherently flawed because character traits are not gender specific. Not all men are pillars of strength and logic nor are all women the epitome of kindness.

Interestingly, women attorneys are often met with conflicting behavioral and personality expectations. Ambition and drive coupled with confidence are admired in a male attorney but those same characteristics are looked upon with disfavor and criticism in female attorneys since they contradict the traditional female image. If a female attorney displays any softness and sensitivity, she is believed to lack the requisite traits to be a successful lawyer. Pierce (2005) found that women attorneys are criticized for being "too nice to the witness," "not forceful enough," "too bashful, and unaggressive," at the same time that they were admonished for being "too aggressive." Also when male attorneys used cajoling and placating strategies to achieve an instrumental end, they received support and encouragement from their colleagues. Women who adopted similar tactics were accused of using their "feminine wiles" to get their way with witness or opposing counsel (Pierce, 1995, p. 113). The end result is a set of confusing and contradictory behavioral expectations for women attorneys.

A related issue is that female attorneys do not receive the same presumption of competence and commitment as their male colleague (ABA, 2011). This presumption of incompetence and lacking in qualification is often used as the rational to support discriminatory practices of hiring, compensation, and promotion. Studies have shown that to the contrary women tend to outshine men academically, receive a disproportionate amount of academic awards, and surpass them in class rankings (ABA, 2011). There is a double standard in assessing professional performance. Research shows that performance of women is subject to greater scrutiny than men and their achievements are attributed to luck and special treatment as opposed to professional qualifications (ABA, 2011). Often is the case where men lawyers are presumed naturally competent while their female counterparts are presumed incompetent (Martin & Jurik, 2007). At the end of the day, a mediocre male attorney will be tolerated and accepted, whereas an organization has little tolerance for an "average female attorney." In 1992, at a symposium for women judges, Justice Sandra Day O'Connor, speaking on gender bias in the profession, said: "You simply have to be better. That is a terrific burden" (Feinman, 1994). Time and time again women are told to work hard, do better and be better than their male counterparts and success and reward will come to them. Disappointingly for women, no matter how hard they work, no matter how much better they are, decades later the legal profession still fails to reward women equally to men for a job well done.

In attempting to enter into historically male-dominated professions, women lawyers encounter many challenges that emanate from traditional hierarchies that often view the male as the dominant gender. Despite gains in gender equality and empowerment, these organizations hold onto gender biases and stereotypes that spill over to organizational policies and structures that serve to marginalize women in the workplace (Martin & Jurik, 2007). Women can only begin to effectuate change though positions of power and leadership in these organizations. Evidence of this transformative leadership is found in women policing where women in greater numbers are ascending into senior positions. These women are acting as agents of change to challenge stereotypes, breakdown barriers, and make progress in effectuating change in policy and culture to support women's successes in these traditionally male-dominated organizations. However, the same cannot be said for women lawyers in leadership positions. In the legal profession, the criticism has been that many women leaders have been lulled into complacency by their individual successes and fail to see the need or urgency for reform (ABA, 2011).

Sex-Based Harassment

Another context in which women lawyers are marginalized and devalued involves sex-based harassment. Although considerable progress has been made over the decades, women lawyers still find themselves subjected to three forms of sex-based harassment: quid pro quo harassment, hostile work environment, and gender-based harassment. "In its broad sense sex based harassment refers to behavior that derogates, demeans, or humiliates an individual based on that individual's sex" (Berdahl, 2007, p. 644). Federal law, Title VII of the Civil Rights Act of 1964, "prohibits employers from discriminating against any individual with regard to. ...employment, because of such individual's ...sex." In the late 1970s, Federal courts recognized cases in which women had lost jobs for failing to comply with their employers' sexual demands as sexual harassment termed "quid pro quo harassment." A decade later, the Supreme Court would rule that "hostile work environment harassment" would constitute unlawful harassment. In *Meritor Savings Bank v. Vinson*, the U.S. Supreme Court described hostile work environment sexual harassment as occurring "[w]hen the workplace is permeated with 'discriminatory intimidation, ridicule, and insult'... that is 'sufficiently severe or pervasive to alter the conditions of the victim's employment and create an abusive working environment.'" Last, also falling under the umbrella of sex-based harassment is gender harassment.

Gender harassment refers to "a broad range of verbal and nonverbal behaviors not aimed at sexual cooperation but that convey insulting, hostile, and degrading attitudes about women" (Fitzgerald et al., 1995, p. 430). Examples of gender harassment include anti-female jokes, comments that women do not belong in the law, and crude terms of address that denigrate women. Unlike the other two categories of sexual harassment, "unwanted sexual attention" and "sexual coercion," with gender harassment there is no sexual interest and no sexual advance. Instead, the degrading terms, antifemale jokes, or telling, among other behaviors, aim to insult and reject women (Fitzgerald et al., 1995, p. 430).

A 2008 survey shows that had to two-thirds of female lawyers report experiencing or observing sex-based harassment (Commission on Women in the Profession, 2008). "Demeaning conduct take a variety of forms" (ABA, 2011, p. 20). Women lawyers are subjected to demeaning forms of address, comments on their physical appearance and clothing, sexist remarks and jokes and unwanted touching, verbal and physical harassment. "Female lawyers were routinely called 'pretty girl, little lady,' 'lawyerette,' 'baby doll,' 'sweetie'" (ABA, 2011, p. 20). "Examples range from the occasional overt comment, such as 'shut up.'" "'Let's hear what the men have to say'" (ABA, 2011, p. 21). Women frequently encountered questions such as whether "they understood all the economics involved in an 'antirust case,' or 'whether their client is satisfied with the representation they had at trial even though the lawyer was a women.'" (ABA, 2011, pp. 20–21) "Though the more egregious forms of these conduct no longer exist, these problems still persist particularly those involving disrespectful forms of address" (ABA, 2011, p. 21).

Almost three-fourths of female lawyers believe that sex-based harassment is a problem in their workplace, research shows that women often will not report incidences of harassment for fear of retaliation or ridicule. Many agencies and private institutions have policies that follow federal regulations prohibiting unwelcomed sexual advances and conduct that create a feeling of intimidation. However, in many organizations the gap between policy and practice is substantial (ABA, 2011). The more egregious forms of harassment have given way to subtle behaviors of harassment and are more difficult to identify and label. In cases of gender harassment, it is seen as inconsequential and less important than unwanted sexual attention in the workplace and therefore even less likely to be reported.

Workplace Structures

Another obstacle for women lawyers' advancement is the workplace structures that fail to support and accommodate women's family responsibilities. In recent surveys, about two-thirds of lawyers report experiencing work–family conflict (ABA, 2011, p. 17). Women find themselves in many institution that do not offer work-life accommodations. This is further compounded by the tendency to view working mothers as less ambitions or less committed. Assumptions about these working mothers can affect performance evaluations and promotion decisions (ABA, 2011). "If she is a good lawyer, she must be a bad mother or vice versa. She can only be a successful lawyer at the expense of her children and she is often seen as failing on both fronts" (Cunningham, 2001, p. 997). "These mixed messages often leave women with behavioral dilemmas" (Martin & Jurik, 2007, p. 127). In sum, like their counterparts in law enforcement and corrections women lawyers must contend with a situation where their work conflicts with their gender identity and other expectations.

Case Study 1: Constance Baker Motley, Civil Right Lawyer, Politician, and Judge

Something which we think is impossible now is not impossible in another decade.

—Constance Baker Motley

Constance Baker Motley was a lawyer, a civil rights activist, a politician, and a judge. During her career, Motley accomplished a number of political and judicial "firsts" that was remarkable for an African American woman given the racism and sexism of the time. As a black woman practicing law in the South, she endured gawking and a number of physical threats. A local paper in Jackson, Miss., referred to her as "the Motley woman."

"Woman lawyers were a joke in most courthouses and unheard of in virtually every place except New York City," Judge Motley wrote in *Ms.* magazine years later. "The whole town turned out to see the Negro lawyers from New York, one of whom [was] a woman."

Notable Firsts:

- In 1944, she became one of the first black women accepted at Columbia University Law School.
- The first African American woman to argue a case before the Supreme Court.
- In 1964, Motley became the first African American woman elected to the New York Senate.

- In 1965, she was chosen Manhattan Borough President—the first woman in that position.
- In 1966, President Lyndon Johnson named her a district judge for the United States District Court Southern District of New York making her the first African American woman federal judge, a position she held, including a term as chief judge, until her death.

Motley earned her economics degree in 1943 from New York University. Motley went on to earn her law degree from Columbia Law School. In 1945, she became a law clerk for Thurgood Marshall and went on to work for the National Association for the Advancement of Colored People's (NAACP's) Legal Defense and Educational Fund, establishing herself as a major player in the civil rights fight. She assisted in drafting the complaint in 1950 for the *Brown v. Board of Education* landmark suit. In 1954, in a unanimous decision, the court ruled in favor of Motley and her colleague and declared that the separate schooling for black and white students was unconstitutional. In the case of *Meredith v. Fair*, Motley became the first African American woman ever to argue a case before the U.S. Supreme Court and won James Meredith the right to be the first black student to attend the University of Mississippi in 1962. Motley was successful in 9 of the 10 cases she argued before the Supreme Court. The tenth decision, regarding jury composition, was eventually overturned in her favor. She was a key legal strategist in the civil rights movement, helping to desegregate Southern schools, buses, and lunch counters. Motley had a number of other legal successes. She fought for King's right to march in Albany, Georgia, and played an important role in representing blacks seeking admission to the Universities of Florida, Georgia, Alabama, and Mississippi and Clemson College in South Carolina.

During her tenure as federal Court Judge, Motley handed down a number of breakthrough decisions. In 1978, she ruled that a female reporter must be allowed into a Major League Baseball locker room. In 1987, she ruled that, without exceptional circumstances, suspects could not be detained more than 24 hours without a court ruling that sufficient evidence exists to justify the arrest.

Sources: http://www.washingtonpost.com/wp-dyn/content/article/2005/09/28/
    AR2005092802525_2.html
http://www.nytimes.com/2005/09/29/nyregion/29motley.html?pagewanted=
    all&_r=0

Women Judges

It is not surprising that women comprise a small portion of the judiciary. When women are restricted to law specialties that are handled in the back room rather than the courtroom, legal research rather than litigation, they are effectively kept out of the eligibility pool for judgeships (Van Wormer & Bartollas, 2013). They are also prevented from establishing the kind of reputation that could lead to judicial appointment (Van Wormer & Bartollas, 2013). Judges have great power, and appointment to the bench usually occurs as a "reward" for a successful career (Martin & Jurik, 2007). Prior to 1920, female judges were a rarity mainly in part because they were ineligible to vote or hold office before the passage of the

Nineteenth Amendment (Belknap, 2007). The first women to ascend to these positions were often appointed to part-time positions as token representatives of their sex (Belknap, 2004).

In 1921, Florence Allen became the first female judge elected to a state supreme court. By 1950, 29 states had at least one female judge (Belknap, 2007). Not surprisingly, "when women were first elected or appointed to judgeships, it was frequently to judgeships consistent with stereotyped gender roles, especially family law, divorce courts, juvenile courts and lower municipal courts" (Feinman, 1984). In 1949, Bonnie Shelton Matthews became the first woman appointed to a federal court by President Truman. In 1971, less than "200 women served on the state courts in the United States and it was not until 1979 that all states had at least one woman serving in some judicial capacity" (Abrahamson, 1998, p. 197).

President Carter appointed more women to the federal bench in his 4 years as president than both President Reagan and President Bush in their 12 years (Abrahamson, 1998). The first woman and 102nd justice appointed to the U.S. Supreme Court was Sandra Day O'Connor who was appointed by President Ronald Reagan. Despite graduating at the top of her class at Stanford Law School and finishing law school in just 2 years, O'Connor was unable to find a job after graduation other than working as a law clerk or secretary. O'Connor's experience typified some of the difficulties and barriers women lawyers faced breaking into the profession in the 1960s. O'Connor went on to serve 24 years as a U.S. Supreme Court Justice prior to retiring in 2005. Though O'Connor's appointment reflected progress in women's efforts to gain a seat on the bench, the true picture of women in the judiciary system reflected a more dismal reality. In 1983, only 5.4% of all federal judges were women and fewer than 5% of all state court judges were women. Out of more than 20,000 judicial appointments in the United States, only 900 were held by women (Morello, 1986). Women attorneys believed that their gender was the reason for the low numbers of women judges and not their ability or lack of skills or temperament. Research supports that the underrepresentation of women in the judiciary is attributable to gender biases in both the selection and confirmation processes (ABA, 2011). One prominent female judge expressed the following: "Male lawyers still only begrudgingly accept decisions that might seriously affect them or their clients…" (Morello, 1994, p. 219). At the National Association of Women Judges convention, there were stories shared of sexism on the bench; "when you are called sweetie or honey in a room full of lawyers it kind of makes your heart stop," remarked Martha Craig Daughtrey, a criminal appeals judge from Tennessee (Morello, 1986, p. 245).

From 1982–1984, the New Jersey Supreme Court created and ran the nation's first official task force on bias on women in the courts and many states followed. By the twenty-first century, some 65 states and federal courts had issued reports on bias in the court systems. The ABA amended both the ABA Model Code of Judicial Conduct and the Model Rules of Professional conduct to include prohibition on bias. While the most severe form of egregious bias was eliminated gender bias had a lasting impact on women's representation in the profession.

In the next decade, three more women would be appointed to the U.S. Supreme Court. President Clinton appointed Ruth Bader Ginsberg to the Supreme Court in 1993. President Obama appointed Sonya Sotomayor to the Supreme Court in 2009 to replace retiring Justice David Souter, and Solicitor Elena Kagan was appointed to replace retiring Justice John Paul Stevens. Although women now make up one-third of the Supreme Court, women still remain underrepresented at the highest levels of the judiciary system. According to the National Women Law Center, only 6 of the 172 active judges sitting on the 13 Federal Courts of Appeal are female, 32% of the U.S. District Court judges are females but there are still 9 District Courts around the country where there has never been a female judge. Today, about 22% of Federal District Court judges and U.S. Court of Appeals judges are women (ABA, 2011). Women continue to be significantly underrepresented in the judiciary system.

Case Study 2: Sandra Day O'Connor—The First Woman on the Supreme Court

The power I exert on the court depends on the power of my arguments, not on my gender.

—**Sandra Day O'Connor**

Sandra Day O'Connor graduated from Stanford University in 1950 with a bachelor's degree in economics and received her law degree in 1952 from the university's law school. Even though she completed her degree in 2 years and graduated top in her class, O'Connor struggled to find work as an attorney. She even worked for the county attorney for California's San Mateo county for free for a time just to get her foot in the door and soon became the deputy county attorney there.

From 1954 to 1957, O'Connor served as a civilian lawyer for the Quartermaster Masker Center in Frankfurt, Germany. She returned home in 1958 and settled in Arizona. There she first worked in private practice before returning to public service. O'Connor acted as the state's assistant attorney general for 4 years, from 1965 to 1969.

Sandra Day O'Connor served as the assistant attorney general for Arizona in the 1960s. In 1969, she was appointed by Governor Jack Williams to the state senate to fill a vacancy. A conservative Republican, O'Connor won re-election twice. In 1974, O'Connor ran for the position of judge in the Maricopa County Superior Court.

Sandra Day O'Connor had a solid reputation for being firm, but fair. In 1979, O'Connor was selected to serve on the state's court of appeals. In 1981, Ronald Reagan nominated her as a justice of the U.S. Supreme Court and she received unanimous Senate approval. O'Connor made history as the first woman justice to serve on the Supreme Court.

As a justice, O'Connor was as a key swing vote in many important cases including the upholding of *Roe v. Wade* and *Bush v. Gore*. O'Connor joined with four other justices on December 12, 2000, to rule on the *Bush v. Gore* case that ceased challenges to the results of the 2000 presidential election (ruling to stop the ongoing Florida Election Recount and to allow no further recounts). This case effectively ended Vice President Gore's hopes to become president.

In *Lawrence v. Texas* [539 U.S. (2003)], O'Connor wrote a concurring opinion contending that state laws that prohibited homosexual sexual conduct violated the Equal Protection Clause of the Fourteenth Amendment to the U.S. Constitution. Substantive due process afforded by the Due Process Clause.

She retired in 2006, after serving for 24 years.

Source: http://www.biography.com/people/sandra-day-oconnor-9426834

Conclusion: An "Unfinished Agenda"

Since the 1960s, the legal world has undergone several major changes. In the 1970s, as part of the changing landscape we saw a growing presence of women lawyers. Women now comprise more than a quarter of the legal profession and about half of all law students are women. Dismayingly, despite substantial progress toward equal opportunity, a century later women in the legal profession remain underrepresented in positions of the greatest status, influence, and economic reward.

In 1986, a NYS Task Force on gender bias in the courts concluded "our very own justice system regularly denies justice to women." Fifteen years later, the report of the ABA Commission on Women in the Profession, The Unfinished Agenda (2001, p. 5), concluded,

> Despite substantial progress toward equal opportunity, the agenda (established by this group in 1987) remains unfinished. Women in the legal profession remain underrepresented in position of great status, influence and economic reward…. The problems are compounded by the lack of consensus that there are in fact serious problems.

In sum, the struggle for equality remains and the agenda "remains unfinished" 15 years after it was set.

Discussion Questions

1. What gender-specific character traits do women bring to the practice of law that allows them to perform their jobs "better" than their male counterparts? Conversely, are there any gender-specific traits that put women at a "disadvantage?"
2. What are some positive and negative images associated with women in law?
3. Does the presence of women lawyers and judges have any impact on women victims or offender and does their role influence the legal outcomes of women issues in the courts (e.g., issues such as sexual discrimination, rape, or domestic violence)?

References

Abrahamson, S. S. (1998). Do women judges really make a difference? The American experience. In S. Shetreet (Ed.), *Women in law* (pp. 75–82). London, U.K.: Kluwer Law International.

American Bar Association (ABA). (2011, January). A current glance at women in the law. Retrieved from http://www.americanbar.org

American Bar Association (ABA). (2012). *The road to independence: 101 women's journeys to starting their own law firms.* Washington, DC: ABA.

Barrett, P. M. (2012, April 23–29). White-shoe blues. *Bloomberg Businessweek*, pp. 6–7.

Barteau, B. S. (1997). *Thirty years of the journey of Indiana's women judges, 1964–1994.* Indianapolis, IA: Indiana University School of Law-Indianapolis.

Belknap, J. (2007). *The invisible woman: Gender, crime, and justice*, 3rd ed. Belmont, CA: Wadsworth.

Bernat, F. (1985). Women in the legal profession. In I. L. Moyer (Ed.), *The changing roles of women in the criminal justice system: Offenders, victims, and professionals* (pp. 307–321). Prospect Heights, IL: Waveland Press.

Commission on Women in the Profession. (2008). *Sex-based harassment: Workplace policies for the legal profession*, 2nd ed. Chicago, IL: American Bar Association.

Cortina, L. M., Lonsway, K. A., Magley, V. J., Freeman, L. V., Collinsworth, L. L., Hunger, M., & Fitzgerald, L. F. (2002). What's gender got to do with it?: Incivility in the federal courts. *Law & Social Inquiry, 36*, 234–270.

Cunningham, K. (2001). Father time: Flexible work arrangements and the law firm's failure of the family. *Stanford Law Review, 53*, 967–1008.

Epstein, C. (1990). Faulty framework: Consequences of the difference model for women in the law. *New York Law School Law Review, 35*, 310–336.

Feinman, C. (1985). Women lawyers and judges in the criminal courts. In I. L. Moyer (Ed.), *The changing roles of women in the criminal justice system* (pp. 271–275). Prospect Heights, IL: Waveland Press.

Feinman, C. (1994). *Women in the criminal justice system*, 3rd ed. Westport, CT: Praeger.

Flowers, R. B. (1987). *Women and criminality: The women as victim, offender, and practitioner.* Westport, CT: Greenwood Press.

Goldberg, S. (1991, July). Token women? The ABA confronts its glass ceiling. *ABA Journal*, 58–63.

Guinier, L., Fine, M., Balin, J., Bartow, A., & Stachel, D. L. (1994). Becoming gentlemen: Women's experiences at one Ivy League law school. *University of Pennsylvania Law Review, 143*(1), 1–110.

Hanson, M. (1992, November). Ninth circuit studies gender bias. *American Bar Association Journal*, 30.

Jackson, L. W. (2007, Summer). Women in leadership positions in the legal profession: Do they face a glass ceiling or clogged pipeline, or is it now a ceiling of lifestyle bubbles. *Forum on Public Policy Online*. Retrieved from http://www.forumonpolicy.com/paperssum07.html

Martin, S. E., & Jurik, N. C. (2007). *Doing justice, doing gender: Women in law and criminal practice occupations*, 2nd ed. Thousand Oaks, CA: Sage.

Merlo, A. V., & Pollock, J. M. (1995). Women in the legal profession. In A. V. Merlo & J. M. Pollock (Eds.), *Women, law, and social control* (pp. 79–95). Boston, MA: Allyn and Bacon.

Morello, K. B. (1986). *The invisible bar: The women lawyer in America 1968 to the present.* New York: Random House.

Motley, C. B. (1998). *Equal justice under law: An autobiography.* New York, NY: Farrar, Straus, and Giroux.

National Association for Legal Career Professionals. (2005). *Women and attorneys of color at law firms.* Retrieved from http://www.nalp.org/content/index.php?pid=253

Pierce, J. L. (1995). Emotional labor among paralegals. In *Annals of the American Academy of Political and Social Science* (pp. 127–142). Berkeley, CA: University of California Press.

Rosenberg, J., Perstadt, H., & Phillips, W. R. (1993). Now that we are here: Discrimination, disparagement, and harassment of work and the experience of women lawyers. *Gender and Society, 7*, 415–433.

Sarver, T., Kaheny, E., & Azmer, J. (2008). The attorney gender gap in U.S. Supreme Court litigation. *Judicature, 91*(5), 238–250.

Schafran, L. (1990). Overwhelming evidence: Reports on gender bias in the courts. *Trial, 26* (February 2), 28–35.

The National Association of Women Judges (NAWJ). (2012). *Welcome to the NAWJ*. Retrieved from http://www.nawj.org

The National Association of Women Lawyers (NAWL). (2011, October). *Report of the sixth annual national survey on retention and promotion of women in law firms*. Retrieved from http://www. nawl.timberlakepublishing.com

Van Wormer, K., & Bartollas, C. (2013). *Women in the criminal justice system*. Upper Saddle River, NJ: Prentice Hall.

Weisberg, D. K. (1982). Barred from the bar: Women and legal education in the U.S. In *Women and the law: The social historical perspective* (pp. 231–258). Cambridge, MA: Schenkman.

Women in Corrections

16

BEVERLY R. CRANK

Contents

Introduction

Corrections is the last stop for offenders in the criminal justice system. Those who manage and supervise offenders in the correctional system are broadly referred to as correctional workers, and the most common positions are probation officers, correctional officers, and parole officers. Both men and women work in these positions and are responsible for two major objectives: (1) ensuring that offenders do not pose a risk to public safety or themselves and (2) assisting with treatment and services for the many offenders who are in need of rehabilitation.

Correctional systems involve the use of jails, prisons, probation, and parole to deter, punish, supervise, and rehabilitate offenders. Institutional corrections refers to facilities used to incarcerate and hold offenders. These facilities include juvenile detention centers or training schools, jails, or prisons. Jail is typically used for those who are awaiting trial or transfer, or for individuals who have been convicted of a misdemeanor and are serving a sentence of 1 year or less. The equivalent term for *jail* for juvenile offenders is *detention center*. Prisons are reserved for adult offenders (and juveniles tried as adults), who have committed a felony and are serving a sentence of 1 or more years. The equivalent term for *prison* for juveniles is *youth training school* or *juvenile correctional facility*. Federal facilities differ from state facilities, as federal facilities are run by the Federal Bureau of Prisons (BOP) and house offenders who are under the legal authority of the federal government. State facilities are run by each state, and inmates in these facilities are under state jurisdiction. Correctional officers are responsible for supervising inmates in all of these different settings.

An alternative to incarceration is community corrections. One common form of community corrections is probation, where a probation officer supervises offenders in the community, and aids in providing offenders access to treatment and services. Parole differs from probation, as it is reserved for those offenders who have been released from prison.

Parole is used to ensure that reintegrating offenders no longer pose a public safety risk, and may include treatment or service components. Similar to probation, parole officers typically supervise reintegrating offenders while in the community.

In 2012, approximately 1 in every 35 adults in the United States was under some form of correctional supervision, with the majority (70%) being placed on some form of community supervision (Glaze & Herberman, 2013). But what about the individuals who supervise all of these offenders?

This chapter is devoted to understanding the challenges of women working in the correctional system. This includes women working as correctional officers, parole agents, and probation officers. This chapter provides a discussion of what is required to work in corrections, the history of women working in corrections, the obstacles that women in corrections face, and the future of their work within the correctional field.

Overview of Working in Corrections

Corrections always has been a male-dominated occupational field, and this trend continues today, although women have gained much traction in terms of employment. Correctional systems tend to emphasize the importance of physical strength, which can be seen as a major obstacle by women, who feel they are at a disadvantage. However, as we will see in this chapter, women have been able to overcome this hurdle, as well as many other obstacles in terms of employment.

Still to this day, women in corrections disproportionately work in more "female-friendly" areas, such as in clerical, nursing, teaching, and other support positions (Flynn, 1999). Although many work as officers within the correctional system, women are still in the minority, and officer positions (compared to support staff positions) hold the greatest potential for advancement.

A total of 148,203 women worked in a correctional facility in 2005 (Stephan, 2008). Women not only work in corrections in the United States, but across the world. In a global survey in 1999, it was reported that 29 countries from Asia, Africa, South America, the Caribbean, Europe, and the Pacific employed women in their correctional systems (Flynn, 1999, p. 24). Outside of the United States, Costa Rica employed the largest number of women in corrections (26%), while some countries in Europe employed the least (10%) (Flynn, 1999). In 2005, 33% of employees working in correctional facilities in the United States were female (Stephan, 2008).

Although much of the discussion in this chapter is focused on correctional officers, women also work in probation and parole positions. Probation officers supervise individuals within the community to ensure public safety, as well as assist in the rehabilitation of offenders. Parole officers work with individuals released from prison, to help reintegrate them back into society. They also help ensure public safety and oversee treatment for parolees. On average, individuals employed as probation officers/correctional treatment specialists (including parole officers) make a median income of $48,190 per year. A bachelor's degree is required, and applicants are usually required to pass written, oral, and/or psychological exams. They receive short-term on-the-job training. However, the predicted job outlook for 2012 to 2022 is unfavorable at –1% (little to no change) (BLS, 2014b).

It is an understatement to note that working in corrections is a demanding job—despite biological sex. Correctional officers are usually required to work 5 days a week for

8–12 hour shifts. Because prisons and jails are open 24/7 for business, correctional officers are required to work holidays, weekends, and nights. Officers usually must be at least 18 or 21 years of age, a U.S. citizen or permanent resident, and have no felony convictions. At minimum, a high school diploma or general education diploma (GED) is required. For employment in federal prisons, an individual must have a college education or 3 years of related work experience (or a combination of the two). In addition, new applicants for federal employment must be appointed before they are 37 years old.

According to the Bureau of Labor Statistics (BLS), the 2012 median pay for correctional officers was $38,970 per year or $18.74 per hour. In 2012, there were 469,500 correctional jobs, and the job outlook from 2012 to 2022 is considered slower than average at 5%. This is due to budgetary constraints, as well as a drop in the crime rate and the number of people being incarcerated. As a result, this could cause jobs in corrections to become more competitive, requiring more field experience or a college education for entry-level positions.

Once selected for hiring, new officers must attend a training academy and receive on-the-job training. Training is based on guidelines from the American Correctional Association (ACA), which is a professional organization comprised of individuals working in corrections, as well as others who are interested in improving the justice system. Subjects covered at the training academy include self-defense, facility policies, regulations, and operations, as well as custody and security procedures (BLS, 2014a). Correctional officers also may receive firearms training, although most correctional officers do not carry firearms. For on-the-job training, new correctional officers usually receive several weeks or months of training and supervision by an experienced correctional officer. On-the-job training can vary widely across facilities. Federal correctional officers are subjected to 200 hours of training within their first year of employment, which includes 120 hours of specialized training at the Federal Bureau of Prisons (BLS, 2014a). In addition, officers must undergo annual in-service training.

According to the Bureau of Labor Statistics (2014a), the duties of correctional officers are as follows:

- Enforce rules and keep order within jails or prisons
- Supervise activities of inmates
- Aid in the rehabilitation and counseling of offenders
- Inspect facilities to ensure that they meet standards
- Search inmates for contraband items
- Report on inmate conduct (Summary Section, Para. 2)

Thus, a correctional officer is required to enforce the rules and regulations of the facility by supervising and monitoring inmates. They are responsible for maintaining security and preventing disturbances from occurring. A day in the life of a correctional officer may include searching inmates for contraband (e.g., weapons and drugs), checking for unsanitary conditions, mediating disputes among inmates, and enforcing rules. Officers check facilities used by inmates, specifically their cells and other areas, for contraband, unsanitary conditions, or signs of a security breach. Correctional officers also inspect inmate mail and visitors of inmates for contraband. On a daily basis, correctional officers write reports and complete daily logs. Officers also escort inmates throughout the facility, in order for inmates to receive treatment, attend court, participate in activities, and see visitors. Unlike law enforcement officers, correctional officers are not responsible for enforcing the law outside of the correctional facility.

Effective correctional officers possess a number of traits that make their jobs easier and more satisfying. Important qualities identified by the BLS (2014a) include:

- *Good judgment*: Officers must use both their training and common sense to quickly determine the best course of action and to take necessary steps to achieve a desired outcome.
- *Interpersonal skills*: Correctional officers must be able to interact and effectively communicate with inmates and others to maintain order in correctional facilities and courtrooms.
- *Negotiating skills*: Officers must be able to assist others in resolving differences to avoid conflict.
- *Physical strength*: Correctional officers must have the strength to physically subdue inmates.
- *Resourcefulness*: Correctional officers often encounter dangerous and unpredictable situations that require a quick response. They must determine the best practical approach to solving a problem and follow through with it.
- *Self-discipline*: Correctional officers must control their emotions when confronted with hostile situations. (How to Become One, Section, Para. 10)

When reviewing these desirable traits, it is important to note that both females and males can make effective correctional officers. Because females possess many of these traits, they have entered the correctional workforce alongside men. Today, female correctional workers play just as an important role in the workforce as men, and a number of females are in advanced positions within the correctional system.

History of Women in Corrections

Corrections has been a male-dominated field since its inception in America, beginning with the first major prison, Philadelphia's Walnut Street Jail in 1773. At the same time, women started playing a role in corrections very early in the United States. After the death of one warden at the Walnut Street Jail, the first female warden was appointed— Mary Weed, the wife of the deceased warden. From 1763 to 1769, Mary Weed was the first female to oversee a correctional facility in the United States (Morton, 1991). It was noted that "she did not fear her responsibilities of maintaining control over 280 male and female inmates with her staff of four male officers who were without whips, chains, leg-irons, guns and canes, security items deemed indispensable in other correctional facilities" (Cohen, n.d.).

Early in the history of corrections, female inmates were not always separated from male inmates. Concerns surrounding the well-being of women and children incarcerated with men led to a reform in the way females were incarcerated. By the 1820s, reformers became interested in hiring women as matrons to supervise female inmates based on allegations that they were being abused, physically and sexually, by male guards. Maryland State Penitentiary was the first to hire a female matron, Mrs. Rachel Perijo, in 1822. She guided female inmates with scripture, while teaching them basic domestic skills.

In addition to female matrons, reformers felt that female inmates may benefit from outside female visitors. The Society of Women Friends was founded in 1823 and members visited female inmates at Philadelphia's Arch Street Prison (Kann, 2005). These visitors established a library and taught classes, such as sewing and writing. They even provided housing to those in need once they were released (Kann, 2005). By 1832, shortly after Matron Perijo was hired, Auburn Prison in New York began to hire female guards. Their purpose was to supervise females who were located in a separate facility from males.

At the end of the nineteenth century, women made their way onto correctional boards in hopes of improving the treatment of female offenders. By 1870, reformers created the ACA, which is still in operation today. Today, the ACA has a special committee, Women Working in Corrections. Members of this committee participate in national conferences on issues surrounding women in the correctional field.

A big shift for women in corrections came in the 1970s. Based on the 1964 Civil Rights Act, discrimination on the basis of biological sex was prohibited, allowing women to enter into all types of work that were once considered "male jobs" (Carlson, Thomas, & Anson, 2004). However, it was not until 1970 in California that female correctional officers were permitted to work in men's institutions. By 1975, the BOP began to use female correctional officers in their male facilities. However, due to a string of violent incidents occurring against female staff in 1977, the BOP amended its policies and only allowed women to work in minimum security facilities with less violent inmates (Feinman, 1986; Tewksbury & Collins, 2006). This policy lasted until 1992, when female officers were finally allowed to work in federal penitentiaries. By 1980, almost all state systems had female officers working in some capacity in male institutions.

The primary forces behind a rise in female correctional workers was Title VII of the Civil Rights Acts extended in 1972 to cover governmental employees, in addition to a number of lawsuits filed by individuals fighting for equal employment opportunities. Many parties contested women entering the correctional workforce, including some male inmates who argued that females infringed on their rights to privacy (Carlson et al., 2004). One of the biggest arguments against women working in corrections came from the male correctional officers who believed it was too dangerous of a job for females (Carlson et al., 2004). Their fear was that females would not be able to control male inmates who were much larger than them, and that feminine traits such as being timid, weak, and seductive "would make them a danger to themselves and to the other men correctional officers" (Carlson et al., 2004, p. 84).

Given all of the obstacles and arguments, why did women want to enter this field? A career in corrections for many women meant job security with a decent salary and benefits, especially for unskilled women. When females first started working in corrections, they were limited in the positions they were assigned, as certain positions were considered more dangerous for females. Male correctional officers expressed concerns that females would not be able to handle and control difficult inmates, and they also would not be able to provide adequate backup for other officers (Carlson et al., 2004). However, women early on demonstrated their ability to deal with difficult inmates verbally (Carlson et al., 2004). Still, men often rated female correctional officers as less superior (Holman & Krepps-Hess, 1983). Interestingly, the majority of male inmates did not view female correctional officers as a problem, and believed that females should be assigned to work in male correctional facilities (Holman & Krepps-Hess, 1983). Further, one study found that the majority of male inmates did not feel like female officers invaded their privacy, nor did they indicate experiencing sexual frustration or resentment toward the female correctional officers (Holman & Krepps-Hess, 1983).

Today, women have made significant advancements in the correctional field, and hold positions in all 50 states, with some women now holding supervisory level positions. The next section is devoted to the experiences of women in corrections today, including the obstacles that women still face.

Women in Corrections Today

As noted by Johnston (2015), "Women continue to prove their value [as correctional workers] and enjoy higher levels of respect and acceptance from their male counterparts" (p. 162). However, even today, women employees still are outnumbered by male workers in the correctional setting. In the current Census of State and Federal Adult Correctional Facilities, male correctional employees outnumbered females at a ratio of 2 to 1 (Stephan, 2008). The largest gender gap in terms of employment is at the federal level. In 2005, approximately 87% of correctional employees in federal facilities were men. In state facilities, men made up about 74% of correctional employees. The gender gap was less at private facilities where men made up 52% of correctional workers. Workers in this survey include not only correctional officers (66%), but also clerical/maintenance workers (12%), professional/technical workers (10%), educational workers (3%), administrators (2%), and others (7%) (see Stephan, 2008, for an overview).

Yet, "Many of the fears of women working in corrections documented from the 1970s seemed to have dissipated" (Carlson et al., 2004, p. 83). In fact, research points to the idea that having female staff present in male institutions is more advantageous than their absence (Tewksbury & Collins, 2006). It is thought that the presence of women may have a normalizing effect on the prison environment, and that women use their verbal skills to their advantage, instead of relying on brute strength to handle matters (Johnston, 2015). Importantly, some research indicates that women experience a greater degree of job satisfaction and personal achievement in their work when compared to men (Carlson et al., 2004).

Although the strengths of female correctional officers is hard to overlook, correctional organizations were still developed and structured after men, with gender divisions placing men at the top of the hierarchy, and women at the bottom of the organization (Acker, 1992). Thus, women still may suffer from working in an environment that was not initially created for them (Cheeseman, 2012/2013). In addition, there also may be perceptions still in place that women inherently display traits that are not conducive to working in a correctional environment, such as being emotional, nonassertive, and dependent. One negative impact from this is that some women report higher levels of job-related stress, and the sources of these stressors are not just inmates, but coworkers, supervisors, and institutional policies as well (Tewksbury, 1999). For instance, Case Study 1 provides an example of one officer's experiences of harassment in the workplace.

Case Study 1: Sexual Harassment in the Workplace

As women continue to enter the workforce and the field of corrections, they may encounter significant adversity, including harassment and discrimination. Although sexual harassment is not solely directed at women, more women than men in corrections are likely to feel the effects of a hostile work environment. Women correctional workers should be aware of the potential sources of sexual harassment: coworkers, supervisors, and even inmates.

Allowing sexual harassment to occur in a workplace is not only immoral but also can be costly for correctional agencies. For instance, in one sexual harassment lawsuit, a former correctional officer was awarded close to $1 million. The lawsuit claimed that sexual harassment occurred, in addition to gender discrimination. The lawsuit cites an unusual source: a handbook passed out to only *female* correctional officers working in the New York State Department of Correctional Services (NYSDCS) system.

From 2002 to 2007, Penny Collins worked as a correctional officer for the NYSDCS, where she was employed at Sing Sing, Sullivan, Auburn, and Eastern prisons. Collins alleged that male correctional officers used profanity around her, openly discussed their genitals and sexual acts, inappropriately touched her, and spread false rumors that she was having sexual relations with inmates. When she discussed the matter with her supervisors, Collins alleged that they took no action.

In addition, a training manual for female officers was distributed by NYSDCS titled *Orientation Handbook for Female Staff Working in an Institutional Setting*. Reportedly, this manual referenced how women should avoid gossiping and being overly bossy at home. Instead, the manual recommended that women should eat ice cream to avoid job burnout (CUSA, 2007). Further, women should "monitor [their] own behavior and eliminate flirtatious mannerisms while on the job" and that women should not use profanity "to be one of the boys" (CUSA, 2007, para 3).

On March 22, 2012, New York State was ordered to pay Collins $650,000 for compensation due to a hostile work environment and lost wages. In October 2012, Collins was awarded an additional $288,000 for attorney fees. In addition, NYSDCS no longer uses the training manual for female staff. This case represents a costly mistake made by a correctional agency that could have been avoided if proper procedures and policies were in place and followed.

Stress in Correctional Work

There is no doubt that employment in the correctional environment is stressful for both males and females. Stressors such as the danger of dealing with violent inmates, working nights and weekends for little pay, and dealing with harassment from both coworkers and inmates can affect both males and females. This is important because stress not only affects mental health, but physical health and work behavior as well (Cullen, Link, Wolfe, & Frank, 1985).

Stress is common in many workplace environments, especially the criminal justice system. The correctional system has unique stressors, as these positions require much employee responsibility in terms of maintaining security and avoiding personal danger (Cullen et al., 1985; Finn, 1998). An added stressor for women is that they are entering the workforce in a male-dominated position. In fact, some studies point to significant harassment and discrimination experienced by female correctional workers (Pogrebin & Poole, 1998; Savicki, Cooley, & Gjvesvold, 2003; Stohr, Mays, Beck, & Kelley, 1998). In addition, some studies also point to female correctional workers experiencing higher levels of stress than males (Auerbach, Quick, & Pegg, 2003; Cheeseman & Goodlin-Fahncke, 2011; Cullen et al., 1985; Wright & Saylor, 1991); although some studies fail to find a significant difference in terms of gender and job-related stress for correctional officers (Griffin, 2006; Grossi & Berg, 1991; Triplett, Mullings, & Scarborough, 1996).

Regardless of gender differences in stress, both male and female workers experience stress in the correctional environment. According to Grossi and Berg (1991), common stressors for correctional officers may include

1. The ever-present potential for physical danger.
2. Hostility directed at officers by inmates, their families, and often even the public.
3. Unreasonable demands and expectations on their role as correctional officers; vacillating political attitudes toward the institutional role of corrections.
4. A tedious and [sometimes] unrewarding work environment.
5. The dependence correctional officers place on one another to effectively work in the institution safely.
6. The reality that one cannot always act the way either one would choose to, or the way the public might expect them to. (pp. 79–80)

Given these potential forms of stressors, the causes of stress have been examined by researchers. For instance, some research finds that a lack of perceived support within the organization is significantly associated with increased levels of stress (Armstrong & Griffin, 2004), especially among female correctional officers (Auerbach et al., 2003). Further, some research finds that coworker support also is an important determinant of correctional officer stress (Armstrong & Griffin, 2004; Triplett et al., 1996). Both of these findings suggest the importance of support from the organization, as well as one's peers.

Another source of stress is the potential for violence in the correctional setting, which is not just limited to violence from inmates, but other sources, such as family and friends of agency staff and offenders. According to the Bureau of Justice Statistics, persons working in custodial care, technical/industrial schools, and law enforcement (including correctional officers) had higher rates of workplace violence than nonworkplace violence (Harrell, 2011). The rate of workplace violence for correctional officers is 33 per 1000 employed persons, which is fairly low compared to other positions, such as law enforcement officers (77.8 per 1000), bartenders (79.9 per 1000), and security guards (65 per 1000) (Harrell, 2011). Although low compared to some jobs, the perception of a dangerous or unsafe workplace can increase perceptions of job stress (Armstrong & Griffin, 2004; Triplett et al., 1996).

Stress related to balancing the work–home relationship also can be a gendered issue. On average, women are thought to be more likely to arrange their employment around family responsibilities, in comparison to men. In terms of positions in corrections, this relationship is no different. According to some research, female correctional officers report higher levels of conflict surrounding balancing time for the work–family relationship when compared to men (Lambert, Hogan, & Barton, 2004; Triplett et al., 1999). Correctional staff are required to work holidays, weekends, nights, and overtime, and females may be more likely to feel the pressure of these time constraints (Lambert et al., 2004). Case Study 2 illustrates another common issue that is specific to women working in corrections—pregnancy.

Case Study 2: Pregnant and in Jail ... Sort of

Historically, women in the workforce who were pregnant were terminated from their positions. However, certain laws in the United States have been developed to protect individuals from discrimination at work. These laws help shield employees from discrimination based on age, sex, race, religion, and disability. These employment laws also cover pregnancy. In particular, the Pregnancy Discrimination Act of 1978 is an amendment to the Title VII of the Civil Rights Act of 1964, making it unlawful for discrimination to occur based on pregnancy or childbirth. According to the law, pregnant women must be treated in a similar manner as other applicants or employees. The employer cannot discriminate against pregnant women in terms of hiring, pay, benefits, job assignments, training, layoffs, promotions, and terminating employment.

Needless to say, being a pregnant correctional officer has its challenges. Not only is the safety of the officer at risk, but so is the safety of the officer's unborn child. Usually if a pregnant woman works within a correctional setting, she can request light duty that will prevent her from having any major contact with inmates. In Niagara County, New York, one correctional officer claims she made this request, but was placed on a leave of absence instead.

The U.S. Justice Department filed a lawsuit in the U.S. District Court in Buffalo alleging that the Niagara County Sheriff's Office discriminated against Correctional Officer Carisa Boddecker in 2007. The lawsuit accuses the Sheriff's Office of violating the Pregnancy Discrimination Act. In September 2007, Officer Boddecker alleges that she informed her supervisors of her pregnancy. At the time, Niagara County Jail had a policy that pregnant correctional officers must be advised of their option to be assigned to a station that does not require immediate contact with inmates. Boddecker was initially transferred to such a position in the jail, but was not allowed to remain in that position very long.

According to the lawsuit, Boddecker was allegedly told by her supervisor, Captain Engert, that she may have to work with inmates again and that she may have to work overtime due to a shortage of female correctional officers. In response, Boddecker produced a doctor's note stating that she should not be in close contact with inmates and that she could not work extra hours. By November 2007, Boddecker received notification that she had been placed on leave under the Family and Medical Leave Act (a law that allows employees to take voluntary leave when needed due to medical situations).

After filing a complaint with the Equal Employment Opportunity Commission, Boddecker was able to receive her job back at the Niagara County Jail; however, the matter was referred to the Department of Justice. The current, ongoing lawsuit seeks back pay and damages. In addition, the Department of Justice is asking for a new county policy that clarifies pregnant officers' right to work, in addition to a policy that handles discrimination complaints. The Department of Justice is pushing for additional employee training on discrimination issues. As noted by Jocelyn Samuels, Principal Deputy Assistant Attorney General for the Civil Rights Division, "Women should not have to choose between their pregnancies and their jobs, and the Civil Rights Division will continue to vigorously enforce the right of pregnant employees to be free of discrimination in the workplace" (as cited in U.S. Department of Justice, 2013). No decision has been made yet in this case.

Special Note: Female Probation and Parole Officers

Most research on women working in the criminal justice system focuses on female law enforcement officers. It is thought that the experiences of women working in the criminal justice system, in general, are similar across positions. However, more women work in the correctional field than law enforcement, and even fewer studies focus specifically on the experiences of female parole and probation officers.

When females first started entering the correctional workforce, female parole agents were rare, so they often supervised same-sex caseloads. In some agencies, females were not allowed to carry a weapon and also had limited work duties. Many females, especially in the 1960s and 1970s, experienced discrimination and harassment. The type of discrimination and harassment could be as small as gossiping and rumors, to being denied promotions and given an unfair work schedule (Mallicoat & Ireland, 2014).

Today, approximately 30% of parole agents are female and have "established themselves as competent" (Mallicoat & Ireland, 2014, p. 316). When specifically examining females in parole, Ireland and Berg (2008) found in their sample that women reported being cautious when dealing with parolees; however, they did not perform their jobs in fear, as noted by one female parole officer:

> Anyone who is interested in this [type of work] and afraid should not get into this line of work; it can compromise quality of work. You have to remember that parolees are not out to hurt staff. (p. 482)

Parole officers in their study also note that they maintain a sense of security by using their communication skills to their advantage by building rapport with parolees, in order to deescalate issues. As noted by another female parole officer:

> We have to have good communication skills; we have to be able to recognize volatile situations; and you have to be able to know how to handle those situations by using your communication skills. I have been involved in situations that could have easily turned volatile, but my manner, my demeanor, my communication skills, and the manner in which I dealt with these individuals has made a very big difference in the way they have responded to me.

Ireland & Berg (2008, p. 483)

Interestingly, the female parole officers in Ireland and Berg's study also indicate that male parole officers over-rely on physical strength, which they felt could be a threat to personal safety.

In addition to female parole agents, female probation officers are also thought to experience greater levels of stress than males (Simmons, Cochran, & Blount, 1997; Thomas, 1998). Probation officers "have contact with more offenders than most other justice employees" (Slate, Wells, & Johnson, 2003, p. 520), and their workplace experiences are probably very similar to other women working in the criminal justice system. Similar to other criminal justice workers, low salaries and a lack of opportunity for advancement have been identified as significant stressors for probation officers (Simmons et al., 1997). Other stressors for probation officers include the relationships with their supervisors, paperwork, and report due dates (Simmons et al., 1997).

Special Note: African American Women Working in Corrections

The issues discussed so far in this chapter are thought to be multiplied for women correctional officers of color. Not only are these women subject to discrimination based on their biological sex, but they also are subject to discrimination based on their race or ethnicity.

There is very limited research focusing on the experiences of African American, female correctional officers. However, one study by Britton (1997) examined the effects of race and sex on job satisfaction and found some interesting results. One of the negative effects found was that African American females were less satisfied with their jobs than white men and men in the "other" racial category. In addition, African American females reported more job stress than white males. At the same time, African American males and females, along with Hispanic males, found more efficacy in working with inmates (i.e., feeling that they can deal with difficult inmates effectively, providing a positive influence for inmates, creating a relaxed atmosphere, and gaining a sense of accomplishment in their work with inmates). As a note of caution, more research is needed to investigate the experiences of African American females working within the correctional system before drawing any definite conclusions on the experiences of these workers.

Future of Women in Corrections

The Management and Training Corporation (MTC) Institute (2008) recommends three major areas in helping women succeed in the correctional setting: training, good supervision, and mentoring. Correctional organizations should continue providing training that is sensitive to gender issues, and promote strategies that help alleviate stress within the correctional environment (Cheeseman, 2012/2013). Cheeseman (2012/2013) makes specific suggestions noting that training led by female correctional workers on cross-gender supervision, health and well-being, and positive coping strategies would be beneficial for all correctional workers.

Same-gender mentoring also may be beneficial for correctional officers, as it helps to "overcome a natural prejudice that may come from working in a traditionally male-dominated environment, encouraging protégés to reach further than what one believes may be possible" (MTC, 2008, p. 10). Many women indicate that receiving supportive mentoring is important in the correctional field, as mentors can serve as inspirations for women and encourage them to advance professionally (MTC, 2008).

The MTC Institute (2008) also advise that women take advantage of opportunities for advancement and suggest the following actions (which also are applicable to men working in corrections):

- Take advantage of all opportunities to learn (e.g. agency training, online training, Internet, etc.)
- Acquire professional credentials (e.g. ACA certification)
- Volunteer for additional assignments, especially those that are very challenging and difficult
- Systematically perform tasks that are designed to provide experiences that demonstrate knowledge, skills and abilities associated with the next higher level… (MTC Institute, 2008, p. 14)

These are all important suggestions to heed, as women are still in the minority in the correctional field, especially in terms of higher level positions. But as women continue to make important strides in corrections, it is inevitable that they will continue to advance.

It is projected that the number of supervisory staff positions in corrections will continue to grow. This provides an excellent opportunity for women working in corrections to continue to advance their career goals. Presently, women working in corrections are more likely to have college and professional degrees in comparison to men, which makes them excellent candidates for supervisory positions. As women continue to enter the workforce in greater numbers, women should capitalize on the strengths they bring to the occupation and recognize the substantial impact that they can have on others, including staff and inmates. In sum, "for corrections, women represent an asset that can no longer be overlooked" (MTC Institute, 2008, p. 19).

Discussion Questions

1. Why do you think corrections is still a male-dominated field? Do you think women will ever be in the majority in terms of employment in corrections? Why or why not?
2. What are some other challenges women working in corrections face that were not addressed in this chapter?
3. Do you think women are subject to more discrimination and harassment working in the correctional system compared to other positions outside of the criminal justice system? Explain your answer. Is there another job where women may experience *more* harassment and discrimination in your opinion? Be sure to justify your responses.
4. What advice would you give to women seeking employment within the correctional system?

References

Acker, J. (1992). *Gendered organizational analysis.* Thousand Oaks, CA: Sage.

Armstrong, G. S., & Griffin, M. L. (2004). Does the job matter? Comparing correlates of stress among treatment and correctional staff in prisons. *Journal of Criminal Justice, 32,* 577–592.

Auerbach, S. M., Quick, B. G., & Pegg, P. O. (2003). General job stress and job-specific stress in juvenile correctional officers. *Journal of Criminal Justice, 31,* 25–36.

Britton, D. M. (1997). Perceptions of the work environment among correctional officers: Do race and sex matter? *Criminology, 35,* 85–105.

Bureau of Labor Statistics, U.S. Department of Labor. (2014a). *Occupational outlook handbook, 2014–15 edition (correctional officers).* Retrieved from http://www.bls.gov/ooh/protective-service/correctional-officers.htm

Bureau of Labor Statistics, U.S. Department of Labor. (2014b). *Occupational outlook handbook, 2014–15 edition (probation officers and correctional treatment specialists).* Retrieved from http://www.bls.gov/ooh/community-and-social-service/probation-officers-and-correctional-treatment-specialists.htm

Carlson, J. R., Thomas, G., & Anson, R. H. (2004). Cross-gender perceptions of corrections officers in gender-segregated prisons. *Journal of Offender Rehabilitation, 39,* 83–103.

Cheeseman, K. A. (2012/2013). Women working in corrections: Where we have been and where we are going. *Corrections Today, 74,* 64–67.

Cheeseman, K. A., & Goodlin-Fahncke, W. (2011). Women working within the walls: The effect of gender on correctional employee perceptions of work stress. *Corrections Compendium*, *35*, 18–19.

Cohen, B. R. (n.d.). *An impact analysis of the* United States of America v. the State of Florida. *Florida Department of Corrections.* Retrieved from https://www.fdle.state.fl.us/Content/getdoc/0303878b-964b-4bf5-8628-196bf049f2cc/Cohen.aspx

Corrections USA. (2007). *CUSA joins IAWIC in calling NY's training manual for female correctional officers garbage; commissioner pulls booklet from training program.* Retrieved from http://www.cusa.org/images/Newsletter/CUSA_October07_Enews.pdf

Cullen, F. T., Link, B. G., Wolfe, N. T., & Frank, J. (1985). The social dimensions of correctional officer stress. *Justice Quarterly*, *2*, 505–533.

Feinman, C. (1986). *Women in the criminal justice system* (2nd ed.). New York, NY: Praeger.

Finn, P. (1998). Correctional officer stress: A cause for concern and additional help. *Federal Probation*, *62*, 65–74.

Flynn, E. E. (1999). Women professionals in criminal justice. In R. Muraskin (Ed.), *Women and justice: Development of international policy* (pp. 11–30). Amsterdam, the Netherlands: OPA.

Glaze, L. E., & Herberman, E. J. (2013). Correctional populations in the United States, 2013. Washington DC: Bureau of Justice Statistics.

Griffin, M. L. (2006). Gender and stress: A comparative assessment of sources of stress among correctional officers. *Journal of Contemporary Criminal Justice*, *22*, 4–25.

Grossi, E. L., & Berg, B. L. (1991). Stress and job dissatisfaction among correctional officers: An unexpected finding. *International Journal of Offender Therapy and Comparative Criminology*, *35*, 73–81.

Harrell, E. (2011). *Workplace violence, 1993–2009.* Washington, DC: Bureau of Justice Statistics.

Holeman, H., & Krepps-Hess, B. J. (1983). *Women correctional officers in the California Department of Corrections.* Washington, DC: National Institute of Justice.

Ireland, C., & Berg, B. (2008). Women in parole: Respect and rapport. *International Journal of Offender Therapy and Comparative Criminology*, *52*, 474–491.

Johnston, C. H. (2015). *Careers in criminal justice.* Thousand Oaks, CA: Sage.

Kann, M. E. (2005). *Punishment prisons and patriarchy: Liberty and power in the early American republic.* New York, NY: New York University Press.

Lambert, E. G., Hogan, N. L., & Barton, S. M. (2004). The nature of work–family conflict among correctional staff: An exploratory examination. *Criminal Justice Review*, *29*, 145–172.

Mallicoat, S. L., & Ireland, C. E. (2014). *Women and crime: The essentials.* Thousand Oaks, CA: Sage.

Morton, J. B. (1991). Introduction. In J. B. Morton (Ed.), *Change, challenge, and choices: Women's role in modern corrections* (pp. 1–12). Lanham, MD: American Correctional Association.

MTC Institute. (2008). *Women professionals in corrections: A growing asset.* Retrieved from http://www.mtctrains.com/sites/default/files/WomenProfessionalsInCorrections-Aug08.pdf

Pogrebin, M. R., & Poole, E. D. (1998). Women deputies and jail work. *Journal of Contemporary Criminal Justice*, *14*, 117–134.

Savicki, V., Cooley, E., & Gjvesvold, J. (2003). Harassment as a predictor of job burnout in correctional officers. *Criminal Justice and Behavior*, *30*, 602–619.

Simmons, C., Cochran, J. K., & Blount, W. R. (1997). The effects of job-related stress and job satisfaction on probation officers' inclinations to quit. *American Journal of Criminal Justice*, *21*, 213–229.

Slate, R. N., Wells, T. L., & Johnson, W. W. (2003). Opening the manager's door: State probation officer stress and perceptions of participation in work place decision making. *Crime & Delinquency*, *49*(4), 519–541.

Stephan, J. J. (2008). *Census of state and federal correctional facilities, 2005.* Washington, DC: Bureau of Justice Statistics.

Stohr, M. K., Mays, L. G., Beck, A. C., & Kelley, T. (1998). Sexual harassment in women's jails. *Journal of Contemporary Criminal Justice*, *14*, 135–155.

Tewksbury, R. (1999). Should female correctional officers be used in male institutions? In C. B. Fields (Ed.), *Controversial issues in corrections* (pp. 187–194). Boston, MA: Allyn & Bacon.

Tewksbury, R., & Collins, S. C. (2006). Aggression levels among correctional officers: Reassessing sex differences. *The Prison Journal, 86,* 327–343.

Thomas, R. L. (1998). Stress perception among select federal probation and pretrial services officers and their supervisors. *Federal Probation, 52*(3), 48–58.

Triplett, R., Mullings, J. L., & Scarborough, K. E. (1996). Work-related stress and coping among correctional officers: Implications from organizational literature. *Journal of Criminal Justice, 24,* 291–308.

Triplett, R., Mullings, J. L., & Scarborough, K. E. (1999). Examining the effect of work-home conflict on work-related stress among correctional officers. *Journal of Criminal Justice, 27,* 371–385.

U.S. Department of Justice, Office of Public Affairs. (2013, May 13). *Justice Department files lawsuit against Niagara County, New York.* Retrieved from http://www.justice.gov/opa/pr/justice-department-files-lawsuit-against-niagara-county-new-york

Wright, K. N., & Saylor, W. G. (1991). Male and female employees' perceptions of prison work: Is there a difference? *Justice Quarterly, 8,* 505–524.

Index